Foundations and Best Practices in Early Childhood Education

P9-DID-954

Do Not Sell

DMACC ECE

Foundations and Best Practices in Early Childhood Education

HISTORY, THEORIES, AND APPROACHES TO LEARNING

Second Edition

Lissanna M. Follari
Sheridan College

PEARSON

Boston   Columbus   Indianapolis   New York   San Francisco
Upper Saddle River   Amsterdam   Cape Town   Dubai   London   Madrid   Milan
Munich   Paris   Montreal   Toronto   Delhi   Mexico City   São Paulo   Sydney
Hong Kong   Seoul   Singapore   Taipei   Tokyo

Vice President and Editor in Chief: Jeffery W. Johnston
Senior Acquisitions Editor: Julie Peters
Editorial Assistant: Tiffany Bitzel
Vice President, Director of Marketing: Quinn Perkson
Marketing Manager: Erica DeLuca
Project Manager: Holly Shufeldt
Senior Art Director: Jayne Conte
Text Designer: Jayne Conte
Cover Designer: Margaret Kenselaar

Photo Coordinator: Carol Sykes
Media Project Manager: Rebecca Norsic
Full-Service Project Management: Sudip Sinha/ Aptara®, Inc.
Composition: Aptara®, Inc.
Printer/Binder: Hamilton Printing Co.
Cover Printer: Lehigh-Phoenix
Text Font: Bembo

Credits and acknowledgments borrowed from other sources and reproduced, with permission, in this textbook appear on the appropriate page within text.

Every effort has been made to provide accurate and current Internet information in this book. However, the Internet and information posted on it are constantly changing, so it is inevitable that some of the Internet addresses listed in this textbook will change.

Photo Credits: Lissanna M. Follari: pp. 1, 4, 7, 19, 37, 55, 57, 61, 66, 72, 75, 81, 85, 90, 99, 103, 111, 114, 133, 141, 150, 153, 157, 178, 181, 183, 186, 187, 192, 194, 195, 203, 204, 212, 217, 219, 222, 227, 233, 247, 249, 252, 253, 261, 263, 267, 269; Scott Cunningham/Merrill: p. 12; Courtesy of the Library of Congress: p. 23; North Wind Picture Archives. p. 27; Used by permission of Scott Bultman, Froebel Foundation USA, http://www.froebelfoundation.org: p. 30; Brittany Campbell; pp. 44, 49, 97, 128, 138, 170; Anne Vega/Merrill; p. 130; Anthony Magnacca/Merrill; p. 162; Katelyn Metzger/Merrill; p. 167; Mick Follari; p. 240

Library of Congress Cataloging-in-Publication Data
Follari, Lissanna M.
   Foundations and best practices in early childhood education: history, theories, and approaches to learning / Lissanna M. Follari.—2nd ed.
      p. cm.
   ISBN-13: 978-0-13-703446-8
   ISBN-10: 0-13-703446-6
   1. Early childhood education. I. Title.
LB1139.23.F66 2011
372.21—dc22

2009030181

10 9 8 7 6 5 4 3

www.pearsonhighered.com

ISBN 10:   0-13-703446-6
ISBN 13: 978-0-13-703446-8

Preface

The field of early childhood education has been growing and evolving for centuries. There is much to be learned from our past as we create a vision for our future. Even more can be learned from exploring the unique approaches and beliefs that shape practices around the world. This book is an invitation to embark on this exploration.

This text is written for beginning educators as well as for those with experience teaching young children who are furthering their education. For the beginning educator, this is an invitation to consider your place in this dynamic field by tracing its history and current trends. For the more experienced educator, this text can provide more in-depth explorations of specific methods and approaches to guide the ongoing process of professionalizing your practice. The overarching goal of this text is for educators to make connections between beliefs and philosophies and practice. To do this, I have included stories or extended vignettes, which come from a variety of classrooms and highlight how teachers and programs are integrating guiding principles and beliefs into applied practice. It is my hope that you will use this text to begin or continue your reflective journey on the evolving path of defining and reshaping your own practice. Go forth and find your voice—the voice you will raise in advocacy on behalf of all children and families.

Features of the Text

The Classroom View cases from the field included in most chapters provide a snapshot of diverse education settings and illustrate the key concepts. I invite you also to reflect on your own observations in light of these stories, comparing your experiences with those included here. The In Your Own Words boxed features encourage you to reflect on specific aspects of your own beliefs and practice. We also pause frequently along this journey to think about specific suggested applications, which are highlighted in the Putting It Into Practice boxed features.

Several themes run like threads throughout the text: teachers' roles, views of children, inclusion, and diversity. These are key aspects of all practice that you, too, must integrate into your thinking and teaching. The reflection prompts, questions at the start and end of each chapter, and application activities are all designed to facilitate the development of your own beliefs about these key themes. The appendixes contain tools that can be used in this process, including samples of graphic organizers and a comprehensive portfolio plan.

Guiding Concepts

Several concepts that guide this text are used as a lens through which we will view the field. First, this text takes a *child-centered approach* to early childhood education. Childhood is a unique and valued period of life, and children are capable, competent, and active participants in their growth and learning. Another guiding concept is the belief, flowing from *constructivist* learning theory, that children are busily and actively building knowledge from their earliest moments. Children continue this lively inner process even when they are quiet. Their learning, thinking, and feeling are expressed in myriad "languages," or ways of communicating. Teachers must be receptive and respectful of them all. Finally, I strongly believe that teaching is a personal as well as a professional endeavor. Adults and children form social bonds and relationships that are at the heart of learning. Above all else, I believe that children deserve to be respected and loved by the adults in their lives. It is with this spirit of love and respect that I present this text to you and wish you a challenging, surprising, rewarding journey.

Professional Preparation

In addition to the overarching themes, two aspects to help you in your professional preparation are woven throughout this book. In each chapter you will be guided to activities that help shape your professional portfolio. Your portfolio is used to present a picture of who you are as a developing teacher and as a teacher education student. The other element woven throughout the text is an emphasis on core content aligning with teacher preparation exams, such as the Praxis™ Early Childhood test. The foundations, key theories, and examples of best practices presented here represent a major part of the content of such exams.

New to This Edition

This second edition reflects recent changes in early care and education practice based on legislative and policy changes as well as the latest research on effective practice. You will find important revisions and updates in the following areas:

- Reorganized table of contents to improve flow of text topics
- Additional lists of application ideas in Chapters 8 through 11 to increase applicability of content
- Expanded Chapter 3 on professionalism, incorporating a variety of associations in addition to the National Association for the Education of Young Children (NAEYC)
- Entirely revised appendices, including all-new graphic organizers in Appendices D, E, and F
- Addition of a comprehensive portfolio rubric and guide, integrating new NAEYC standards in Appendix E
- Key legislative updates and reauthorizations to IDEA and Head Start in Chapters 1 and 6
- Updates from NAEYC's newly revised Developmentally Appropriate Practice and Standards statements in Chapters 1, 3, and 12
- New research on Waldorf Education and student outcomes in Chapter 11
- Expanded Chapters 1 and 12 to provide more in-depth support for professional portfolio creation
- Integration of Pearson's MyEducationLab assignable video-based assignments and activities throughout each chapter (see margin notes) with the addition of an

all-new student activity, Building Teaching Skills and Dispositions, at the end of each chapter

- Streamlined summaries for student accessibility

Ancillaries Accompanying This Text

All ancillaries are available online. To download and print ancillary files, go to **www.pearsonhighered.com.** and then click on Educators.

Online Instructor's Manual This manual contains a glossary handout, chapter overviews, additional Web resources, and additional application activities for in-class and out-of-class which are designed to enhance students' understanding of chapter concepts and build students' professional portfolios.

Online Test Bank The Test Bank includes a variety of test items, including multiple choice and essay items.

Pearson MyTest is a powerful assessment generation program that helps instructors easily create and print quizzes and exams. Questions and tests are authored online, allowing ultimate flexibility and the ability to efficiently create and print assessments anytime, anywhere! Instructors can access Pearson MyTest and their test bank files by going to www.pearsonmytest. com to log in, register, or request access. Features of Pearson MyTest include:

Premium assessment content
- Draw from a rich library of assessments that complement your Pearson textbook and your course's learning objectives.
- Edit questions or tests to fit your specific teaching needs.

Instructor-friendly resources
- Easily create and store your own questions, including images, diagrams, and charts using simple drag-and-drop and Word-like controls.
- Use additional information provided by Pearson, such as the question's difficulty level or learning objective, to help you quickly build your test.

Time-saving enhancements
- Add headers or footers and easily scramble questions and answer choices—all from one simple toolbar.
- Quickly create multiple versions of your test or answer key, and when ready, simply save to MS-Word or PDF format and print!
- Export your exams for import to Blackboard 6.0, CE (WebCT), or Vista (WebCT)!

Online PowerPoint Slides Colorful PowerPoint slides prompt student engagement with reflective questions, highlight key concepts and strategies in each chapter, and enhance lectures and discussions.

Acknowledgments

I wish to offer my heartfelt appreciation to all my students. It is for you that I undertook this project. I hope that the inspiration and collegiality we share in our classes continue to fuel your work as they do mine. It continues to be an honor to travel this road together. I wish you all a successful and nourishing journey.

I would like to thank Luci Coke for all her assistance in gathering the tremendous research that went into this book and Julie Peters and Kerry Rubadue for their continued support and valuable feedback. This project is stronger for your caring involvement.

I would like to thank the following reviewers for their helpful comments: Elaine Camerin, Daytona Beach Community College; Virginia Carey, Columbus State Community College; Deborah Ceglowski, University of North Carolina, Charlotte; Elizabeth Elliott, Florida Gulf Coast University; Susan Johnson, Northern Virginia Community College; Herman Knopf, University of South Carolina; Jyotsna Pattnaik, California State University, Long Beach; Nancy Payne, Northern Virginia Community College; Margarita Perez, Worchester State College; Jeri Sorosky, Nova Southeastern University; Harriet Sturgeon, University of Houston, Clear Lake; Andrea Zarate, Hartnell College; and Pauline Davey Zeece, University of Nebraska, Lincoln.

A very special thank you also goes out to the dedicated teachers and families at the Northampton Community College Child Care Center, the East Stroudsburg University Child Care Center, and the Sheridan, WY, YMCA Child Care Center.

Finally, I lovingly dedicate this project to Greisan, the motivation behind it all.

myeducationlab

THE POWER OF CLASSROOM PRACTICE

"Teacher educators who are developing pedagogies for the analysis of teaching and learning contend that analyzing teaching artifacts has three advantages: it enables new teachers time for reflection while still using the real materials of practice; it provides new teachers with experience thinking about and approaching the complexity of the classroom; and in some cases, it can help new teachers and teacher educators develop a shared understanding and common language about teaching. . . ."[1]

As Linda Darling-Hammond and her colleagues point out, grounding teacher education in real classrooms—among real teachers and students and among actual examples of students' and teachers' work—is an important, and perhaps even an essential, part of training teachers for the complexities of teaching in today's classrooms. For this reason, we have created a valuable, time-saving website–MyEducationLab–that provides you with the context of real classrooms and artifacts that research on teacher education tells us is so important. The authentic in-class video footage, interactive skill-building exercises and other resources available on MyEducationLab offer you a uniquely valuable teacher education tool.

MyEducationLab is easy to use and integrate into both your assignments and your courses. Wherever you see the MyEducationLab logo in the margins or elsewhere in the text, follow the simple instructions to access the videos, strategies, cases, and artifacts associated with these assignments, activities, and learning units on MyEducationLab. MyEducationLab is organized topically to enhance the coverage of the core concepts discussed in the chapters of your book. For each topic on the course you will find most or all of the following resources:

CONNECTION TO NATIONAL STANDARDS

Now it is easier than ever to see how your coursework is connected to national standards. In each topic of MyEducationLab you will find intended learning outcomes connected to the appropriate national standards for your course. All of the Assignments and Activities and all of the Building Teaching Skills and Dispositions in MyEducationLab are mapped to the appropriate national standards and learning outcomes as well.

ASSIGNMENTS AND ACTIVITIES

Designed to save instructors preparation time, these assignable exercises show concepts in action (through video, cases, or student and teacher artifacts) and then offer thought-provoking questions that probe your understanding of theses concepts or strategies. (Feedback for these assignments is available to the instructor.)

---

[1]Darling-Hammond, l., & Bransford, J., Eds. (2005). *Preparing Teachers for a Changing World.* San Francisco: John Wiley & Sons

BUILDING TEACHING SKILLS AND DISPOSITIONS

These learning units help you practice and strengthen skills that are essential to quality teaching. First you are presented with the core skill or concept and then given an opportunity to practice your understanding of this concept multiple times by watching video footage (or interacting with other media) and then critically analyzing the strategy or skill presented.

IRIS CENTER RESOURCES

The IRIS Center at Vanderbilt University (http://iris.peabody.vanderbilt.edu–funded by the U.S. Department of Education's Office of Special Education Programs OSEP) develops training enhancement materials for pre-service and in-service teachers. The Center works with experts from across the country to create challenge-based interactive modules, case study units, and podcasts that provide research-validated information about working with students in inclusive settings. We have included this content on your MyEducationLab course to enhance the content coverage in your book.

TEACHER TALK

This feature links to videos of teachers of the year across the country discussing their personal stories of why they teach. This National Teacher of the Year Program is sponsored by the Council of Chief State School Officers (CCSSO) and focuses public attention on teaching excellence.

GENERAL RESOURCES ON YOUR MYEDUCATIONLAB COURSE

The *Resources* section on your MyEducationLab course is designed to help you pass your licensure exam, put together an effective portfolio and lesson plan, prepare for and navigate the first year of your teaching career, and understand key educational standards, policies, and laws. This section includes:

- *Licensure Exams:* Access guidelines for passing the Praxis exam. The *Practice Test Exam* includes practice questions, *Case Histories,* and *Video Case Studies.*
- *Portfolio Builder and Lesson Plan Builder:* Create, update, and share portfolios and lesson plans.
- *Preparing a Portfolio:* Access guidelines for creating a high-quality teaching portfolio that will allow you to practice effective lesson planning.
- *Licensure and Standards:* Link to state licensure standards and national standards.
- *Beginning Your Career:* Educate yourself–access tips, advice, and valuable information on:
  - Resume Writing and Interviewing: Expert advice on how to write impressive resumes and prepare for job interviews.

- Your First Year of Teaching: Practical tips to set up your classroom, manage student behavior, and learn to more easily organize for instruction and assessment.
- Law and Public Policies: Specific directives and requirements you need to understand under the No Child Left Behind Act and the Individuals with Disabilities Education Improvement Act of 2004.

- *Special Education Interactive Timeline:* Build your own detailed timelines based on different facets of the history and evolution of special education.

Visit www.myeducationlab.com for a demonstration of this exciting new online teaching resource.

Brief Contents

Contents

Foundations and Best Practices in Early Childhood Education

CHAPTER 1

Welcome to the Field of Early Childhood Education

The journey of a thousand miles begins with one step.

—LAO-TZU

Being an early childhood educator is a constant journey. It is exciting, challenging, tiring, invigorating, and always changing. Above all else, it is rewarding. There is no more influential period of life than the first 8 years. Because of the tremendous leaps that occur in development during the early years, early childhood educators are positioned to have profound impact on children's lives. The role of the teacher of young children is, therefore, crucial to our future generations. As early childhood educators, we take on many different roles in the course of our days: teacher, researcher, lifelong learner, caregiver, family and child advocate, provocateur (provoking children's thinking), playmate, and many others. We are called upon daily to face many daunting challenges and tasks.

Early childhood settings can be diverse, including large or small center-based programs, in-home or out-of-home family care, faith-based programs, intervention programs, or in-school programs. The children and adults in those settings also bring vast diversity to the program in terms of ability, interests, culture, values, languages, and so on. Developing sensitivity to diversity and attitudes and skills to celebrate all members of a group is vitally important. In any setting, relationships are the heart of education. Teaching occurs in a social context, in which we continually negotiate a complex system of relationships (schools, families, colleagues, beliefs, practices, communities). Teachers are required to make a myriad of decisions in selecting the most appropriate tools and methods from an astounding array of choices (technologies, ideologies, theories, materials). Teachers also use those decisions to carefully create learning environments that plan for universal norms and also validate and support individual development and choices. Increasingly, teaching also involves assessment and accountability to internal and external audiences. To be successful requires that you have a strong foundation of knowledge and skills, as well as dedication and commitment.

STARTING POINTS: QUESTIONS AND REFLECTIONS

1. What role do teachers play in children's lives? In the lives of families? In the community?

2. How do you define and envision yourself as a teacher? Describe who you are or who you want to be as a teacher. (Start by listing five characteristics you want to embody as a teacher.)

3. How can you integrate what you know and believe and who you are into one resource?

MyEducationLab

Go to the Resources section in the MyEducationLab for your course and explore Portfolio Builder. This guide will familiarize you with how to create your own portfolio based on national standards.

Professional portfolio

An organized collection of work that reflects your beliefs, experiences, and competencies as a teacher.

Your Role as a Teacher-Education Student: Finding Your Professional Identity

Your task at this point in your career is to embrace a reflective perspective. You must learn about the history of early childhood education in order to envision the future and a variety of practices to be able to cultivate your own style. Through your studies and work, you will learn from the past and present, from sound research, from children, from families, from colleagues, and from yourself as you develop your professional identity. The topics in this text provide a foundation from which you can start to build your own teacher identity. Throughout this book and during your teacher-education studies in general, you will be called upon to create a body of work that represents your beliefs and abilities as an educator. Creating a **professional portfolio** is your first (and an ongoing) effort to define and redefine yourself as an educator.

A portfolio is a collection of work, or artifacts, that represents you: your beliefs, your abilities, your goals, and your accomplishments. It will change throughout your studies and practice. Many people choose a binder, an expanding folio, or some other material that will allow artifacts to be added or withdrawn. You must carefully and thoughtfully select items to include in your portfolio that reflect your progress, highlight your experiences, and demonstrate your abilities related to state and national teaching standards (Gelfer, Xu, & Perkins, 2004). Your portfolio may be used to assess your progress in your studies, to demonstrate your competencies in interviews, and to document your professional development throughout your career. Periodically reflecting on your portfolio in presentations or interviews will prompt you to summarize your work, learn from your experiences, and articulate who you are or will be as a teacher (Bullock & Hawk, 2001). Throughout this book, you will have opportunities to explore options and strategies for creating your portfolio. Take a moment to review the many informational resources about portfolios and state and national standards, as well as the Portfolio Builder guide at MyEducationLab. This guide will familiarize you with the process of creating your own portfolio based on national standards.

Reflecting on a variety of learning theories and teaching methods and critically examining how they can inform your own practice are important tasks of an education professional. As you read on, continue thinking about general and specific elements presented in each chapter. Find elements that you can envision integrating into your own unique

Your Professional Portfolio

Consider aligning your portfolio around standards such as those from the National Association for the Education of Young Children (NAEYC; recommended by the National Council for Accreditation of Teacher Education, or NCATE) or the Interstate New Teacher Assessment and Support Consortium (INTASC; Campbell, Cignetti, Melenyzer, Nettles, & Wyman, 2004; NAEYC, 2008). The headings for each standard, including examples of possible artifacts to include, are as follows (artifacts are described throughout the text):

NAEYC

Standard 1: Promoting Child Development and Learning
Artifacts: analysis of metaphor describing children; statement of beliefs about teaching and learning; brochure highlighting development in each domain

Standard 2: Building Family and Community Relationships
Artifacts: family workshop outline; family brochure or newsletter; community needs survey; community resource list/brochure collection of agencies serving families and children

Standard 3: Observing, Documenting, and Assessing
Artifacts: observation reports; program comparison report; assessment tools; rubrics and checklists created to evaluate classroom environments and children's progress; child study

Standard 4: Using Developmentally Effective Approaches to Connect with Children and Families
Artifacts: lesson plans; review of journals or self-evaluations; learning center designs; planning webs and charts; photo documentation panels

Standard 5: Using Content Knowledge to Build Meaningful Curriculum
Artifacts: content-area lesson plans; planning webs and charts

Standard 6: Becoming a Professional
Artifacts: multiple intelligence self-test and response; NAEYC membership; NAEYC position statement review; journal article reviews; theorist studies; conference attendance records; teacher interview report, including questions on law and policies affecting families and children

INTASC

Standard 1: Knowledge of Subject Matter
Standard 2: Knowledge of Human Development and Learning
Standard 3: Adapting Instruction for Individual Need
Standard 4: Multiple Instruction Strategies
Standard 5: Classroom Motivation and Management Skills
Standard 6: Communication Skills
Standard 7: Instructional Planning Skills
Standard 8: Assessment of Student Learning
Standard 9: Professional Commitment and Responsibility
Standard 10: Partnerships

NCATE also recommends using standards from the Association for Childhood Education International (ACEI) for elementary education programs. Find their standards at www.ncate.org/public/programStandards.asp?ch=4.

Using tabs or dividers of some kind, you can create separate sections for each standard, including a section for personal data such as a résumé, educational philosophy, reference letters, and transcripts. In the standards sections, you can begin to include class assignments such as papers, teaching lessons or units, family newsletters, and any field experiences, including any observation reports or evaluations that fit within the standard topic. As an introduction to each section, consider writing a one-page self-reflection analysis in which you write about any of your experiences that helped prepare you for that standard. This summary and the reflection statement demonstrate not only your writing skills but also your knowledge of standards and your self-awareness.

philosophy and practice. Critically examine your own beliefs and potential biases in light of your readings and discussions. Reflect, adapt, or allow yourself to change your beliefs and expectations of teaching, children, and families as you learn about historic and current educational theories and practices. This ongoing process of exploring research and practice, while examining your own beliefs, is an essential part of becoming a reflective practitioner.

Roles of the Early Childhood Professional

As you travel through the history, theories, guiding frameworks, and approaches presented in this book, you will delve further into the many roles embodied by early childhood teachers. Think about how you fit into these roles in the evolving future of the field.

Teacher

Your role as a teacher may seem the most clear, embodied in the following activities:

- Facilitating children's development
- Valuing children's play as important to their development as well as intrinsically enjoyable

Working directly with children on hands-on activities is a primary role of the early childhood professional.

- Creating beautiful and engaging learning environments that welcome all children
- Providing learning experiences that pique children's curiosity and spark their imagination
- Asking questions to encourage children to think and sometimes to challenge their thinking
- Building strong relationships with children and families
- Being a learner alongside children as co-constructors of curriculum, knowledge, and classroom community

The meaningful, interesting, challenging learning experiences you design should also integrate all **developmental domains** and span both **child-initiated activities** and more structured, **teacher-directed activities**. Finding a balance among developmental domains, structure of activity, context, and group or individual time is the task of every skillful teacher. In each of the approaches we discuss in this book, you will see how teachers manage this important task.

Good teaching is built on a solid understanding of developmental theories, which include universal expectations and awareness of individual differences (Bredekamp & Copple, 1997). Teachers understand that learning environments are designed to facilitate development in all developmental domains. Developmental domains include

- Physical development: small motor skills (picking up, pinching), large motor skills (walking, skipping), balance, coordination, and movement control
- Socioemotional development: getting along with others; understanding, regulating, and expressing feelings; developing moral and ethical beliefs; becoming independent and able to work within a group
- Cognitive development: thought process, language, intellectual skills, creativity

Developmental domains

The major areas of human development: physical, cognitive, socio-emotional.

Child-initiated activities

Activities that are chosen and directed by children.

Teacher-directed activities

Activities that are planned, selected, and directed by teachers.

Teachers need to be aware of the paths that children's development should take so that learning experiences may be planned to enhance that development. For example, infants begin to refine their physical control by lifting their heads, then sitting up, and eventually walking and running. Development in all domains generally follows predictable sequences, although it progresses at individual rates (Allen & Marotz, 2003). Although some skills may be categorized within one domain, development should always be viewed as integrated and interrelated. That means that competencies and abilities within each domain impact and are impacted by other domains. For example, learning to walk can be categorized within physical development but is also impacted by the infant's social interactions through encouragement, models, and support. In fact, nearly any developmental milestone you can think of is probably related to the child's environment just as to their internal drive. Children should be viewed holistically, as whole people living and growing among a range of influences (Noddings, 2005).

Although developmental theories remain an important foundation for teaching, teachers must also become careful observers of individual children and classroom dynamics. For example, teachers often overhear children in dramatic play remarking that two girls or two boys cannot participate in a dramatic play wedding sequence because only boys and girls can marry. Or teachers may notice some children excluding other children of different ethnic backgrounds. Teachers often see preferences in terms of gender as well; boys may gravitate toward certain materials that girls do not play with. On the surface these may seem like typical behaviors. When these scenes are viewed more critically, however, insights

Valuing Extended Families

I will share with you a personal story from my early days in the field that showed me just how far I had to go to truly understand and respect family culture. Soon after I started directing a medium-sized center in a diverse community, an Asian family enrolled their 2-year-old son in our program. The parents spoke English, but the son and the grandmother did not. In an effort to ease the boy's transition to a new country, culture, language, and school, the child's grandmother came to school with the boy each day. At first the teacher tolerated her presence, although she was not particularly pleased with the situation. Whereas her goals for the children included fostering increasing in-dependence, this child was held on his grandmother's lap and spoon-fed at meals, spoke in his home lan-guage to her and did not speak to other children, and played with her during choice time. The teacher wor-ried that he would not achieve the same goals as the other children.

She made several failed efforts to encourage the grandmother to let the boy reach out and commu-nicate with the teacher and other children. Finally she requested that we meet with the parents and ask them to not allow the grandmother to come to the school. They agreed and kept her home, but I felt their hurt and reluctance. The boy remained with-drawn and appeared uncomfortable but slowly learned some familiar words in English.

One evening when the child's mother came to pick him up, I asked her to talk to me about their family life. She shared with me that, in her family, the grandmother has a very important place as the child's care provider when the parents are working. She talked about how close bonds between them are highly valued in their culture and said that the caretaking of their young children is an important family goal. As she spoke, I began to realize just how much we had hurt the grandmother personally by denying her role as the boy's caretaker and also how disrespectful we had been to the family's culture. I shared my sincere appreciation with her for helping me learn this lesson and assured her that we would make efforts to support the family as a whole.

Soon after, another child enrolled who spoke only French. Her father had transferred jobs, and the family had recently moved. I had deeper insight this time into the diversity of family culture, the needs of English language learners, and the stress of a new en-vironment. I spoke to the girl in French and provided the staff with translation dictionaries and French nursery songs on tape, and I encouraged them to use English and French words to label the shelves and the schedule. We encouraged the child to share with us photo albums of her home and family and special items from home. The child's mother joined the class on many occasions and taught everyone songs and poems. We all had a better understanding this time about the importance of valuing and maintaining the family's home culture and language. We were so pleased to see how quickly the child and family be-came comfortable at the center and how much more easily she was able to learn English.

into gender biases, stereotypes, or dominant culture can be revealed. Reflective teachers must become aware of these more complex realities of the early childhood classroom (Ryan & Greishaber, 2004). Children's play is highly complex and a critically important window into their lives and development.

Something that may be a less obvious facet of the role of the teacher is that al-though teaching is highly professional work, it is also deeply personal. You must love what you do; children deserve to be loved just as they deserve to be respected and val-ued. Genuine enthusiasm and caring will make you a truly inspiring educator. Your per-sonal commitment and love of teaching also ensure that you will continue to find satisfaction and nourishment in your work. At any age, students need to feel that their teachers care about teaching, about their learning, and—most of all—about them as people (Noddings, 1995). With young children, a loving bond formed with teachers is important for healthy emotional development as well as healthy brain development, especially in infancy (Baker & Manfredi/Petitt, 2004). You may spend long hours with children, sometimes even more waking hours than children spend with their families. It is natural and healthy that close bonds be formed.

Keep in mind that children's attachments are not exclusive. They form personal bonds with any caring, responsive adults who spend long periods of time with them. This is a normal and healthy response, one that actually strengthens the parent-child bond (Baker & Manfredi/Petitt, 2004). Also keep in mind that your role as a teacher is to form close connections to families. Let families know that you both share the same goal: to provide the best environment possible for their children. Reassure them that your relationship with their children supports each child's development as well as the family as a whole. When families and teachers know they are working together, everyone's satisfaction improves. Amid all the work you do as a professional, never lose sight of the fact that teaching is personal. Remember that the heart of this work is about relationships. This includes relationships with both children and families (extended families too).

A meaningful way to form close bonds with children can be through their play. Play has been valued throughout our history and across international practice as the primary vehicle for children's learning and socialization (Fraser, 2007). In particular, teachers need to preserve children's right to spontaneous, child-initiated play and recognize not only the intrinsic joy but also the power of play (Jenkinson, 2001). Although we may strive to "make learning fun" (a common theme among my students' professional philosophy statements), we must also hold fast to children's right to time and space for play in their lives. Their

Communications with families happen in both formal and informal ways every day.

spontaneous, imaginative self- and cocreated worlds that emerge in their play serve to nourish them in body, mind, and spirit and give them opportunity to create social bonds in a way that cannot be achieved as meaningfully through other adult-controlled activities. This nourishment is essential to children's development and a natural and valuable part of early childhood programs.

Researcher

Throughout this book, you will read about the various theorists' views of the teacher as a researcher. For centuries, educators have been advocating and practicing their role as researchers. Now it's your turn:

- Explore innovations.
- Learn from others' work by observing and reading journals, joining informal discussions, and attending conferences.
- Stay current with what other professionals are doing.
- Approach your own work in your own classroom with an inquiry stance—question, try, watch, reflect, and try again.

In the spirit of our field's great pioneers, take every opportunity you can to observe children and reflect on what you see. Everything we know about children has come from the willingness of researchers to observe children and analyze what they do. Learn about your children from your analyses of their actions, behaviors, and conversations. If you experience tough days in the classroom, approach these as challenges to be investigated; there are vast resources for working through various classroom situations, including your colleagues, the faculty, books, and websites. Take suggestions from all the sources you can find and try them out in your work. Not all the ideas you learn about will be the right fit for you, your children, or your families, but embrace the try-and-reflect process. There is no end to what you can learn through research, observation, and reflection throughout your career. As a researcher, you not only become a better educator, you also open yourself to being a lifelong learner.

Lifelong Learner

Although your tenure as a student may officially end when you receive your degree, certification, certificate, grade, or course completion, your role as a learner never ends. At times books, lectures, discussions, and projects may be your education. As you embark into the professional world, experience, collaboration, and reflection become your education. Just as you hope to instill in your children an enthusiasm, curiosity, inquisitiveness, and desire to learn, so too you must cultivate these qualities. One of the most motivational aspects of teacher education programs—and your work thereafter—is the chance to learn by seeing and doing. Cultivate a habit of seeing the potential for growth, learning, and development all around you. Look to your own hobbies and interests for inspiration in your teaching. Share your personal interests with your children. Engaging educators also seek to integrate children's personal interests into the classroom. Continue to expand your teaching by expanding your own interests, skills, and knowledge. Try new things, visit new places. Remember that who you are as a person is how you teach. This truly makes all life's experiences adventures in personal and professional growth.

Child and Family Advocate

Overarching everything teachers do is the guiding principle that we are advocates for children and families. We respect them. We believe in them. We want to empower them to succeed. We strive to foster healthy growth as individuals and as a family unit with unique and shared culture, beliefs, and goals. The day-to-day practice of working with young children further demands a heightened sensitivity to the unique qualities of childhood. Recognizing that experiences in the early years can greatly impact later developmental outcomes reminds teachers of the care and forethought that must go into each decision we make on behalf of our children. Viewing infancy and childhood as periods of particular vulnerability reminds us that the nature of our behavior affects children and families in many ways. This realization, perhaps more than any other, endows teachers with a tremendous responsibility to hold themselves to the highest standards of professional demeanor and ethical behavior.

Our work and influence stretch far beyond the classroom walls and the end of the school day or school year. We teachers have an impact on children's lives, and they have an impact on ours. As a teacher, you have a voice in forums where children do not. It is your role to advocate on their behalf in larger public forums through participation in community groups, professional organizations, and other networks. Being an advocate for children means that you must understand public policies affecting children and families. It also means that you may be called upon to help shape those policies in ways that promote a positive impact for all children and families (Jalongo et al., 2004).

The view of the "family" as strictly a nuclear unit consisting of a mother, a father, and child(ren) has expanded. Many children live with single parents, extended families, blended families, and nontraditional family members. These may include grandparents, aunts and uncles, other relatives, stepfamily members, partners, or other people who share the child's life. Some children also live with foster families or appointed guardians who become the child's family. Keep in mind that all the people in children's lives have an impact on them and are valued members of their world. It is also important to consider that different generations, just like different cultures, may have different styles and roles in children's lives. The emphasis on teaching as relationship building encompasses all the influences that create a child's unique world. Appreciate the vast potential for learning and development provided by children's families. Working together will make your experience richer and provide great opportunities to enhance everyone's learning.

Current Issues Facing Early Childhood Professionals

Before you step back in time on a historical journey, take a moment to explore our present cultural context. Many issues that early theorists wrestled with remain topical today. In addition, there are new and complex issues that face teachers and guide our practice. Changes abound all around us: social changes, political changes, technological changes, and demographic changes. As our world becomes increasingly more complex, diverse, and global, teachers' responsibility to educate children capable of navigating this complex world becomes all the more urgent.

Changing Traditional Practice: One Size Does Not Fit All

Traditionally, classrooms have been places for rows of desks with students quietly receiving instruction from a teacher. Students complete an abundance of prescribed activities at their seats. Teachers transmit information while students passively take it in (Stanford, 2003). Within this model, there is an unspoken expectation that "one size fits all" in terms of classroom instruction style (Burchfield, 1996; Eisner, 2004). There is very little challenge to higher-level thinking (Pool, 1997). This picture may seem more appropriate for some elementary school levels, but there has been a trend toward pushing down this kind of instructive, academic-focused classroom style to kindergarten and preschool programs. The unfortunate result of this classroom style is that children are placed in a passive role that does not align with the way in which children learn best (Hirsh, 2004).

Active Learners Need Interactive Teachers

Young children are naturally active, social, exploratory beings and generally seek out opportunities to manipulate objects in their world. They are often so engrossed in their own explorations that they do not attend to classroom schedules, lengthy lectures, or even peers' feelings. When children have something to say or something they want to do, their natural inclination is to satisfy their needs. This kind of sometimes boisterous, self-directed behavior does not mesh well with restrictive classroom environments in which teachers expect a schedule to be kept and focused attention to be maintained. It is a common goal of early childhood teachers to want to instill some sense of order and adherence to rules in a classroom. Also common is the desire to increase children's attention on learning and skill-building tasks. Although these are worthy goals, they are not successfully achieved through a restrictive style of teaching.

Whole-group and teacher-directed instruction for extended periods of time most often results in teachers having to resort to restrictive responses to children's fussiness. Classroom time is wasted in redirecting attention and behavior at the exclusion of interactive dialogue. This kind of restrictive teacher-child interaction becomes the norm within a transmission teaching style. This then perpetuates less child initiation, language, and active exploration (Cassidy & Buell, 1996; Girolametto, Weitzman, & Greenberg, 2003). Restrictive teacher practice in early childhood settings may control children's actions and preserve order in the room; however, the cost is children's initiation, deeper learning beyond memorization, and development in a meaningful, active learning process. Although some teacher-directed and whole-group activity is important in any classroom, restrictive practices rely on these methods for too much of the children's day. This denies the opportunity for emergent, authentic, meaningful experiences that children can easily relate to their own lives.

Restrictive teaching styles preserve teacher authority, validating the teacher as the keeper of the right answer and subjugating the child as the seeker of the right answer (Pool, 1997). If there is a right answer, then there is a wrong answer. This equation can restrict the willingness of many children to generate possibilities, to test ideas, and to solve problems by manipulating different media and materials for fear of being wrong. Children in a "right answer" classroom may be inhibited from exploring concepts and phenomena and sharing their discoveries in their own individual style. It is essential that teachers acknowledge and validate each individual child's contribution to the class. Each member of the classroom community should be valued for his or her diverse perspectives.

Changing Demographics

As a first-year second-grade teacher, Brendon felt ready to take on the challenges of being a teacher. His school used a mentoring system, and he was paired with SallyAnne, a 21-year veteran of the public schools. In one of their meetings before the school year officially started, SallyAnne reminisced about the changes she'd seen over the years. "I remember when this community was a small farm town. The kids here didn't have much sense of the world outside the town. In some ways it was hard to get them to imagine what life could be like elsewhere. But slowly, over the years, more and more people moved here from the city. Small pockets of immigrant families began to shape the community. Back then, we didn't really have any plan for kids who didn't speak English or who couldn't keep up with the class. They were on their own." Brendon couldn't imagine such a time. With all the classes he'd taken that talked about the importance of making plans for each individual child's abilities and valuing home culture, he was glad to be reminded of how far education had come.

SallyAnne agreed. "At first it was hard for all of us. But we were lucky that our principals have been progressive enough to want to make change happen and that we were able to find resources to make it possible. So many schools still struggle today to make programs accessible for children with diverse needs. We all had workshops and formed collaborative teams to work on new ideas and plans. We started to rely on our parents and community to help us. Once they started to see they could have an impact on the advisory board, they really became involved. I learned a lot from them—even day-to-day things like new words in Spanish and Russian to communicate with several immigrant children. We became a team—real partners. Like I said, we were lucky. I know some schools that really resisted these demographic changes. In the end, it was hard not only on the kids, but also on those teachers. They didn't have anyone to rely on, no partnerships like we did. Now we see almost one third of the class representing different cultures and languages. I love being able to rely on parents to bring a richness and liveliness to our culture studies. I see my kids getting excited about the differences out there. It makes them want to explore their world and understand each other."

Brendon was glad they had met that day. SallyAnne reminded him about the beauty of their diverse community. She also reminded him about the importance of coming together as a community to create a responsive, stimulating, collaborative learning environment.

Valuing Diversity: The Richness of You

Early childhood environments of today reflect the rich diversity of our communities. The need for teachers to continue to develop ways to create environments that celebrate shared and individual cultures is at an all-time high. As educators, we must begin our work from a place of respect, sensitivity, and genuine interest in knowing and valuing our children and families. It is important for their development now, but it is also essential for their development later as they move out into the world beyond our classroom walls. The diversity around us holds many opportunities to bring meaningful, authentic experiences into the classroom. Partnerships with families and communities allow teachers to expand learning beyond the classroom and more realistically mirror children's lives. Sometimes teachers avoid recognizing differences in an attempt to promote equality ("we're all the same and equally welcome here"; "we're color-blind in this room"); however, this does not actually value what makes each individual special. It is our rich diversity that makes life so interesting and colorful. Celebrate what makes each person unique while exploring the ways in which we share common experiences.

Many educators start by exploring their own unique cultures. Think about what life was and is like in your family. What unique traditions, norms, values, and experiences make you special? What life experiences do you and your family carry within yourselves that are defining features of you? Celebrate them! They are what make you special. Also think about the shared cultural traditions you carry within yourself. What are the things that connect you to other people in your school, your community, and your geographic location? It is how your shared and unique qualities align that color your experiences and perspectives. Exploring them, as you can do with your children, reveals the richness that is you. It is a shared and individual richness that each of us possesses. Allowing yourself and your children to explore yourselves as individuals within a richly colorful group creates bridges within your school community.

In addition to sometimes downplaying differences, teachers also sometimes avoid topics or situations with which they are inexperienced. Unfortunately, this only leaves teachers unprepared to handle situations when they arise. For example, many early childhood teachers are uncomfortable discussing issues of reproduction, gender identity, gender bias, or ethnic and racial biases in children's behavior. They may not seek to challenge children's assumptions about how children play, what kinds of roles they can play, or the materials with which they can play (for example, two boys getting married in dramatic play, an Asian child pretending to be a white cartoon character, or a child with a visual impairment playing the bus driver on the playground). Children are surprisingly astute at internalizing social rules and norms. As teachers we need to be aware of certain biases in these norms,

Inclusive classrooms support active participation for all children.

perhaps even in our own beliefs, and challenge them so that all children become aware that they are empowered with choices and self-direction (Ryan & Grieshaber, 2004).

Equality: Everyone Has a Place at the Table

Educators have been advocating for the inclusion of all children in classrooms for more than a century. It has been only a little more than a quarter of a century, however, that **inclusive classrooms** have become mandatory in schools. Today educators rely on the **Individuals with Disabilities Education Act** (IDEA) as a foundation for inclusive practices, but they go beyond the laws to fully embrace the spirit of inclusion. That law, dating back to 1975, has been reauthorized over the years to make provisions for schools to address the needs of children with limited English proficiency and homeless children as well as children with disabilities (Gargiulo, 2006). The law provides guidelines for schools to offer intervention services, specialized staff, and technologies to students in need of assistance to help them succeed in school.

Inclusive classrooms

Classrooms that meaningfully integrate all children, including those with disabilities.

Individuals with Disabilities Education Act

The 1975 law that ensures access to equal learning environments for all children with disabilities.

In the same way that we believe in the value of diversity to enhance and enrich our lives, so too we value the unique contributions children at all developmental levels bring to the classroom. By viewing all children as important members of the classroom with something special to share, we can begin to create authentic communities of learners who rely on each other and validate each other. When classrooms are viewed as a community, there is an opportunity for all children to feel valued. Communities are connected by the interrelationships of their systems, structures, and members. Within this framework, each individual contributes to the identity of the whole. Children can be unique and special at the same time that they are part of a shared culture. It is important for teachers to look for ways in which to encourage each child and family to have a role within the classroom community. A growing body of research reveals that children in inclusive classroom settings hold more positive attitudes about children with diverse abilities, especially when teachers take an active role in helping to facilitate acceptance and inclusion (Dyson, 2005; Nikolaraizi et al., 2005). This underscores the important role teachers play in promoting and modeling a culture that celebrates of diversity within the classroom.

An important element of celebrating diversity is to view children as unique and on individual developmental paths. Not all children achieve the same milestones at the same time, just as not all children speak the same language or prefer the same activities or foods. Each child has capabilities to achieve meaningful goals. Our task as educators is to help identify what goals children are working on at the moment and to develop ways to facilitate their progress toward realizing their highest potential. Once again the partnerships with families and community support become important in this quest. When additional support and help are needed for individual children, teachers must be able to connect with the community resources that offer such help. At the heart of all we do, we must view all children as capable and always remain committed to finding ways to unlock their amazing potential.

Aligning Standards with Good Practice

Our current educational climate is influenced by new emphases on holding schools accountable for children's performance. The belief is that if schools and teachers are held to high standards and made responsible for whether children succeed, then the quality

Systems of Influence

In 1979, Urie Bronfenbrenner developed his ecological systems theory. In this theory, he identified the many direct and indirect influences that impact children. He designed a diagram to represent the interrelationships, which looks like a series of concentric circles. At the core, representing the strongest influence, are the child and immediate family. From here the child's extended family, school, community, political systems, and so on, branch out to show the widespread systems that impact children (see the following figure). A key element of Bronfenbrenner's theory that is particularly important for early childhood practice is that the influences are bidirectional; this means that the many layers of influences shaping the context of children's lives are also impacted by the child (Darragh, 2007). Children impact their world in the following ways:

- Parents' choices and decisions are based on goals for their children and their children's needs.
- Employers often create policies in light of family needs (family leaves, family health insurance).

- School district policy and practice are shaped by parent input and enrollment.
- Community parks are placed in neighborhoods where children reside.
- Operation of child-care facilities is based on family needs.
- A variety of child-welfare issues are regular features of political platforms.
- Public funding and support for social service agencies serving children and families varies, in part based on parent lobbying.

Think about this in relation to your own life. Using small adhesive notes, write down each person, agency, institution, and system that influenced your life along its course. Once you have as many as possible down, organize them by how direct the influence was. Try to design your own visual representation to convey the dynamic, fluid, interdependent way these influences helped shape who you are.

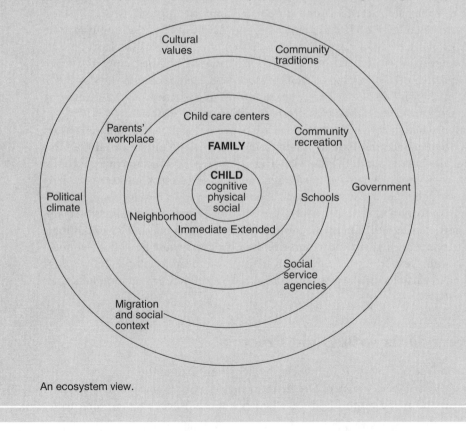

An ecosystem view.

Putting It Into Practice

The Potential in All Children

Creating a class book is one way to highlight each child's potential within the class as a whole. Children can create pages about themselves, what they like, and what they are good at through dictation, signing, drawing, writing, selecting pictures, and so on, which then can be combined into a larger class story. A similar classroom community project is to create a documentation panel on large cardboard sheets. The panel can include photos, children's work, stories, quotes, and family notes. Viewing the classroom community as a patchwork of individuals coming together to create a unified whole can also be represented in a class quilt, in which each child creates a square with his or her family and unites them with others in a quilt at school.

of instruction will improve. Accountability and standards have, at their core, the goal of ensuring that all our children have access to the very best educational experiences.

The quality of education in America has been at the fore of the political agenda and public financial responsibility since the 1965 passing of the Elementary and Secondary Education Act (ESEA). In 2001, President George W. Bush included the **No Child Left Behind Act** (NCLB Act) in a reauthorization of the ESEA (passed in 2002). The NCLB act seeks to improve the quality of education and improve outcomes for all students, particularly lower income students, by increasing the quality of teachers and the schools' accountability for student achievement. NCLB addresses teacher proficiency by requiring that all teachers be *highly qualified*. This means that all teachers must hold a bachelor's degree and state teaching license, as well as demonstrate competency in the subject matter they teach. A strong emphasis on developing good literacy skills by the third grade is a key feature of NCLB (U.S. Department of Education, 2004a). At the heart of the NCLB mission is the belief that students will strive to attain the standards and expectations set for them. Set low standards, and they will underachieve; set high standards, and they will perform better and achieve more. There are four key pillars of NCLB:

No Child Left Behind Act

The 2001 law that seeks to improve the quality of education and improve outcomes for all students, particularly lower income students, by increasing the quality of the teachers and the schools' accountability for student achievement.

- Stronger accountability for results
- More freedom for state and communities
- Proven education methods
- More choices for parents

Within these four pillars lie what policy makers hope to be the motivation and guidance necessary to support improvements in schools and student outcomes: tracking and publishing results of student achievement on annual tests as a reflection of school effectiveness, connecting student achievement scores/school effectiveness to annual progress expectations, and parent choice for where they enroll their children (U.S. Department of Education, 2004b).

Student scores are tied to standards in math, science, and literacy, and they govern schools' access to funding. Under NCLB, parents are given the opportunity to transfer a child to another school if the school their child attends is rated as underperforming for at least 2 years (U.S. Department of Education, 2004b). This kind of accountability has led to the term *high-stakes testing*: Student test scores are determining factors for public support of schools. Although in theory NCLB provides federal dollars for education, many people share serious concerns over its implementation and impact on education (Hyun, 2003; Noddings, 2005).

Many educators are concerned about the unbalanced emphasis placed on students' scores on standardized tests. As good educators know, fair and accurate student assessment, particularly assessment of young children, should include a variety of assessment measures and be viewed as an ongoing process (Geist & Baum, 2005). Test scores alone do not provide an accurate picture of a child's learning (Jones, 2004). The overreliance on standardized test scores to prove schools' passing performance has left many educators feeling extremely pressured to align teaching with the tests, as opposed to teaching based on holistic, child-centered, proven practices. Many educators also express concerns over the stress the climate of testing places on children. This pressure and stress has led many educators to protest the NCLB implementation (Geist & Baum). Other educators express concerns over the narrow emphasis on academic skills and performance. They cite an interest in creating classrooms that view children holistically, and they seek to foster their development in academic, social, personal, and other areas (Noddings, 2005). NCLB continues to be a hotly debated issue with evidence of success and struggle.

Although some of the means for achieving NCLB's goals are questionable or even harmful, teachers must work to create learning environments that align with its requirements but also uphold high standards of quality and developmentally appropriate practice as advocated by professional organizations and supported by our current research base. It is not an easy task, but it is of paramount importance for our children. Our task as teachers and advocates is always to find a balance in teaching and assessment. We must find a balance between

- Accountability by schools, prekindergarten state standards, national and local standards
- Authentic assessments and standard tests and measures
- Individual interests
- Developmental needs and appropriateness; integrated social, emotional, cognitive, and physical learning and development
- Divergent theories and expert beliefs
- Expert advice and our own intuitive knowledge
- Ourselves, our children, our families, and our society

Standards in Early Childhood Education

Early childhood programs (infancy through early elementary grades) should be integrating developmental theories with active learning experiences. Standards—in the form of the Developmentally Appropriate Practice framework, Head Start Performance Outcomes, various state standards, and national content-area standards—seek to provide overarching goals for what young children should learn. Many teachers struggle with feeling limited to teaching only to standards. This creates a limited view of children's lives. In a time when we are recognizing the importance of the context of children's lives and experiences—meaning that children learn and grow in a dynamic system of influences, including home, family, school, and community—teachers must understand how to use standards effectively as one of many tools for teaching.

Although it can feel limiting to use standards as a starting place for instruction, teachers can instead start with elements of good practice and then fit standards into practice. Good practice means (Jalongo et al., 2004)

- Understanding broad developmental trends while planning for individual development
- Balancing instruction to engage diverse learning styles and address all domains
- Creating environments that are safe, stimulating, and welcoming for children of all ability levels
- Meeting children's basic need for sustenance, shelter, clothing, and health care
- Encouraging processing and representation in a variety of ways
- Helping children make personal connections and find meaning in their experiences
- Supporting families with respect for family diversity

Standard learning goals within each domain or content area, such as math, literacy, science, or arts, can be successfully addressed in a balanced approach to teaching. Figure 1–1 shows the cycle of planning, teaching, and assessment.

Standards can even be addressed through children's play. As noted previously, play is pure enjoyment for children but also a powerful vehicle for active, meaningful learning

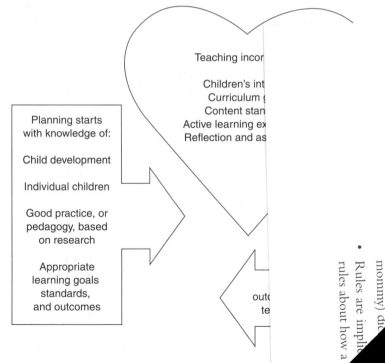

FIGURE 1-1 Map of the Planning, Teaching, and Ass

(Elkind, 2003; Fraser, 2007; Hirsh, 2004). It is through play that children are engaged in authentic activity, stemming from their own internal interest, and building strengths in all areas of development. For example,

- Pretend play promotes social development through shared creation of play scenarios and role negotiation.
- Building with blocks helps children develop spatial abilities, counting, and shape recognition.
- Painting helps children learn colors, develops imagination and creativity, and enhances spatial thinking,
- Dictating, writing, or acting out stories promotes language arts development (reading, writing, speaking, listening) and understanding of story structure, as well as valuing personal experiences and ideas.
- Moving water or sand in a sensory table develops children's knowledge of physics, how different materials behave and change form, and sense of touch.
- Climbing on a play structure promotes physical development, coordination, and balance.

Furthermore, giving children time to choose activities develops choice making and initiative. All these goals are part of learning standards but, more importantly, are part of quality practice. When viewed as a part of the picture, standards do not have to be at odds with what teachers believe about the best ways to educate young children.

Tools of the Mind

Newly emerging research on the benefits of play-based, constructivist approaches to early care and education is guiding current views of "best practices." Based on the work of Russian-born psychologist Lev Vygotsky, the *Tools of the Mind* curriculum "is a novel approach emphasizing intentional development of specific academic skills and self-regulation of behavior and emotions with play featured in a leading role in the curriculum" (Barnett et al., 2008). Mental tools are strategies that children integrate into their thinking and processing that then allow them to become more capable to regulate themselves (thought, behavior) and their environment (Bodrova & Leong, 2007). Vygotsky valued language (a mental tool) as a pivotal tool in learning, memory, and self-regulation as well as a key component of how teachers can support, prompt, and challenge children's learning (scaffolding their learning and development as they reach higher and higher levels of independence). Through the mastery of language as an organizer of thought, children can learn to talk themselves through challenges, connect new ideas to existing mental frameworks, and elaborate on existing ideas to expand knowledge. Additional examples of mental tools include using symbols to represent something, creating rhymes to remember content, and ___ with rules and roles of sociodramatic play. When viewed through a constructivist ___ dren's play is viewed as a key means for children to organize and regulate their be- ___ e this in the following aspects of play:

- ___ defined and guide behaviors (pretending to be a teacher, a horse, or a ___ tate actions.
- ___ d and at times negotiated and are based on play roles (there are ___ eacher behaves).

Standards can be appropriately integrated into learning activities and assessment so that children's experience remains authentic and enjoyable.

Furthermore, research has revealed that in play children's mental skills, such as attention, memory, recall, and imagination, are at a higher level than during any other activity (Bodrova & Leong). Connecting these important findings, the *Tools* curriculum guides teachers to facilitate children's acquisition of essential mental tools through play, carefully guided activities, and systematic observations. With the strong connection between self-regulation and school success, the *Tools* curriculum has important implications for early childhood practice. For more information about this curriculum, visit www.toolsofthemind.org.

Assisting us in facing the challenge are volumes of writing from centuries of thinking about childhood, learning, teaching, and society as well as our own reflections and experiences. The challenge for teachers now is first to inform ourselves about the voices from history—their messages, meanings, and teachings. Equally important is the hand-in-hand effort to learn about ourselves, our assumptions, our own beliefs, and our own personal histories through continued self-reflection (Landerholm, Gehrie, & Hao, 2004). Through this outward and inward learning, you, as future teachers, must find your own unique way to bring together the sea of professional knowledge and recommendations with your own personal passions and drives. The work of the educator is at once both highly professional and deeply personal. It is about thinking, feeling, and doing. In essence, this is work we do with our heads, our hearts, and our hands.

Beginning the Journey

As you move forward through this book, keep in mind your developing beliefs about teaching, your image of yourself as an educator, and the issues that impact the field of early childhood. Whereas some issues, such as use of the Internet, are uniquely modern issues, there are others that echo throughout our history. You are entrusted with the task of continuing the dedicated march toward reshaping practice, improving professionalism, embodying lofty

---

Putting It Into Practice

The Internet and Teaching

You no doubt use any number of technological tools throughout your day and throughout your life as a student. You may not even really think twice about many of these tools. As an educator, however, you must make careful decisions about what tools are beneficial to children. For example, you may have access to computers for your classroom. Numerous games and educational programs are available for children's use on the computer. Many programs call themselves "educational," although this may not necessarily be true. It is your job to be a careful consumer of all the materials you select for your classroom. Many of the programs and computer applications work on skills that can be addressed in other, more active ways. Think carefully about why you select materials, always looking for the most active, meaningful, healthy choices.

Technological improvements have also come a long way in improving the functioning of many children with disabilities. Hearing aids for children with hearing impairments, talk devices for children who cannot speak, computer-driven wheelchairs for children with limited mobility, and language-translation software are a few examples of the assistive technology tools that make it possible for children to participate in inclusive classrooms. Teachers should familiarize themselves with these tools to be able to better serve all families. I also encourage teachers to become skilled in using technology as a tool for their own use. There is a wealth of information (reliable and not so reliable) available at the click of a mouse that can help you become a better teacher. There are forums where you can network among other educators across the world. There are ideas, plans, and strategies you can find to assist you in your work. For all of the valuable ways to use these technologies, you must maintain a critical eye and carefully select applications that best serve your children and families.

---

ideals, and empowering children and families. Through this work, our ultimate goal of ensuring that all children live successful, meaningful lives can be realized. Each chapter presented here is a story, a voice from the field that shares new ideas and experiences. Let these stories inspire you as you begin creating your own story. Welcome to the journey!

> *The mediocre teacher tells.*
> *The good teacher explains.*
> *The superior teacher demonstrates.*
> *The great teacher inspires.*
>
> —WILLIAM A. WARD

SUMMARY

The path of the early childhood education professional is continually changing and reflects the dynamic nature of development in the early years. At no other time of life do we see greater leaps and changes in human growth, making early childhood educators profoundly important in children's lives. A key task of the professional is to hone the skills, attitudes, and knowledge necessary to meet high standards of quality practice and to demonstrate these in a professional portfolio. Your portfolio is representative of your professional identity and capabilities, and may be aligned with one of several national standards frameworks. In the course of developing your professional identity throughout this text, you will explore the roles early childhood professionals play in the lives of children and families, including

- Teacher
- Researcher
- Lifelong learner
- Child and family advocate

You will also explore the current issues that guide our practice, especially the complex nature of

- Working with diverse children and families
- Meeting national and state standards
- Promoting developmentally appropriate practice
- Exploring and integrating concepts and strategies from a wide variety of methods, theories, and approaches to early childhood care and education

Application Activities

On the Web: MyEducationLab   Locate the Resources link on MyEducationLab. Review the links on Preparing a Portfolio, Standards, and Beginning Your Career. Pay particular attention to the NCLB and IDEA links in the Beginning Your Career section. Make notes of specific items you find particularly useful and share your thoughts in small groups.

In Class: Describe Your Favorite Teacher   Think back to when you were in school—any age or grade. Think about one of your favorite teachers. What do you recall? What was it about this teacher that made you respond? Write a few phrases, words, or sentences to describe your memories. Share them with your class or small group. What common threads emerge? How do your memories and points from the class discussion fit into your vision of the ideal teacher—the kind of teacher you hope to become?

When I do this exercise with my own students, it is always the personal qualities that come through as the most memorable: someone who cared, someone who went out of his or her way for you, someone you felt you could talk to about anything, someone who felt like a friend and teacher, someone who truly wanted to see you succeed as a person and a student. Did you find the same thing in your memories and in your class discussion? Keep in mind your memories of your favorite teacher and the impact he or she had on you as you develop your own teacher identity.

In the Field   Create a list of questions about NCLB, managing a classroom, guidance strategies, and promoting success in meeting standards for all children (children with disabilities included). Arrange to interview a preschool through third-grade teacher to find answers to your questions. Choose a teacher who has been teaching for at least 4 years.

MyEducationLab

Go to the Resources section in the MyEducationLab for your course and explore Preparing a Portfolio, Standards, and Beginning Your Career. Pay particular attention to the NCLB and IDEA links in the Beginning Your Career section. Make notes of specific items you find particularly useful and share your thoughts in small groups.

For Your Portfolio As you begin your journey into this introduction to early childhood education, you may already bring with you years of experience and prior coursework, or this may be the start of your professional path. In either case, a good starting point for your portfolio is to create a brief autobiography, including basic information about yourself as well as a section describing why you want to be in this field. Once you decide on a specific portfolio organization plan (perhaps based on standards, your teacher education department's own framework, or the CDA content areas), your autobiography fits nicely into an introductory section along with a resume and transcripts. Your autobiography is also a useful document to share with classroom teachers when you complete field hours or student teaching.

RELATED WEB LINKS

Association for Childhood Education International
www.acei.org

National Association for the Education of Young Children
www.naeyc.org

Council for Professional Recognition
www.cdacouncil.org

CHAPTER 2

Historical Overview: People and Beliefs That Shaped the Field

Education, then, beyond all other devices of human origin, is the great equalizer of the conditions of man—the balance-wheel of the social machinery.

—HORACE MANN

The field of early childhood care and education has a long history involving divergent viewpoints, dedicated educators and theorists, and a pattern of pendulum swings in terms of popular practice. The study of how young children have been viewed, treated, and educated is rich and complex. It is entwined with the histories of social welfare, cultural movements, religion, and politics. This chapter provides you with an overarching historical backdrop in order to help you understand where we are today and why we believe what we do about best practices.

The backdrop of early childhood education's past and evolution will help you understand the more detailed approaches, frameworks, and theories that you will explore throughout the rest of this text. The history of education is a bit of a roller-coaster ride, so hang on! Use the charts in Appendixes A, B, and C to help you keep names, dates, and important theories straight. Think about what values, beliefs, and practices stand out to you as elements that may guide your own eclectic practice.

STARTING POINTS: QUESTIONS AND REFLECTIONS

As you read about all the people, places, and beliefs that influenced practices throughout the past few centuries, ask yourself what you know about early childhood practices today.

1. What are your beliefs about the innate nature of children? How should children learn and how should they be taught?

2. Do you think parents or schools are best equipped to care for and teach their infants, preschoolers, and school-age children?

3. What do you believe should be the primary goals and functions of early childhood programs? Are your ideas different from what you think is actually happening in regard to these areas of concern?
   • Service to working parents
   • Parent education
   • Child education
   • Child welfare
   • Parenting and caregiving
   • Keeping children safe or busy
   • Preparing children for society, elementary school, and careers

Historical Trends

Several hotly debated issues run like threads through the patchwork of U.S. early childhood history. At some times more prominent than at others, these are the underlying trends that have influenced practice. As you travel along the historical time line of this chapter, the following issues will be your traveling companions:

• The prevailing views regarding children

• The role of families, particularly women at home and in society

• International theories, research, and trends that influence American educational programming

• The effects of **socioeconomic status** (SES) on early care and education practice

• Early childhood settings as **custodial care** or education; the goals and purpose of the programming

Think about children's experiences throughout history as you think about what you want your own practice to be like and what experiences you hope to provide for children.

Life in the 1600s: Harsh Traditions and New Ideas

In Colonial America, children were generally treated as small adults, and childhood was not necessarily valued as an important phase of life. Colonial American society generally agreed that children should be taught to read the Bible from an early age, initially at home with their fathers as teachers (Spodek, 1985). According to Colonial society, it was desirable to curb children's sinful nature early in life. In 1647 Massachusetts enacted a law requiring the establishment of local

Socioeconomic status

The status within community and society based on income level, family economic stability, and social acceptance.

Custodial care

Type of program for young children that emphasized care and service to parents but did not have strong educational components.

schools for young children. These schools were often called **dame schools** because they were run by the women of the community (Beatty, 1995). The schools were places to care for children while adults worked and to instill piety through readings of the Bible. School activities stemmed from a desire to teach children the value of hard work, strong moral character based on religious beliefs, and trade skills they would use as adults (Hacsi, 1995).

Dame schools

Early local, public schools established in the mid-1600s to provide basic care for children of working mothers.

Influential People, Contexts, and Ideas

By the earliest decades of the 1600s, philosophers and educators were beginning to focus their attention on early childhood as a distinct stage of life. Several key theorists emerged with ideas that countered the harsh educational practices being used in Europe and America (Matthews, 2003). Eastern European religious leader **Johann Amos Comenius** (1592–1670) was one of the earliest authors to produce a text outlining a modern system of education for all children (Beatty, 1995). He continued to advocate for universal education, which Martin Luther (1483–1546) had successfully promoted in some European countries (Sandsmark, 2002). Comenius's vision of education as a means to promote social harmony and end the war and political strife he had witnessed in his life reflected his deep religious convictions and commitment to working toward peace. He saw nature as a prime method of fostering children's growth and advocated letting children play and grow in natural, harmonious settings. He was among the first to propose that young children had a great potential for learning and ought to learn through active means (Schickedanz, 1995).

Comenius also promoted the role of mothers—not school—as the best educators of children under the age of 6, and he wrote a guidebook outlining all the concepts, skills, and activities he felt children should be taught. Although his guide was quite specific in its details, Comenius nevertheless insisted that mothers individualize instruction because children develop at different rates, and he warned against excessive academics too early. Does it surprise you to realize that some of these modern beliefs (individualized instruction, parents as the child's first teacher, young children as capable learners) were being written in his book in the 1650s? Best practices in our field have come a long way, but as you can see, the historic roots run deep.

A scant 40 years later, a doctor and philosopher, **John Locke** (1632–1704), produced another guide to education that had a great impact on educational practices in America. Much of his work contradicted customary practices and promoted views of children that were more favorable, free, and playful. Locke strongly emphasized the importance of first-hand experiences as a means of learning. This viewpoint gave rise to the concept of experiential education, which is still in favor today. Locke emphasized the importance of education (less emphasis on innate drives) and proposed that children were like blank pages or wax that should be molded and shaped by experience (Henson, 2003). For Locke, experience was education.

Locke believed that the development and education of young children were best served by parents as educators. He advocated instructing children as young as 1 or 2 in literacy, but he cautioned that academic instruction should feel more like play to children (Beatty, 1995). He also encouraged parents to use children's internal need for approval and guilt to manipulate them into desired behaviors, preferring reasoning with children to physical punishment (Hulbert, 1999). He differed from previous theorists in that his beliefs were more centered on children and less centered on religion.

The beliefs of Comenius and Locke did much to counter the negative view of children that generally pervaded the 17th century. The pendulum had begun to swing toward more favorable beliefs about children's innate character. Fortunately for children, this trend toward a deeper awareness of the nature of young children and a respect for childhood as a unique stage of life formed the foundation for the vision of the next round of influential theorists.

Education in the 1700s: Romantic and Radical

For the romantics, or some of the enlightenment thinkers who permeated the 1700s and 1800s, education was a naturally unfolding process. However, this naturally unfolding process needed to involve careful teaching to come to fruition and to create balanced individuals who could operate in society (Kontio, 2003). Many people believed that children were best educated in rural settings through authentic experiences that were interesting to them. The following example illustrates the harmonious, respectful, natural education advocated by these philosophers.

CLASSROOM VIEW

A small child bursts forth from a little stone cottage on a sunny green hillside dotted with grazing sheep. The child decides to fill the small trough from which the sheep drink. He knows the stream is through the trees behind the cottage, and he sets off. Once there, he scoops some water up in his hands and begins to make his way back to the trough. As you are probably already thinking, the water has seeped through his fingers by the time he gets back to the trough. His clothes and shoes are wet. He stops and looks at his hands for a while. His teacher watches from a distance, careful not to scold the child or direct him to the pail by the side door. The look on the child's face shows that he is processing his experience, trying to formulate some kind of plan that will successfully achieve his goal. His gaze turns from his hands to the trough. He reaches out and touches it, feeling the wooden sides. The teacher patiently waits and watches. The child looks at his hands again, spreading his fingers. Slowly, he looks around him, searching for something more like the trough than his hand—something that can carry the water.

The child sees his teacher and approaches him. He tells the teacher about his plan and about his experience with the water running through his hands. The teacher listens. The teacher asks the child if he can think of anything he has used before to hold water. The child pauses. "A cup at supper," he remembers. The teacher and child talk about the child's cup, how it works, and what it looks like. As they talk, the child decides to look for something with tall sides and a bottom, like his cup. With a start, his eyes alight on the pail, and he runs off to give it a try. The teacher continues to observe the child's self-initiated actions.

Influential People, Contexts, and Ideas

French philosopher **Jean-Jacques Rousseau** (1712–1778) authored influential books that spawned educational reforms in Europe and America (Beatty, 1995). His founding principles are seen as threads running through the beliefs of many prominent educators throughout history (Lascarides & Hinitz, 2000). In one of his books, *Emile*, he proposed the radical idea that children were innately perfect and optimal development would unfold naturally without the corrupting influence of some elements of society (Null, 2004). Rousseau did, however, validate the importance of each person maintaining individual will while also promoting the will of society (Kontio, 2003). In his view, the individual learns to operate within and for the social group. Happiness is derived from individual freedom and the capability to develop attainable goals.

Johann Heinrich Pestalozzi, 1746–1827.

Although Rousseau's book was fictional, it did serve as something of a guide in which he encouraged manipulating and directing children's actions and thought indirectly (Procher, 1998). He took care to caution against exerting direct control and authority over the child, which would lead to anger and rebellion. The concept of individual freedom and aversion to dominance was of prime importance to Rousseau (Kontio, 2003). Rousseau validated children as pure, fundamentally different from adults, and in need of protection from corruption (Henson, 2003). He advocated that childhood be prolonged and reserved for activities of interest to children, not those imposed by direct adult instruction. Unlike earlier theorists, he believed that young children should not be pushed into academic instruction but rather be allowed to develop naturally and harmoniously (Null, 2004). Rousseau did not believe that mothers were capable of properly educating their children. Instead, he advocated that mothers turn over their children to male tutors for proper upbringing (Beatty, 1995). Here we see the first major pendulum swing relating to parents' role in young children's education.

In another shift in perspective, Swiss educator **Johann Heinrich Pestalozzi** (1746–1827) focused on the welfare of poor children. His concerns grew out of the increasing industrialization of society and the dramatic rifts among upper, middle, and lower classes in urban areas. Unlike earlier theorists, he worked directly with children, experimenting with new methods (Schickedanz, 1995). Inspired by the romantic view of childhood, Pestalozzi followed some of Rousseau's ideas and designed schools and curricula based on a holistic approach to teaching the whole child physically, mentally, and emotionally (Henson, 2003).

Pestalozzi strove to instill a strong community-minded consciousness in students and valued active involvement with the environment. One of his enduring innovations was a system of teaching that fostered learning through reflection on experience (Adelman, 2000). Growing up with few resources himself, Pestalozzi designed an original method of teaching children living in poverty that centered on several key beliefs (Null, 2004):

- All children are capable of learning.
- Learning begins at birth with parents as the first teachers.

- Teacher–student discourse and activities should focus on hands-on manipulation of real objects.
- Natural experiences in the course of daily living are the source of learning.
- Arts and physical education are essential components of a comprehensive education.

Unlike Rousseau, Pestalozzi validated the mother and home as the most natural learning environment and held a low opinion of schools for young children. He envisioned all children learning through hands-on manipulation of objects with loving, affectionate mother figures, a view based on his own early experiences (Bowers & Gehring, 2004). His application of concrete objects remains visible today with the many manipulable materials lining preschool shelves (wooden and plastic blocks, puzzles, and unit cubes). Although his initial efforts were directed toward educating children and mothers in poverty, his method became popular with all classes of society abroad and in the United States. Many Pestalozzian schools were opened in U.S. cities in the early 1800s (Beatty, 1995).

Education in the 1800s: Kindergarten Is Born

Influential People, Contexts, and Ideas

British educator **Robert Owen** (1771–1858), who shared Pestalozzi's concern for impoverished children, became a pioneer and champion of educating children outside the home. He fueled the British infant school movement, in which he sought to create institutions where kindly teachers would encourage large groups of children to explore actively and amuse themselves. Owen also embraced beliefs about the importance of learning from nature and concrete objects. Owen's chief mission was to create moral adults through education promoting cooperation and social cohesion (Beatty, 1995). He firmly opposed the harsh, punitive practices common in his day (Owen, 1857).

In the 1820s Owen became increasingly interested in spreading the infant school movement in America. One of the earliest intervention programs (like the Head Start programs of today), infant schools targeted comprehensive services for children in poverty as a means of social reform (Spodek, 1985).

A parallel social movement, which was developing in the United States at about the same time, was to have a great impact on the decline of the infant school movement (though infant schools continued to flourish in England). As social life continued to change with industrialization, the role of men as the economic providers and the place of women in the home became increasingly promoted as the proper family dynamic (Spodek, 1985). This shift in domestic responsibilities led many experts, as well as mothers, to reject the practice of sending children to schools outside the home in place of in-home education (Dombrowski, 2002). This family dynamic was possible only for upper- and middle-class families; however, many working-class mothers simply could not stay at home to embody this ideal.

Care versus Education and the Separation of Early and Elementary Education

Day nurseries

Group day-care programs providing basic care and designed as a service to working parents.

For working-class mothers who had to work to survive, **day nurseries** were the only option for keeping their children safe and off the streets while they were at work. Often organized by middle- or upper-class women, the day nurseries' mission was to provide welfare and care to children on the days when their mothers were working. A pervasive attitude of blame was placed on these working mothers, who were often made to feel deficient (O'Connor, 1995). Also, the programs had no real educational goals, and a stigma developed over the social welfare-oriented programs (providing custodial care) versus education-based programs. This stigma remains today to some degree; however, today there is ample evidence to support the importance of quality, comprehensive programming for all young children. The day nurseries managed to remain an institution primarily because they filled a pressing social need.

Romantic views of children and childhood as godlike and of womanhood as the domestic ideal led not only women but also policy makers to reject including infant schools with public schools for older children. With the ousting of early childhood programming from the public schools, the funding problems began (and still plague the field today). Once again the pendulum was swinging as previous beliefs about the importance of early academic instruction shifted to a fear that it would do harm to young children's development. It became customary by the 1840s to refrain from any reading or academic instruction until children were 6 years old (Beatty, 1995; Schickedanz, 1995). A familiar theme remained, however, which was the importance of good moral upbringing from infancy.

Amid this rocky period, one of the most famous and influential people in early childhood history began to make his mark. **Friedrich Froebel** (1782–1852) is best known as the father of the kindergarten. Froebel's initial training in forestry and his rearing in a strict religious home gave him a closeness to God and nature that can be seen throughout his educational philosophy and methods, much like previous educators (Lascarides & Hinitz, 2000). Indeed, translated from his native German, the name he chose for his method—kindergarten—means "child's garden." Froebel sought to build on previous theories and create a formal system of education for young children that would uplift human society (Adelman, 2000).

Laying a foundation that remains in place today, Froebel advocated a play-based learning environment in which children would actively engage with special materials he created, called *gifts*. Teachers were to observe and guide children's activities, not to interfere in their naturally unfolding processes. The teacher's role was that of a careful gardener, nurturing children as tender seedlings growing naturally and harmoniously (Lindqvist, 1995). It was through directed play that Froebel sought to keep children's interest so that they could become engrossed in learning activities with hands-on materials (Saracho & Spodek, 1995).

Theories About Knowledge

Froebel based his kindergarten on rationalism. In this view, knowledge is not derived from experience but is gained by logically thinking through concepts from a given premise. In practice, this is evident in Froebel's method of having children work through prescribed activities with his gifts and occupations as the starting place. By working and thinking through prescribed tasks, children would acquire the knowledge that was symbolized in the materials and activities.

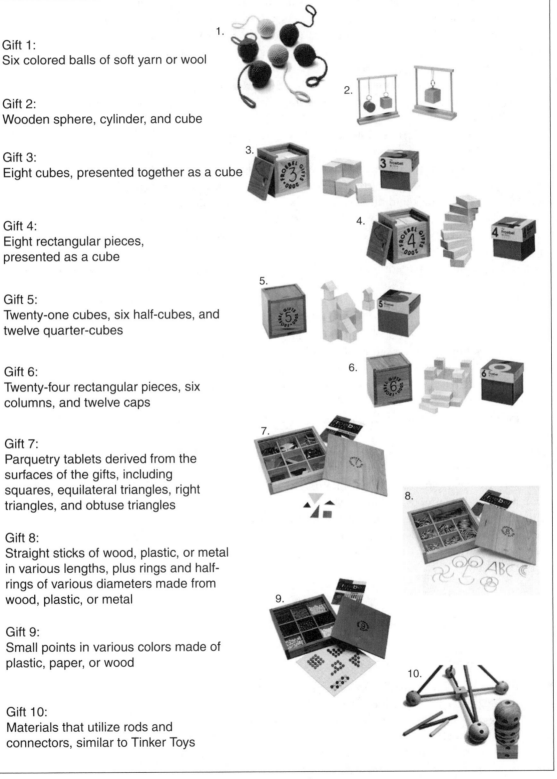

Gift 1:
Six colored balls of soft yarn or wool

Gift 2:
Wooden sphere, cylinder, and cube

Gift 3:
Eight cubes, presented together as a cube

Gift 4:
Eight rectangular pieces,
presented as a cube

Gift 5:
Twenty-one cubes, six half-cubes, and
twelve quarter-cubes

Gift 6:
Twenty-four rectangular pieces, six
columns, and twelve caps

Gift 7:
Parquetry tablets derived from the
surfaces of the gifts, including
squares, equilateral triangles, right
triangles, and obtuse triangles

Gift 8:
Straight sticks of wood, plastic, or metal
in various lengths, plus rings and half-
rings of various diameters made from
wood, plastic, or metal

Gift 9:
Small points in various colors made of
plastic, paper, or wood

Gift 10:
Materials that utilize rods and
connectors, similar to Tinker Toys

Froebel suggested 20 gifts and occupations and gave detailed instructions for their presentation and use with children (Saracho & Spodek, 1995), including

- Solid, three-dimensional geometric shapes fashioned of wool and wood
- Flat shapes of wood, wire, and other natural materials
- Handwork activities such as weaving, sewing, paper folding, cutting, and modeling
- Gardening
- Finger plays, songs, and games

Influenced by Pestalozzi's view of the important role played by mothers in children's education, Froebel also advocated strong family involvement. However, he preferred educational settings outside the home that served as extensions of the home. Here, mothers held key positions and status and infused maternal love throughout the school setting (Read, 2003). His repositioning of women in valued roles outside the home struck a chord with many upper- and middle-class women, who took up the cause of promoting kindergartens with great passion. Kindergarten programs began to open across Europe and spread through other continents as well. Froebel did not necessarily trust modern women's abilities to raise their children properly, however, and so also created a training program for mothers and teachers (Beatty, 1995). It was the close bond of mothers and children that opened the door for Froebel's kindergarten method to find favor in the United States, despite the concerns about out-of-home schooling that had caused infant schools to fall out of favor.

A German immigrant started the first U.S. kindergarten in 1856 in Wisconsin. In fact, German immigrants started most of the early kindergartens, thanks to Froebel's influence (Beatty, 1995). The early kindergarten programs and published guidebooks carefully outlined exact instructions for proper Frobelian methods, continuing the tradition of harmonious, natural learning instead of academic instruction. Although these programs earned some public attention, the onset of influential U.S. educators paved the way for more widespread acceptance as well as fierce rivalries between Froebelian purists and those who would change the kindergarten to fit American culture (Spodek, 1985).

One such American educator who became a champion of the kindergarten was **Elizabeth Palmer Peabody** (1804–1894). Inspired by the Wisconsin kindergarten, Peabody opened the first English-speaking kindergarten in Boston in 1859 (Swiniarski, 2005). She traveled to Germany, where she studied Froebelian methods, took her new knowledge back to America, and firmly opposed early academic instruction in favor of teaching through hands-on objects (Beatty, 1995; Peabody, 1877). Peabody adapted Froebel's ideal child's garden to include **individualized instruction**, in which she adapted activities to suit particular children's abilities. Based on her wealth of experience with children, she believed children needed careful direction to develop fully (Swiniarski, 2005).

Assisted by the efforts of **Susan Blow** (1843–1916) to remain true to Froebel's theory and practice, the kindergarten movement gained ground and implemented programs for children and quality training programs for teachers across the United States (O'Connor, 1995). Blow was particularly concerned about inferior teacher-training programs because she believed that qualified, quality teachers were essential for the continuation of the Froebelian kindergarten movement (Blow, 1900). Peabody created the American Froebel Society to regulate the quality and authenticity of kindergarten programs, and she advocated

Individualized instruction

The process of adapting learning experiences or material selection based on the unique needs and abilities of individual children.

for inclusion of African American women in the new kindergarten training programs (Dombrowski, 2002). She worked tirelessly to provide educational opportunities for post–Civil War slave children in the South as well as Native American children (Lascarides & Hinitz, 2000).

Moving Education Forward in the 1900s: Progressive and Developmental

Didactic materials

Materials that are specifically designed to be used in one way or focused to teach a particular concept. Opposite to *open-ended* materials, which are less defined to allow for many uses.

Over time, Froebel's method became increasingly rigid and formal, so that children's activities were directed by teachers and by the self-correcting, **didactic materials**. Kindergarten practices still included play, but Froebel's own writing that undirected play was frivolous and wasteful contributed to more direction of children's activities— even their play (Lindqvist, 1995). This was the start of the "push down curriculum" problems that are still debated today and that gave rise to the Developmentally Appropriate Practice statement, which we discuss in the next chapter. The rigid practices that were taking over kindergartens led to criticism by new progressives and proponents of the child study movement, who were beginning to take their place as the leaders in the field in the 1900s.

CLASSROOM VIEW

On this crisp autumn day you are taking advantage of the new lab school on a nearby college campus to peek into the lives of children. The classroom is set up with a one-way window, which allows you to observe without the children knowing you are there. This is a real opportunity to see them in a natural setting. You settle in at the window and start to notice the room and materials. The most prominent feature, which takes up a large portion of the room, looks like a house, but in miniature. There is a kitchen area with a small wooden stove and icebox, a table and chairs, and a hearth. There is also a social gathering place with sofas and chairs. Children are busy acting out scenes from typical daily life at home. Some are making food, some are at the table eagerly waiting for a meal, and two children are cleaning up with small brooms. The children are talking among themselves as they act out this little drama.

You notice that the teacher has been watching them, writing in a notebook. She acknowledges two other adults in the room who are also interviewing a child and taking notes. They are engrossed in this child study. The teacher leaves her notebook and begins to interact with the children. She elaborates on their dialogues and asks the children if they think the table should be set for supper. Two children jump up from the table and run to get table settings. The room hums with activity, but you're wondering about all this playing and whether the teacher is going to start directing the children on academic tasks soon. Later, when you have an opportunity to talk with the teacher, she describes her view on education as "progressive."

Influential People, Contexts, and Ideas

The 1900s mark a dynamic period of change in early childhood theories and practice. As the new millennium approached, discourses on education shifted from the religious influences to more scientific approaches. Charles Darwin's pioneering work in developing his theory of evolution significantly influenced the new social scientists who were leading the field of childhood development and education.

The Rise of Child Study

G. Stanley Hall (1844–1924), the first American to receive a doctorate in psychology, integrated Darwin's ideas with those of the romantics and created the child study movement. His approach to education emphasized aligning the educational curriculum with the stages of development. He began the effort to elevate education into the ranks of respected science with his scientific approach to studying children (Null, 2004). Hall's systematic research yielded volumes on children's development and introduced classroom teachers to a new role as researchers. He also became an advocate for modifying the Froebelian kindergarten to align more with his developmental theories; for example, placing more emphasis on large motor development early as opposed to Froebel's emphasis on fine motor skills first (Beatty, 1995).

Hall supported an interdisciplinary approach to working with young children that integrated supports and services for health and education (Hall, 1907). Through his observations of children, he voiced concerns about children spending too much time in classrooms, at the expense of time outside playing freely in fresh air (Hulbert, 1999). His concerns that schools were making children nervous and pushing them ahead of their time remain concerns today.

Arnold Gesell (1880–1961), a student of Hall's, placed great emphasis on the developmental importance of the early childhood years and promoted the role of parents and teachers as researchers (Gesell, 1940). He emphasized the importance of careful, documented observations and made the university lab school a popular feature of the child study movement. The classroom visit at the start of this section illustrates the lab school in action:

- Observers making **naturalistic observations**
- Teachers chronicling their observations and using them to guide children's education
- Researchers interviewing children to gather data on developmental trends

Visit MyEducationLab to observe children using different materials; use your observation skills to make assumptions about their development as if you were part of this child study movement.

Much information was gleaned in these settings about how children develop and respond to educational environments, although the children studied represented mostly the upper-middle class. Gesell wrote prolifically about his research findings, pioneering the use of photographic research. His work defining the stages of infant development, as well as his support of connections between home and school, remains influential today (Lascarides & Hinitz, 2000). The child study movement was challenged by behaviorists (promoting education as habit training), who dismissed the role of teachers and parents in the research process and questioned the scientific integrity of the child study movement. Behaviorists, such as Edward Thorndike, sought more quantifiable data and devised the earliest standardized subject achievement tests (Trotter, Keller, Zehr, Manzo, & Bradley, 1999). The tension between educational psychology schools of thought continues today (Takanishi, 1981).

Naturalistic Observations

A research method of directly observing subjects in their natural environment.

MyEducationLab

Go to the Video Examples section of Topic 4: Observation/ Assessment in the MyEducationLab for your course and watch the video entitled *Sensory Activities*. Keep in mind how observation is a teacher's most powerful tool in becoming aware of children's development and learning.

The Progressive Era Dawns

At the turn of the 20th century, another movement was afoot—one that sought to synthesize old ideas with new discoveries in an effort to move education forward. **John Dewey** (1859–1952) cultivated his role as one of the most influential contemporary American education scholars and popularized the progressive movement in education (Henson, 2003). Dewey was influenced by the discourse on educational philosophies of his predecessors (including Hall) and by Darwin's theories of evolution. He valued the child's psychological and social dimensions and believed that education should emerge from the child's own unfolding development and interests rather than be rigidly imposed upon the child by the teacher (Matthews, 2003). He emphasized three key factors of education (Dewey, 1938; Powell, 2000):

- experience with authentic materials
- Meaningful to the individual student
- Based on problem-solving activities

Contrary to previous perspectives of early childhood programs as protective gardens, Dewey suggested that the classroom environment mirror society (Henson, 2003). In his writing on the role of democracy in education, Dewey presented the idea that social engagement was central to the development of responsible citizens (Archambault, 1964). Dewey firmly believed that the environment exerts great influence over the child, especially the social environment (Antler, 1987). Furthermore, the disposition of the learner began to emerge as an area of concern for modern educators.

In addition to focusing on the acquisition of skills, Dewey believed that the development of a love of learning and a desire to continue learning ought to be the primary aims of the educational environment (Dewey, 1899). He believed that the intellect and interest of students were best engaged through collaborative, critical inquiry in an environment that supported the learner as a shared authority with the teacher. In his progressive view, learning occurred through the direct interaction of students, teachers, and materials in experiential, problem-solving endeavors. A key role of the teacher was to uncover children's interests, thoughts, and feelings and to plan engaging educational experiences based on them (Hyun & Marshall, 2003). **Emergent curriculum** methods of today, such as the Project Approach (Chapter 8), integrate Dewey's ideas. The results of this learning environment were expected to be the raising of independent thinkers, fully capable of making meaning out of their world through critical inquiry, collaboration, and judgment (Gregory, 2002).

Emergent curriculum

Learning experiences and plans that emerge from children's interests and lives.

Amid fierce rivalries over conservative Froebelian methods and more Americanized kindergartens, Dewey sought a balance between too much teacher direction and leaving children to go forth unguided in their education (Beatty, 1995). He advocated more open, unstructured play and careful guidance in developmentally appropriate activities, such as the dramatic play in the classroom view (Saracho & Spodek, 1995). Kindergarten teachers such as **Patty Smith Hill** (1868–1946) designed new child-centered, interest-based methods that integrated ideas from Froebel, the child study movement, behaviorism, and progressive approaches to education. Hill also laid the foundation for today's National Association for the Education of Young Children through her efforts to professionalize the field in the 1920s (Bredekamp, 1997). One enduring belief promoted by Hill was the universality of early childhood education and the integration of all social classes together in the classroom. She lamented the loss of kindergarten's strong social welfare ties as public schools became more and more involved, although she was pleased with the improvements made to earlier, more rigid Froebelian methods (Hill, 1941).

Despite Dewey's view of education for social justice and Hill's dedication to improving conditions for impoverished children and Native American children, many programs fell short of these goals. In relation to Native American children, the goals of education were to assimilate children into mainstream American culture at the expense of their home language and culture, a practice that is strongly opposed today (Beatty, 1995; Lascarides & Hinitz, 2000).

Assimilation of Native American Children

As settlers moved westward across the United States, clashes with the indigenous people became frequent and violent. By the 1900s, Indian schools had been created by Protestant and Christian Anglos (European Americans) with the purpose of assimilating Native Americans and sometimes Hispanics into the new white American culture. The goal of Americanizing, which was regarded as a salvation for the so-called barbaric and savage natives, was to enable such students to step into the new society as fully functioning members. Children were removed from their homes and families to be raised in boarding schools or with surrogate white families. Their hair and dress were changed to match those of the dominant culture. They were forbidden to speak their native language or recognize any cultural traditions other than those practiced by the new settlers. This "systematic programme of cultural extinction," a common and accepted practice at the time, was funded by the government as a public service (Margolis & Rowe, 2004).

Natives, considered worthless, were dehumanized by how they were described and treated. The prevailing view felt it was necessary to erase all vestiges of the Native American in order to create a civilized human in his or her place. It was decided that it was less expensive to reprogram or reeducate the natives than to kill them (Margolis & Rowe, 2004). The school programs differed from state to state, but it typically included occupational training for boys (farming and woodworking), domestic tasks for girls (cooking and knitting), and heavy manual labor for all children. Activities, including recreational activities, were strictly regimented to ensure complete deference to authority.

By the 1920s, however, the goal of assimilation to integrate Native Americans into society had been lost. The expectation for the reeducated Native American was not to find an equal, or functional, place in society. The new goal of assimilation programs was to train Native Americans (along with many immigrants) to accept their lesser status in a racist system (Hoxie, 1984). The skills learned in the schools would provide jobs as servants working for white families (Margolis & Rowe, 2004).

Slowly, beginning in the late 1920s, the culture of assimilation in Indian schools began to change. Public schools were encouraged (with financial incentives) to include Native American children. These schools began to include studies of native culture and arts along with academic subjects. The practices that had previously stripped Native American tribes of their autonomy, financial self-governance, and land ownership were starting to change. The practice of corporal punishment (physical abuse) in schools was outlawed in 1929, changing the previous system of abuse that had run rampant in Indian schools.

As kindergarten methods progressed and changed, advocates of early childhood education continued to push for public acceptance and universal kindergartens. Many debates ensued as states slowly began to integrate kindergarten programs into the public school arena. Areas of debate included the following:

- Methods and scope—literacy instruction, play, and worksheets
- Mission—social reform, individual development, academic training, and first-grade preparation
- Salaries for teachers
- Half-day versus full-day, double sessions

As kindergarten programs aimed at 5-year-olds became more entrenched in public schools and universal in scope (and perhaps more narrowly focused on elementary education goals versus broader developmental goals), a new wave of early childhood programming began to rise: nursery schools for 2- to 4-year-olds.

Nursery Schools Emerge

In the years following World War I (1914–1918), concerns over a child's overall welfare became a driving force for various organizations and agencies to come together to meet children's and families' needs. The nursery schools forming at this time, influenced by growing voices in the psychodynamic field, sought to provide caring and nurturing as well as educational programming. At that time, nursery schools, which served diverse populations, had roots firmly planted in social welfare for needy children. Once again integrating trends from international circles, the work of sisters **Margaret** (1860–1931) and **Rachel McMillan** (1859–1917) in London became influential in American nursery schools.

With backgrounds in social welfare and an interest in alleviating the challenges faced by children living in poverty, the McMillans created an open-air nursery school where hygiene, outdoor play, and active hands-on learning were primary goals (Beatty, 1995). In addition to the emphasis on nurturing and welfare, Margaret McMillan envisioned nursery schools as fueling children's imagination and curiosity. The sisters felt these were attributes children would need as future leaders of society (Spodek, 1985). Margaret wanted her schools to be lab schools where professionals from a variety of disciplines could explore new methods to influence their own practice (Lascarides & Hinitz, 2000). Throughout the 1910s and 1920s, many nursery schools and teacher-training centers were opened based on McMillan's insights. In her writing, she emphasized the impact that nursery school teachers have on the brain development of young children during the brain's most plastic and formative period (McMillan, 1919). These words were truly insightful and prophetic in 1919, considering research on brain development and education have come to the fore just within the last few decades.

Amid the burgeoning Progressive movement and with more and more attention being afforded to the education of young children, two dynamic and highly influential women were poised to change the field. Firmly committed to validating children's play as the most powerful force in their learning, **Caroline Pratt** (1867–1954) opened the Play School (later renamed the City and Country School) in New York City in 1913. Her primary goal was to create an education system that would teach children how to think—to generate knowledge that they would carry over from the classroom to the world (Antler, 1987). Her philosophy of **intrinsic motivation** and education for oneself ran like a current throughout

Intrinsic motivation

The desire, interest, and motivation that are driven by internal forces, as opposed to external rewards.

Active, meaningful, social experience develops children's love of learning.

the school. Absent formal, teacher-directed, passive activities, children at the Play School chose their own paths. In effect, the children directed their own learning through free choice with materials and activities. The ultimate vision of the Play School was to engender social reform through education. Above all else, Pratt valued not obtaining information, but rather the process of learning information. This belief was also emphasized by Jean Piaget (Lascarides & Hinitz, 2000).

Early in the life of Pratt's Play School, a long and fruitful collaboration with Lucy Sprague Mitchell began. After many years of working in academic environments at the university level, **Lucy Sprague Mitchell** (1878–1967) became an integral founding member of the Bureau of Educational Experiments. She remains one of the most influential people in contemporary early childhood history. Through Mitchell's tireless work, the bureau's early emphasis became the exploration of experimental educational methods and philosophies. The bureau served as a lab school for the study of child development (Antler, 1987).

The systematic study of children's growth was, in turn, used to inform practice and refine child-centered methods. Mitchell's own interests in social reconstruction, the influence of friend and teacher John Dewey, and a personal interest in geography guided her belief that children's education in history and geography ought to stem first from their own life experiences. It should begin with the children's own neighborhoods, for example. Overriding everything, she felt, was that education was about each student's finding relationships—of concepts, people, events, or places (Antler, 1987).

Building on her lengthy work with and research involving children through the Play School, Mitchell embarked on an expansion bureau project at its new location on Bank Street in New York City. In the new location, a teacher-education facility was built with the lab school and research center. The goal was to develop teachers who would think—who would observe, reflect, and experiment actively in their own work and would value the social context of education (Grinberg, 2002). Today the importance of well-trained, educated teachers continues to be a key to the quality of education and children's success. In fact, the training and level of education of teachers remains the top predictor of program quality (Horn, Caruso, & Golas, 2003).

Mitchell practiced education as both a science and an art, and she strove to instill the same commitments in her student teachers (Lascarides & Hinitz, 2000). The influence of the Bank Street innovations had moved beyond experimental schools and into New York City public schools by the mid-1940s. The once radical ideas and experimental practice of progressive schools continued to become widely accepted, mainstream elements in education (Sullivan, 1996).

Education and Emotions

As has always been the case, early childhood education has been greatly affected by various sociopolitical events. During World War II (1939–1945), public interest in young children was renewed for several reasons:

- Habit training and behaviorism were giving way to more child-centered, affectionate, nurturing beliefs about how children needed to grow.
- Encouraging children to express their feelings became an educational goal.
- More women were entering the workforce, giving rise to an increased need for out-of-home care. (Public views that mothers ought to raise their children at home still reigned, contributing to many guilt-ridden working mothers.)
- As more out-of-home care opportunities opened for children, more women were able to find employment.

The increased need for early childhood programs translated into federal involvement in the form of legislation securing public funding for children's centers in the areas most impacted by the war efforts. More than 130,000 children were served daily, on average, in publicly funded programs at the time (Lascarides & Hinitz, 2000); however, only a fraction of the eligible children were involved. After the war ended, much of the federal funding for early childhood programs did too. It wasn't until the national War on Poverty campaign of the 1960s that federal funding was once again on the increase. The Head Start program, discussed in Chapter 6, is one of the enduring initiatives of that campaign.

The unique considerations for children's emotional needs, especially during traumatic events such as war or family crises, influenced several researchers during the middle of the 1900s. **Erik Erikson's** (1902–1994) developmental stage theory of socioemotional development remains a foundation of current beliefs about children's personality development (Vander Zanden, 2003). Erikson's theory has been used to guide interactions with infants and children. The early stages of his lifespan development theory are presented in the text box along with implications for early childhood professionals and practice. Young children are highly susceptible to the impact of relationships with adults in their lives, including families and caregivers. Early childhood professionals must strive to form close relationships with children and always remember the emotional nature of young children.

Another influential psychologist of the time was **Susan Isaacs** (1885–1948). Isaacs used richly detailed qualitative reports, mostly objective observation reports, in an effort to illuminate children's development (Isaacs, 1966). She advocated the importance of applying the growing knowledge base in psychology to children's education (Goswami, 2001). She also founded the Department of Child Development at the University of London in 1930, where her work,

Bank Street College of Education: The Developmental–Interaction Approach

Blending psychology and education (primarily Dewey's theories) in the creation of the curriculum for young children, development, and interaction were at the forefront of the interdisciplinary approach to education at Bank Street. In this active, hands-on, child-centered learning approach, all forms of interactions served as the basis for learning, including children's interaction with

- Peers
- Adults
- Materials
- Society/community
- Ideas

This led to renaming the program the Developmental-Interaction Approach.

Pervading all Bank Street's work was the mission to foster a new collective society that would nurture all members—young and old alike. This often meant that student teachers were engaging in observation and volunteer work in the community. This mission also guided the curriculum emphasis on social studies—that is, of the experiences of human life across all disciplines. The research on children, practices, theories, and society—as opposed to being a separate entity within the school—ran as a thread throughout both children's programs and student teacher programs. The research and innovations generated through Bank Street's efforts contributed significantly in terms of theory-to-practice applications (Grinberg, 2002).

Lab School

Starting with an interest in researching innovative and experimental practices, Bank Street integrated a nursery school program into the organization's structure. The lab school served as a place to study children, teachers, and learning environments as well as a place where student teachers gained valuable classroom experience. The nature of the curriculum was open-ended, where children learned through play and work using a variety of materials.

Teacher Education

The teacher-education branch of Bank Street evolved during a time when discussions of politics and education were at their height. Although much effort was being exerted on the generation of theories and exploration of international approaches and influences, Bank Street became a leader in implementation and practice. Here teachers were inducted into a culture of learning through experience; student teachers were encouraged to approach their teaching as artists but also to employ a scientific approach to inquiry, action, and reflection. Above all else, the progressive approach used at Bank Street sought to open teachers' minds to explore the possibilities in the complex social context of children's lives. The faculty at Bank Street served as in-class models as well as teachers for the student teachers—students could learn through discussions with them and learn by watching them in action. Student teachers took a variety of classes in child development as well as arts and personal development courses.

building on the ideas of Dewey, Freud, and Piaget, influenced methods aimed at promoting social and cognitive development (Aldrich, 2002). She promoted the belief that children's contact with the world around them formed the basis for their learning, de-emphasizing their internal constructive process (Hall, 2000). On this point, her ideas differed from Piaget's.

Although learner-centered education enjoyed much support from educators and began to garner research support as well, events from across the globe were about to change the educational landscape. In 1957, Russia made headlines when it launched the *Sputnik* satellite into space. At this point in history, this "space race" represented technological advancements, progress, and national pride. The shock of being behind in this leg of the race spurred Americans to look for answers. Their attention and blame turned to current progressive education practices, which some viewed as being permissive and chaotic (Henson, 2003). The pendulum of popularity was swinging again.

Erikson's Life-Span Theory of Socioemotional Development		
Birth–1 year	Trust vs. mistrust	Early experiences with parents and caregivers foster feelings of trust and security or mistrust in self and others. Responsive caregiving is essential. Give appropriate stimulation; respond to infant's cues for nourishment, love, play, and sleep.
2–3 years	Autonomy vs. shame and doubt	Newly mobile, children seek to assert their will and control their actions. Supporting children's choice making and encouraging self-direction are important. Think about the toddler who angrily grabs a shoe, crying, "I do it!" This child needs to build confidence in his or her abilities.
4–5 years	Initiative vs. guilt	Children become curious and want to explore their world. Children need to be encouraged to manipulate objects and direct their own activities.

In response, more scientific, skills-based approaches to education were embraced. One such self-proclaimed scientific method, which gained favor in the early decades of the 1900s and, after a brief fade, regained popularity after *Sputnik* and throughout the latter half of the 1900s, was Maria Montessori's method. Montessori based her method on systematic observations of children's spontaneous activities (Montessori, 1966). She then designed materials through experimentation and reflection. She was highly influential in her homeland of Italy and later throughout the world, and her methods have been influencing early childhood practices since her first early childhood school opened in 1907 (Montessori's life and method are discussed in Chapter 10.) The academic, skill-and-drill training emphasis ruled many public school programs until the introduction and enduring impact of constructivism in the latter half of the 1900s.

Educating Thinkers

Constructivist theories influencing practice today are grounded in the highly influential work of a 20th-century Swiss psychologist, Jean Piaget, and a Russian psychologist, Lev Vygotsky (discussed in more depth in Chapter 4).

Jean Piaget (1896–1980) spent his long life studying children's cognitive development, primarily through observation and analysis of children's answers to problem-solving tasks. Piaget observed that children think in qualitatively different ways at different ages, giving rise to his stage theory (Piaget, 1961). Piaget wrote prolifically about cognition, language, intelligence, and children's development (Piaget, 1929, 1954, 1969, 1975). His work has become a foundation for programs like High/Scope, and it has inspired countless educators and psychologists. He proposed that children seek **equilibrium**, or balance, in their beliefs and understandings of experiences. New information is processed through **assimilation** and **accommodation**, which involves either fitting it into a child's existing belief or by the child's changing his ideas to accept the new information (Piaget, 1969). Piaget regarded these cognitive processes as ongoing ones, such that a balance or equilibrium at one point would give way to disequilibrium with more new experiences that challenge the child's thinking.

You can see from this brief synopsis that Piaget valued the role of experience as well as the internal processes engaged in by the child on his or her quest to know the world. One important aspect of his work is that Piaget believed that both nature (biological growth) and nurture (people, experiences, events) influenced development (Piaget, 1975). This both-and thinking, as opposed to either-or thinking, has become an important feature of current theory and practice.

Although Piaget's work remains foundational, his work has been challenged in some areas. Many critics believe that changes in thinking occur more as trends, not as steplike stages. Some also believe that the cognitive processing of infants and children may be more advanced than Piaget thought (Sameroff & McDonough, 1994). Proponents of emergent curricula methods, such as interest-based projects, also disagree with Piaget's belief that young children are not capable of advanced thought sufficient to generate hypotheses and propositions (Hall, 2000). New research has shown that, with the help of adult guidance, children demonstrate higher levels of thinking at younger ages than Piaget proposed (Vander Zanden, 2003). Although they were contemporaries, the work of Lev Vygotsky has taken us beyond the theories of Piaget.

Equilibrium

Presented by Piaget, the cognitive state of balance, where the child feels comfortable with beliefs, ideas, and knowledge.

Assimilation

Integrating new experiences, ideas, or beliefs into existing knowledge structures (schemas).

Accommodation

Changing existing beliefs based on new information or experience that challenges current knowledge, so that new knowledge or understanding is created.

Piaget's Stages of Cognitive Development (adapted from Vander Zanden, 2003)

Birth–2 years	Sensorimotor	Infants realize the relationship between sensations and their motor actions. Infants reach and grab items they see; they put items in their mouths; they move their bodies to make objects move, such as a mobile. Around 9 months, infants also learn that objects exist even when they can't see them—called object permanence.
2–7 years	Preoperational	Children begin to think symbolically. They begin to use and master language—a symbol system. Symbolic dramatic play, in which children use an item to represent something else, such as a block for a car, emerges.
7–11 years	Concrete operations	Children begin to think rationally, and they begin to be able to understand conservation—that while an item's shape may change, the mass, weight, number, length, or volume does not. For example, a younger child will see a ball of clay flattened and think the flat one has more because it is longer. Children in this stage understand that the lump may be longer but that it remains the same amount. Piaget believed this happens because older children can reverse the flattening action in their heads and imagine the lump as a ball again.
11–older	Formal operations	Abstract thinking develops. Children can now think on the basis of hypotheses and propositions, not just on concrete objects. Children can master more complex scientific and mathematical operations using reversibility and reciprocity.

Putting It Into Practice

Model Language

During the early childhood years, children's language arts development blossoms, including speaking, listening, reading, writing, and thinking. You can help facilitate this development by engaging children in conversations, by expanding their verbalizations, by repeating and extending their ideas, and by modeling your own use of language as a tool of communication and thinking. Talk about your thoughts. Talk yourself through tasks. Explain what you are doing. Show children how you use reading and writing in numerous ways in your own daily life. Keep the language environment rich.

Lev Vygotsky (1896–1934) spent his relatively short life writing works that were not available to the public until long after his death. Political oppression in his native Soviet Union and late translations into English kept his work from the West for many years. Vygotsky's ideas differ from those of Piaget due to his emphasis on the importance of language development as a tool for facilitating and organizing cognitive development. More than just the primary vehicle for communication among people, according to Vygotsky (1978) language is the primary means by which children begin to organize their thinking. With the onset of coherent receptive and expressive speech, children begin to notice how people use words to share ideas as well as talk themselves through problems or think out loud, which later becomes silent thought.

Private speech

Children's use of language to organize their thinking, first by talking aloud and later as silent, internal talk.

This self-talk, which Vygotsky termed **private speech**, is often intuitively modeled by adults and, in turn, utilized by children. As children are given verbal cues, directions, or strategies from adults, they often repeat these or similar verbalizations to themselves while they work through problems independently. In this way, they use language not as a means to communicate with others, but as a means to organize their thoughts. Vygotsky believed that private speech was a powerful organizer that became silent and internal as children aged but continued to influence thought (Berk & Winsler, 1995; Vygotsky, 1978).

Zone of proximal development

Vygotsky's theory of learning, which posits that learning occurs when children are supported in working on challenging activities that are beyond what they can achieve on their own.

Firmly opposed to teacher-directed, habit-training modes of education, Vygotsky saw great potential for education to lead development within appropriate limits. His **zone of proximal development** theory suggests that each child has a developmental range within which he or she can be assisted in operating at higher levels than are possible alone. Key features of this theory include an awareness of the child's independent ability, as well as what is beyond his or her ability, and the assistance of a teacher to guide, coach, and prompt the child's thinking. This assistance, called **scaffolding**, changes based on each child's need and current cognitive level. Scaffolding treads a fine line between offering too much help (too easy, doing it for the child) and not enough help (too challenging for the child; Vygotsky, 1962).

Scaffolding

A teaching technique that involves giving verbal cues, prompts, and suggestions on appropriately challenging activities.

Vygotsky's work also emphasized the role of society and culture in children's development, underscoring the social, group nature of education. This makes sense when you think about why a child raised in England learns to speak English, whereas a child raised in Italy learns to speak Italian. In many more subtle ways, children's family and community culture impact the way they grow, think, and develop. Some cultures value group interdependence, but other cultures emphasize personal independence and self-reliance. These norms and values greatly influence the course of children's development in all domains, particularly social and cognitive. This reflects an interdependent view of growth and development that has great implications for parents and teachers.

Current constructivist theorists, including **Jerome Bruner** (1915–), continue to build on and refine ideas about how children think, process and store information, and learn (Bruner, 1991). Bruner valued self-discovery as the most important process for learning, emphasizing that children should be given freedom and autonomy to explore their interests (James, 2008).

Another influential theory that emphasizes the influences of a child's cultural context is **Urie Bronfenbrenner's** (1917–2005) ecological systems theory. Bronfenbrenner has suggested that children live within a system of influences at many levels. The interrelationships among children, family members, neighborhoods, schools, and peers impact the children's growth most directly and profoundly. He also has suggested that larger systems, such as government, broader educational systems, media, and larger social and cultural beliefs, exert influences on children, although perhaps in less direct ways (Bronfenbrenner, 1986). Within this view, illustrated in Chapter 1, you can see how complex and dynamic the overt and less obvious influences on children are and just how much is involved in children's development. As you read in previous sections, families and children also influence society and policies, as in, for example, Head Start legislation, school desegregation laws, and the Individuals with Disabilities Education Act. These represent the many layers of influences impacting children's lives.

Vygotsky's Zone of Proximal (or Potential) Development

The lower level of the zone of proximal development (ZPD) is where children operate independently; the upper level children can do only with help (it is beyond their current abilities); and the space in between is where children are engaged in challenging activities with the varying assistance of a more capable partner (Vygotsky, 1978). It is within this central area where learning and knowledge construction occur.

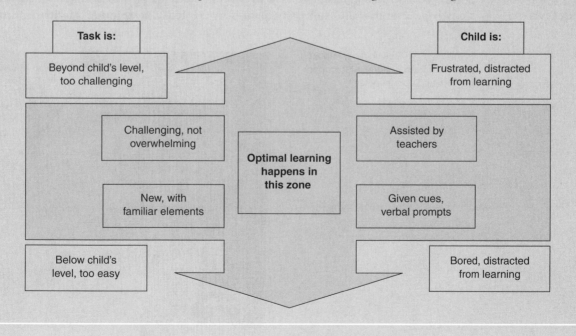

Modern Movements and Trends

The multiple influences of families, children, and society are apparent in some of the events of our recent past. The history of education is full of inequities such as separate classrooms and even separate schools for different social classes, ethnicities, races, and abilities. Current laws and beliefs, however, call for integrated, responsive programs that meet the needs of all children and respect all children. Some of the most influential legislation affecting schools has come from the sacrifice, tireless work, courage, and blood, sweat, and tears of parents and children.

Against the backdrop of the growing civil rights movement in the 1950s, African American families raised their voices and stood up for the rights of all children, regardless of race, to equal schools. The landmark 1954 Supreme Court decision in *Brown v. The Board of Education of Topeka, Kansas* paved the way for the desegregation of U.S. schools. Included in the overarching equality movement of the last part of the 20th century, public policy makers, families, and educators alike sought to even out the disparities affecting children living in poverty.

Throughout history, society has looked to early childhood education as a vehicle for social reform. The 1964 Head Start legislation was enacted to combat poverty and to meet children's diverse needs through comprehensive preschool programming and parent involvement. Other early intervention programs, such as the Chicago Parent Child Centers, which were launched in 1966 and run by the Chicago public schools, are enduring and successful examples of the tremendous positive impact high-quality programming can have on children and families (Reynolds, Miedel, & Mann, 2000).

Continuing the work of breaking barriers to equality in education, families once again were instrumental in changing established practices of institutionalizing children with disabilities. At one time, children with disabilities were relegated to unsatisfactory programs or even sometimes to prisonlike institutions. After much lobbying, IDEA became law in 1975. This law includes provisions for equal access to education for children with disabilities. The law has been revised in recent years in an effort to continue the process of providing educational opportunities and full participation in the **least restrictive environment** for

Least restrictive environment

Part of the IDEA, the goal that children with disabilities be provided with educational programming and services in classroom environments that reflect their highest functioning level, ideally in regular education classrooms with supports as needed.

Families, as well as society, impact children's lives; children also impact families and communities.

children with special needs (Turnbull & Cilley, 1999). This means that children with disabilities should be included in regular classrooms whenever possible to allow them to reach their fullest potential. They may be included in regular classrooms with assistance or in special classes, as dictated by individual needs.

Today's Issues

Few countries can boast of the richness of diversity that thrives in the United States. Although as a nation and society we have made great strides in realizing the centuries-old dream of social equality, we still have work ahead of us. Understanding and respecting diversity is currently a top priority for all early childhood educators. After decades of viewing schools as places for **Americanizing** children from diverse ethnic backgrounds, we are finally embracing more **culturally responsive practices**. The history of the Indian schools you read about before illustrates some of the hostile practices of assimilating people into U.S. culture.

Some educational practices are not intentionally discriminatory but still result in adverse effects on segments of the population. The challenge in receiving an equal education faced by many English Language Learners (ELL) (non–English speaking students) is another area that has been socially and legally challenged by families for many decades. The landmark 1974 Supreme Court case of *Lau v. Nichols* was filed on behalf of nearly 3,000 Chinese-speaking students in the San Francisco school system who were receiving instruction only in English. Although the schools provided some assistance to Spanish-speaking students, no assistance in other languages was provided. The case was based on the premise that, due to the students' linguistic diversity and lack of native language support from the schools, the students were being denied equal access to public education as protected under the Civil Rights Act.

The Supreme Court ultimately agreed, indicating that an English-only curriculum could discriminate against non-English-speaking students, even if unintentionally. The courts requested that the schools provide language assistance and instruction in other languages in addition to English. Although the *Lau* decision remains in place, over the decades the legal basis for the decision has been eroded on the grounds that unintentional adverse effects may not be grounds for legal action (Moran, 2005). Even though the legal battle continues, the contribution to our beliefs about best practices for diverse students is clear.

Culturally responsive practices mean acknowledging and respecting diversity and supporting all students' unique family cultures, including

- Linguistic diversity
- Ethnic and racial diversity
- Diversity in developmental abilities
- Diversity in beliefs, customs, and traditions
- Religious diversity

Current guidelines for quality practice include the following research-based suggestions (NAEYC, 1995):

- Maintain children's home language (which assists, not hinders, in learning English)
- Foster home-school connections, using translation software or community services when needed

Americanizing

The practice of actively diminishing and erasing diverse backgrounds and influences in an effort to promote dominant U.S. beliefs and culture.

Culturally responsive practices

An approach to programming that values, supports, and embraces diverse racial, ethnic, linguistic, and cultural influences and backgrounds.

- Invite families to participate in class activities whenever possible
- Seek out resources and information that will help you understand and value individual cultures
- Include a child's home language in your classroom whenever possible (label shelves, incorporate numbers and simple words into the class vocabulary)
- Give all children opportunities to represent their knowledge and experiences in a variety of ways (verbal, visual, kinesthetic, etc.)

In addition to practices in the classroom and within centers and schools, early childhood professionals need to keep child and family culture, language, and special needs in mind when researching and selecting materials and professional resources. The wealth of available resources to assist professionals in working successfully with diverse families is a good start, but we must also adapt materials to suit our own unique families (Corso, Santos, & Roof, 2002). Suggestions for adapting materials include

- Adding graphics or additional explanations when presenting material
- Using different formats and technologies
- Translating languages as needed
- Selecting parts from a variety of sources (individualizing)
- Asking community members to review materials for authenticity and value

MyEducationLab

Go to the Building Teaching Skills and Dispositions section of Topic 1: History in the MyEducationLab for your course and complete the activity entitled *Using History to Inform Current Practice*.

Conclusion

Along the winding road of the history of early childhood education, many prominent people have contributed, influenced, and informed current beliefs about best practice, particularly in learner-centered approaches to educating young children. We've certainly come a long way, but the road is laid out before us too. It may be bumpy in places and not well traveled, but ours is a profession built on innovation and on a willingness to take risks and change practice for the better. Although we stand on a foundation laid over centuries, we are still pioneers ever committed to the quest of improving practice and life for our children. At the heart of all early childhood practice is the enduring belief in the worth of all children, the value of play as a means of learning, and the potential for quality early education to improve children's lives. Our task as educators is to continue reflecting on our beliefs, challenging ourselves to improve practice, and dedicating ourselves to ensuring success for all children.

REFLECTION QUESTIONS: LOOKING BACK AND LOOKING AHEAD

Think about the rich, complex history that guides our current practices; reflect on how far we've come but also about how far we still have to go.

1. Do any of the people you read about or beliefs presented in this chapter support your own beliefs?
2. Does anything you read challenge your beliefs or assumptions?

3. What are your visions of the ideal learning environment?

4. What is your own theory of knowledge? How do you think children learn about the world?

SUMMARY

Throughout the long and complex history of early childhood education in the United States, there have been overarching trends that have distinguished various periods.

- During the 1700s in Colonial America, religious dogma reigned and children's upbringing was harsh and rigid. Schools were designed to instill moral and religious values through the reading of the Bible, and at home fathers were regarded as the guiding influence.

- In the 1800s, the role of mothers as the primary providers of child care came into the spotlight. As life began to change and move toward a more industrialized society, class structures became a new concern for educators. As more women entered the workplace, the need for early childhood education outside the home increased, and early childhood education emerged as an important profession. English, European, and U.S. educators called for education as a key to social reform and as a means of ameliorating the negative impact of living in poverty. This goal still remains important today.

- In the 1900s new scientific views of the study of children and childhood took hold and expanded the knowledge base. Now families were guided by scientific experts who took the place of religious leaders as persons who exerted an influence over parenting and educating. Changes in practice were also emerging as the Progressive era reigned. Many enduring practices and beliefs formed at this time, including learner-centered programming, interest-based project curricula, lab schools, and teachers as researchers.

- Amid the scientific revolution of the middle to later 1900s, education continued to grow as a science worthy of study and an important profession. Early childhood education became a public concern as federal legislation was enacted to meet the needs of children living in poverty or with disabilities.

- With the new century, accountability and standards took center stage and continue to be prominent aspects of early childhood practice. As evidence emerges that demonstrates the lifelong value of high-quality early care and education, it will continue to be important to evaluate practice and demonstrate evidence of success.

Application Activities

On the Web: MyEducationLab Watch the *Quality Child Care Settings* video at MyEducationLab. In this video segment, a variety of child-care environments are presented to illustrate the options in today's early childhood field. As you watch the video, try to make connections to the evolution in the field over the course of the long history presented in this chapter.

MyEducationLab

Go to the Assignments and Activities section of Topic 5: Program Models in the MyEducationLab for your course and complete the activity entitled *Quality Child Care Settings*. Keep in mind how observation is a teacher's most powerful tool in becoming aware of children's development and learning.

In Class In small groups, create a timeline of events, beliefs, and people to represent the history of early childhood education. You can select highlights from the chapter—key people and theories that show change and trends throughout time. You do not have to include every name and date. Use whatever materials you have available. Here is your chance to make the sometimes dry reading of history more lively and colorful.

In the Field Visit an area child-care center or school, or visit the center or school's website. Arrange to interview the program director or school administrator. While exploring the site, find the program's mission. Ask the administrator to explain the school's philosophy, mission, and prevailing views of children and families. Make notes about your impressions of how the environment supports the responses. For example, a center that speaks of the importance of family involvement in children's education may have a parent bulletin board, family resource room, family welcome space, and the like. What visible signs do you see of the philosophy, mission, and view of children? Write a brief reflection paper that summarizes the interview responses, includes the school's mission, and presents your perspective and impressions, integrating your thoughts on the chapter opening and closing questions about early childhood programs. Include any brochures or other literature that is available to you on your visit or from the website.

For Your Portfolio This activity could be used as an artifact in your portfolio under knowledge of the field or development. Throughout this journey through history, there were swings in beliefs and practice related to the following issues. For each issue, write a brief statement about your own beliefs, including what influenced them.

- The prevailing views of children and how children develop and learn
- The role of families, particularly women at home and in society
- International philosophers or educators and trends influencing American programming
- Effects of socioeconomic class divisions on programming
- Early childhood settings as custodial care or education; the goals and purpose of the programming

RELATED WEB LINKS

A History of American Education Web Project
www.ux1.eiu.edu/~cfrnb/index.html

Digital History, Children in History
www.digitalhistory.uh.edu/do_history/young_people/index.cfm

The Gilder Lehrman Institute for History
www.gilderlehrman.org/teachers/modules.html

Info USA
Comprehensive site for facts, information, and resources about the U.S. education system provided by the U.S. Government
usinfo.org/enus/education/index.html

CHAPTER 3

Professionalism in Early Childhood Education: Framing Best Practices

The aim of education must be the training of independently acting and thinking individuals who, however, can see in the service to the community their highest life achievement.

—ALBERT EINSTEIN

The field of early childhood education has a long history of reflecting on evolving practice. Throughout the history of early childhood education, evidence has emerged highlighting the importance of appropriate experiences in the early years for healthy development. Because of the increasing numbers of children entering early childhood programs and the growing numbers of children from homes where English is not the primary language, the need for articulated professional standards emerges as an essential emphasis for providers. An array of professional associations exists to guide providers in the many facets of professional practice, which include curriculum planning, teacher education, learning standards, inclusion, ethical practice, and more. One of these, the National Association for the Education of Young Children (NAEYC), offers a channel through which to generate and disseminate information and guiding frameworks about practices serving children from birth through age 8 and their families. NAEYC has worked closely with a variety of other professional associations to create many joint position statements in an effort to ensure an integrated, collaborative approach to working with and for children and families.

Nearly 20 years ago NAEYC addressed the need for standards of practice by writing their Developmentally Appropriate Practice (DAP) and Code of Ethical Conduct (also referred to as the Code) statements. The statements present standards of best practices and standards of professional behavior, respectively. In concert, the revised statements provide a solid foundation for making sound decisions about practice and meeting professional responsibilities in teaching and caring for young children. Today, NAEYC continues to provide support for early childhood professionals through research, publishing, conferences, and accreditation of quality early childhood programs.

STARTING POINTS: QUESTIONS AND REFLECTIONS

Think about the following questions as you read through the chapter and explore the purposes, goals, and possibilities of professional associations and what it means to be an ethical and professional early childhood educator:

1. What do you believe are the most important rights of children, parents, and teachers?

2. A professional credo is a set of defined beliefs and commitments. What would you write if you were writing your own professional credo? How do you believe teachers of young children should conduct themselves with other teachers, with young children, and with families?

3. Recall observations you have made for this or some other education class or think back to your own schooling. Try to remember the nature of the teacher-child interactions. That is, how did the teachers and children speak to one another? Would you characterize these interactions as warm, loving, responsive, and engaging? Did you hear more directive comments (telling children what to do)? How do you think this element of the classroom would affect the overall program quality?

CLASSROOM VIEW

Director Interview: Ethics in Action

It's a warm, clear morning in May as you prepare to visit a mid-sized infant, toddler, and preschool center in a small suburb. The center, a franchise, has a capacity of 125 children, and the owner/director, Lisa, is committed to child-centered practices. She finds resource and inspiration in constructivism and diverse learning styles as well as in her own experience as a teacher.

The center fully supports NAEYC's DAP and program accreditation guidelines, which have more stringent facility and program standards than the center's state regulations. Lisa describes how she learned about DAP in college and how she conducted many observations of programs to understand what DAP really means in practice. As a new teacher, she worked in a center that relied on a lot of teacher-directed, whole-group activities. She became frustrated with having to redirect the children many times during the day to sit quietly and pay attention to the teachers.

After several years, she left her first center, knowing that she needed to do things differently. She found another position in a center that encouraged child-initiated activities almost exclusively. Teachers prepared the environment and materials and stepped back to observe how children interacted with their materials. At this center, Lisa learned a lot about how to design spaces that invite children to explore and how to use observations effectively to assess and plan.

Over the years, though, she came to realize that children need some guidance and active support to make the most of their explorations. She opened her own center and made a commitment to a balanced, holistic approach to educating and caring for young children. First and foremost, Lisa describes the importance of balancing the following key factors:

- *Teacher-directed activities and child-initiated explorations*
- *Whole-group, small-group, and individual experiences*
- *Skill-based lessons and interest-based projects*
- *Teachers and children sharing control over classroom activities and topics*
- *Integration of principles of child development*

Staff Meeting at the Center

Lisa explains that all the staff comes together for bimonthly planning and sharing meetings. "Building a feeling of mutual respect and open sharing of knowledge has really helped make this center a place where teachers want to work. So many centers have a difficult time with teacher turnover, which is hard on the children. Particularly our infants and toddlers, but all children in general, need the stability of regular teachers in order to form close attachments. Without a strong, secure emotional foundation, their learning and development here at the center are jeopardized. I take every opportunity I can find to remind teachers just how important their influence is on our children and to validate the work they are doing." She goes on to talk about the early days of the center when teachers were used to doing their jobs and no more.

There was a pervasive feeling of disconnect among the teachers; each took care of his or her own room and did not network with others. Lisa knew this situation wouldn't change unless she directly addressed it, and she called a full staff meeting to air her concerns. The meeting quickly turned into a complaining session in which teachers shared similar issues with Lisa and each other. They turned to Lisa to fix their problems. Lisa saw an opportunity to use what she learned about resolving staff conflicts through the Code of Ethics guidelines, and she took it.

She focused on the kindergarten teaching team. Lisa facilitated a brief conflict-resolution session in which each teacher listened to the others as they openly shared their issues. The teachers each shared several things they thought were working well and a few things with which they were dissatisfied. Lisa then told them that it was their responsibility to work out their issues directly with one another in a respectful, supportive way and that she was there to facilitate that direct approach. She reminded them that this was their center as much as anyone else's and that the children depended on each of them working as a team. Lisa recalled how nervous she was when she said to them, "You are professionals. You are here because you chose to be a positive influence in the lives of your children. It is up to you to see that commitment through in all the big and little things we, as teachers, do. It may mean cleaning up or staying a few minutes late one day, and it certainly means respecting the need for families and teachers to work together. It is up to all of you to take pride in your work."

As she spoke, she saw their demeanor change. She saw them sit up straighter and nod their heads. In fact, all the staff seemed to become a bit more open. One teacher said, "I am so glad you said that." The kindergarten teachers agreed that they did not like their room to look dirty and made a schedule of tasks to complete during their shifts. They often felt disconnected from parents because drop-off and pickup times were often rushed. They agreed to keep a "back-and-forth" journal in which they could leave notes about things to share with parents when either of them was not there. Other teachers began to share ideas that they could use and then ideas that they themselves wanted to try. They decided to schedule a time for parents to come in for group activities. They rearranged morning and evening tasks so that they would have more time to linger with parents.

"By the end of our first meeting, the teachers seemed energized and excited. After a long day's work, this was a new sight for me! They usually were tired and ready to bolt out the door. But here

Putting It Into Practice

Knowing When to Step In

In the opening classroom visit, Lisa decided not to solve the teachers' problems, which is what they wanted her to do. She recognized how important it was to facilitate problem solving among the teachers so that they would ultimately be able to work together. This is also true for children. Too often teachers step in and implement their own solution to a conflict, such as taking away a toy, separating children, or removing a child to a cool-down area. Although these strategies probably solve the immediate problem, they alone won't teach children how to solve problems on their own. It is important for teachers to watch conflicts carefully to determine whether children will be able to work through them. If things escalate, teachers can facilitate mediation between the children, asking each one in turn to talk about the situation while the other child listens. Then ask the children to generate some ideas for how things could be resolved. Ask them to agree on one choice and implement it. When solutions come from their own ideas, children are more satisfied with the outcome and also learn how to problem solve for themselves.

they were lingering, talking, and praising each other's ideas. As conversations wound down, I told them all how proud I was to be working with such a dedicated, enthusiastic team. The tone of the center has become one of teamwork and of personal and professional integrity and one in which we always remember why we are here: to provide the absolute best possible environment for our children. Remembering why we chose this work in the first place is humbling and makes us appreciate ourselves and each other for our shared commitment."

Lisa reflected on the process by saying, "It certainly has been hard work to get where we are today, but our staff, parents, and community have no doubt about the rewards. Seeing our children developing into capable, healthy, curious people who embrace challenges and work together to solve them reminds us every day that there is no more important work."

At this point, the toddler teacher, Lauren, stops by the office to leave an anecdotal record in a child's mailbox. In this way, she can communicate stories from a child's day to his or her parents if schedules do not allow for time to chat at pickup. Lauren invites you to visit her classroom to see DAP in action.

Toddler Classroom: DAP in Action

There are eight toddlers and three teachers in the room this morning. On some days, there are 12 toddlers with 3 teachers. Lauren explains that they use a primary caregiver system, in which each teacher is assigned 4 children. Although all the teachers work with all the children, the primary caregivers maintain responsibility for observation reports, assessments, parent communication, and generally overseeing the children's daily activities. They are sort of the keeper of official information about their four children and are the parents' main contact person.

The goal of their primary caregiver system is to promote strong bonds between one teacher and the child and family. "Being a primary caregiver lets me really focus on a smaller number of children in some ways, although the other teachers and I share information about all the children so we can answer any parents' questions. I like being able to do more in-depth observation reports and assessments too. By sharing these tasks we are each able to do more for our children. I know my primaries so much more deeply than I did when we were all responsible for all the children. And sharing the responsibilities makes us [the teachers] all feel like equals. We really work as a team."

As you continue to observe the room, the last few children are just finishing up with a snack and are on their way to wash their hands. The toddlers enjoy splashing in the sink while a teacher cheerfully talks to them about the sensation of the bubbly soap and the warm water. Another teacher is encouraging a small group of toddlers to put their coats on by themselves. The children are intently focused on getting their arms through the sleeves while the teacher patiently watches, praising their efforts. You notice how responsive the teachers are with the children. Even during mundane tasks such as hand washing and coat dressing, the interactions feel warm and personal. The teachers do not talk above the children's heads or speak at them. They express a genuine interest in being there with them and exploring all the wonders of their world. The children respond with curiosity, confidence, and delight at their discoveries and achievements. You feel a sense of love and joy in this room; it reminds you of why you want to be a teacher.

The children and teachers prepare to go outside. They are excitedly talking about what they think they will see in the garden. Some of the children reach their hands over their heads and stretch out their fingers. One teacher translates the movement by saying, "Yes! I think we might see flowers blooming! Our bulbs are growing more and more each day, just like you!" The three teachers and most of the children sing a song about flowers growing as they make their way outside. Later on, Lauren explains their interest in the garden.

Framing Professionalism: Associations That Guide and Support Best Practices

> *"For practice to reach professional status, both head and heart need to meet at the interface of reflection."*
> —(MOYLES, 2001, P. 90)

Lisa's memories of conflicts, resolutions, and becoming a team of professionals underscore the heart of what professional associations strive to promote. It is about setting high standards of professionalism and practice, about meeting challenges as a community of partners, and about maintaining a high degree of personal integrity in handling any situation that arises as we ensure the very best in early care and education. Achieving these goals is an ongoing process that demands continued reflection, self-assessment, partnerships, and outreach. In addition, four common threads have been identified that serve to define essential components of professionalism in early care and education (Caulfield, 1997):

- Specialized knowledge of children's development
- Partnership with families
- Observation and assessment
- Code of ethics

Meaningfully integrating these common threads requires teachers to be well prepared, dedicated, motivated, and passionate about their profession (Moyles, 2001). In concert with quality teacher education and professional development training, becoming familiar with early childhood–related associations and organizations can support both new and experienced teachers. There are scores of associations and agencies working to enhance the practice and professionalism of early care and education, just a small sample of which will be highlighted in this chapter along with the work of NAEYC. For a sizeable list of related associations, visit NAEYC's website at www.naeyc.org/links and explore the many links highlighted there. The associations listed are specifically chosen for early childhood teachers and can help you prepare for your first days of teaching as well as provide options for enhancing your professional development.

ACEI (Association for Childhood Education International) was founded in 1892 on a platform based on the work of Friedrich Froebel and sought to promote quality professional preparation of kindergarten teachers (ACEI, n.d.). Today ACEI has an expanded mission to enhance development of young children (infancy through middle childhood) all over the world and to support high standards of professional development for early childhood educators. These standards of practice are outlined in the 2006 document Global Guidelines for Early Childhood Education and Care in the 21st Century (ACEI, 2006), which guide early childhood practice in the following areas:

- Environment and physical space of settings for children
- Curriculum content and pedagogy
- Early childhood educators and caregivers
- Partnership with families and communities
- Services for young children with special needs
- Accountability, supervision, and management of programs for children

The guidelines provide clear, concrete indicators of quality ethical practice within a comprehensive approach that emphasizes the larger context of children's lives. In addition, they correspond to a program assessment tool that, like the guidelines, is freely available in several languages on the ACEI website. The program assessment tool offers teachers and administrators the opportunity to self-evaluate, rate practice, and reflect on how practice compares with these key indicators of quality. These tools support teachers in the ongoing process of self-reflection and assessment, but the association also publishes research-to-practice journals aimed at reviewing and informing policy and best practices.

Whereas groups like ACEI and NAEYC take a comprehensive, global perspective on guiding practice, other organizations focus on supporting segments of the early childhood population such as infants and toddlers, family child-care providers, or children with exceptionalities. The Division for Early Childhood (DEC) of the Council for Exceptional Children represents the largest association serving the latter (DEC, n.d.). With a mission to promote policies and best practices serving families and children with or at risk for disabilities, DEC publishes position statements, journals, tools, and tips for administrators, teachers, and parents and provides training opportunities across the country. The "tools you can use" section of the DEC website includes free checklists and workbooks to assist providers in integrating successful inclusion strategies and to help parents evaluate the inclusiveness of early childhood programs.

Just as inclusive practices and valuing the diversity among children and families have become hallmarks of quality early care and education, the past several decades have yielded scores of reports emphasizing the critical importance of the first 3 years of life. Since 1977 ZERO TO THREE has utilized a multidisciplinary approach to supporting and enhancing

Putting It Into Practice

Visit the DEC website at www.dec-sped.org and click on the About DEC link. Under the Tools You Can Use link, you will find information and checklists to help professionals and families understand and advocate for quality inclusive practices. Open the Parent Checklist and review the list of quality indicators. Think about these indicators in relation to your own practice, classrooms or programs you have visited, or your own future practice. Print a copy for your portfolio to have as a reference and resource to share with families.

the health and development of infants and toddlers through research, advocacy, publications, and practical tools for families and professionals. The scope of work encompassed within the ZERO TO THREE organization demonstrates a truly comprehensive, multidisciplinary approach by integrating current research-based recommendations from relevant fields, which cover topics such as

- Mental health
- Nutrition
- Disaster relief
- Child welfare
- Language and literacy

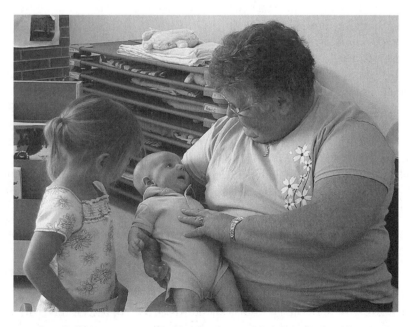

Supporting caregivers' efforts to promote healthy development in infants and toddlers is also an important aspect encompassed within the scope of early childhood education.

- Abuse and neglect

- Developmental screenings

- Early education, brain development, play

- Behavior and temperament

The multipronged approach of addressing professionals, parents, and public policy is a hallmark of professional associations and reflects the importance of a systemwide approach to optimizing developmental outcomes. You may have noticed that the emphasis on policy advocacy and especially on including families in the early childhood professional effort is a common thread throughout these associations, and you will see it emphasized in the work of NAEYC. Before exploring more about NAEYC, take a moment to view infant and toddler programs at MyEducationLab and think about the interrelated nature of the context of children's learning and development even at these youngest ages.

MyEducationLab

Go to the Assignments and Activities section of Topic 5: Program Models in the MyEducationLab for your course and complete the activity entitled *Infant and Toddler Setting*. Observe the spatial design, materials, and strategies the teachers use to promote learning, development, and relationships with infants and toddlers.

Foundation and Scope of NAEYC

Evolving out of the progressive era and the founding of the National Association for Nursery Education by Patty Smith Hill, NAEYC was officially established out of Hill's efforts in 1926 (Bredekamp, 1997; NAEYC, 2004). Even at this early stage of the organization, the goals included a desire to promote high-quality programs that met certain accepted standards and a desire to remain flexible and responsive to innovations in the field.

Since the 1960s there has been a growing concern about the lasting effects of early childhood experiences. Whether the effects are positive or negative depends on the quality and appropriateness of the program. As more and more children entered early childhood programs in the 1970s and 1980s, new research on the effects of such programming emerged. From this research arose a need for the crystallization of a guiding framework to help early childhood professionals align their teaching with sound theory-to-practice suggestions (Dunn & Kontos, 1997). In response to this long-standing concern about quality, NAEYC developed a system for evaluating and accrediting programs in 1985 and the first DAP framework in 1987. Both were based on high standards of good practice that emerged from developmental theories (and later sociocultural theories) of growth, learning, and teaching. The Code of Ethical Conduct was adopted in 1989 (Baptiste & Reyes, 2002).

At the heart of these statements is a set of *core values*, which are foundational to the DAP and the Code statements. NAEYC's core values translate into a mission "to promote high-quality, developmentally appropriate programs for all children and their families" (Bredekamp & Copple, 1997, p. 8). The core values include a commitment to (Bredekamp & Copple, 1997)

- Appreciate childhood as a unique stage to be valued in the present, not just as a time of preparation for the future

- Use knowledge of child development as the basis of all work with children

- Appreciate and promote the bonds between children and family

- Maintain a view of the child that encompasses the context of their family, culture, and community experience

All children learn best through sensory, hands-on experiences.

- Interact with all individuals with respect
- Make every effort to ensure that children and adults reach their full potential

The DAP and Code of Ethical Conduct frameworks have become cornerstones in defining ideals in the practice of early childhood care and education.

The DAP Framework: Theory and Practice

The original and revised versions of the DAP framework were undertaken in response the trend toward academically focused programming (pushing down elementary education curriculum; Bredekamp, 1997; Bredekamp & Copple, 1997). With a theoretical basis relying heavily on the work of Jean Piaget (Spodek & Saracho, 2003), the original DAP statement advocated the use of a child-initiated, play-based, integrated curriculum that reflected both age and individual appropriateness. Age appropriateness was defined as the awareness of universal progressions of normal development (developmental milestones) in each domain that are expected in all children. NAEYC also recognized that not all children develop in precisely the same ways or reach milestones at the same times. Therefore, teachers were also cautioned to incorporate awareness of individual differences in their environmental design and teaching (Bredekamp, 1987).

Embracing the process of debate, reflection, and revision, NAEYC members and an appointed revision committee made several key changes in the document at both the 1997 and 2009 revisions (Bredekamp, 1997; NAEYC, 2009). Research reviews spanning the decade between the first statements (1987 to 1997) indicate that children in more developmentally appropriate programs achieve higher academic success than children from less developmentally appropriate programs regardless of cultural, economic, or linguistic background (Jambunathan, Burts, & Pierce, 1999).

> ## *Putting It Into Practice*
>
> Accurate assessment is an area that is sometimes challenging for teachers but is increasingly emphasized in our standards-driven era. Best practices guide teachers to engage in systematic authentic assessments that are used to inform curriculum-planning decisions and evaluations of children's progress (Bredekamp & Copple, 1997). Appropriate assessment strategies include observations, work-sampling portfolios, and performance on authentic tasks, such as stacking blocks and pouring water into a cup for younger children or orally presenting a group project for older children. The assessment process is also an important time to foster reciprocal relationships with families. Families have a wealth of information to provide about their children in the broader context of their lives, which, when paired with information from the classroom context, presents a more accurate picture of the child (Moore, 2000). Validating the contributions families make to enhance children's learning and development is a key thread that runs throughout the DAP statement.

Revisions to the DAP Framework in 2009

The dramatic increases in children's enrollment in center programs, the ever-changing demographics of those children, and the contributions of ongoing research on development and learning demand that professional practice must continue to evolve. In response, NAEYC engages in a major revision process to the DAP statement at roughly 10-year intervals, with the most recent revision completed in 2009.

Recognizing the risks in either-or thinking (such as in teacher-directed versus child-initiated curriculum), the new NAEYC DAP statement promotes the use of a both-and approach to working with children. For example, the original version's strong cautions against the use of direct instruction on rigorous academics have softened somewhat. In regard to instructional strategies, teachers are now encouraged to follow several basic goals, including (Dickinson, 2002; NAEYC, 2009) the following:

- Skillfully balancing child-initiated activities and direct instruction
- Recognizing universals and individuality in children's development
- Providing routines, boundaries, and limits and allowing children to make choices
- Supporting children's need to work in groups and alone on individual tasks
- Preparing children for successful lifelong learning by fostering the foundational skills and attitudes they need to be successful in school and beyond (especially literacy and mathematics)

There remains an emphasis on the importance of social-emotional factors in predicting later school success, especially the development of self-regulation (NAEYC, 2009).

In the director interview with Lisa at the start of the chapter, we can see some of these changes taking place. Lisa first found herself teaching in a heavily teacher-directed program. She then switched schools and taught at a center with a strictly child-initiated program.

When she balanced both approaches to more effectively meet the children's needs, she settled into a style that felt right.

Shifting the Emphasis to Acknowledge Culture

The other major shift in the revised statements appears in the prevalent emphasis on the diverse cultural contexts of children's lives (NAEYC, 2009; Quick, 1998). Research on early brain development, early intervention programs, and economic diversity continues to raise awareness of the importance of family culture in children's development (Diamond & Hopson, 1999; Serpell, Sonnenschein, Baker, & Ganapathy, 2002). The emphasis on sensitively responding to economically, culturally, and linguistically diverse children moved to the forefront of the DAP statement's focus (Bredekamp, 1997; NAEYC, 2009). This shift occurred in response to changing demographics in schools and communities and the necessity of being prepared to teach all children in any context. The 1997 revision integrated evidence of exemplary practices from around the world, including those of Reggio Emilia, Project Approach, and Montessori and such national educational policies as Head Start/Early Head Start (Dickinson, 2002). (You will read about all these methods and approaches in later chapters.) The 2009 revision continues to highlight the increases in the number of English Language Learner families and children while also calling for stronger collaborations between early care and education programs and elementary schools

Changing Demographics

Across the nation, schools are seeing increases in diversity in student populations with the percentages of African American, Hispanic, Asian/Pacific Islander, and Alaskan/Native American students increasing, as reported by the U.S. Department of Education (2007a; 2007b), National Center for Educational Statistics (retrieved from nces.ed.gov/pubs2007/minoritytrends/ind_2_7.asp and nces.ed.gov/ccd/tables/2009305_02.asp). By 2007, public school enrollment of nonwhite students had increased from 34% (in 1991) to 56%. Although changes in national averages may seem relatively minor, there is also great variation based on specific state and locale (city, rural, or urban fringe). By 2003, non-White students made up 65% of public school enrollment in cities, with the largest increase being in Hispanic students. State-by-state comparisons demonstrate the wide range of student enrollments, with the District of Columbia reporting 95% enrollment of students who were non-White in 2007 (African-American students made up 83% of the student population) and Vermont reporting 5% enrollment of nonwhite students. In the same year New Mexico reported that Hispanic students (55%) made up the largest segment of their student population.

These changes, variety in student populations, and diversity from one area to another require teachers to be prepared to work sensitively and effectively with all unique family cultures and backgrounds.

Key Principles of Developmentally Appropriate Practice

The DAP statement both affirms a set of agreed-upon standards of good practice and validates early childhood teachers' experience of children as individuals and their need to tailor care and education accordingly (Bredekamp & Copple, 1997). The key principles and decision-making guidelines encompassed in the statement are viewed as foundations on which to build quality programs in the community context. Read the complete 2009 DAP statement for a more detailed discussion of principles and guidelines at www.naeyc. org/about/positions.asp.

All professionals working with and for young children must continually make decisions about how best to meet children's needs and enhance development. Several sources of information should guide those decisions (especially the first three; NAEYC, 2009):

- Knowledge of universal norms in child development and learning
- Knowledge of each individual child
- Knowledge of each child's unique social and cultural background
- Awareness of the sequence in which concepts and skills are learned
- A repertoire of teaching effective strategies

Because each of these elements is continually changing, teachers must continually learn from research, from each other, and from children and families. The roles of the teacher as a knowledgeable reflective practitioner, thoughtful decision maker, and learner define the teacher as a professional (Bredekamp & Copple, 1997). NAEYC continues to advocate for high standards of teacher preparation and ongoing professional development as essential elements for ensuring quality programming (NAEYC, 2009).

Knowledge of Child Development

Integrated learning experiences

Including activities that build skills and foster competency in more than one area.

The nature of human development is such that the distinct domains—cognitive, social, emotional, and physical—are interdependent and interrelated. Teachers must be aware of the complex interplay among domains in order to fully support development across domains through **integrated learning experiences** (Bredekamp & Copple, 1997). Planning integrated experiences refers to including activities that build skills and foster competency in more than one area. For example, as children develop the cognitive ability to combine sounds into words, their social development is affected by the ability to interact with the people around them. Similarly, as infants' physical development allows for more refined, purposeful grasping of objects, their cognitive development is enhanced by the opportunity to explore and learn about those new objects in their hands. When teachers think about children's development from a holistic (whole person or system) perspective, they create learning environments and experiences that meaningfully foster all areas of development.

In the opening visit to the toddler classroom, Lauren explained some of the class activities that fostered development in all areas through the garden project. The children experienced the physical sensation of digging in the dirt and the texture of the cool water moistening the ground. They talked about how it felt, looked, and smelled. They delighted in singing songs with movements that represented the growing plants. They visited with the older children at the center to hear stories about the garden. Each day the children looked for changes in the garden. Many of them enjoyed looking at pictures of plants and flowers in gardening books.

Some of the children also painted flowers on the easel like the ones they saw in the books. Throughout these meaningful experiences, the classroom activities ensured that the children's cognitive, physical, and social-emotional development were all supported.

Knowledge of Individual Children

As a teacher with a solid knowledge of what to expect at certain age intervals, you will be prepared to present appropriate experiences to individual children at different ages and stages. You will also be better equipped to notice how individual children differ in their abilities to master certain tasks or understand certain concepts. Being able to recognize norms and differences will allow you to individualize instruction and assess children's individual progress toward developmental goals. Individualizing for each child also allows children with special needs to be naturally supported in the regular classroom. Teachers are encouraged to validate children's different ways of knowing and representing knowledge. Echoing language and concepts from Howard Gardner's multiple intelligence theory, Lillian Katz's writing on the project approach, and the philosophy of the schools of Reggio Emilia, developmentally appropriate practices support the many ways in which children think, explore, understand, and represent their ideas (Bredekamp & Copple, 1997).

Knowledge of the Child's Unique Social and Cultural Background

The revised DAP statement also includes several principles emphasizing the unique cultural and social contexts of children's lives and their effects on development and learning. This revision reflects a new emphasis on sociocultural constructivist theory in addition to

Teachers use everyday experiences as opportunities to get to know children and strengthen relationships.

Putting It Into Practice

Individual Development

Although your studies will give you a background in developmental theories, the only way to really see individual diversity is by carefully observing individual children. Observing children and making notes must be a regular part of your day. You can create a rotating schedule so that you have made observation notes on each child within a week or two. Then you can use your notes to tailor individual plans to maximize each child's development, notice emerging interests, and assess progress. Whenever you individualize instruction in this way, be sure to start your observations by noting what the child likes or is interested in, then what he or she is good at or can do well, and, finally, what he or she is learning to do or what developmental goals he or she is working on at the moment. Use what you know about the child's likes and abilities to address what he or she is working on.

developmental theory. Concepts from Lev Vygotsky's writings, about which you will read more in Chapter 4, are prevalent in the 2009 statement. In particular, DAP encourages teachers to use play as a framework for children's learning and to present experiences that challenge children within the upper limit of their current developmental level (NAEYC, 2009). The revised DAP statement also embraces unique family culture as a key influence on children's development. The role of the family as an integral part of the teaching process marks a shift toward more culturally responsive teaching. The awareness, validation, and

Children's Choice Making

The High/Scope system of plan-do-review is an excellent example of how some programs are integrating children's choices into the curriculum. During group discussion time, children in High/Scope classrooms are prompted to choose activities that they will work on during their choice/center time. This actively promotes initiative, responsibility, and self-direction. Children then disperse and work out their plans in centers. After their choice time, the children come together again and reflect on their work. This review phase instills a sense of accomplishment in the children while they reflect on the results of their work and choices, validating their ability to direct their own actions. Teachers facilitate children's self-direction and support their activity in the classroom, but they respect children's developing self-discipline and self-regulation. In this way, teachers foster relationships with children that reflect trust, respect, and a belief that children can take active roles in guiding their own learning. Self-regulation is promoted in the new DAP statement as a key foundation for later success in school.

celebration of the richness and power of diversity among children's families and communities have become overarching themes in teaching today.

The Code of Ethical Conduct: Key Principles

The process of reflecting on and rethinking your own beliefs while embracing and validating many different perspectives is a requisite for being a professional educator. This is why you may find yourself writing reflective statements, generating personal philosophies, and exploring so many different approaches and beliefs about teaching and learning throughout your studies. This reflective habit should continue as you move throughout your professional career. The commitment to high standards and making equitable decisions as you carry out the duties of the profession are the hallmarks of professional ethics.

The conversations regarding professionalism in early childhood education and the request for guidance from practitioners in facing challenging situations began to take shape formally in the 1970s. With the growth of the field and reports of wide variations in practice, the need to professionalize early childhood education practices became clear. By the end of the 1970s, the conversations on professionalism and ethics had crystallized into published books on ethics in early childhood education. Lillian Katz and Evangeline Ward's *Ethical Behavior in Early Childhood Education* (1978) was one of the first. By 1988 an official Code of Ethical Conduct had been drafted by a NAEYC working group, which the NAEYC Board then adopted in 1989 (Baptiste & Reyes, 2002). NAEYC retains an Ethics Panel, whose responsibility is to review and revise the Code every 5 years (Freeman, 2000). The adoption and widespread dissemination of the NAEYC Code has given practitioners a research-based framework for making sound decisions in their work, especially when faced with ethical dilemmas.

Ethical dilemmas are complex situations that cannot be solved by research or law, and for which there is more than one possible course of action. For any course of action taken, there are potentially positive and negative implications (NAEYC, 1995). The difference in power and authority between teachers and children presents an added need for standards of ethical practice. Teachers, by definition, are in positions of authority over children, and conflicting situations arise for which there are no clear-cut answers. These realities of teaching prompted NAEYC to respond to teachers' requests for guidance in handling ambiguous situations where they felt multiple responsibilities created conflict (Freeman, 2000).

An example of an ethical dilemma a teacher might face is being asked by parents to withhold snacks or naps from their 3-year-old, even if the child is tired or wants what other children are eating. The parents explain that they need the child to eat and sleep earlier in the evening for the mother to be able to get rest herself for her night job. Conflicts between the responsibility to respect parents' choices for their children, their family needs, and the child's needs at school present a challenge in handling such ambiguous situations. In another example, a teacher witnesses a more senior colleague carrying out questionable practices that do not align with the goals of the center. The conflict between the responsibilities to promote the center's goals, maintain a respectful and supportive relationship with colleagues, and promote the best learning environment for the children can leave teachers unsure about the right thing to do.

Ethical dilemmas

Complex situations that are not solved by research or law and for which there is more than one possible course of action. For any course of action taken, there are potentially positive and negative implications.

IN YOUR OWN WORDS

If you have ever found yourself in a situation you would characterize as an ethical dilemma or ever been unsure about the right thing to do, how did you feel and how did you respond? In retrospect, would there be anything you would change about how you handled the situation? Can you think of other possible ethical dilemmas and how they could be handled?

Key Ideals and Principles

The NAEYC Code is a series of ideals and principles that outlines professionally responsible behavior in the care and education of young children. The Code is divided into sections addressing professionals' ethical responsibilities to children, families, colleagues, and community and society. It is not designed to be an answer sheet that spells out exactly how to handle any situation a practitioner might face. NAEYC policy makers have always affirmed that there is tremendous variability in the situations teachers face that are based on the unique and complex contexts of children's lives (Feeney & Freeman, 1999). However, the Code does provide guidance on what constitutes ethical and unethical practices in the same way that the DAP framework outlines basic standards of appropriate and inappropriate practice. You can read the entire Code on the NAEYC website at www.naeyc.org/about/positions.asp.

Ethical Responsibilities to Children   There is an understanding that in any professional relationship in which a difference of power exists, meaning that one partner maintains a role of power and authority over another, the importance of professional ethics is heightened. In the case of a teacher-child relationship, the power differential is extreme, with adults having an advantage of size, strength, authority, and power of persuasion over children.

With children's vulnerability in mind, the ideals related to responsibilities to children include a call for teachers to (Feeney & Freeman, 1999)

- Preserve each child's right to live in safe, healthy settings
- Respect and empower the potential of each individual child
- Remain current in research advances in an effort to continually improve practice
- Ensure that all children have access to necessary support in the path to healthy development

The principle that achieves these ideals, above all others, is that teachers "shall do no harm" to children. This seemingly simple statement includes the responsibility to recognize the signs of abuse, know the procedures for documenting and reporting suspicions of abuse, and access the social welfare resources for assisting children and families who may need them.

During your visit to the toddler playground, Lauren discussed her experiences with ethics. "When Lisa gave us all a copy of the Code, it was my first experience with the statement," Lauren said. She shared her own story of a child who consistently took more snacks than the portioned amount and who had been caught trying to take food from other children's plates as they cleaned up or threw out their leftovers. "We reminded him that he could have two crackers or five pretzels each snack, and we scolded him for reaching in the trash. We started to become frustrated with the child and were pretty disgusted that he was

Putting It Into Practice

Knowing Your Resources

Take a moment and locate your own state's child services Web page. Make a note of the link. Go on the page and locate the toll-free number you can call if you want to talk to someone about or report a suspicion of abuse, neglect, or resources for families needing food, clothing, or shelter.

eating from the trash. In one of our staff meetings we asked for ideas to deal with him. Teachers asked about the contents of his packed lunch, his clothing, and what mom or dad said about the situation. As we explained more about him, we realized that his clothes were sometimes quite dirty, that his packed lunches were usually a can of spaghetti or soup, and that we had few interactions with the teenage sister who picked him up and less contact with the parents. Some teachers wondered if there might be some issues of neglect. We realized that we needed to know more about the boy's home life in order to understand his behavior at school." Lauren looked down for a moment and said, "I was pretty ashamed to think I had been frustrated with this child, when in reality his family may not have enough to eat or proper clothes to dress him in!"

"I stayed a little later the next day and talked to the sister. She explained that the child's mother had left them 6 months ago and that the father was struggling to provide for her and the toddler. I went to Lisa right away to talk about what resources we could find for this family. Together we were able to initiate contact with the father and put him in touch with an agency that provides clothing, in-home support, learning materials, and paperwork for food vouchers. We also were able to organize a coat drive in the winter, which helped this family and others in the community. As soon as this boy started having a balanced breakfast and lunch with us, he stopped reaching for scraps in the garbage. His whole outlook changed, really. He is doing well, and his dad has even been able to come to parent nights and participate in some class activities. I feel like we are a team now, working together to help support this child's development."

Lauren's story illustrates the importance of a teacher's positions in families' lives. Scolding the boy for misbehaving served only to add to his problems. Experienced teachers immediately considered signs of a family in need of resources and recognized the importance of finding out more about the child's home life. When the teachers came together to understand the context of the child's life, they were able to start a course of action that supported the boy and his family.

Ethical Responsibilities to Families   Echoing the DAP statement's validation of the importance of family involvement in children's education, the Code includes ideals and principles related to a responsibility to families, which call for teachers to (NAEYC, 2005)

- Respect the child's family values and cultures
- Share knowledge of development and knowledge of their child in meaningful ways
- Help families build valuable support networks

Respecting parents as children's first teachers is part of being a professional educator.

Principles for supporting families include administrative tasks such as developing confidentiality policies. They also include practical strategies such as including families in decisions affecting their children and maintaining a network of professional resources (Feeney & Freeman, 1999). Many teachers struggle with forming reciprocal relationships with families owing to time constraints or mismatched schedules. However, the responsibilities to preserve family confidentiality and maintain a respectful attitude are absolutes of professional practice. Take a moment to view a teacher-parent conference at MyEducationLab and think about the interrelated nature of influences in the context of children's lives.

Ethical Responsibilities to Colleagues and Community   The commitment to work with an attitude of respect, genuine caring, and professionalism applies first and foremost to the children and families directly involved with the teacher. The nature of educational settings is such, however, that they also involve colleagues and the larger community outside the center. The ideals of ethical practice call for teachers to conduct themselves with the same spirit of respect and collegiality with one another and related community agencies and partners. With many early childhood centers experiencing increasing demands on teachers, finding the time to perform primary teaching and caring functions is a challenge. Adding in the responsibility to promote positive relationships with families, colleagues, and the outside community poses significant challenges for teachers and administrators. Collaborative partnerships within schools can be achieved by

- Creating communities within centers and within schools that remain up to date on current research as it pertains to teachers' work
- Welcoming the respectful and open sharing of divergent views
- Working collaboratively to solve problems through a stated conflict-resolution policy
- Creating policies that promote the well-being of employees
- Cooperating openly with partner agencies

MyEducationLab

Go to the Assignments and Activities section of Topic 3: Family/Community in the MyEducationLab for your course and complete the activity entitled *Parent-Teacher Conference*. Observe the strategies the teacher uses to promote collaborative discussion with the parent and the efforts she takes to prepare for the meeting.

Practitioners must continually reaffirm their core commitment to provide the highest quality programs possible for all children and their families. To this end, they use the professional statements as their guiding framework to make thoughtful, rational decisions in the best interest of the children in their care.

Meaningful Applications: Using DAP and the Code

First and foremost, teachers seeking to align their teaching with NAEYC's benchmarks of quality practice must become familiar with the content and underlying goals of the statements. Teaching is becoming an increasingly complex profession. Teachers are daily faced with a variety of challenges demanding thoughtful, deliberate decisions. As a teacher of young children, you are a powerful force shaping their development and laying a foundation for later school and life experiences. Given such an influential position, all teachers must acknowledge and adhere to high standards of practice.

Your Knowledge of Development: The Foundation for Practice

Standards of professionalism require teachers to cultivate a solid foundation of key theories of development and learning and remain current on important research findings. Therefore, reading textbooks for class, completing research papers, and catching up on current events impacting children and families will give you knowledge needed to make sound decisions on behalf of children. In addition to reviewing literature, teachers must develop their skills as researchers. Making regular observations and careful documentation that allow for interpretation are activities teachers may not consider part of their daily routine. They are, however, important activities for the reflective practitioner and one of the most important sources of information about the children in your care.

Systematic Observations: Teachers as Researchers

You will undoubtedly be asked to complete many observations as part of your teacher-education program. Although this may seem repetitive, honing your observation and documentation skills is an essential part of becoming a good teacher. When teachers develop their skills of observation and analysis, they build an ability to gather pertinent information, which they can then use to guide their practice. An important part of implementing a program that is developmentally appropriate involves being keenly aware of the interests, abilities, habits, and routines of each individual child. This awareness is best developed through carefully observing and listening as children interact with each other and their world. The observation and analysis process is perhaps the best tool teachers have to guide their environment and curriculum planning as well as to assess children's progress. Keep this in mind as you undertake the many observation assignments you are given as part of your education classes.

Putting DAP and the Code Together in the Classroom

With a theoretical base informing expectations and an awareness of individual differences, teachers are equipped to make plans and decisions to prepare optimal environments, schedules, activities, and material selections. DAP guidelines, which rely on socioconstructivist learning theory, suggest that optimal learning environments are those that challenge children within the upper limits of their individual developmental abilities. Engaging children in meaningful classroom activities is achieved by presenting interesting materials and worthwhile projects that reflect their individual and group interests. When learning experiences align with the context of their lives, children see the meaning and value in them and are more deeply engaged in the experience (Moore, 1999). Your observations of children's play and conversations provide insights into their experiences.

The garden project of Lauren's toddler class provides an example of how teachers maximize children's interests through observations. Earlier that spring, as the children went out for their daily outdoor time, the small tulip shoots popping up from their playground garden had captured their attention. The preschoolers had planted bulbs the previous fall, and the tulips were just beginning to peek up out of the ground. The toddlers became interested in the phenomenon in the garden and made daily visits to assess the growth progress. They invited the preschoolers to visit their classroom and talk about the planting process. The toddlers kept a journal of their observations, which the teachers wrote down from their dictation. They took photos and drew sketches. They heard stories describing seeds growing into plants, their parents shared stories about gardening at home, and they planned how to plant their own garden. The teachers planned movement activities where the children curled up like sleeping bulbs and slowly stretched their limbs as they grew into plants. (Remember the toddlers in line, ready to go outside, stretching their arms overhead? They were telling the teachers that they were thinking about those bulbs growing.) They explored seed packets and learned how to care for plants. The teachers scoured libraries for books on planting, plants, and gardens and shared them during story time.

The children's interest in gardening and plants, which lasted for 4 weeks, resulted in a chronicle of the growth of the tulips and a new, small garden on the edge of the toddler playground. The children's interests guided the classroom activities, and the teachers engaged them with directed, skill-building activities in literacy and science. "There were some challenges that arose during the project that sent me back to the Code," Lauren explains. "One child became visibly upset when we got out the potting soil and little shovels. She became upset because she wanted to plant, too, but had been forbidden by her parents to get dirty. We wanted to respect the parents' wishes but were sorry that the child could not engage in the activity. After a morning of tears, we decided to talk to the parents about the value of our messy activities." Lauren explained that it was hard at first because the parents felt criticized. The teachers shared their goals for the children and their knowledge of active learning experiences, taking care to validate the parents' concerns about the child's clothing. The parents explained that it was customary in their culture to send children to school in their finest clothing and that they had only a few such outfits. After discussing the matter for some time, the parents agreed that the teachers could change the child's clothes for messy activities. Lauren explained that the teachers embraced the project because they know that toddlers are naturally active and love sensory experiences like playing in the garden dirt. But it was only when they understood some parents' concerns did they realize how important it is to be sure that they are both listening to parents and explaining their practices.

Conclusion

The NAEYC DAP and Code of Ethical Conduct statements serve as valuable partners in upholding the commitment to provide high-quality programs for all children. Ultimately, however, each individual must choose to take responsibility for embracing these ideals and principles in his or her own life and work. The satisfaction of knowing that this commitment will enhance the lives of countless children is a reward well worth the effort.

Embracing high standards of quality and ethics also calls teachers to develop a professional identity. Unlike in other levels of education, early childhood teachers endure public perspectives that do not endow them with the same degree of professional respect as other teachers (for example, classrooms referred to as day care and teachers referred to as babysitters). As a new teacher, you need to present yourself as a well-prepared, capable, knowledgeable professional. This is the only way we can continue making efforts to update and upgrade the view of early childhood education as an important profession pivotal in laying the foundation for later healthy development. This aligns with the view of teachers as reflective, deliberate decision makers who use foundational theories of development and learning and apply them to individual situations and students. The heart of the DAP and Code statements seeks to do just this: to give you clear, articulate goals and strategies for developing yourself as a prepared, confident professional practitioner working on behalf of each and every child.

REFLECTION QUESTIONS: LOOKING BACK AND LOOKING AHEAD

Now that you have a clear understanding of NAEYC and the DAP and Code of Ethical Conduct statements, think about the following questions as you continue on the path to becoming a professional educator:

1. What professional ideals do you value?
2. What key principles of the DAP or Code of Ethical Conduct statements do you think would be the most challenging to implement? What can you do to alleviate those challenges?
3. Revisit the questions at the beginning of the chapter. How have your responses changed?

SUMMARY

The NAEYC promotes high-quality early childhood education programming through the publication of guiding frameworks and position statements. The DAP statement presents key principles that guide teachers' work with and for children and families by addressing basic knowledge of developmental trends and expectations as well as diversity among individual children. As the educational research base continues to grow and contribute to our understanding of how children grow and learn, new and revised statements are presented to continue to inform teachers' practice. The important role of the family and community

MyEducationLab

Go to the Building Teaching Skills and Dispositions section of Topic 3 to 12: Professionalism/ Ethics in the MyEducationLab for your course and complete the activity entitled *Becoming an Early Childhood Professional*.

culture and collaborations with elementary schools present a newer facet to the statement, reflecting changes in early childhood education research and practice.

The overarching principles presented in the DAP statement include a validation of play as an important vehicle for learning and balancing classroom activities between interest-based, or child-initiated, and skill-based, or teacher-directed, experiences. Underscoring everything teachers do in their work with children is a view of children as

- Developing based on norms but with great individual variability
- Capable of learning, endowed with tremendous potential
- Worthy of respect and dignity
- Influenced by their family culture

The Code of Ethical Conduct statement serves as a valuable counterpart, guiding teachers in skillfully navigating the tumultuous waters of sensitive ethical dilemmas. The Code presents guidance for maintaining obligations to children, families, colleagues, and the community while handling situations in which these obligations may be in conflict. The Code serves as a valuable tool in the ongoing effort to maintain high standards of professionalism even in the face of conflicting, challenging situations where the right thing to do may not be readily apparent. By upholding the DAP commitment to respecting all children and families, the Code reiterates these goals while providing suggestions and examples of professional practice.

MyEducationLab

Go to the Assignments and Activities section of Topic 8: DAP/Teaching Strategies in the MyEducationLab for your course and complete the activity entitled *Designing Developmentally Appropriate Days*. Keep in mind the recommendations of the professional associations highlighted in the chapter.

Application Activities

On the Web: MyEducationLab Watch the *Designing Developmentally Appropriate Days* Video on MyEducationLab. Considering the recommendations of the professional associations highlighted in the chapter, respond to and discuss the corresponding questions in small groups.

In Class In small groups, analyze the following teacher scenarios. Based on what you know about children's development, DAP, and the Code of Ethical Conduct, analyze these situations and decide what you would do in these situations and discuss why you made your decision. Identify specific principles and ideals from the Code that helped guide your decision making (available on the NAEYC website at www.naeyc.org/about/positions.asp).

Holiday Play: The teacher in the 5-year-olds' room in your center is preparing to present her annual holiday play. She has written a long script with parts, lines to be memorized, and group songs. The children have been spending 90 minutes each day practicing their lines, moves, and songs. When you pass by you see some children rolling on the floor, and some are standing in front of the teacher, emotionlessly repeating the lines. Two children are standing at the window looking at the playground. You notice that on her posted schedule, this is the children's outdoor time. With the performance only one week away, however, the children have to focus on rehearsals.

Craft Project: The assistant teacher in the 4-year-olds' room has spent 15 minutes reading the story of Fredrick to his class. Then he directs the children to the tables where he has laid out various precut shapes of colored paper. The children sit at the tables and watch the teacher as he instructs them about how to assemble their mice from the precut shapes. All children are instructed to complete the project in the same way, although some children seem to be struggling with managing the glue and with grasping and placing the small paper pieces. The teacher redirects their efforts with the same instructions, pointing out that other children are able to complete the task without problem. He finishes by reminding the struggling children that they are "big boys and girls" and should keep working until they finish their craft projects. In the end, he completes the project himself so that each child has something to take home at the end of the day.

Student Teaching You are student teaching in a preschool class, and your classroom teacher gives you a lesson that you feel is not age appropriate for the children in the class. Feeling obligated as a student teacher, you start the lesson. After several minutes, a few children indicate that they are scared by the activity and don't want to continue. The teacher tells them that they're fine and that you should continue.

In the Field Using the Internet or your local phone book, locate a family services agency in your area. This may be listed as child welfare, maternal child and health, family assistance, healthy communities, or a resource and referral agency. Find the contact information and make an appointment to interview a representative. Ask the representative about their services, how families access programs, and what resources are available, and gather any printed information (brochures) that are available. Write a brief summary of your conversation, the scope of the services for families, and the materials you gathered. These resources will be useful to you as a teacher and are also items you can include in your portfolio to demonstrate professionalism and awareness of community resources.

For Your Portfolio Locate the NAEYC website and explore their online list of position statements located under the Publications link (www.naeyc.org/about/positions.asp). Make some notes about the kinds of topics that are reflected therein. Locate and print the DAP and Code of Ethical Conduct statements. Read them through and make notes summarizing the statements and some personal reflections about how the statements impact your practice with children and families. Create an informational brochure to highlight and promote the values and guidance for practice in the statements, as if you were creating an advertisement. This activity can be added to your portfolio in the section on professionalism.

RELATED WEB LINKS

National Child Care Information Center
www.nccic.org

National Association for Family Child Care
www.nafcc.org

Association for Childhood Education International
www.acei.org

Zero to Three
www.zerotothree.org

4

Constructivist Learning: Building Knowledge from Within

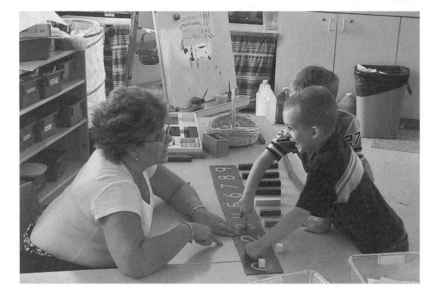

You cannot teach a man anything; you can only help him find it within himself.

—GALILEO

Education is a field in which theory and practice are continuously evolving through dialogue, reflection, synthesis, and experimentation. As you know from Chapter 2, for centuries educators have been attempting to create learning environments that maximize children's potential in terms of skills, knowledge, attitudes, and lifelong habits. Learner-centered theories of teaching have contributed to the landscape of classroom experience in powerful ways that have great potential to positively shape practice. For the past two decades, educational practice has been influenced by the theory of learning known as constructivism and its recent application to teaching. This chapter presents an overview of the theory of constructivism and an analysis of the possibilities and challenges of applying the theory to educational practice. Strategies for meaningfully making the theory-to-practice leap are presented as a starting point and as a guide to constructivist-inspired teaching and assessment.

STARTING POINTS: QUESTIONS AND REFLECTIONS

Take a moment to identify things you believe or already know about learner-centered teaching or constructivism as well as any questions you might have. Reflect on your own classroom experiences or observations and think about the role of students, teachers, environment, materials, and the community in those settings.

- Think about things you recall from your own education or things you have seen during classroom observations that you particularly liked or disliked. What were they, and why did you think of them as positive or negative?

- How would you define *knowledge* and *truth*?

- Think about a time when you were allowed to choose a topic to explore— perhaps a group presentation or a report. How did you feel about this? Was your ability to choose the topic meaningful?

- Recall a moment when you learned something particularly meaningful. How did you come to that knowledge? What was the context surrounding that learning experience? Was there something personal that made you choose that memory?

- Do you prefer simply to be told something, or do you prefer to test ideas out for yourself? How would you test them (for example, that baking soda and vinegar make an explosive reaction when mixed)?

CLASSROOM VIEW

The Constructivist Teacher in Action: An Observation

This morning a small group of second-graders are having an art class as part of their regular school program. The program takes place at a small local museum and creativity center. The classroom walls are adorned with displays of local artists' work. The students' worktables are stocked with small baskets of glue, a variety of scissors, markers, and hole punchers. While sitting in pairs at the ample tables, the children and teacher are introduced to the resident artist, Gail. Gail will be their partner, teacher, and guide for a series of visual arts explorations. After telling the children to close their eyes, Gail takes the students on a guided imagery journey and asks them to imagine themselves in a place that is very special to them. They are asked to think about the time of day, the colors and light, what they see around them and in the distance, and how being in their place makes them feel.

After a few moments, the students are asked to open their eyes and write down a few key words that describe what they saw and felt on their imaginary journey. The teacher helps the students write in their journal books. Gail prompts them to think artistically by using terms such as color, depth light, hue, and shape. Students are shown several prints of professional artists' landscapes, and their attention is focused on specific elements of line, color, shape, and composition. Contrasts between the different techniques, colors, and styles are discussed as the students comment on the pieces. Gail briefly discusses the color wheel, reminding the students of colors that are neighbors and those that are complements.

With pieces of tissue paper, students are asked to begin to choose a color palette that represents the colors they saw in their special place. Gail calls the students' attention to a pile of textured papers (papers painted in the style of Eric Carle, with patterns in one color or similar shades of color, that the class had painted that morning). The students are prompted to look over the papers and begin to select ones that reflect the colors they chose in their tissue paper palette. Students are then invited to create a landscape collage with the textured papers to represent their special place. As the students begin to work, Gail moves around the room and briefly stops at each table.

Putting It Into Practice

Teacher-Child Interactions

The important influence of the way you talk to children cannot be overemphasized. Throughout your day, stop and take time to really listen to your children. Ask questions that reflect how attentively you are listening and how deeply you care about their lives. This is a foundation to demonstrating your respect and commitment to children.

At each table, Gail carefully looks at what the students are creating. After examining the students' work for a few moments, Gail comments on specific elements of the work. She asks questions, uses artistic terms and answers students' questions with examples of what some artists do or what else the student might want to think about. For example, Gail suggests to one student that she might want to include a thin contrasting line of dark color between her sky and ground to make the distinction stand out. Gail models teaching strategies for the teacher, who is working alongside her students. Gail acts as a more knowledgeable guide and collaborator in the creative problem solving. These are some of the comments she makes:

"Think about contrast as you work on this part. If you step back and look, do you think a darker strip in between these pieces would make it stand out more?"

"Think of your original color palette as a starting point. You may want to expand it as you work."

"I see you have made yours very textural. You've used a mosaic technique here with these small square pieces."

"Collage is about layers, building details, and making compositions with large and small shapes."

"Consider your point of view in this landscape. Are you looking from below, straight on, or from the sky?"

"Think about depth. Imagine that you were walking into the landscape."

After a little over an hour at work on their landscapes, Gail encourages the class to wrap up their work and prepare for whole group discussion. After about 15 more minutes, the class reorganizes as a whole group. Gail instructs the students to arrange their landscapes on a long table at the side of the room. The class then takes several minutes to observe each other's work. The class is invited to share their experience with the activity.

Several students express satisfaction at working through the challenges of developing an idea and forming it on paper. Several students comment that the collage technique is more familiar to them, so they feel more competent and are more pleased with their work. One student indicates things she would do differently now that she has stepped back and looked at her work. Gail facilitates this dialogue, but she now takes a secondary role to the students' interactions. She lets them drive the direction of the conversation.

Constructivism

A theory of knowledge and learning that posits that children actively engage with their world—people, experiences, materials—and build their beliefs and knowledge through interaction and internal processes.

What Is Constructivism All About? The Big Picture

With a long and rich history, including discourses in philosophy, psychology, and—more recently—education, the theory of **constructivism** continues to be dynamic and evolving. As the translation of constructivist theory to educational practice gains increasing popularity among teachers, concerns about misapplication of the theory have been raised

Teachers facilitate children's internal process of knowledge construction through hands-on experiences.

(Green & Gredler, 2002). Applying theoretical principles to actual practice in effective ways can pose significant challenges for teachers, especially new teachers.

Roles of the Learner

At the heart of the theory of constructivism is the belief that knowledge is constructed through an active process in which the learner engages in

- Exploration with materials
- Inner processes of reasoning
- Interaction with peers and teachers

The learner is valued as an important part of the knowledge construction process, which is shaped by prior experience, learning, and beliefs. Constructivists believe that when ideas are challenged by new information, the learner interprets and makes sense of the new information in the context of previous experience. This process of making sense involves building a new cognitive framework that meaningfully incorporates the old and new information in ways that make sense to the learner (Davis & Sumara, 2002). When constructivist theory is applied to classrooms, it generally involves engaging learners in a cognitive process that includes such activities as (Low & Shironaka, 1995; Schuh, 2003)

- Asking and answering questions
- Making hypotheses
- Testing those hypotheses
- Dialoguing with teachers and peers
- Confronting challenges to one's own and others' thinking
- Exploring and reflecting on results

Learners in a constructivist classroom are not viewed as passive recipients of knowledge handed out by teachers. Rather, students are viewed as active partners in problem solving through the asking, testing, considering, and answering of questions. Learning is viewed as a dynamic inquiry process (Gregory, 2002). At the core of this process is that the students are *thinking*. Students are not merely given answers, nor are they sent forth alone to face challenges they are not equipped to meet. Students are supported as they find ways to navigate through challenging and interesting problems and reflect on their own processing and solutions.

Roles of the Teacher

The nature of student-teacher interactions in the classroom observation at the beginning of the chapter is very different from such shallow complimentary comments as "That's pretty" or "Good job." Gail's comments are not the same as handing out directions about where to place cotton balls or precut shapes on paper and how much glue to use. Her comments, which include technical artistic vocabulary, are thoughtful and reflect both a careful analysis of the students' work and a sharing of ideas from a more expert knowledge base. Gail uses comments that are designed to encourage students to think about what they are doing. Her comments and questions encourage the students to become deliberate, thoughtful, and reflective about their artwork. She also prompts students to discuss their work together and share decisions they made about their creations. This teaching style illustrates an example of constructivist scaffolding, where the teacher acts as a guide and facilitator of students' thinking and activities within learning experiences.

By varying the degree to which she directly guides or indirectly supports the students' work and discussion, Gail embodies the careful balance of a constructivist teacher. At times she directs students' work and attention by teaching them strategies of artistic techniques, and at other times she steps back and lets the students discuss and reflect on their own processes and work. Through this balance of a direct and indirect presence, Gail fosters a community among the students and encourages them to be thoughtful and engaged with their own work and with their peers. This thoughtfulness, reflection, and deeper cognitive engagement with one's own work and with one's peers are hallmarks of constructivist classrooms.

Scaffolding

Scaffolding involves the dynamic and active assistance from the more expert partner, who relies heavily on verbal cues, prompts, and questions. The teacher provides clues that "nudge" the child's thinking or actions in solving a problem or completing a task. Be careful to give just enough help to avoid overriding the child's own process. Scaffolding requires that teachers know how children are capable of thinking—what their developmental level is at that moment. As children become more capable, the assistance is reduced. In this way, the teacher's help acts as a stronger support as children need more help and as a lesser support as they become more independently capable in the task.

Constructivist teachers strive to balance their teaching style to include (Powell, 2000)

- Posing engaging questions and challenging problems
- Giving students necessary information
- Supporting students' research to find information for themselves
- Prompting students to try new problem-solving strategies
- Focusing student attention on particular aspects of the activity
- Observing and considering students' actions and dialogue
- Promoting collaboration among peers and teachers
- Assessing students' processing through careful dialogues

In the constructivist classroom, teachers and students are viewed as partners in critically thinking about phenomena in their world and exploring them on a personal level (Castle, 1997; Richardson, 2003). This personal, active involvement is what makes constructivist learning meaningful, real, internal, interesting, and accessible to even the youngest students. To fully understand how teachers create learner-centered, constructivist-inspired classrooms, the origins and metamorphosis of constructivist theory should be briefly explored within its historical context.

Historical Perspectives: How Constructivism Emerged

At its heart, constructivism values a learner-centered perspective. This educational pedagogy, which has been in service in Europe and America for centuries, has endured the tide of popular fads in teaching practice. Most of the recent attention on constructivist teaching centers around applying the theory to teaching practice. However, the underpinnings of the theory of constructivism have roots that date back thousands of years, beginning with the onset of formal education (Henson, 2003). Remember from Chapter 2 that certain beliefs have run like threads throughout the centuries, from one influential philosopher to the next. Think about how the following elements evolved and grew in importance over the centuries:

- Active and hands-on experiences—children are encouraged to explore hands-on **manipulatives** and sensory materials.
- Children's interest—when children initiate activities, choose materials, or are allowed to play freely, they are more engaged and learning is more meaningful.
- Capability of children—all children are capable of learning, questioning, problem solving, and generating ideas.
- Holistic approach—education should be emotional, physical, and cognitive and exist within the context of children's lives.

Manipulatives

Hands-on materials that are designed to illustrate and demonstrate such concepts as shape, series, categorization, grouping, and so on.

Current constructivist beliefs draw on the work of several prominent philosophers and psychologists. Philosophers who lived as long ago as Socrates in 400 B.C. have pondered the processes of human thinking, learning, and teaching. In the 1500s, Francis Bacon introduced a new way of thinking that embraced problem solving and consideration of multiple possibilities. Recall from Chapter 2 that through the 1600s and 1700s John Locke created experiential learning and Johann Pestalozzi created an early learner-centered model of education (Henson, 2003). Contemporary philosophies of education remain heavily influenced by these rich traditions of discussion, debate, and open testing of ideas. Active exploration and discourse as methods for learning were the foundations that shaped progressive teaching practices in the 20th century.

In the Progressive Era, the disposition of the learner began to emerge as an area of concern for modern educators. The belief that learning occurred through students' interactions with peers, teachers, materials, ideas, and work on solving problems set the stage for modern concepts of best practices in active learning (Dewey, 1938). As research in the first half of the 1900s reinforced the effectiveness of learner-centered models of education, active learning held favor in educational trends (Henson, 2003; Matthews, 2003; Simpson, 2002). The progressive emphasis on critical thinking, shared authority, and learning within a social context paved the way for contemporary constructivist theory.

Whereas philosophers explored the nature of human thinking, psychologists in the 20th century assumed a primary role in designing methods of teaching that would develop and foster learning. Jean Piaget and Lev Vygotsky, who brought the theory of constructivism and the application of constructivist principles into its modern age, were responsible for defining two branches within the theoretical framework (Berk & Winsler, 1995). In Chapter 2, you were introduced to the work and impact of Piaget and Vygotsky in a general perspective, but here you will explore their contributions to constructivist theory and practice more specifically.

Cognitive-developmental constructivism

A theory of knowledge as an individual construct built through maturation and new experiences that challenge the learner's existing knowledge.

Sociocultural constructivism

A theory of knowledge as socially coconstructed and then internalized; as such, the social and cultural environment heavily influences knowledge construction.

Here and Now: Contemporary Constructivist Beliefs

In a broad sense, there are currently two main branches that use different lenses to view the nature of learning and knowing:

- Cognitive-developmental constructivism
- Sociocultural constructivism

Each branch has its primary advocate, Piaget and Vygotsky, respectively, and central perspectives (Simpson, 2002). Considered to be branches of the same overarching theory because they share several core beliefs, there is nonetheless a clear distinction between the two. **Cognitive-developmental constructivism** seeks to explain how learners shape their world, whereas **sociocultural constructivism** seeks to explain how the world shapes the learners (Davis & Sumara, 2002). The difference is one of perspective and position, and it is the differences, combined with the similarities, that present a more complete, detailed picture.

Piaget's Influence

Cognitive-developmental constructivists, like Piaget, believe that children actively construct knowledge through cognitive processing of their experiences, driven by an innate desire to explore and manipulate materials in their world. More than just the sum of experiences or the sum of innate ideas, constructivists view knowledge acquisition as an active, dynamic cognitive process in which children build, rebuild, discard, and change their ideas.

Piaget's Contributions to Constructivism

Within the cognitive-developmental perspective, heavily influenced by the work of Jean Piaget, knowledge is an individual construct built through maturation and new experiences that challenge the learner's existing knowledge. Recall that Piaget proposed that children actively seek to make sense out of their experiences. He felt that this active search for meaning is what leads to the child's developing ideas and changing them as new experiences bring new knowledge (Berk & Winsler, 1995; Davis and Sumara, 2002; Piaget, 1969). Piaget also suggested that as children mature, their thinking changes as their cognitive development goes through stages (Piaget, 1929). These stages were presented in Chapter 2.

A key concept in constructivism is the notion of **cognitive conflict**, in which the individual child is made aware of discrepancies between existing beliefs and new information that presents a different perspective. In essence, cognitive conflict is finding out some new information that contradicts currently held beliefs. When this contradiction is realized, some testing of the old and new ideas happens to come to a new understanding. For Piaget, the processes and resulting changes associated with cognitive conflict are driven by the internal capacities of the individual, particularly assimilation and accommodation (Piaget, 1975).

Cognitive conflict

When new information contradicts currently held beliefs, which then prompts the child to rethink existing beliefs.

Much of Piaget's theories of cognitive development arose from his extensive work observing children's processes and abilities as they worked to accomplish certain tasks at different ages. Piaget noticed that children's actions changed qualitatively over time as their development progressed through levels of understanding. He believed that these changes and activities contributed to the child's knowledge construction. He believed that development leads learning as children engage in spontaneous exploration and discovery using processes and abilities naturally available to them (Berk & Winsler, 1995).

Piaget's influence on current practice, particularly on the practice of teaching young children, is illustrated in the reliance on discovery centers as a primary vehicle for children's active exploration in the classroom. Think about observations you have made or videos you have watched of early childhood classrooms. Did you see children engaging in active explorations like building with blocks, putting puzzles together, or mixing paint colors and drawing at an easel? Did you see children sitting at desks silently working on worksheets or listening to the teacher lecture? If your observation was a recent one, chances are you saw children busily working with hands-on materials and projects. As children become involved with their materials, they learn firsthand how they work, and they begin to develop ideas about cause and effect.

Although social exchanges are a part of the picture, they are valued in terms of the impact on the individual's engagement with ideas and materials. Piaget did not necessarily believe that social dialogues played as important a role in shaping children's cognitive development as active exploration of materials. Social interactions may provide the catalyst for the child's cognitive conflict and resolution when a partner provides new information based on his or her experience or understanding. Social exchanges may also serve as a forum for testing ideas when partners debate conflicting beliefs or jointly engage in testing new information (Richardson, 2003). The role of the social environment is a subtle, but key, distinction between the two branches of constructivism. This is also an area in which many current researchers and educators differ with Piaget's theory. Piaget himself, late in his career, began to question the universality of his earlier

Vygotsky's Influence

Vygotsky's work expanded existing beliefs about constructivist theory. He influenced the sociocultural branch of constructivism, which believes that knowledge is constructed through active mental processes but is greatly influenced by one's social and cultural environment. The role of experience remains important, but interactions with people (such as teachers and peers) and society (cultural norms, traditions, and beliefs) are viewed as essential influences in knowledge construction.

stage theory, acknowledging diversity in cognitive development based on diverse environment and experience (Knight & Sutton, 2004).

MyEducationLab

Go to the Assignments and Activities section of Topic 2: Child Development/ Theories in the MyEducationLab for your course and complete the activity entitled *Scaffolding Emergent Literacy*. Notice the strategies the teacher uses to scaffold the child's emerging writing skills.

Vygotsky's Contributions to Constructivism

Lev Vygotsky continued the process of shaping constructivist theory, but his work was particularly useful in applying constructivist principles to teaching (Davis & Sumara, 2002). For sociocultural constructivists like Vygotsky, knowledge is socially coconstructed and then internalized as opposed to being independently constructed within the individual working solely with materials (Berk & Winsler, 1995; Simpson, 2002; Vygotsky, 1978). Vygotsky's work represents a shift in constructivist thinking; he placed a heavy emphasis on the value of social collaborations, particularly with more expert partners. Within this framework, knowledge is a shared construct influenced by prior experiences, cultures, environments, people, and beliefs. Vygotsky believed that the purpose of learning was to lead development. As Vygotsky noted, "Learning awakens a variety of internal developmental processes that are able to operate only when the child is interacting with people in his environment and in cooperation with this peers" (Vygotsky, 1978, p. 90). When applied to classroom environments, this translates into teachers engaging the children in discussions and activities a step ahead of their current developmental level. Recall from Chapter 2 that it was in what he defined as the zone of proximal (or potential) development (ZPD) that Vygotsky felt growth could occur. Working in the ZPD means working with more expert help on challenging activities that are neither too easy nor too hard (Berk & Winsler, 1995). The nature of learning and development is cyclical in that once the process is internalized, the teacher adjusts learning experiences to reflect a new zone of development. View how teachers and children can engage in learning together through active projects at MyEducationLab.

IN YOUR OWN WORDS

Can you recall a time when you have been bored in class? (Though not this class, of course.) Did you feel tired or restless? Did you stop paying attention to what you were doing or to what someone was saying? Can you recall a time when you just didn't understand something, feeling as if it were way over your head? Did you get annoyed or frustrated because you could not figure out a solution or because someone was explaining something in a way that did not make any sense to you? In these situations, you probably did not learn much; maybe you cannot even recall what topic you were studying or the materials you were using. You probably "checked out" mentally and didn't think deeply or actively about what you were working on. For constructivists, deep cognitive engagement is an essential part of the learning process. It is something that must be carefully and skillfully fostered by attentive, observant teachers.

Beyond Piaget: Social Learning, Language, and Culture

Inherent in the framework of the ZPD is the emphasis on the nature of the interaction with a more expert partner (a teacher in role if not in title). In a Vygotskyian framework, the teacher deliberately assesses the child's level and provides interaction just beyond it, even though still within reach. In Piaget's framework, the partner may unwittingly be a source of conflicting information so that the child is thrown into the cognitive conflict-knowledge construction process. Vygotsky, on the other hand, viewed the partner as a deliberate actor in the purposeful engagement of the child's thought. It is an active role, one that requires expertise in both content and teaching technique.

The teacher must understand the child's current thought process in order to provide appropriate support for the child's process of working through challenging problems. Furthermore, the teacher must remain active and attentive during the child's processing so that the form and level of assistance can be continually adjusted based on the child's place within his or her individual zone. Highly interdependent, this scaffolding process is at the heart of a Vygotskyian view of knowledge construction.

Teachers give suggestions and ask questions to guide children's thinking and work.

Language Development as a Promoter of Cognitive Development

Vygotsky promoted the milestone of language use as the most influential event in shaping the child's cognitive development (Berk & Winsler, 1995; Vygotsky, 1978). Children use language to develop ideas socially, which are then internalized (Vygotsky, 1978). First, children think out loud verbally, which slowly becomes internal, private speech, which they use to organize thought (Dixon-Krauss, 1996). When children have a reasonable mastery over language, the dynamic of the learning environment is one of collaboration among children and adults in which the group negotiates meaning and socially constructs knowledge. For Piaget, the child's use of private speech was not particularly meaningful developmentally, and it was attributed to the child's cognitive immaturity (Berk & Winsler, 1995).

The Role of Culture in Cognitive Development

New research testing elements of Piaget's stage theory have led to modifications and expansions in beliefs about how cognition is influenced by culture (Knight & Sutton, 2004). Piaget believed that as a course of normal maturation, cognition progresses through distinct levels of processing. New research exploring thinking using subjects from diverse cultures—industrialized and nonindustrialized societies—indicates that the unique experiences of specific cultures can greatly impact the level of cognition achieved (Suizzo, 2000).

Although the Piagetian and Vygotskian branches of constructivism have different emphases, they nevertheless maintain several commonalities and present a more comprehensive picture of constructivist theory when explored together. Contemporaries familiar with

TABLE 4-1   Key Distinctions Between Branches of Constructivism

Branches of Constructivism	Cognitive-Developmental	Sociocultural
Primary Advocate	**Jean Piaget**	**Lev Vygotsky**
Learner's role	Learners' explorations and actions shape their knowledge of the world.	Interactions with their world and the people in it shape learners' knowledge.
View of knowledge construction	Knowledge is individually constructed, shaped by processing new experiences.	Knowledge is coconstructed, shaped by interaction with people, and influenced by culture and environment.
Role of peer/social partner	Peers can unwittingly provoke cognitive conflict (passive role).	More expert partner purposefully guides the exploration of ideas (active role).
Relationship of development and learning	Development leads learning.	Learning leads development.
Relationship between language and thought	Language-knowledge construction connection is not emphasized.	Language is promoted as strongly influencing thought.

each other's work, Piaget and Vygotsky traveled different theoretical paths within the same field. Both theories

- Are learner-centered models of how thinking and knowledge acquisition develop
- Emphasize children as active creators of knowledge
- Recognize innate and social influences on thought processing
- Value the child's environment for its influence on thought (Berk & Winsler, 1995)
- View knowledge as a subjective, constructed reality (Richardson, 2003)
- Validate the child's internal motivation to explore and manipulate his or her world as a means of understanding it (Matthews, 2003)

When used in concert as complementary subsets of the overarching theory, cognitive-developmental and sociocultural constructivist views provide educators with a viable framework for both understanding children's developing thought and creating learning environments to support that development. However, just as constructivists promote the critical analysis of new information in relation to prior understanding, it is important for educators to carefully consider and reflect on any theory presented to them. As you read through all the chapters in this text or learn about any new aspects of educational theory and practice, you must continually reflect on what you are learning and examine how it fits into your own developing philosophy.

Criticisms and Challenges of Translating Theory Into Practice

There are several potential problems in translating theory into practice under constructivist-inspired teaching. One concern that is raised by commentators on current constructivist-inspired practice is that the work of the key philosophers and psychologists mentioned previously was not intended to be taken as prescriptions for practice. In other words, constructivism emerged as a *theory* of human knowing, not as a *method* of teaching (Davis & Sumara, 2002; Ray, 2002). In spite of this, for at least two decades, educational practice and teacher-education programs have adopted the vocabulary, interpreted the spirit of constructivism, and applied it to classroom teaching.

Teacher-Directed or Student-Initiated

Critiques of constructivist teaching revolve around the confusion in teachers' understanding and application of constructivist theory to classroom practice. Based on the belief that knowledge is constructed within the learner through interaction with the world (material and social), constructivism supports the sharing of authority. Teachers and students bear collective responsibility for guiding learning (Ray, 2002). In other words, teachers are the ones with the right *questions*, not the right *answers*. Transmission models in which the teacher directly shares information are often regarded as contradictory to constructivist theory (Davis & Sumara, 2002; Powell, 2000).

We can see the dilemma: If knowledge is individually or socially constructed through a collaborative inquiry or exploration process, what knowledge or information could teachers share directly? How should teachers evaluate whether a student's knowledge is valid, deep, and broad? In addition to dealing with the quandaries involved with what knowledge or information is exactly, teachers may avoid directly teaching children facts and information and thus not deal with children's misconceptions.

In fact, Piaget's theoretical framework of cognitive development proposes that children interact with their environment as well as their own misconceptions (Powell, 2000). Interpreting this aspect of his theory in the classroom may lead teachers to refrain from correcting children's erroneous beliefs. The potential pitfall of applying theoretical constructivist principles directly to practice is revealed in these issues. For the novice teacher attempting to embrace a constructivist teaching style, this sharing of authority and jointly constructed knowledge poses significant challenges when faced with accountability to content standards and learner assessment.

Reconciling Content Standards and Assessment with Constructivism

If you, as a new teacher, were attempting to embody a constructivist approach, you would support children's questioning, curiosity, experimentation, and reflection. You would encourage children to explore challenging problems and work collaboratively to find solutions. What happens, though, if children's reflections and inferences from their experiments or solutions are simply not accurate or miss a key concept? How do you address core content and basic information?

In practical terms, there is a concern that widespread misapplication of constructivist theory might translate into passive, laissez-faire teaching. The key principles of constructivist teaching can sometimes seem to leave teachers in the role of semi-active participants (Dewey, 1938; Simpson, 2002):

- Value children's conceptions even if they are misconceptions from the teacher's perspective.
- Promote collaborative problem solving where children can generate their own answers.
- Work in partnership with students.

Denying their role as experts or authority figures, teachers are in a quandary when it comes to judging students' progress. When teachers misunderstand the premise of learner-centered, constructivist teaching to mean there can be no direct instructing of students on core content or valid assessment of student learning, there exists a potential that children will not become competent in the basic set of standards deemed educationally necessary (Gregory, 2002). Remember from Chapter 1, however, that guiding principles of best practices call for teachers to balance child-directed and teacher-directed activities. On the surface, perhaps this feels like a challenge in constructivist classrooms.

Balance

Critics of child-directed learning cite research showing that some children perform better on measures of academic achievement when exposed to direct-instruction methods, particularly children from lower socioeconomic status backgrounds (Marcon, 1992;

Teachers use systematic observations to assess children's progress and plan for future learning experiences.

Matthews, 2003). Much of this argument centers on teacher-directed instruction or child-initiated exploration; however, most educators recognize the importance of balancing both instructional methods. Dewey himself recognized the need for some teacher authority and for widely accepted standards of skill and content within disciplines, and he saw these as existing in concert with inquiry-based, collaborative problem-solving learning environments (Dewey, 1938; Gregory, 2002). Equally compelling is the voluminous body of research that provides evidence of academic, intellectual, and attitudinal success in learner-centered, constructivist classrooms (summaries cited in Berk & Winsler, 1995; Marcon, 2002; and Schweinhart, Barnes, & Weikart, 1993).

Putting It Into Practice

Balance

Remember from the classroom visit how Gail skillfully "danced" between giving the children directions and suggestions on their collages (whole group and individual) and giving them room to explore their own ideas and the materials? This is a great example of how this balance between teacher-directed instruction and child-directed exploration can be accomplished. It is the teacher's role to share expertise with the students, giving them skills, tools, and experiences that they can then use in their own active explorations.

What these studies show is that a balanced approach, including some direct instruction paired with an emphasis on child-initiated exploration (including hands-on, problem-solving activities), leads to the biggest gains in a variety of developmental measures. Consider a Vygotskyian framework in which teachers create environments that allow children to share ideas, test conceptions, and build meaning from experience—all while remaining active in scaffolding children's experience. The Vygotskian approach also validates the use of whole-group direct instruction on techniques, strategies, or use of new materials in moderate amounts as deemed appropriate by the teacher (Berk & Winsler, 1995).

Within this more compromising, balanced approach, children can engage in the meaningful, inquiry-based, constructive process while still gaining proficiency in a core set of standard content. At first glance, the constructivist teacher may appear to be less active than a transmission-style lecturer. In reality, he or she is continually active, sometimes in the foreground, sometimes in the background, leading and following children's development in a collaborative, mutual, dancelike process. Principles of constructivist theory can be viewed as one of many frameworks that can guide practice in teaching young children in learner-centered, developmentally appropriate, meaningful ways.

Strategies for Applying Constructivist Theory to Early Childhood Education

The overarching goals of constructivist theory can translate into teaching pedagogy and shape practice in appropriate ways. Appropriate translations you can use include (Powell, 2000; Schuh, 2003)

- Being an active participant with children ("let's find out together")
- Supporting children's connections to prior experience ("that photo looks like the bridge you were building with the long blocks last week")
- Empowering children as contributing members of the classroom community ("that's a great idea; let's all see if we can figure that out together")
- Facilitating children's questioning, testing, exploring, and reflecting ("What do you think will happen if/when . . .?")
- Observing and assessing children's ongoing processes
- Stocking the classroom with open-ended materials that invite exploration and multiple uses
- Holding back from providing answers, solving problems, or resolving conflicts for children

Interpreting constructivist theory from an educator's perspective yields several specific suggestions for practice.

Share the Road

First, believe the principle that classrooms can be communities of learners. This means that teachers must relinquish much of the control, power, and authority endowed in them in a

MyEducationLab

Go to the Assignments and Activities section of Topic 2: Child Development/ Theories in the MyEducationLab for your course and complete the activity entitled *Using Constructivism to Modify the Environment.* Observe the strategies teachers use to create shared spaces with children and let the children's unfolding projects guide daily activities.

traditional model (Low & Shironaka, 1995). Again, be willing to have more questions than answers. A willingness to share power in the classroom must start with mutual respect. Children respect teachers and peers, and teachers respect children, including children's ideas, prior experiences, and processing of new experiences. When children are validated as having valuable contributions to make to classroom learning, they are prompted and encouraged to share. You can encourage children to take an active role in the direction of their learning and the forming of the classroom community in many ways. Recall how Gail did this as she facilitated the students' reflection and let them engage in group discussion of their work. Observe how teachers use knowledge of and experience with the children in their class to create authentic environments.

Using a simple what we already **know** what we **want** to know–**how** can we find out–what did we **learn** (KWHL) chart or group web allows children to share their prior knowledge and decide what new knowledge they want to explore. In keeping with constructivist theory on children's misconceptions, include all statements children make about what they know, even if they are incorrect. Through their own process of inquiry and exploration, they will come to see their misconceptions. The "what we learned" section of the chart can be a venue for highlighting new, corrected knowledge. The KWHL technique validates individual past experiences, and it empowers children to shape future classroom endeavors. Asking children to generate ideas for how they will find out what they want to know places them more in control of their own learning activities. By reflecting on the KWHL chart, children can see the progress or transformation of their own learning.

KWHL Chart on Flowers, Pre-K

What Do We *Know*	*What Do We Want to Know*	*How* Can We Find Out	**What Did We *Learn*** (New Words in Bold)
• Grow from seeds	• How do they grow?	• Visit a flower shop.	• Bees do not eat them. Some other bugs do, such as beetles.
• Come in different colors	• Do they eat? What?	• Find some books.	• Flowers need sunlight, water, and **soil** to grow.
• Are tall and green	• Why do bees eat them?	• Grow flowers on the windowsill.	• Some are short, some are tall.
• Bees eat them	• How many colors do they come in? • Why do they die? • How tall do they get? • Where do they go in the winter?	• Ask a flower grower.	• Some grow from seeds, some from **bulbs** • They can't grow in frozen **temperatures** • The flower store had more red flowers than any other color. • There are many colors from all the rainbow colors. • Our class favorite flower color was yellow. • Our class favorite flower was the **sunflower** • You can eat some flower seeds. • Some flowers grow fast, some grow slower.

Children can also direct the social climate of their classroom. For example, allow children to create desired classroom rules. This is an important part of creating a classroom that is psychologically safe and allows for risk taking, mistake making, exploration, and reflection. When children are empowered to create rules, they are more likely to internalize them, follow them, and remind each other of them (DeVries & Zan, 2003). When children understand and value the role of the individual within the classroom community, they are more likely to create fair rules that preserve the harmony of the community and serve the collective good. The experience of being a member of a cooperative, mutually validating system itself fosters positive moral development in children and is a primary benefit of constructivist classrooms (DeVries & Zan, 1995).

Refrain from Doing Too Much

Scaffolding can be used to increase children's self-regulation and autonomy in social interactions and task activity. When conflicts do arise or rules are broken, many teachers are quick to resolve the conflict for the children. Imagine this situation: Two children are working with the blocks, and one grabs an item from the other, saying, "I need that!" The first child becomes upset and reaches for the item, crying, "Mine! I had it first!" The argument becomes physical when you come over to intervene. The methods used to resolve conflicts in traditional classrooms often include the teacher's stepping in, separating children, reminding them of the rules, demanding an apology, and redirecting behavior. However, keep in mind that, in many ways, conflict is a prime opportunity for learning.

Constructivists view conflicts, particularly cognitive conflict, as a necessary impetus for exploring and changing one's ideas and misconceptions (Piaget, 1975). By prompting children's dialogue instead of telling them what to do, using active listening as they explain their sides and modeling respectful negotiating of a mutually satisfying resolution, children can learn to work through their own problems. Teachers can also start small- or whole-group discussions as a means to share ideas on how to resolve individual or group problems. Teachers start as facilitators, models, and mediators and ultimately reduce their presence as the children become more capable of resolving conflicts autonomously (Arcaro-McPhee, Doppler, & Harkins, 2002). This process embodies the scaffolding techniques used by constructivist teachers to promote children's self-regulation of learning as well as behavior.

Balance, Balance, Balance

A third suggestion for applying constructivist principles is to emphasize child-directed experiences but include instruction when necessary. This ensures a weighted balance of classroom experiences that allow children to act on their world to build understanding but also to learn conventional knowledge (DeVries & Zan, 1995; Schuh, 2003). Simply telling children things is not enough experience for them to build real understanding. They may be able to memorize facts but will not really understand what they mean or how they relate to their lives. It is the emphasis on this deeper, meaningful knowing that is foundational to constructivist theory and practice. Likewise, leaving children to journey without a map (guidance) also inhibits their learning.

Combine brief instruction with ample opportunity to explore, test, and manipulate materials. These experiences put abstract concepts into their hands and afford children the chance to understand concepts and phenomena (Richardson, 2003). Particularly when you are working with young children, it is always important to keep in mind their need to be active and explore their world with their own two hands. If you find yourself continually reminding them to not touch something, sit still, or be quiet, you need to reevaluate your methods and environment. Chances are you are expecting them to behave and learn in ways that do not align with their naturally curious, social, active nature. Long circle time with too much teacher-talking time is often a disaster. Gauge your children's interests and read their cues. Give children plenty of time to engage in activities and with materials that they design and choose.

Authentic Assessment Is a Must!

Finally, teachers using a constructivist framework need to reconceptualize the type and use of assessment. **Authentic assessment** seeks to capture a richer picture of

- Who you are
- What you are thinking
- How you have changed
- Your learning process and style
- Your ability to communicate through a variety of forms of expression
- How your experiences, thinking, and engagement with your world impact you

> **Authentic assessment**
>
> Methods of assessing children's progress, knowledge, and accomplishments within a naturalistic context. Portfolios, observations, and work samples are examples of authentic, contextualized assessments.

Dissatisfied with focusing only on children's existing competency, as in standard testing, Vygotsky carried his ZPD concept from teaching through to assessment practices. *Dynamic assessment* strategies were developed to capture children's learning in motion. In keeping with the premises of the ZPD and the teacher's role as scaffolder, dynamic assessment utilizes a three-step system to gather information on how children complete tasks alone as well as how they respond to instruction (Berk & Winsler, 1995):

1. The children complete a new task alone.
2. The teacher intervenes with some form of scaffolding instruction.
3. Children then complete the task again.

The changes from step 1 to step 3 in the child's performance and process are explored to determine the child's potential for learning with adult assistance. Observational notes on the child's performance and transcriptions of the child's dialogue can be used to explore the child's task mastery and thought processing. Like dynamic assessment, **performance assessment** provides valuable information that can be included in overall assessments of children. In performance assessment, teachers record and evaluate children's responses on certain authentic tests (McAffee, Leong, & Bodrora, 2004).

> **Performance assessment**
>
> Methods of evaluating what children know and can do by observing their performance and responses on authentic (real-life) tasks.

The differences between the assumptions in traditional versus alternative assessments parallel the theoretical differences in traditional versus constructivist teaching. Traditional transmission models of teaching and assessment focus on decontextualized discrete skills and bits of information, the final product, objective facts and truths (a "right answer"), and assessment as a tool to document previous learning.

Authentic assessment techniques include teachers observing children during typical activities and analyzing their performance.

Alternative or constructivist assessment focuses on (Anderson, 1998)

- Context and individual
- Past changes and future potential
- Subjective meaning of experience and information
- The processes students employ to make sense of their world
- Learning as an active process and assessment as a tool to facilitate learning

One of the more widely used alternative, authentic assessment formats is the portfolio. Just as children are involved in creating classroom rules and guiding interest-based learning activities, children are also involved in the creation of their portfolios. Teachers and children together decide on the samples of work to be included—samples they both feel appropriately represent the child's learning process. This might include drawings, stories, paintings, photos of sculpture or block buildings, collages, journals, and so on. Teachers also select observation reports, anecdotal records, notes from children's conversations, developmental checklists, or notes from family conversations (Ediger, 2000). By gathering key pieces of authentic work spanning a variety of activities over a period of time, a more richly detailed picture of the child's growth in progress can be captured.

Rubrics

An outline of expectations for assignments, including evaluations of basic, moderate, and advanced performance or quality.

One drawback to the use of portfolios, aside from the time needed to gather and sort the work, is that they are more subjective than most standardized tests. The interpretations from one evaluator (parent, teacher, etc.) to another as to the rate and direction of a child's progress can vary widely. To standardize or grade a portfolio, teachers develop **rubrics** that identify key elements and broad levels of competence (Anderson, 1998). Rubrics are expectations of what you want to see in an assignment. The highest grade or points are given to pieces that meet those expectations. Partial or no points or lower grades are

FIGURE 4-1

Preschool Social Skills Rubric (Partial)

Sample Rubric Used to Assess 4-year-olds' Social Development

Skill/Milestone	Advanced—3	On Level—2	Emerging—1
Plays well with other children	• Plays collaboratively with individuals and groups • Creates and engages in complex play scenarios	• Plays with others • Engages in simple to complex play scenarios	• Plays next to others • Interrupts others' play when seeking companionship
Follows classroom rules	• Always follows classroom rules • Reminds other children of rules	• Follows classroom rules most of the time • Needs few reminders of classroom rules	• Needs 3+ reminders of classroom rules and routines much of the time
Initiates and maintains conversations	• Skillfully integrates into groups using appropriate requests • Listens and responds appropriately to several members of a group • Engages several members of a group in conversation	• Appropriately asks to play with others • Understands conversation patterns, knows when to interject • Is able to take turns in conversation	• Approaches others or groups but does not yet use language to request integration • Interrupts others, not yet taking turns in conversation
Expresses wants/needs with words	• Able to create solutions to conflicts over wants/needs • Understands impact of own wants/needs on others	• Mostly uses appropriate words to express wants/needs • With prompts, understands impact of own wants/ needs on others	• Uses few words to express wants/needs • Uses physical actions to express wants/needs

assigned to pieces that meet some expectations but not all (see Figure 4-1 and Appendix E for sample rubrics). With the use of rubrics to evaluate portfolios or other kinds of learning activities, the process, depth, and detail remain a part of the assessment while standard criteria and a placement within broader expectations provide important information about the child's development. Simple checklists based on developmental expectations and performance goals can also be used to evaluate children's progress and performance (see Appendix F for a sample checklist).

In this way, teachers can use assessments to glean insight into children's ongoing processes and interests as well as their progress on defined learning goals. This twofold use for alternative/authentic assessments allows teachers to use the information gathered to plan instruction and guide children's learning while also documenting the outcomes of their classroom experiences.

From an overarching understanding of constructivist theory, more specific strategies of teaching and assessing can be developed and utilized. Vygotsky's framework, in particular, provides inspiration for many learner-centered, constructivist teaching strategies. Specific theoretical principles with related teaching and assessment strategies are presented in Table 4-2.

TABLE 4-2   Constructivist-Inspired Teaching and Assessment Strategies

Constructivist Principles	Teaching Strategies	Assessment Strategies
Children learn through guided problem solving of challenging tasks.	Determine each child's developmental level and ZPD. Present interesting tasks and challenging problems within their ZPD and form groups to work through them collaboratively.	Keep observational records of children's responses to challenging problems. Note how much help was needed at periodic points. Use labeled photographs of children's work in stages to chronicle process.
Children use language to organize their thinking.	Model self-talk, active listening, and problem-solving dialogue. Encourage children's dialogue. Facilitate children's dialogue when needed. Ask children higher level questions (open-ended, seeking elaboration).	Capture children's dialogue through transcripts. Analyze their conversations for clues of cognitive processing. (For example, ask children how they arrived at a solution or observe dialogue between children as they explain their reasoning.)
Scaffolding involves using verbal cues, questions, and prompts to engender inquiry.	Use open-ended, higher level questioning. Ask children to make predictions and hypotheses, explain observations, and elaborate on ideas of self and others.	Record child–teacher conversations and code for evidence of higher level responses. Document number and complexity of responses to open-ended questions.
The goal of education is to lead to increasing self-regulation and independence.	Begin by exploring new problems together; slowly reduce help as children become more capable.	Use children's work samples and anecdotal records to document progress toward independent task mastery. Use performance assessment to demonstrate independent task mastery.
Overbearing, authoritarian adult influence minimizes children's active exploration, problem solving, and social relationship building.	Remain in the role of guide and facilitator providing challenges, assistance, support, and resources as needed. Determine need by carefully observing children's activity and language. Keep the classroom climate free, allowing children to take risks, make mistakes, and share authority over making decisions. Allow children to make classroom rules and meet as a group regularly to discuss children's feelings about classroom community.	Reflect on the nature of interactions between teachers and children and children and children. Record group discussions to assess children's feelings about the tone of the classroom. Use photos of children interacting paired with dialogue transcripts to capture children's process and progressions.
Children's conceptions and misconceptions are all part of the knowledge construction process.	Validate children's attempts to understand and accomplish tasks. Use children's errors to assess thought progress and direction. Pose questions that guide children in different directions if they are off track.	Ask children relevant questions and ask them to support their ideas with a rationale. The children themselves may discover misconceptions as they explain their thinking. Observe and record children's responses and reactions.
When children are interested in the tasks at hand, learning is more meaningful.	Present tasks, experiences, and materials that relate to children's individual and group interests.	Keep notes during small- or large-group discussions for clues to children's interests. Ask children to identify prior knowledge and current questions. Record children's responses. Use children's prior knowledge to inform the group and connect to current experiences. Revisit the list when explorations are in progress. (Using a KWHL chart is helpful.)

Putting It Into Practice

Portfolios

Now you are familiar with the basics of the portfolio; perhaps you have even started to put one together for yourself. If not, you will soon! Even if you don't need it for school, you can definitely use it when you apply for jobs. Review artifacts that you would put into a binder or folder as if that portfolio were all you had to use to describe yourself. Make a list of items that you would include. If you already have one, write down what is in it. Review your list and write a few sentences about WHY you selected each item in your portfolio. For example, perhaps you put a résumé in to show people what work experience, education, and skills you possess. Maybe you included an observation report or a paper on which you did well to demonstrate your writing and analytical strengths. Perhaps you put in photos of a learning center you created with an accompanying lesson plan to show your competence as a teacher. Just as important as doing a portfolio in the first place is that you choose which items to include *deliberately* and you reflect on them. You may want to even attach your why statements. These things not only show your deeper reflections, but also are handy topics to talk about during an interview.

Conclusion

For many teachers, being in the role of cocreator, jointly learning from students while skillfully guiding their explorations, is exciting and refreshing. The possibilities for reinventing the classroom climate as a place alive with activity and enthusiastic learners are vibrant within constructivist theory. Unlocking that potential is possible with thoughtful, collaborative translations of theory into practice. Appropriate application of constructivist principles to teaching practice requires that teachers be empowered with the knowledge, skills, tools, and room to renegotiate the classroom into a collaborative community of learners. When teachers consider the realities of classroom life, children's development, and the impact of interactions with peers, adults, and their environment, principles of constructivist theory dovetail nicely with the overarching goals of education.

REFLECTION QUESTIONS: LOOKING BACK AND LOOKING AHEAD

Consider the following questions in light of what you have learned in this chapter as well as what you know from other sources.

1. What elements of a constructivist-inspired classroom do you most agree with? What aspects do you disagree with? Why?

2. Think about classroom experiences that made you feel particularly capable or that were particularly meaningful for you. What is it about these experiences that made them positive? What did the teacher, other children, and you do in these experiences?

3. Do these experiences align with constructive theory? How?

SUMMARY

- Constructivists believe that knowledge is constructed within the individual, shaped by experiences with the materials, phenomena, and people in their world.

- Teachers skillfully provide more or less support as needed, encouraging children to become deeply engaged in the cognitive process.

- All members of the constructivist classroom are active thinkers. Students think about challenging problems and tasks, teachers think about sparking students' interests and reflect on their activities, and all members reflect on their processes and evaluate outcomes. A key element of constructivist learning is that children learn through firsthand exploration of challenging activities.

- The roots of constructivism can be traced back to early philosophers, but more recent contributions from Dewey, Piaget, and Vygotsky have shaped current constructivist theory and practice. An active, discovery-based learning process reflects the key principles in Piaget's work.

- Key principles of Vygotsky's work include an emphasis on how the learner's interactions with people and materials shape his or her knowledge construction. Vygotsky believed that the role of the teacher was to scaffold children's learning by providing varying support and guidance as children work through challenging tasks within their zone of proximal development. To Vygotsky, language served as a primary vehicle for both communication and organization of individual thought.

- Among the potential challenges of applying constructivist theory to classroom practice is the ability of teachers to find a careful balance between learner-initiated activities and teacher-directed lessons.

- In the same way that learning experiences are structured to be authentic and meaningful to children, assessing their processes and progress toward goals must be authentic and meaningful.

MyEducationLab

Go to the Assignments and Activities section of Topic 2: Child Development/ Theories in the MyEducationLab for your course and complete the activity entitled *Cognitive and Language Development*. Observe how the teacher uses scaffolding to guide the children's activity and thinking.

Application Activities

On the Web: MyEducationLab Complete the activity entitled *Cognitive Language Development* on MyEducationLab. Observe how the teacher uses scaffolding to guide the children's activity and thinking. Make some notes about specific teacher prompts and strategies that you feel align with constructivist practice.

In Class Constructivists believe that one way knowledge is more deeply understood is through the process of teaching. With a small group, take a key concept from the chapter and create a demonstration that teaches the main components of the idea or concept. You can be creative with this one—think about a short skit, media tools, documentation panels, activities, songs, or whatever other strategies you can think of to engage your audience in a learning experience about your concept. Topic ideas include Piaget's contributions, Vygotsky's contributions, assessments, and classroom community.

In the Field Observe a program for young children in your area. Identify elements that align with constructivist theories of learning and teaching. For this assignment, you should take a broad view as you observe, keeping in mind the following questions:

- How would you describe the teacher's role?
- How would you describe the children's roles?
- How are materials displayed and used?
- How are learning experiences presented and implemented?
- How are conflicts handled?

Take notes on these and any other elements you feel are important. Prepare a brief presentation on how the program you observed compares to the constructivist practices you have read about.

For Your Portfolio Choose either older toddlers (2–3 years) or preschoolers (3–5 years) as your target age group, and create a series of simple rubrics or checklists you could use to assess children's performance on tasks in the following learning centers: literacy corner, block area, and manipulatives. Think about expected performance, advanced responses, and responses that would fall below age expectations. Create sample responses that would earn advanced, average, and below-average ratings. Keep in mind that milestones represent broad expectations but that some variation in children's responses and performance is expected.

In a book and writing corner, children may have access to books, books on tape, paper, crayons, markers, pencils, magazines, and puppets. In a block area, children may have access to different-shaped blocks, cars, and animal and people figures. In a manipulative center, children may have access to sorting bears in different sizes and colors, colored connecting beads, puzzles, lacing cards, matching and memory games, plastic building blocks, peg boards, unit blocks, and geometric-shaped blocks with pattern cards. Start this project by researching classroom materials. Refresh your memory about expected developmental milestones in language, cognition, social, fine motor, and gross motor skills for your selected age group. (A child development textbook, early childhood journals like *Young Children* from www.naeyc.org, and observations can assist you in this. In addition, the following websites may be useful: www.pbs.org/wholechild/abc/, www.howkidsdevelop.com/developSkills.html, www.growingchild.com/milestones.html, and www.zerotothree.org). Share your rubrics in class and discuss them in groups. Your rubric series can be an artifact in your portfolio section on observation and assessment.

RELATED WEB LINKS

Fuderstanding
www.funderstanding.com/about_learning.cfm

Constructivist Teaching and Learning Models
www.ncrel.org/sdrs/areas/issues/envrnmnt/drugfree/sa3const.htm

Developmental Checklist for 3-Year-Olds
www.gigglepotz.com/pres_checklist3.htm

Developmental Checklists for Children Birth Through 5 Years
www.arcdallas.org/docs/family/checklist.PDF
ecdc.syr.edu/checklist_download.html

CHAPTER 5

Multiple Intelligences Theory: Applications in the Early Childhood Classroom

"It's not how smart you are, it's how you are smart."

—HOWARD GARDNER

Since the beginning of formal educational settings, language skills and logical thinking have been the focus of learning and assessment. For the children who "get it"—those who think with these methods—academic experiences are generally positive and successful. For many children, however, learning, school life, and standard assessment are not so easily navigated. Twenty years ago a Harvard University professor, Howard Gardner, offered the world an alternative view of how children can "be smart" when he published his theory on multiple intelligences (MI).

Today, the theory continues to evolve, and is becoming a staple of how educators view children's individual abilities and strengths. MI theory offers teachers an alternative to traditional classroom climates in which students passively receive information presented by the teacher. A clear understanding of the principles of the theory and appropriate applications is essential to ensure success for all students.

STARTING POINTS: QUESTIONS AND REFLECTIONS

Take a moment to consider the following questions and reflection opportunities. The journey into exploring MI is an important time to think about how you process, think, and communicate. As a teacher, it is essential that you be aware of your own styles in order to ensure that you are teaching to all kinds of thinkers. It is not uncommon for teachers to teach through their own style or passion (Carlisle, 2001). So, if we're not fully aware of our own strengths and weaknesses, we will teach to our strengths and leave many children behind.

1. What kinds of activities do you prefer? Take a moment and consider your own way of thinking, perhaps evident in the types of activities you enjoy and choose to do in your free time.

2. How do you solve problems? Consider how you approach solving challenging situations or problems like being lost or stuck on a schoolwork problem. Identify some methods you use to help you through challenging situations and see if you can identify your own intelligence strengths as we explore each one in turn.

CLASSROOM VIEW

On this snowy afternoon in Mr. Washington's kindergarten classroom, the children are working on a project about the weather. The class decided to produce a weather-reporting station during the course of their science unit. Mr. Washington is one of a team of teachers in the K–3 school who started a pilot program aimed at integrating MI theory into the classroom. He meets you at the door and welcomes you to the classroom.

"When I started teaching here 4 years ago, things were very different. NCLB had just come out, and the whole school was really focused on standards and testing. Things were getting pretty stressful. In our January staff meeting the principal talked about a program that used a multiple intelligences curriculum and asked if a pilot group wanted to explore the possibility of us doing that. I signed up, and the journey began! Over the past 3 years we've continued to expand schoolwide. It's been a great learning experience for us. And the students' classroom experiences are so much more active and lively. I'm sure you'll see that this afternoon. The best part is that even though we've adopted a portfolio assessment method, the state test scores are also improving. I've seen how we are able to meet all our state standards in a rich, meaningful way that really engages the kids. This weather channel experience will really show you that."

Most of the children are working in groups, although one child is sitting at a table writing in his personal journal. A small group is working with a student teacher to build a background for the weather reporter's desk. The teacher is working with four children on setting up a video camera for the daily weather report recording. Two children are sitting by a window making notes with pictures about current weather conditions and reading a thermometer and a precipitation gauge on the outside of the window. Four children are sitting at another table excitedly talking about a script for their report. A teacher's assistant takes dictation. One girl is compiling the previous week's forecasts into graphs on poster board using picture symbols to track weather. Another team is working in a music center selecting music to accompany their weather reports. They are debating about which selection best represents how the cold, grey, snowy weather felt when they were outside this morning. For three weeks, the children have been working on their weather station each afternoon.

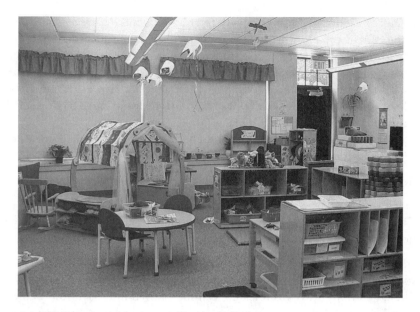

Children work in small groups at a variety of learning stations.

Around the room you notice a series of signs posted on the walls that describe the different ways of thinking in MI theory. The signs include positive statements that cover all the MI categories: word smart, number smart, picture smart, body smart, nature smart, people smart, me smart, music smart. You also notice individual charts on which the children's names are written; pictures and notes are attached. The pictures and notes describe ways in which each child is smart. As you think about the categories, you start to see them represented in the children's activities. Some children are writing, drawing, taking measurements, building, listening to music, and talking. The classroom is set up with group tables, not rows of desks, and there are stations around the room. They, too, align with the MI framework. There is an outside observation station, a music center, a writing and drawing station, a numbers and math area, and an open carpet space with boxes, blocks, scarves, and other large motor materials.

You also notice how many different activities the children are engaged in related to their science unit on the weather. Even though it is a science unit, the children are still working on all their skills and subject areas: mathematics, language arts, social skills, and creative arts. The student teacher later explains that, as part of their weather station reporting, the children also research weather conditions in other states. In this way, geography standards are covered within the weather project. Both teachers look as excited about the weather station as the children when they explain that the children periodically interview school staff and other classes about their weather experiences. The children also decided to start a weather newspaper with the help of the third-graders, in addition to their video program, which they will distribute daily to the school. As you prepare to leave the class, there is no doubt in your mind that Mr. Washington was right about how lively and active the students are.

Overview of Gardner's Work

Many teachers can identify with the frustration of being faced all year with those kids who just don't seem to get it. Although most of the class is moving along, there are some students who cannot understand directions, cannot seem to behave within the confines of a school setting, or cannot seem to complete their assignments. Many teachers give up and focus on the rest of the class, wondering what will become of those students. Stories abound of individuals who were once school failures, who performed low on standardized tests, but who later went on to achieve great success and make outstanding contributions to society. Concerned and interested in this phenomenon, Howard Gardner began the journey down the "precarious path" toward a more realistic, broader view of thinking, learning, and intelligence (Gardner, 1993a, p. 60).

This journey took him well outside the confines of the current theories of intelligence. He started with many far-reaching questions, such as

- How do we define intelligence?
- Do all people know, think, and learn in the same way?
- If **intelligence tests** (IQ tests) are really testing for aptitude, why are they not predictive of later success (Gardner, 1993b)?

Intelligence tests

General, standardized tests of current cognitive functioning. IQ tests are mostly used to predict short-term academic function.

Later, when Gardner began to define different kinds of intelligences, he started asking questions about exactly what competencies ought to be classified as separate intelligences. These questions drove his research. Gardner delved into data from brain research, psychological profiles, and cases of ordinary people who had extraordinary moments of insight (or "aha!" moments), where the solution to a problem became clear or an innovation became illuminated. Through this research, he explored the possibilities of a variety of potential human intelligences. In Gardner's view, the foundational requirements of any intelligence are that it must entail a set of problem-solving skills and must also entail the potential for creating new problems (Gardner, 1993a). Even though he ultimately defined the currently accepted eight classifications of intelligence, in his writing he points out that there can be no definitive list because this research is ongoing and potentially ever changing.

Intelligence and Creative Thinking

At the heart of Gardner's work are the notions of creative thought and creative problem solving. Creativity involves the ability to make something new out of stored information. Creative thinking likewise involves the ability to brainstorm many new ideas that are flexible and relevant to the task at hand and then to elaborate on those ideas in useful ways and to communicate the results of this process (Torrance, 2003). Applied to real-life situations, it is seen in the ability to

- Solve problems by seeing new solutions
- Create new problems or scenarios
- Find new uses for existing products, ideas, or tools
- Invent entirely new products, ideas, or tools

The emphasis on creative problem-solving ability as applied to authentic, real-life situations is essential in understanding Gardner's working definition of intelligence. This problem-solving process forms the context for acquiring new skills and knowledge.

Defining Intelligence

The definition of intelligence, often interpreted as talent or skill, is, according to Gardner, more about individual thought process than about skill performance. Our abilities to use words, pictures, diagrams, song, drama, classification, or dialogue to understand our world or work through an authentic problem demonstrate the thought process we use to engage with the world. Two ways our thought processes reveal themselves in performance and skill are by singing a beautiful piece of music in perfect tempo and pitch or by delivering an articulate and convincing argument; Gardner's definition of intelligence then is about how individuals process information and experiences. In essence, intelligence refers to the many different possible ways in which individuals think about their world, process experiences, and function within their own daily lives. Above all, Gardner emphasized that the parameters used to define intelligence "are a way of ensuring that a human intelligence must be genuinely useful and important" (Gardner, 1993a, p. 61).

Gardner also presented his theory as flexible, changing, and adaptable based on the cultural and knowledge lens within which it is used. Since his original work was published in 1983, he has continued to expand and revise various elements of the theory. His most recent expansion is the addition of the eighth intelligence, with a ninth possible. He cautions that his work be viewed as a framework from where we can begin the journey into the vast and diverse capabilities of human potential. Gardner further reminds teachers that MI theory offers a way to reenvision teaching to ensure that all possible ways of thinking are stimulated. He cautions that it is not intended to be used as a way to label or track children as one kind of thinker or another. Observe how teachers can plan curricula that integrate the many ways of thinking and representing knowledge at MyEducationLab.

For example, in the classroom view, you saw groups of children working on different tasks related to the weather station project. Mr. Washington later explains that the children often select the activities on which they want to work. Their selections usually align with their stronger thinking styles. He also sometimes selects tasks for them that will strengthen all their intelligences. He selects groups who have complementary strengths to work together, such as the team working on the music selections. One child in that group has strong music ability, another has strong number intelligence, and the other child understands feelings and motivations (the "me smarts"). Each brings a thinking style to the project that is different from those of the others and strengthens the team. As they work together, they are able to see that other people think differently than they do but still work together to accomplish a shared task.

The Eight Multiple Intelligences: Many Kinds of Smart

Gardner recognized that although one or more types of intelligence may be particularly more developed or natural, we all possess varying strengths in many or all of these areas. As educators, it is particularly important for us to develop an understanding of all the ways in which people are smart. The current list defined by Gardner (see Table 5-1) offers a snapshot of the scope of human intelligence (Gardner, 1993b).

MyEducationLab

Go to the Assignments and Activities section of Topic 7: Curriculum/Content Areas in the MyEducationLab for your course and complete the activity entitled *Integrating the Arts in the Early Childhood Curriculum*. Observe the different kinds of learning experiences and content areas integrated in these lessons.

TABLE 5-1   Summary of Gardner's Eight Intelligences

Intelligence Type	How People Demonstrate Intelligence
Verbal/linguistic (word smart)	Well-developed language skills and a sensitivity to the sound, meaning, and rhythm of words
Logical/mathematical (number smart)	Ability to think abstractly in concepts and to discern numerical patterns
Musical (music smart)	Appreciation for or the ability to produce rhythm, pitch, and tone quality
Visual/spatial (art smart)	Thinking in pictures or images or the ability to visualize abstractly
Body/kinesthetic (body smart)	Ability to use and control one's movement or a sensitivity to handling and manipulating objects
Interpersonal (we/people smart)	Awareness and sensitivity to the moods and motivations of other people
Intrapersonal (me smart)	Self-awareness and a connection with one's own feelings and thought processes
Naturalist (nature smart)	Appreciation and ability for recognizing and sorting objects in nature

Verbal/Linguistic Intelligence

"The use of words to communicate and document, to express powerful emotions, to set to music in song sets human beings apart from other animals" (Campbell, Campbell, & Dickinson, 2004, p. 2). It is our ability to use words both internally and externally, written and orally, that is one of the greatest measures of human evolution. It is one of the primary means by which we are connected as a species across distance and time. It is a mechanism that is so strong that we develop the physical ability to hear while still in the womb, at around 4 months (Vander Zanden, 2003). Considering this developmental and social emphasis, it becomes clear how vitally important it is for young children to be surrounded with rich language experiences from the beginning.

Verbal/linguistic intelligence

Well-developed language skills and sensitivity to the sound, meaning, and rhythm of words.

Individuals with strong **verbal/linguistic intelligence** are likely to exhibit aptitude in listening, reading, speaking, and writing. In Chapter 4, we saw that children use language both as a means of organizing their thoughts and as a means of communicating effectively with others (Carlisle, 2001; Vygotsky, 1978). Children's private speech offers parents and teachers a rich opportunity to gain a window into children's thought processes. It is also an opportunity to get clues about children's language abilities beyond just the ability to repeat letters, sounds, or words. This is an example of the difference between a processing ability and a performance skill. As Gardner points out, the true nature of a child's knowledge is to be found in his or her processing.

The verbal/linguistic child may show an interest in

- Listening to, telling, or reading stories
- Poetry
- Playing with words in riddles and rhymes
- Talking
- Creating and explaining complex play scenarios
- Persuading others or negotiating

Mnemonic Devices

Mnemonic devices include creating acronyms for strings of information—like the one my mom and music teacher taught me. She used the letters F-A-C-E to help me remember the sequence of whole notes within the written musical staff, beginning with the space between the bottommost lines. Perhaps you remember one about the planets that your teacher used.

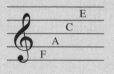

These children may also use language to remember information through **mnemonic devices** such as HOMES to remember the first letter and, hence, name of each of the Great Lakes.

Children with linguistic delays or disabilities are still able to develop methods of communicating effectively and eloquently, often through other intelligences. Helen Keller is an excellent example of an insightful communicator and writer. Despite being blind and deaf, she was able to experience the sensory richness of the world through alternative means. The books she wrote are truly inspirational and demonstrate the amazing potential for learning and success in all humans. Other examples of the embodiment of well-developed verbal/linguistic intelligence can be found in poets, authors, lawyers, storytellers, public speakers, and linguists (translators, multilingual individuals).

Mnemonic devices

Mental tricks like rhymes and acronyms used to remember strings of content.

Children in MI classrooms are given many opportunities to express their thinking and knowledge.

Logical/Mathematical Intelligence

Logical/mathematical intelligence

Ability to think abstractly in concepts and to discern numerical patterns.

Logical/mathematical intelligence involves an affinity for numbers, calculations, and deductive and inductive reasoning and an understanding of patterns and relationships. "At the core . . . is the ability to recognize and solve problems" (Campbell et al., 2004, p. 32). In a logical/mathematical thinker, we would be likely to see (Campbell et al., 2004)

- Ability to understand the function of objects (physics)
- Familiarity with concrete and abstract concepts of quantity, time, and cause and effect
- Ability to perceive and appreciate patterns and relationships among items in the world
- General enjoyment of numbers and calculations
- Creating diagrams and patterns to connect information
- Building patterns with various materials and blocks
- Wrestling with open-ended problems
- Predicting logical outcomes

Our understanding of logic and mathematics starts from a concrete foundation where the concept of numbers and counting is learned through manipulating objects. This could include lining up a string of 10 plastic bears and touching each one while counting 1, 2, 3, and so on. Our mathematical understanding then moves into the abstract realm of actions, reactions, hypothesis statements, and numerical manipulation completed mentally (Gardner, 1993a).

Logically/mathematically inclined individuals are particularly capable of handling long strings of ideas and reasoning, and they are able to recognize key problems and solve them. They are both explorers of object and phenomenon and discoverers of relationships and sequences. They offer the world great contributions in both the creation of new problems and ideas and explanations for concrete, physical realities (Gardner, 1993a). "Perceiving the patterns in the universe and organizing them into meaningful forms is the logical/mathematical mind working" (Calvin-Campbell, 1998, p. 20).

Logical/mathematical thinkers may gravitate toward puzzles, pattern blocks and cards, graph paper, rulers, compasses, and protractors that make linear patterns on paper and may take delight in experimenting to test their hypotheses. They can benefit from using diagrams or words to identify and explain relationships and ideas and enjoy an environment that offers room for questioning, exploring, and discovering (Campbell et al., 2004). Mathematicians, scientists, accountants, and computer programmers are examples of individuals who use logical/mathematical intelligence in their work.

Musical Intelligence

Musical intelligence

Appreciation for or the ability to produce rhythm, pitch, and tone quality.

As with verbal and mathematical disciplines, the realm of music is like a language with unique symbol and notation systems. As an information-processing ability, however, its consideration as intelligence goes beyond mastery of the functions of playing or creating music. Individuals with strength in **musical intelligence** often explain that they hear music and lyrics in everyday events and situations. The pattern of the rain as it hits

---

Putting It Into Practice

Graphing

Facilitate children's use of graphing as a means to promote logical/mathematical thinking. Even young children can count and color in boxes on a teacher-made chart. For example, children can count class preferences (colors, foods) or things such as frequency of certain family pets. This allows children to make a visual display of their mathematical thinking.

Class Pets		
Fish	**Dog**	**Cat**

Number of Students

---

different surfaces, the rhythm of branches in the breeze, the cadence of voices and beats of footsteps can all conjure music within the mind of the musically intelligent individual. An affinity or interest in rhythm, tone, and music may appear earlier than many of the other intelligences. We even may see this in a newborn's ability to show preference for the specific pitch or melody of the mother's voice (Calvin-Campbell, 1998).

In their earliest years, young children are often drawn to and excited by music as a creative outlet and source of pure enjoyment, but they also use it as a tool for remembering information and understanding concepts. Consider some of your early memories of Mother Goose rhymes set to music or your ability to sing the alphabet song. As with the mnemonic devices discussed in the verbal/linguistic section, setting academic knowledge to music is an easy way for teachers to make learning memorable.

Music is a highly emotional genre. It engages not only our aural (hearing) sense, but also our sense of touch through vibrations and rhythms, and it can have remarkable effects on our emotional state, too. Music can be used as a tool to set the mood in a classroom, to expose children to soft, soothing music at meal and rest times. At other times, we can use faster, upbeat selections to give children an opportunity to move about and develop connections between their bodies and the music. Children who grow up in environments that offer a rich range of opportunities to be exposed to and actively engage with music and instruments are more likely to have well-developed musical intelligence than children who do not have these experiences (Fox, 2000). Although research on brain development and music is ongoing, some reports indicate that actively listening to and exploring music

---

Putting It Into Practice

Feel the Rhythm

One of the best ideas for enabling children to feel the rhythms of music, even deaf children, is to give them an inflated balloon. (Do not overinflate to reduce the risk of popping, and be sure to monitor carefully.) Let them hold the balloon between their hands, with palms and fingers laid out on the balloon. As the music plays, they will feel vibrations in the rubber. Children can be prompted to feel (to listen with their hands) for stronger or more subtle vibrations.

---

enhance brain development and contribute to academic achievement in several other discipline areas, such as math and English (Flohr, 1999). We are still learning about the impact of music on brain functioning; however, it is clear that the inclusion of rich and varied music experiences has benefits for all young children.

Children who are particularly musically inclined may demonstrate the following (Campbell et al., 2004):

- Becoming excited and physically active around music
- Using their bodies to express a connection to the music through conducting or dancing
- Becoming affected emotionally when listening to various works
- Singing to themselves
- Seeking out and enjoying playing musical instruments
- Describing interpretations of music in terms of colors, moods, scenery, or other imagery

Even though music may enrich all our lives, a true musical intelligence is about more than technical competence in performance. The rare musical prodigy may show remarkable natural abilities at a very young age without formal training. Consider the musical genius of Mozart, for example, who was astounding audiences with his technically and emotionally superb compositions as a 5-year-old child. Also worthy of note here is the physical nature of music—the rhythm and vibrations that can be felt and enjoyed by all people, even by individuals who suffer from hearing loss. In rare cases of individuals with particular developmental disabilities like autism, a compelling, clear connection to musical pieces can be seen in the individual's ability to hear a piece once and repeat it back perfectly (Gardner, 1993a).

Visual/spatial

Thinking in pictures or images or the ability to visualize abstractly.

Visual/Spatial Intelligence

The human capacity for representing our **visual/spatial** understanding of the world is truly our oldest form of communication. It was the very earliest recorded history of man, evidenced in cave drawings made tens of thousands of years ago, that paved the way for the later development of writing as a means of communication and representation (Rush, 1998). Along with the history of the written language, we see the reliance on visual/spatial ability in the evolution from pictures or imagery to pictographs (like Egyptian hieroglyphics) to an abstract symbol system (like our alphabet).

It is important to consider the many facets of visual/spatial processing at work in each of these activities:

- Creating images in one's mind
- Using visual images to express ideas and tell stories
- Recognizing and discriminating among visual input
- Accurately representing the world visually
- Moving through complex paths
- Manipulating images

The key function of using vision as an external process to enhance one's internal, mental image is only one part of this intelligence. Indeed, individuals who are visually impaired or suffer from some forms of brain damage often have highly developed spatial abilities and are extremely capable of navigating their way through their world (Campbell et al., 2004; Gardner, 1993a).

Artistic ability can also be a clue that an individual possesses a strong tendency in this intelligence. The artist uses various media to make external representations of the visual imagery conjured in their minds. Often this is the most satisfying way for them to fully express themselves. Artists are capable of manipulating media to create a visual representation that can evoke emotion, recognition, and connection with the viewer. Visual artists use their representations to communicate and evoke strong emotional response from appreciators. Visual representation, however, is also a highly cognitive, intellectual endeavor (Davis & Gardner, 1993). Visual representation is another tool or language used to make sense of experience as well as to express or share ideas. Children who cannot attend as well to verbal cues (for example, instructions or lectures) may demonstrate rapt attention when pictures, symbols, charts, or videos are presented to them. This point validates the importance of using multiple modes of instruction.

Visually/spatially inclined children are stimulated by pictures and images in their environment and may naturally gravitate toward charts and graphs as a means of categorizing or explaining information. These children may also show a heightened interest in artistic endeavors or in working with manipulatives to build complex structures. A strong spatial ability allows individuals to see, touch, and manipulate objects in their mind's eye. This allows them to map out actions and reactions prior to the physical experience. This processing style is particularly evident in successful chess players, who have to imagine what moves their opponent might make several steps ahead depending on their own next move. Surgeons, engineers, scientists, sailors, architects, athletes, and sports coaches all use this ability to see in their mind's eye the relationship between objects in space and how they move dependent on one another.

The cultural underpinnings of Gardner's theory (and working definition of intelligence) are perhaps most evident in this realm of intelligence. Consider tribal life in remote locales where hunter-gatherers must provide food for the members of the tribe. They fulfill this most basic function solely by their ability to navigate extreme and complex terrains using only their visual map (Gardner, 1993a). Gardner's original emphasis on

Putting It Into Practice

Picture Labels

Because young children respond more readily to pictures as their literacy develops, labeling classroom materials, shelves, centers, name charts, or schedules with picture icons is an important way to communicate. For example, use individual symbols (like a star or heart) paired with children's names on cubbies and job charts. Have children make their own stamps from sponges or erasers, so they can "sign" their names with their symbols. This is particularly useful when children want to write letters to their friends. Also consider labeling shelves with words and pictures of materials to help children identify where the materials are housed. A picture or drawing of the blocks on the block shelf encourages children's independence at cleanup time, too.

the cultural value of the intelligences can be understood in a context such as this one, where the processing ability of the individual has great consequences for the members of the entire community.

Body/Kinesthetic Intelligence

Body/kinesthetic

Ability to use and control one's own movement or a sensitivity to handling and manipulating objects.

One of the earliest mechanisms humans use to explore their world, **body/kinesthetic** processing, begins in infancy. Babies respond to touch and use their bodies to express likes and dislikes, wants, and needs. Consider the happy baby whose entire body tightens in excitement at the sight of the mobile overhead and then bursts into jerking and waving of the arms and legs as he giggles or the bright-eyed 9-month-old who haltingly reaches out

Putting It Into Practice

Mapmaking

Facilitate children's visual/spatial development by encouraging them to make maps and visual charts. They can map their classroom, their playground, or their route home (ask parents to help). Children can also use a map to plot out a new school garden as a class project. Free programs that make garden layouts may be found at www.lowes.com/lowes/lkn?action=pg&p=Down_to_Earth/GardenPlanner/garden_planner_launch.html or www.bhg.com/gardening/design/nature-lovers/welcome-to-plan-a-garden/

Montessori's Materials

Montessori's method emphasizes the use of sensory education. Maria Montessori designed sandpaper letter cards that allowed children to feel letters in addition to seeing them. She developed sensory matching games that honed listening, smelling, touching, hearing, and seeing skills. These games can be easily recreated with the use of small sealed containers, such as film containers. Fill pairs of containers with a variety of items that make different sounds when shaken (bells, beads, sand, pebbles, rocks). Be sure to glue the lids on for safety! Children then take turns shaking one container and then trying to find its match by sound discrimination. The same procedure used with cotton balls soaked with different smelling extracts (be sure all substances are nontoxic). You can glue small pieces of screen or mesh to the top (still use a lid over that) to ensure that the cotton ball is not removed. You will read more about Montessori's method in Chapter 10.

her arm toward a block, clumsily grasps it, and brings it to her mouth to receive the sensory input necessary to begin to understand the nature of this object. These are but the beginnings of children's use of body/kinesthetic intelligence to learn about the world around them. It is further developed as preschoolers engage in hands-on, sensory exploration of the materials in their environment.

Our physical abilities are divided between gross motor (large muscle) actions and fine motor (small muscle) actions. We use our bodies to move around in the world, to communicate and express ourselves, to reach and grasp for objects we want to see up close, to seek and give comfort through gentle embraces, and to identify things in our world. It is our ability to grasp and purposefully manipulate tools so delicately and effectively that sets us apart from many other living species on the planet (Gardner, 1993a). For individuals with an inclination toward body/kinesthetic processing, the opportunity to touch, manipulate, move, and feel as they learn is essential. They use information gathered from their fingertips to identify, classify, or recognize materials. Or they may use movement or dance to represent information or communicate.

Individuals who use their hands or bodies to process information and solve problems are exhibiting strong body/kinesthetic intelligence. Skilled artisans or craftspeople, athletes, dancers, actors, and surgeons exemplify body/kinesthetic intelligence.

Children who learn through this realm will often (Campbell et al., 2004)

- Gravitate toward experiences and materials they can manipulate and touch
- Show sensitivity to physical stimuli in the environment
- Demonstrate skill in handcrafting or moving
- Appear graceful and fluid in their body movements

Because all children learn through sensory experiences, it is natural to integrate hands-on, tactile, kinesthetic experiences into classrooms for young children. In addition, the period from birth to 3 years of age is a time of unprecedented physical development. It is a time when a focus on physical activity and the honing of physical abilities is essential.

Environments for Moving

Young children have lots of energy. At this time of life, physical development blossoms and must be refined. When creating environments for young children, toddlers in particular, it is important to plan for movement. Toddler classrooms should include some kind of gross motor equipment such as a small climber and slide. Classrooms should be designed to encourage free flow among centers, but be careful not to include too much open space, which encourages running indoors. Plan ample outdoor time in the morning and afternoon. Also plan for tactile experiences like making play dough and clay, exploring funnels and shovels in sand bins, identifying sinking and floating items in water bins, and using manipulatives to develop small motor skills. Consider making small sand and rock gardens, much like Zen gardens, which children can rake and design. Also encourage children to trace shapes, letters, and words in sand or shaving cream.

Through the ongoing inclusion of these kinds of tactile and physical experiences, children's body/kinesthetic intelligence can be strengthened, and the preferred processing mechanism of body/kinesthetic learners can be supported.

The Personal Intelligences

Often presented together, the two personal intelligences refer to the proclivity of some individuals to seek out and exhibit great ability to engage with emotions, moods, intentions, and human connections. Either turned outward or inward, inter- or intrapersonally intelligent individuals have a keen sense of the complex personality characteristics in others or in themselves that are at the heart of human existence. "Both of these capacities are based on the importance of the self and self-knowledge. Intrapersonal competence promotes one's personal agenda and interpersonal intelligence works to ensure the smooth functioning of the wider community" (Calvin-Campbell, 1998, p. 25). The roots of this ability may have ties in the quality of the child's earliest attachments to parents or caregivers.

Loving, warm, responsive caregiving early in life helps infants develop healthy emotional bonds to the adults in their world. Being able to trust that needs will be met—that caregivers will love, protect, encourage, and support them—is the foundation for later healthy social and emotional relationships. Being cared for by adults who support children's attachment and independence promotes feelings of social connection with others and confidence in themselves (Salter Ainsworth, 1989). Attachments lay the groundwork for later strength in both interpersonal and intrapersonal intelligences (Gardner, 1993a). Although the personal intelligences are entwined with one another to some degree, there are areas where they differ. It is entirely possible to have strength in one area and not the other.

Interpersonal Intelligence   In cultures that value the community or collectivist aspects of their society, individuals who are particularly adept at forming relationships and navigating social situations are at a particular advantage. Individuals with a strong **interpersonal intelligence** are most comfortable interacting in groups, are attuned to the moods and desires of the people around them, and are naturally capable of influencing peers. Because the intelligences are related to culture, individuals who are living in socially oriented societies will be more likely to develop stronger interpersonal intelligence. This is because the environment can serve to enhance or diminish an individual's natural inclinations.

Some developmental theorists have classified young children as *egocentric*, or not yet able to understand or sympathize with the feelings of others (Vander Zanden, 2003). But more recent evidence suggests that many children are quite in tune with the feelings of others around them. They will seek to ease pain in peers who have been injured emotionally or physically. The preschooler who tearfully holds the hand of a friend with a skinned knee demonstrates a capacity to understand how that friend is feeling. She provides comfort by acknowledging his pain and feeling unhappy about his suffering. There are also those children who are social butterflies, who exhibit more skill than many peers in navigating social situations and commanding a group of peers in complex play scenarios.

Interpersonally intelligent children may demonstrate the following:

- Sensing and identifying the moods of caregivers and peers
- Interest in social play either in leading or following roles
- Leading group dramatic play sessions
- Organizing peers during group games, influencing peer groups

In more developed forms, this inclination allows individuals to use their sensitivity to others' emotions and act upon it to influence the actions of groups of people. Politicians,

> **Interpersonal intelligence**
>
> Awareness and sensitivity to the moods and motivations of other people.

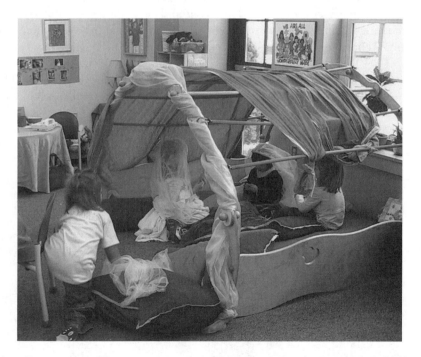

Social interactions are one of the many ways some children process and represent their thinking.

religious leaders, comedians, psychologists, and teachers generally exhibit a strong interpersonal intelligence (Gardner, 1993a).

Intrapersonal intelligence

Self-awareness and connection with one's own feelings and thought processes.

Intrapersonal Intelligence   Interrelated with the "outward" personal intelligence, **intrapersonal intelligence** relates to a sensitivity to and understanding of those personality characteristics that lie within us:

- Motivation
- Goal setting
- Integrity
- Empathy
- Sense of self
- Attunement with internal emotional states

Like interpersonal intelligence, our ability to know ourselves, our wants and needs, and our interests develops from the beginning. Infants quickly learn to identify and respond to their own needs and to the emotional security of strong attachments. Developmental theorists point to a child's progression through several stages in his or her social and emotional development. Erikson's stages, discussed in Chapter 2, include early stages in which the young child must acquire increasing autonomy, independence, and self-sufficiency if positive developmental outcomes are to follow. When children are supported and encouraged to take initiative and to master tasks, they internalize positive feelings of efficacy, accomplishment, and motivation (Erikson, 1950). These early experiences, along with positive parental and caregiver models, lay the foundations for children to develop a clear understanding of their feeling states as well as a healthy self-image.

The individual who has a well-developed intrapersonal intelligence enjoys being introspective, is naturally comfortable identifying and responding to internal states, and often is uniquely capable of expressing cognitive or emotional processes eloquently and compellingly. Reflective journaling writers—for example, Anne Frank, whose classic personal story of her life while hiding from Nazi forces put a face to millions of people who perished during World War II—demonstrate a clear awareness of themselves. They also demonstrate an ability to express their feelings and thoughts in ways that other people can

Putting It Into Practice

Goal Setting

In Chapter 7 you will read about the High/Scope curriculum's plan-do-review framework. This system encourages children to start each day by making a purposeful plan for how they want to spend their time, what centers they want to work in, and what materials they want to experiment and play with. This is a simple way to facilitate children's directionality, intentionality, and goal setting. After center time, children regroup with teachers and reflect on how their plans played out and what they learned.

relate to. Counseling therapists often exhibit strong intra- and interpersonal intelligence when they use their own intimate knowledge of their inner processes to understand and assist others (Gardner, 1993a).

Naturalist Intelligence

Although naturalist intelligence was originally included in the logical/mathematical and visual/spatial intelligence realms, Gardner selected particular aspects of this thinking style for its own category. **Naturalist intelligence** refers to individuals who gravitate toward engaging with the environment, nature, and natural phenomena and who demonstrate skill at "identifying members of a group or species, distinguishing among the members or species, recognizing the existence of other species, and perceiving the relationship among several species" (Campbell et al., 2004, p. 220).

Once again, we can trace the roots of the evolution of this intelligence to our early ancestors. Their very survival was contingent on their ability to successfully differentiate between viable and harmful natural sources for food, shelter, and clothing. Naturalist thinkers maintain a connection and a deeper understanding of the immensely broad scope of the

Naturalist intelligence

Appreciation and ability for recognizing, sorting objects in nature.

MyEducationLab

Go to the Building Teaching Skills and Dispositions section of Topic 6: Curriculum Planning in the MyEducationLab for your course and complete the activity entitled *Planning the Curriculum: Methods, Effective Teaching Strategies, and Standards*

Putting It Into Practice

Webbing Activities

Taking children outdoors to gardens, on nature walks, or even just to the playground are all important parts of any child's life. To encourage naturalist thinking, try making idea and relationship webs on topics from nature. For example, in a gardening project, children can classify types of flowers based on certain characteristics, such as color or the time of year when they bloom. Or children can chart differences in trees based on evergreens and deciduous varieties (those that lose their leaves).

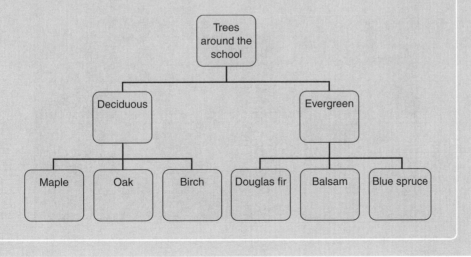

natural world. These abilities are strong in natural scientists such as botanists, zoologists, and biologists. Chefs, gardeners, and hunters also demonstrate aspects of the naturalist intelligence in the way they are able to classify organisms in the natural world and find practical, valuable uses for natural elements.

Children who exhibit strength in this realm will often be entranced with (Campbell, et al., 2004)

- Sorting and classifying pictures or replicas of bugs, plants, or animals in a science center
- Collecting specimens on nature walks
- Seeking to understand how things work
- Making frequent observations using such tools as microscopes, telescopes, and notebooks
- Growing gardens
- Spending ample time outdoors looking for plant and animal life
- Researching environmental issues in books or on the computer

The children working at the observation window in the classroom visit were using and strengthening their naturalist intelligence. All the intelligences are innate to some degree, but children born with a natural sense of wonder and interest in their world must be exposed to experiences and people who can fuel that development in order for them to develop strengths in their unique combinations of intelligences.

Space, time, and encouragement are ways that teachers support children's many forms of representation.

All the Intelligences Work Together

Through varied, active experiences teachers can foster learning in all children, support development in all ways of thinking, and provide opportunities for all children to engage in meaningful activities that

- Expand their thinking processes
- Encourage active collaborative construction of understandings
- Promote activities that foster higher level thinking

At first glance, this expectation may sound inappropriate for young children. However, reviews of innovative early childhood centers are finding that in project-oriented programs that validate multiple ways of thinking and representing knowledge, children's demonstration of deeper learning and higher order thinking is several steps beyond that in traditional practice (Edwards, Gandini, & Forman, 1996). In essence, traditional preschool practice may expect too little of children and teachers in terms of what is possible within the classroom (Bredekamp, 1993).

Self-reflection: Developing Our Intrapersonal Strength

As you move into a discussion of strategies for integrating Gardner's theory into working with young children, it is important to take a moment to consider these many ways of knowing in relation to your own intelligence strengths. Reconsider the processes you use to solve problems, the kinds of skills you use in your life and work, or the kinds of activities in which you choose to engage. Review the notes you made earlier and compare them with your ideas now. Take a moment to consider what you imagine your teaching style will be like, taking care to note particular intelligences you may be omitting.

Rethinking Education: A New Vision of Active Learning

Historically, the American education system has systematically validated verbal and logical ways of thinking, processing, and sharing but has marginalized other ways of thinking (Emig, 1997; Gardner, 1993b). When children with different intelligences (or different ways of thinking) are placed in this environment, they may be identified as failing in school. These are the children who don't seem to get it or who go on to perform poorly on standardized tests and struggle with school activities. Ensuring the success of all children requires a shift in how teachers view children's thinking capacities as well as how they view the roles of teachers and children in the classroom.

Shifting Images: Possibilities for Teaching Young Children

Since the original publication of Gardner's theory and the promotion of more developmentally appropriate early childhood teaching, preschool programs have begun to embrace practices that are more suitable for young children. Using activity centers that target different content areas (for example, science, art, or literacy) allows children to engage with materials that tap into specific intelligences. Centers also allow children to engage in small groups and actively construct understanding through hands-on interaction with materials and firsthand experience of phenomena. This approach to classroom structure, based on a developmental perspective of children, illustrates a view of children as active explorers of their environments. Remember how the children in Mr. Washington's class were actively exploring the weather? They then represented their new knowledge in the form of their weather station and newspaper. The children tapped into the many ways of thinking to research and learn as well as to share their findings.

A center-based approach is certainly a step in the right direction from overly instructive styles; however, it relies on a theoretical perspective that all children develop through universal stages. According to MI theorists, this view denies the great diversity that exists in the ways children think and process their experiences (Krechevsky, 1991). Simply arranging furniture and materials in centers, without careful planning for individual learners, does not truly embody MI-inspired teaching. A lack of planning for individual diversity demonstrates a shortcoming that must be addressed in order for MI-inspired practice to be successfully applied. Mr. Washington accomplished this by guiding some children's choice of activity as well as by grouping certain children together who could share unique strengths.

Contemporary MI-inspired practice contrasts sharply with traditional teacher-directed styles and builds on center-based approaches (Stanford, 2003). Gardner's advice to teachers committed to applying MI theory meaningfully and appropriately in the classroom is to recognize, value, and celebrate the many ways in which children think and understand their world. He suggests teachers do this by presenting diverse, engaging learning opportunities (Gardner, 1995). Schools that employ an innovative, MI-inspired approach view the teacher as a

- Facilitator of children's explorations
- Coach guiding their investigations and creations
- Reflective, deliberate decision maker

MI schools have been compared to the approach in children's museums, where children are able to manipulate and actively explore authentic materials (Armstrong, 1994). Many content areas are integrated to promote connections between content and contexts, such as the weather station project. In these settings, children and teachers learn in more informal ways, and children's inquiry and exploration are the primary vehicles for learning experiences. Teachers also serve as careful observers of children's unfolding learning. They listen as children explain their choices of materials and activities and value their unique ways of representing their thinking. Teachers in MI schools use their observations of children's interests and strengths to plan daily experiences in all eight intelligence areas, taking care to give equal value to all ways of thinking (Armstrong, 1994; NEA, 1998; Stanford, 2003).

Roles of the Teacher

A key responsibility of teachers in MI classrooms is the ability to shift from being the keeper of the right answers to being the generator of the right questions. Young children need to be guided in the inquiry process. Teachers' use of thought-provoking, open-ended questions serves as a model as well as stimulation. In MI classrooms, the teacher's and the children's questions are the starting point for exploration and the driving force behind this inquiry learning process (Campbell, 1997). Once the children are engaged in meaningful activities to investigate the answerers to their questions, teachers can move about the room and observe or support the children's explorations. Teachers provide resources, materials, and suggestions as needed to help children work through challenges and guide children toward exploring many possible ways of processing and thinking. The classroom environment may present a more informal appearance; however, teachers remain thoughtful and deliberate in their planning and guidance of young children's activities.

Another feature of MI schools that differs from traditional programs can be found in the area of curriculum planning. Early childhood teachers frequently use preplanned curricula that lay out the topics to be covered and specific activities to be completed days or even months in advance. MI schools view the curriculum as more organic and emergent, taking direction from the topics that are relevant to the individual group of children (Guild & Chock-Eng, 1998). As with the project approach to teaching young children promoted by Lillian Katz (discussed in Chapter 8), children have an active role in directing the topics of study and in choosing activities and representations to crystallize their learning (Katz & Chard, 2000).

Teachers work with children to support their investigations and explorations. They facilitate interactions among children (and with the community) and provide resources to spark their interest and satisfy their curiosity. Teachers may arrange the classroom into centers, but they are also thoughtful and reflective about how children are engaging with their environments and each other. Materials in centers are chosen and updated to encourage and provoke children's thinking and are often **open-ended materials** to allow children to use them for their own design. Teachers still include directed, skills-based learning experiences, but the bulk of children's day is spent in active, child-initiated exploration and problem solving.

Open-ended materials

Materials that are designed to be used in many ways.

Assessment

A unique element of MI teaching is that both the teacher and students reflect on classroom learning and experience (Guild & Chock-Eng, 1998). Children are encouraged to discuss the investigations, choices, and discoveries they make. They explain why they selected various materials with which to explore and create. It is through this guided self-reflection that children begin to understand their own learning style and thinking processes. These reflection sessions are prime opportunities for teachers to make notes about children's thoughts, which then serve as insightful elements to assess children's progress.

Children are also encouraged to evaluate their own learning in concert with the teacher. Children can reflect on samples of their work, discuss what they were doing at that particular stage, and identify things that they have learned since. The process of portfolio assessment lends itself well to evaluation in MI classrooms because it is individual, personally meaningful, and reflective—all key elements of MI theory. By reviewing documentation of previous learning experiences, children can more clearly see the progression of their skills and knowledge. Being aware of their own learning processes and progress is a level of involvement that is not often enough integrated into early childhood programs. It is an important part of your learning, too. You'll have a chance to identify your own processing styles at the end of the chapter.

Perhaps one of the most liberating and daunting challenges presented by MI theorists to practicing teachers is the notion that there is not necessarily one right model or prescription for applying MI theory in the classroom (Campbell, 1997; Gardner, 1995). As with the nature of emergent curricula, the specifics of MI classroom design must emerge from (Guild & Chock-Eng, 1998)

- The interplay of the teacher's theoretical knowledge bases
- Thoughtful observation and reflection of the children
- Desired learning outcomes
- Creativity and risk taking

Emergent curriculum empowers children with a voice in making decisions about the direction of their learning. So, too, MI teaching endows teachers with a freedom to explore new, innovative ways of teaching while remaining active learners. Just as children need the freedom to take risks and try new ideas (Pool, 1997), teachers need the space and support to embrace a new vision of learning and explore new potentials in interactive, learner-centered teaching.

Applying Multiple Intelligences in Early Childhood Education: Personalization and Diversity

At the heart of the application of MI theory is the validation that there are many ways to think about common phenomena. Gardner proposes that there are many ways in which children approach learning about content—even the same content. In other words, children can understand mathematical concepts through metaphors in other media. Visual or linguistic activities can illuminate mathematical content for children who do not think in strictly mathematical/logical ways (Gardner, 1993b). Teaching to multiple intelligences is about expanding classroom experiences for all children and not about classifying children's processing styles. The teacher's role is to provide rich, meaningful, and varied opportunities that support and encourage all learners (Gardner, 1997).

Teaching to All Children: Basic Principles

Children are naturally energetic and curious to touch and manipulate things in their path, and it is essential that early childhood educators encourage this natural desire to learn and explore through the development of appropriate, interesting, meaningful experiences (Miller, 2003). Grounded in a solid understanding of child development and current beliefs about developmentally appropriate practice, much of the foundation of a classroom that aligns with Gardner's theory may be familiar to many teachers:

- Provide children with a variety of hands-on materials that they can explore and manipulate.
- Offer distinct and varied areas in the room that focus on one or a few intelligence areas, such as a small group storytelling or puppet station where children can employ and develop verbal/linguistic, interpersonal, and intrapersonal abilities.
- Ensure that adults or older children serve as role models meaningfully engaged in work and play as the children are, in a sense, offering children the experience of an apprentice learning from observing and working side by side with a master (Gardner, 1993b).
- Include basic skills in concert with active, application type experiences.
- Strive to understand each learner as an individual (Guild & Chock-Eng, 1998).

Putting It Into Practice

Careful observations of children's choices and approaches to solving problems can guide teachers in their planning for children's learning. For example, a child who spends most of the time in the science discovery area grouping animal cards or figures into classes of species (naturalist) but who rarely explores the musical instruments and listening area might be encouraged to explore music by classifying different pieces by such categories as soft, fast, sleepy, or energetic or by categorizing the instruments according to the kind of sounds they make when played by fellow classmates. In this way, the child is able to engage with music and instruments through his or her preferred thought processes and also engage with a new peers group.

Or, consider the solitary child who enjoys listening to stories, scribbling in the writing center, and spending time in the book corner (verbal/linguistic, intrapersonal) but who rarely engages with other children and prefers to sit on the bench during outdoor time. This child might benefit from activities in which he or she is able to explore stories about nature and go on a nature story hunt outside. One idea is to have a group of children go on an expedition to hunt down a story either through chronicling their own outdoor adventures or by searching for and gathering printed words or pictures that the teachers have hidden on the grounds. After the words or pictures have been collected or phrases from the adventure have been dictated to the teacher, the children can gather inside to create poems and stories using the materials from their hunt. Encouraging the children then to illustrate their poetry and story can further engage and develop their visual/spatial intelligence.

Understanding these theoretical components and translating them into practice requires careful consideration, an appreciation of the time involved in a change process, and a willingness to embrace an alternative view of learning and thinking. By becoming familiar with specific strategies and ideas for teachers to align their practice with MI principles, you can begin to envision the classroom as a place where all children are able to succeed in learning. This new vision affects the roles of the teacher and the child, the kinds of learning opportunities offered, the design of the environment, and the kinds of materials children can access.

In selecting manipulative materials for children to handle and explore, it is important to look for collections of both natural and constructed items. Children can use all kinds of boxes, packing materials, cardboard pieces, caps, jugs, disks, broken toys, and so on, to discover and create. Open exploration of such materials allows children to take apart, put together, classify, make connections, and creatively act on the material as opposed to having only one use for the item.

It is in this creative activity that children learn about the properties of materials and find new ways to use their environment, materials, and thought processes to construct meaning, solve problems, and develop skills. It is also through this use of open-ended, varied materials and experiences that children can find and develop their unique intelligence strengths. Gathering materials, analyzing relationships, and generating new uses for common objects give opportunities for practice in higher level thinking which is practical and useful throughout our lives (see Figure 5-1 for specific teaching strategies).

FIGURE 5-1

Activities to Support All Learners

The following table presents practical applications of MI theory and explores examples of specific activities that illustrate ways to support skills in each of the eight intelligences. The following items should be viewed as suggestions for starting the process of developing activities and experiences based on the specific interests, capacities, and strengths of individual children.

Key Skills	Activities and Experiences to Support Verbal/Linguistic Intelligence
Listening	• Reading and telling stories and poetry aloud • Listening games • Sound discrimination games like guessing among various objects in a shaker or guessing the instrument being played • Listening to stories on tape • Giving directions, plans, and instructions verbally or in song/rhymes that allow for playing with words
Speaking	• Repeating chants and rhymes • Reading stories • Storytelling • Allowing classroom and individual discussions • Asking many open-ended questions • Allowing show and tell; word plays and riddles • Creating dialogue with children • Allowing dramatic play • Allowing group activities
Writing	• Dictating stories • Tracing letters in sand or stencils • Forming letters out of dough • Creating stories and poems as a group based on classroom experiences • Using journals, either dictated or written, to let the children reflect on their day and plan for tomorrow • Making paper bag stories (Label bags with the words for characters, settings, and plots; then ask children to come up with suggestions for each element of the story and place them in the bag. In groups, children pull several slips from the character bag, a couple from the settings bag, and one from the plot bag. The children then combine their elements to create an original story to write or tell the class.)
Reading	• Incorporating quality children's literature into the curriculum several times a day • Supporting curricular concepts with stories, songs and rhyming games that relate to subjects • Playing recognition games and "word hunts" • Integrating written language into classroom materials such as food boxes and menus • Making picture-word association boards where preliterate children can create stories using pictures and can pair select words with the pictures • Taking student dictation to create a class story or poem for the children to read • Modeling reading behaviors
Key Skills	Activities and Experiences to Support Logical/Mathematical Intelligence
Calculating	• Counting • Measuring • Number corresponding

	• Cutting out geometric shapes • Cooking • Sorting • Providing pattern blocks and cards, puzzles, blocks, and measurement devices for children to explore • Recognizing series of sizes
Strategies for Problem Solving	• Using open-ended questions and materials that support many possible solutions • Predicting outcomes • Engaging children in deep, investigative projects and experiments that allow them to hypothesize, research, test, and explore their world • Having children make charts or graphs to categorize, compare, and represent information • Creating games with rules • Identifying patterns or creating new ones with various blocks • Explaining actions • Creating treasure or scavenger maps • Creating sand and water activities that explore different-sized containers to see how many it takes of one to fill another; volume; cause and effect
Key Skills	**Activities and Experiences to Support Musical Intelligence**
Listening	• Developing songs for transitions or directions • Discussing different sounds, combinations of instruments, styles, speeds, etc., from selected audio recordings • Discussing how certain sounds, instruments, or pieces make us feel • Arranging a class trip to a performance • Going on a "listening walk," where children are instructed to collect as many sounds as they can (like a nature walk collecting leaves and things) • Using music strategically; constant background music may prompt children to tune out
Singing	• Singing favorite songs as groups and at transition times • Chanting and humming to feel different sensations of vibrations • Instituting "singing-only time," where, for a limited period of time, everyone must use lyrical utterances to communicate
Composing	• Allowing children to create their own musical works (But do not pressure them into too many structured lessons.) • Allowing children to create rhythms, patterns, melodies, and songs • Going on a "composition walk," where children play materials like tapping on a tree trunk or clinking on a fence to create an original song • Making up songs to favorite rhymes
Playing	• Providing a variety of instruments, and having children make their own, to be used individually and as a group • Trying to recreate sounds heard in nature by creating and playing child-created instruments • Exploring authentic instruments from various cultures
Key Skills	**Activities and Experiences to Support Visual/Spatial Intelligence**
Visualizing, Mental Imagery	• Using guided imagery • Describing the images in their mind's eye • Using imagination and make-believe games • Describing hidden objects by touching—"feely" bag/box

(Continued)

FIGURE 5-1 CONTINUED

Working Visually and Spatially	• Giving children pattern blocks and cards to visually represent concepts in geometry, math, etc. • Letting children develop a treasure-hunt map using the school/playground as the parameters and then follow the map • Recognizing shapes • Using mazes, mapping, and puzzles • Building with blocks, creating towns, solving traffic problems with blocks and ramps • Playing spatial navigation games that allow children to move around the room/space • Making flowcharts or maps to outline information • Using a camera to select and take pictures
Making Images, Visual Art	• Creating their own storyboards or illustrations for stories • Using paper, paint, crayon, pencil, etc., to create pictures from their mind's eye after a guided imagery journey • Allowing children to make whole-class murals to depict a class trip or story • Using graphic symbols to represent a process, flowcharts, graphs • Creating 2-D art using drawing, painting, collage, printing • Creating 3-D sculpting/modeling
Key Skills	**Activities and Experiences to Support Body/Kinesthetic Intelligence**
Motor Skills and Coordination	• Using obstacle courses • Using large motor equipment • Playing games like Head, Shoulders, Knees, and Toes and the Hokey Pokey, which allow children to use their bodies to identify body parts • Creating carnival tossing games (hand-eye coordination) • Taking exercise breaks to focus on energy release/energizing
Hands-On Activities	• Using materials like sandpaper letters to allow children to feel the shape and use their tactile sense and motion to understand the letters • Creating sensory projects and games like shaving cream tracing • Using tools • Cooking • Creating touchy-feely boxes that allow children to guess what they are feeling without looking at the object • Going on nature walks • Gardening • Sculpting with various forms of dough and clay • Using manipulatives
Using Body for Expression	• Having children paint or trace letters or short words on wall-mounted, mural-sized paper, which requires a full range of motion of their arms • Dancing to different tempos, rhythms, and sounds to integrate abstract concepts into physical experiences • Providing props and time for creative movement experiences so that children can develop their own choreography and dances to stories • Playing the writing a letter/word on your back game, where children have to guess what you've written only by feeling the shapes you trace with your finger on their backs • Forming parades, marching to rhythms • Using gestures, pantomime • Role playing, acting, dramatic play

Key Skills	Activities and Experiences to Support Interpersonal Intelligence
Using Social Skills	• Modeling prosocial skills by teachers • Feeling games like "guess what I'm feeling by my expression" • Playing active listening games encouraging children to listen and paraphrase what they heard • Practicing conflict resolution with puppets and role play • Defining and agreeing on classroom rules by the children • Using collaborative learning to remove win/lose emphasis • Sharing classroom responsibilities • Allowing show-and-tell time, where children can share and learn about one another
Working in a Group	• Allowing plenty of time for working in small groups on project-oriented activities that allow children to investigate, explore, and solve problems together • Playing team games and scavenger hunts • Playing group sports • Having class meetings, where children plan their activities, engage in their play, and then regroup to review and share their experiences • Role playing and dramatic playing, where children learn to divide roles and responsibilities, work out conflicts through play, and redefine social norms and rules • Mural making by the whole group • Making a class quilt, where children collect information about themselves and turn it into a square in the class quilt • Collective story and poetry writing, where each child contributes a line • Creating paper bag stories, described in verbal/linguistic activities • Creating enjoyable, collaborative learning with discussions, brainstorming, planning together, and majority-rule decisions • Using peer tutoring/coaching

Key Skills	Activities and Experiences to Support Intrapersonal Intelligence
Self-Identity, Self-Management	• Setting goals, planning activities, reviewing experiences • Identifying self-control strategies • Developing self-care skills such as hygiene habits • Exploring books, pictures, and materials that convey diverse identities and cultures • Working independently, providing individual activities and centers, along with nooks where children can go to be alone for a few minutes • Planning "my favorite thing about you is . . ." game, where children toss a soft ball to the peer next to them while telling him or her the favorite thing about the person • Acknowledging and respecting each child each day • Viewing children as active participants in the running of the classroom
Making Personal Connections	• Journaling, reviewing choices and experiences • Providing support for children's poetry writing, taking dictation for prewriters • Identifying likes and dislikes • Playing "imagine if you were . . ." game, where children close their eyes and imagine to be something/someone other than who they are; discuss their vision and feelings as a group • Discussing how new knowledge personally affects them
Processing Emotions	• Identifying and express emotions • Recognizing appropriate and inappropriate responses to emotions • Exploring emotion puppets or masks

(Continued)

FIGURE 5-1 CONTINUED

	• Planning board games that identify emotions and behaviors • Including art activities as a means to express and explore feelings in an effort to develop intrapersonal intelligence. (This can include not only hands-on activities but also discussions about professional art and music and how different pieces make us feel.)
Key Skills	**Activities and Experiences to Support Naturalist Intelligence**
Observing and Using Senses to Gather Information	• Recognizing plants and animals • Describing and recording observations using graphs and charts • Creating patterns to classify objects • Using microscopes, binoculars, telescopes, and computers to study organisms • Watching processes and cycles, such as in growing plants • Sorting sequenced picture cards displaying natural processes like the life cycle of a butterfly
Interacting with Nature	• Caring for a classroom pet • Caring for the environment—recycling, composting • Creating a school garden by finding a plot of land, tilling and preparing the soil, discussing and deciding what to grow, sowing and watering seeds, weeding and fertilizing, and then harvesting • Going on nature walks, collection walks • Taking field trips to the zoo, planetarium, arboretum, park, aquarium, museum • Exploring collections of natural materials in the science area, including rocks, shells, seeds, leaves, cleaned feathers, pictures, fossils
Making Relationships and Connections	• Sorting natural objects • Classifying and categorizing • Matching and comparing • Arranging objects to form associations and connections • Identifying relationships among species using picture cards • Creating charts and webs to represent information and relationships

Source: Adapted from Campbell et al., 2004; Carlisle, 2001; Gardner, 1993b; Nuzzi, 1997; Reiff, 1996.

Conclusion

For many teachers, the first introduction to Gardner's innovative theory generates much excitement and energy as the possibilities for all children's success in some area or another emerge. Beginning to understand the many ways in which humans can "be smart" is just the first step in exploring and discovering the complex nature of human thought and learning. As teachers continue down this path, the excitement of charting new courses and discovering new horizons generates an energy and a creative challenge that are truly very rewarding aspects of the field of education.

As the educational climate continues to emphasize standardized tests as indicators of children's success in learning and schools' success in educating them, concerns continue over the viability of MI-inspired practice. Recent case study research indicates that whole-school reforms shifting toward teaching to MI can increase children's test scores. Continued research on both culture- and intelligence-fair assessment and children's achievement in core content standards will be important in validating the efficacy of MI practices (Greenhawk, 1997; Hoerr, 2003).

Care must be taken, however, in the kind of assessment and the inferences drawn from the results. Changing traditional practice to an MI framework but continuing to assess based solely on traditional testing measures is counterproductive. It undermines both the teaching and the testing processes. The tension between individualized education, which supports and values many ways of thinking, and systems emphasizing standardized scores (high school graduation and college entrance standards) is a deeply ingrained part of the American psyche.

The importance of assessment and evaluation exists even in MI practice, and a compromise is available. Authentic assessments, which include performance evaluations, work sampling, representative portfolios, and real-life problem-solving activities along with test scores, allow children to demonstrate their acquired knowledge and skill proficiency while applying what they have learned in meaningful ways (Campbell, 1997; Krechevsky, 1991). As more and more teachers find ways to reach all the children in their classrooms, the potential for increases in successful student achievement presents an enticing call to continue exploring the possibilities offered by the application of MI theory.

REFLECTION QUESTIONS: LOOKING BACK AND LOOKING AHEAD

Think about the following questions in light of your reading as well as your reflections on your own ways of thinking:

1. Which intelligence areas do you think are your strengths and which are areas you do not feel as strong in?

2. Imagine being a student in a classroom where the teacher uses instruction methods that do not align with your intelligence areas. What impact would this have on your learning and your feelings about school?

3. How do you think your specific thinking style might impact your teaching?

4. What can you do to ensure that your strengths do not dominate your teaching?

5. Do you believe there are other kinds of intelligences that have not been identified? What would they be and why would you choose them?

SUMMARY

Unsatisfied with the narrow definitions of intelligence and schools that were failing to address the many ways children use to think and process experiences, in 1983 Howard Gardner presented the first version of his theory of multiple intelligences. He used a more flexible framework for his definition of intelligence—a framework of the ways in which people solve problems and create new problems. Maintaining his flexible view, he presented, in his original publications, seven intelligences, which he later expanded to the current eight: verbal/linguistic, mathematical/logical, musical, visual/spatial, body/kinesthetic, interpersonal, intrapersonal, and the more recently added naturalist.

Although it is tempting to use Gardner's theory to identify particular kinds of thinkers, or the ways in which certain children think, it is important to consider that many or all of the eight intelligences may be present in any individual. There may be a few that are stronger, but in general we all possess capacities in each area. It is equally important to continue to reflect on your own style and preferences in an effort to ensure that you are reaching all children and not just teaching to your own strength.

Traditional teaching practices of lecture, seatwork, and narrow assessments are not adequate to promote optimal development in young children or to capture their ever-changing progress and abilities. By balancing the kinds of activities, teaching strategies, and materials children work with, you can ensure that all children use their strengths and engage in activities that help develop less preferred ways of thinking. In the course of teaching and assessment, personalizing instruction and evaluation to maximize individual and group success is a key goal of using MI theory appropriately. By maintaining a commitment to value and celebrating the many ways in which people think and learn, you can begin to unlock each child's potential for successful learning.

Application Activities

MyEducationLab

Go to the Assignments and Activities section of Topic 2: Child Development/ Theories in the MyEducationLab for your course and complete the activity entitled *Applying Multiple Intelligences Theory.* Watch the first graders reflect on their 'simple machines' project and note how teachers foster their learning.

On the Web: MyEducationLab Go to the Video Examples section of Topic 7: Curriculum/ Content Areas in the MyEducationLab for your course and watch the video entitled *Group Time: Inquiry Activity.* In this video segment, children engage in several different activities as they explore, process, and represent their experience with a terrarium. Observe the different types of activities and the ways the teacher supports many ways of thinking and representing. Discuss how MI theory applies to this classroom scene in small groups.

In Class Take a multiple intelligences inventory to identify your own particular combinations of processing preferences on one of the following websites:

Interactive MI Test:

www.ldrc.ca/projects/miinventory/miinventory.php

or

www.mitest.com

Discuss your results with your group. Was your profile what you expected? Think about the areas in which you scored higher and lower. Do they reflect your preferences?

In the Field Visit an early childhood classroom (pre-K through third grade). Using the MI framework as a lens, analyze the classroom environment and observed activities. How many ways of thinking or intelligences do you see occurring in the environmental design or class activities?

For Your Portfolio In small groups develop a learning unit on an agreed-upon theme that would be suitable for an early childhood class. Brainstorm related topics and activities that would appeal to all of the intelligences. You can use the web in Appendix D in your planning, or create your own graph or chart to have a visual representation that clearly shows activities for all kinds of thinkers. This plan can be added to your portfolio section on teaching and learning.

Related Web Links

Interactive MI Tests

http://www.ldrc.ca/projects/miinventory/miinventory.php

http://www.businessballs.com/howardgardnermultipleintelligences.htm#multiple%20intelligences%
20tests

Howard Gardner—Biography

www.pz.harvard.edu/PIs/HG.htm

Project Zero Website

pzweb.harvard.edu

CHAPTER 6

Head Start and Early Head Start: Empowering Change from Within

Teaching should be such that what is offered is perceived as a valuable gift and not as a hard duty.

—ALBERT EINSTEIN

Across the nation, communities are suffering under adverse conditions, including poverty, unemployment, and poor access to community services. These conditions, existing in urban, suburban, and rural locales, may put children at risk for later school and life problems. Research on early brain development has revealed the importance of healthy environments and experiences for young children as well as the benefits to society of raising strong, healthy children. Children with special needs or disabilities are also considered to be at risk for developing later school problems. In an effort to combat poverty and increase all children's chances for life success, national initiatives and programs have been created. *Early intervention* is the term widely used to refer to the comprehensive programs for young children who are living in conditions that include one or more risk factors for possible future problems in school or life. The overarching goals of early intervention programs are to provide developmentally appropriate, stimulating, individualized learning experiences and comprehensive health services for families and children living in poverty or with disabilities.

This chapter traces the history of intervention programs, explores definitions and effects of risk factors, assesses the current status of children living with risk factors in the

United States, and identifies specific elements of current early intervention programming. The federally funded Head Start and Early Head Start programs and policies are presented to illustrate key components of intervention programming. Research on the effectiveness of Head Start in reaching program goals is presented, and current trends and changes to federal policies are reviewed.

STARTING POINTS: QUESTIONS AND REFLECTIONS

As you prepare to explore the history and scope of early intervention programming in the United States, carefully consider the following questions. Use them to reflect on your own beliefs about the kind of environments in which you think children should be raised. Be honest in this reflection activity, and become aware of any **biases** you might have based on your beliefs or personal experiences. As you read through this and later chapters, keep in mind that becoming aware of the foundations of your beliefs can lead you to question and change as you explore new methods and issues in early childhood.

Biases

Beliefs, often deeply held and sometimes subconscious, that stereotype a person or group based on perceived defining characteristics. Biases may be about race, intelligence, behavior, or culture.

1. List at least five things you believe are necessary for children's healthy overall development. Consider what you believe to be the optimal home, school, and community environment for children.

2. What would you do if a child in your preschool class consistently appeared in dirty, ill-fitting, or torn clothing and hoarded food?

3. Who do you think should be responsible for providing food and medical care for children?

4. How do you feel about welfare or social service programs like food stamps, housing subsidies, or child-care subsidies? Why do you feel that way?

CLASSROOM VIEW

Today you are visiting a small preschool program operating out of a community church in an urban neighborhood. The center has three rooms, each with 15 preschoolers and 2 teachers. There is a small playground, which is fenced in on the other side of the parking lot. The church is a small stone building with long windows at the top of the walls. These windows provide plenty of natural light but afford no view to the outdoors. The church also serves as a community resources center, with counseling services in another room down the hall. A smiling face pops out of a doorway and welcomes you to the school. An African-American woman with grey streaks in her dark brown hair gives you a wave. "Hi there! I'm Ida. The kids call me Grammy Ida. Come join us!" she laughs in a warm voice.

The preschool teachers invite you to sit at the small table and observe a typical morning in the "threes room." The children are finishing their snack of fruit salad and milk. The teachers encourage the children to serve themselves with fruit and use their small spoons to eat by themselves. Some children are using their fingers to hold the fruit on the spoon, and some are using their hands to eat while they hold the spoon in their free hand. The teachers do not correct the children but rather model eating with a spoon themselves. They have lively chats with the children about their morning and what activities they will be doing for the rest of the day. Occasionally a child proudly holds up a spoon loaded with fruit, pleased at being able to keep the fruit on the spoon. The teachers cheer the children in their efforts to master the utensil.

Promoting community connections is important for all children.

When they finish, the children take their bowls and spoons to the low sink while the teachers wash the tables. The teachers thank the children for being such good helpers and remind them about washing hands after eating. There is a new procedure for cleanup now: The tables must be sprayed with disinfectant and allowed to sit for 2 minutes before being wiped clean, and the children must wash their hands for 15 seconds. These health and hygiene regulations are mandated by the state. The teachers and children sing songs to count the time.

After snack cleanup, the children move around the room and choose activities. They have 45 minutes of uninterrupted time, during which the teachers support children's play and use of such materials as blocks, push toys, homemade play dough, books, counting bears, and puzzles. After this free-time segment, the group will go outside. Today the teachers have brought in a large basket to collect items that interest the children during a community walk. The mother of one of the children is a local artist and is coming to class tomorrow to help the children create a mural with their collections. Their walk will take them through a downtown area and a local park. The children routinely visit some of the shops (the Spanish and Korean food markets, the bakery, the butcher, the florist), and the shopkeepers talk to them about their work.

"These places are a part of the children's home lives, so it's important that we integrate them into school activities too. The store owners love having the kids come around. They have even visited the classroom. We can barely keep up with the children on those days. They are all talking and sharing stories so fast! They really love investigating the stores on a deeper level."

During the children's choice time, one of the teachers sits at the table and makes notes in a few of the children's files. She is using observations from snack to document children's developing self-care, social, and fine motor skills. The file seems thick. You ask her about paperwork, and she comments that it sometimes seems like a lot. But she quickly adds that it really helps when she's meeting with parents and program supervisors. She can readily find plenty of examples of how children are developing and what they have been working on. She also uses the files to help plan for new materials or activity ideas. "We make general plans for the group, but we also make individualized plans," she explains. "The individualized plans can be simple, such as introducing a new material to the child. Sometimes they are more complicated and involve therapists. It all depends on the specific child and what they're working on at the moment. Having all these notes about what a child said one day or did another helps me get ideas about what skills they need to work on and what things are interesting them."

Just then one of the girls starts screeching and crying. It looks as if every muscle in her small body is tensed up; her face is deep red, and her screaming rings through the halls. The other children look at her for a moment but quickly go back to their work. They don't seem surprised by her behavior. One of the teachers goes over and speaks softly to her. The child begins to slam her legs against the floor. The teacher puts her arms around the screaming child and holds her gently but firmly. The child flails her arms and legs for a few moments and then begins to quiet. After several minutes, her body relaxes into the teacher's rocking and soothing voice.

Ida smiles and explains that this child's family is working with a therapist referred by Head Start because of her emotional disturbances. The therapist also comes into the classroom to work with the teachers and show them the techniques the family is using at home with the child, such as the embrace. "This kind of consistency among all the networks in the child's life is so important. At Head Start, being a teacher is just one role we play. We have lots of trainings on things like special needs and community resources. Most times we are the first and only contact for the families. They need me to guide them to health and welfare networks. Doctors, dentists, therapists—we help families find whatever services they need, especially families who don't speak English. Most of the teachers here speak Spanish or Portuguese, too, so that we can communicate in a way that is comfortable and effective for them. We're all from this neighborhood, so we know what's what here. And I need them to keep me included in family plans. We're really lucky that family partnerships are such a focus from day one. It benefits the children more than anything we could do alone."

Soon all the children are busy working in their chosen areas. Some are building structures with blocks and driving the cars around them. Four girls are preparing dinner in the kitchen area. Ida works with one child on a puzzle. Three children are working together on a collage of their favorite foods, sparked by a recent trip to the food market. They page through old magazines and newspaper circulars, tearing and cutting out pictures of foods for their collage. Periodically they call out to the teacher, "Mira! I found carrots. I found pollo! I found ice cream!" The teacher responds by rubbing her stomach and saying, "Mmmmmm! Try to put the different foods in sections, like we see at the market. Then we'll have to show Mr. Ramirez the collage when we visit the market later."

This visit highlights Head Start teachers' efforts to keep the curriculum balanced, culturally relevant, and individually tailored to each child's particular developmental level. A strong emphasis is placed on authentic assessments of children in the form of observations, portfolios, and parent meetings.

Historical Perspective: The Start of Early Intervention

In Chapter 2 you read about how social renewal has been a goal for educators throughout the centuries, but it wasn't until the 1960s that current **early intervention** preschool programs were formalized in the United States. At that time, new research fueled a growing belief among American policy makers, civil rights activists, psychologists, and sociologists that a strong start early in life could have lasting positive effects on all children (Bloom, 1964; Gershoff, 2003). This applied especially to children from low-income backgrounds. With this growing awareness, the early intervention movement received support over the following decades (Kagan, 2002; Schweinhart, Barnes, & Weikart, 1993). It was during this

Early intervention

Early intervention is the term widely used to refer to the comprehensive programs for young children who are living in conditions that include one or more risk factors for possible future school or life problems.

Head Start

Part of the 1965 War on Poverty initiatives, Head Start provides comprehensive programs to families living in poverty. Programs include education, health and wellness, and nutrition services.

time that the **Head Start** initiative was created. Other early intervention programs, such as the High/Scope Perry Preschool Project, were also designed at this time. The High/Scope curriculum is also used in programs serving families from all economic levels. Currently a significant number of Head Start programs use the High/Scope curriculum (the High/Scope curriculum and research information are presented in Chapter 7). The impetus for programs focusing on improving outcomes for disadvantaged children was also closely tied to the overarching social climate of the time.

Influence of the Social Climate of the 1960s

The late 1950s marked a new, growing demand for equality for all people, beginning with the emotionally charged struggles for racial equality. Other socially marginalized groups, one being the women's movement, then began to voice their opposition to being treated unfairly and insist on equal freedoms and rights. Advocates championed for expanded educational and employment opportunities for women, which were previously afforded only to men. Do you recall from Chapter 2 how increases in the numbers of working mothers impacted the field of early childhood education? Along with increased employment opportunities for women outside the home came the need to expand early childhood programs quickly to meet the requirements of a changing society.

Half-day nursery schools catering to the interests of wealthier families were not appealing to a working mother who needed all-day care for her children. Many families, especially *lower-socioeconomic-status* (SES) families, did not have access to high-quality programs. Placing children in low-quality care that lacked appropriate stimulation only amplified the problems facing children living in families with limited income. Many programs lacked rich language environments, materials to manipulate, indoor and outdoor play spaces, and appropriate curricula taught by trained teachers. The concern over quality in early care environments was further fueled by research in the new field of brain development.

MyEducationLab

Go to the Assignments and Activities section of Topic 2: Child Development/ Theories in the MyEducationLab for your course and complete the activity entitled *Physical Development*. Focus your observation on the different developmental milestones demonstrated by the two children in the video.

Influences of Brain-Development Research

Researchers in the 1950s began to investigate the idea of *critical periods*, also called sensitive or key periods, in human development. New connections were made between genetically influenced development and how environmental stimuli affect the outcomes of those critical periods. These influences are often referred to as *nature* (biological influences) and *nurture* (environmental influences, including relationships). Researchers carefully observing large numbers of children promoted the belief that there are key times, especially in very young children, in which the brain is primed to make certain developmental leaps (Bloom, 1964; Diamond & Hopson, 1998).

For example, at birth infants are unable to clearly see things in their world. Their visual focus sharpens over the first 8 months or so. With adequate visual stimulation in the first year of life, most infants will achieve nearly adult-level visual acuity during this time (Vander Zanden, 2003). Conversely, visual development can be hampered by a lack of stimulation, such as living in perpetual darkness or not having interesting objects to look at and reach for. The first year of life, then, would be considered a critical period for the development of aspects of vision. Visit MyEducationLab to watch two children of different ages playing outside to compare physical development.

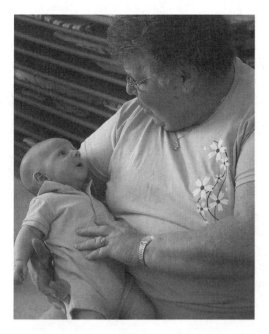

Stimulating experiences fostered through relationships with caring adults are essential for optimal development from infancy.

Likewise, anyone who has been around a toddler can attest to the amazing leaps in physical and language development that occur between infancy and the preschool years. Researchers, including Jean Piaget, Erik Erikson, and Maria Montessori, made major contributions to our understanding of the periods and stages through which children develop. The discoveries in brain research continue to shed light on the complex nature of human development, offering practitioners clues into how to optimize children's developmental paths.

Research evidence mounted during the decades following the 1950s and supported the belief that appropriate stimulation in the early years was critical to positive developmental outcomes and later school success (Bloom, 1964; Gershoff, 2003; Hanson, 2003; Kagan, 2002; Nord & Rhoads, 1992; Peth-Pierce, 2000; Schweinhart et al., 1993). Evidence also emerged from early High/Scope research that suggested children growing up in families with limited incomes were more likely to continue to need costly welfare services (Schweinhart et al., 1993). Educationally based programs for families with limited incomes were created in response to achievement and behavior gaps in school-age children (Kagan, 2002).

Early Intervention Programming Takes Shape

Government intervention efforts to address gaps in socioeconomic status as well as children's achievement became part of the national agenda in the 1960s. Political goals focused on keeping America globally competitive, whereas social welfare plans focused on decreasing poverty. In 1965 and 1966 a large number of laws were passed that targeted such social issues as voting rights, urban renewal, subsidized medical care, and improved education. Part of President Lyndon Johnson's War on Poverty initiatives, the first Head Start pilot program appeared in 1965 (USDHHS, 2002a). The primary goal of the Head Start initiative was to alleviate the risks to children and families associated with living in poverty (later including children with disabilities). This goal was addressed through comprehensive

Putting It Into Practice

Suggestions From DAP

Recall from Chapter 3 that the Developmentally Appropriate Practice framework calls for teachers to base their teaching on a solid knowledge of child development. The awareness of critical periods aligns with this belief. In order to maximize toddlers' blossoming language of development, for example, you must be aware of what trends, norms, and milestones to expect at that age. Knowing what to expect enables you to plan stimulating activities, experiences, and environments that support and lead development as it is ready to unfold. Another example would be basing instruction on the awareness that preschoolers and kindergarteners are ready to refine their fine motor control through focused activities, whereas toddlers need more support for gross motor development. Keep in mind that you must use your understanding of universal trends in development together with expected variations between individual children to plan optimal learning environments and experiences.

health, wellness, family involvement, and education programming. Key goals for the programs were to increase children's developmental outcomes, particularly social and academic achievement, and strengthen families' status within the community (Smith, 1988).

From early in Head Start's history, programs have been tailored to diverse communities, including American Indian (AI) tribal communities, migrant families, and Alaska Native (AN) communities. Unique challenges, such as remote rural locations and limited transportation, are issues these programs alleviate to provide comprehensive services to AI and AN families with limited incomes. Throughout changes in administration of program funds, of primary importance in the AI-AN program is to preserve community involvement and governance. To that end, tribal governments remain active in grant money authorization (USDHHS, 2006). By addressing unique challenges while preserving control within the community, Head Start programs validate the key role community members play in the empowerment cycle.

Project Head Start has become the country's largest provider of education and medical services to disadvantaged children and families with limited incomes. As of 2008 statistics, Head Start programs serve more than 908,400 children annually, and more than 25 million children have participated in programs since its inception. The annual national budget for Head Start is now more than $6.87 billion, although threats of budget cuts continue to be part of political debates and the 2008 appropriation is less than the 2007 funds (USDHHS, 2008). Even with these impressive numbers, Head Start programs are serving only three out of every five eligible children (with Early Head Start serving fewer) owing to limits in funding (Children's Defense Fund, 2003). Eligibility for program enrollment is most closely related to family income. Children who are homeless and families with income at or below the federal poverty level categorically qualify and under the 2009 reauthorization programs are able to serve families with incomes under 130% of the poverty level up to 35% of the program enrollment

(USDHHS, 2009a). Despite reauthorizations in the legislation and funding concerns, Head Start has always maintained a commitment to innovation and responsiveness to changing trends in the field. The inclusion of children with disabilities is an example of this responsiveness.

Expanding the Scope of Head Start

When racial segregation practices of "separate but equal" became unacceptable after the civil rights struggles of the 1950s, parents of children with disabilities began to demand equal educational opportunities for their children. Supported by strong advocacy of parent groups, federal legislation was enacted in 1968 to provide adequate educational experiences for young children with disabilities. This law was originally titled the Handicapped Children's Early Education and Assistance Act.

Head Start programming has always been based on comprehensive services for families with limited incomes. In 1972 Head Start initiatives were expanded to include comprehensive educational and welfare services for children with disabilities. Providing adequate services for children with disabilities, integrated into programs for all children, continues to be at the forefront of today's Head Start educational goals. By law, at least 10% of enrollment must be children with disabilities (USDHHS, 2009a). In 2006, children with disabilities constituted 12.5% of Head Start enrollment across the nation (USDHHS, 2008). Research continues to emerge that demonstrates increased positive outcomes for children with disabilities who have access to intervention before age 5 and who are included in classrooms with typically developing peers (Hume, Bellini, & Pratt, 2005).

Individuals with Disabilities Education Act

Further evolutions of federal legislation emerged with the 1975 Education of All Handicapped Children Act (later renamed the Individuals with Disabilities Education Act of 2004). Combining earlier legislation for preschool-age children, revisions in the 2004 act govern how states provide early intervention services for infants, young children, and school-age children with disabilities. Provisions call for ongoing improvements in the access to free appropriate public education for children with disabilities, specifically including (IDEA, 2004; Lascarides & Hinitz, 2000)

- Teachers and parents to jointly create individualized plans for children
- Children to be educated in the least restrictive environments
- High expectations for all children
- Schoolwide support and aid to ensure maximum success for children with disabilities
- Fair educational decisions for all children
- Accountability of professionals to children and families
- High-quality preservice teacher education designed to prepare teachers to meet students' unique and diverse needs with research-based teaching approaches

On the heels of continuing research on the critical nature of the early years in terms of children's development came a new initiative, developed in 1994, to serve pregnant women and infants. **Early Head Start** marked an expansion of programs and services and underscored the importance of optimizing the earliest years of development, even prenatal development, to ensure later positive developmental outcomes (USDHHS, 2002b). Early Head Start programs maintain a strong emphasis on family education and prenatal health care services. In 2007 Early Head Start programs served 62,000 children under age 3 with a budget of nearly $700 million (USDHHS, 2008). Visit MyEducationLab to view an infant and toddler setting and consider the unique needs of this age group and the ways teachers plan for their needs.

This is a brief synopsis of the history of early intervention and Head Start programming. In order to fully appreciate the goals and need for Head Start and Early Head Start, it is important to understand definitions and characteristics of target populations.

The Need for Social Renewal: Defining Characteristics

For decades the term *children at risk* has been used to describe children from lower socioeconomic families or those with disabilities. Many theorists and educators object to the negative connotation implicit in labeling children at risk (for later school failure) and now prefer the more hopeful term "at promise" (Bondy & McKenzie, 1999). As early childhood educators, we believe all children have tremendous promise within them. It is our responsibility to provide opportunities, environments, and experiences to help them realize that promise and potential. In the spirit of that belief, the term *at promise* will be used here, too, in concert with descriptions of risk factors.

Risk Factors: Definitions and Impact

Although it is impossible to draw up one complete profile to fit every situation, it is possible to establish commonalities shared by many families living in low socioeconomic situations. Research has identified the following factors that may pose challenges to optimal developmental outcomes (Knitzer & Lefkowitz, 2006):

- Living at or below the federal poverty guidelines
- Living in a single-parent household
- Being born to a teenage mother
- low education level
- Having unemployed parents
- Having low birth weight
- Living with a disability

The potential effects on a child living within these conditions can be lifelong and severe. It is important to remember that simply living with one or more of these factors does not necessarily determine a child's school or life outcomes. These factors represent the potential for increased school problems. Living with more than one risk factor compounds the potential for negative outcomes. Whereas half of American preschoolers face at least one risk factor, 15% of preschoolers are coping with three or more (Beasley, 2002).

Early Head Start

This 1994 expansion of Head Start services targets pregnant women and infants.

MyEducationLab

Go to the Assignments and Activities section of Topic 5: Program Models in the MyEducationLab for your course and complete the activity entitled *Infant and Toddler Settings*. Focus your observation on the ways teachers need to adapt programming to meet infants' and toddlers' unique needs.

Poverty as a Risk Factor

Most young children who demonstrate negative effects of one or more of the risk factors noted previously are living in poverty (Knitzer & Lefkowitz, 2006). Poverty is periodically assessed and annually defined by the U.S. Census Bureau and the Department of Heath and Human Services (HHS). In 2009 the HHS national poverty guidelines were defined as follows (guidelines are slightly higher for Alaska and Hawaii):

2009 National Poverty Guidelines	
Size of Family Unit	Income at or Below
1	$ 10,830
2	14,570
3	18,310
4	22,050
5	25,790

Source: USDHHS, 2009b.

The term *poverty* is defined by these thresholds. The term *low income* is used to refer to families whose income is at or less than twice the federal poverty level (NCCP, 2008). For example, a single mother with two children earning less than $32,000 would be considered *low income.*

Family income is considered a crucial element in determining children's developmental outcomes because of several associated factors. Children living in poverty or low-income

Putting It Into Practice

Knowing Your Children

The rise in child poverty rates only underscores the importance of knowing your children's family and home context. You know it is important to support linguistic and cultural diversity, but support becomes even more urgent when families are struggling to provide food, shelter, or medical care for their children. Making connections between homes and schools requires that teachers embrace family-friendly practices. The following are strategies you can use to get to know your children and families:

- Invite parents into the classroom; find ways for them to contribute meaningfully.
- Encourage dialogues.
- Share helpful resources (first of all, be knowledgeable about local resources).
- Offer sensitive responsiveness when parents do talk about life at home; don't judge their parenting skills.
- Maintain professional confidentiality.
- Participate in a home-visit program.

families more frequently suffer from inadequate nutrition, are more likely to be exposed to environmental toxins such as lead, may suffer abuse or neglect, and are the least likely to be placed in quality child-care settings (Aber & Palmer, 1999). Finding safe housing, providing adequate nutritious foods, and being able to afford quality child-care can be a challenge for any family, but for families with limited incomes, the stresses are even greater. Sometimes parents work more than one job to try to make ends meet, which diminishes the time they can spend with their children and increases their stress. After a period of decline, the rates of children living in poverty are now increasing. Statistical data from 2008 reveals that more than 10.6 million children (age 6 and under) are living in low-income households, and more than 5.2 million of those are living at or below the federal poverty level (NCCP, 2008).

There is additional evidence that being raised in a low-income household increases the likelihood that children will exhibit behavior disorders (Elliot, Prior, Merrigan, & Ballinger, 2002). Remember the child's outburst during the classroom visit? She was not yet able to handle conflict with a classmate and lost control. She deteriorated into disruptive and unsafe behaviors (yelling, kicking) when the stress of social conflict, on top of the stresses of home life, was too much for her. Lack of coping skills, social skills, and the ability to handle classroom conflicts compounds school problems for our children at promise. Social maladjustment further exacerbates problems with schoolwork and forming social connections with teachers and peers. These impediments to successful classroom interactions, particularly underdeveloped social skills, all increase the likelihood for school problems.

Increasing children's social competence has been identified as the single most important area of development for children's school success. The ability to get along with diverse groups of people, to accept new people into their world (both new adults and children), and to be comfortable trying new activities in small and large groups are all rated as the highest priority in terms of kindergarten and first-grade readiness skills. In keeping with their mission to grow and expand as children's needs do, in recent years Head Start programs have placed a stronger emphasis on social competence (Powell, 2000).

Learning to work together and develop strong social skills is an essential part of Head Start programs.

Other Risk Factors

More than half of the children in families receiving public assistance have mothers who began childbearing when they were teenagers. Teenage mothers are also more likely to have only a high school education level, compounding risk factors for their children. Being a child of a teenage mother itself appears to be a risk factor for later school problems, health problems, and behavior problems. Young mothers are less likely to seek prenatal medical care, and they are less likely to maintain healthy habits during pregnancy. Inadequate prenatal and neonatal care can lead to lower birth weight (a risk factor for negative developmental outcomes) and undernourishment (Blair, Peters, & Lawrence, 2003). These inappropriate prenatal care habits may be due in part to lower education levels, lower income, fewer support networks, or a lack of awareness of healthy self-care and parenting skills (Nord & Rhoads, 1992; Peth-Pierce, 2000). Early Head Start seeks to address these issues as early as possible during pregnancy through comprehensive health and education support services.

Children of immigrant parents are also more likely to be living in low-income households (61% versus 40% for native-born parents; NCCP, 2008). These statistics illustrate the importance and need for intervention programs that target children and parents as early as possible and within their own community and cultural context. Many immigrant families do not yet have strong English-speaking skills. This can limit their employment options as well as limit their access to social services. Also, even when immigrant parents held professional jobs in their home countries, the transition to a new job market can track them into lower paying jobs. Simply focusing on addressing children's needs, independent of the family unit, is not an effective way to address larger social and economic issues. It is important to validate the child's home culture, parent involvement, and unique background in an effort to support success for the whole family.

Many families who are receiving some form of public assistance are struggling with a combination of the risk factors mentioned or even struggling with some factors not mentioned. In light of this reality, it becomes clear that families living with risk factors are in need of high-quality, comprehensive, early intervention services. What specific elements constitute a successful, quality early intervention model?

IN YOUR OWN WORDS

Before you read about the specific elements of Head Start programming, take a moment to think back to the questions at the beginning of the chapter. As you envisioned what you believe to be an ideal learning environment, had you considered the risk factors just mentioned? Were you surprised by the effects of the family's poverty status on children's development? Did you think the numbers of children living in poverty were as high as they are? Continue to reflect on your own beliefs about optimal environments for children, public assistance, and family economic status.

Head Start Program Standards

The kinds of early experiences that are identified as the most suitable to foster healthy early development for all children include (Smith, 1998)

- Developing warm and caring relationships with care providers who model positive behaviors, such as compassion, cooperation, and curiosity

- Exposure to authentic literature experiences daily, such as reading stories together, noticing signs, and using maps and menus
- Exploring materials, such as blocks, water tables, and clay, in a hands-on way
- Plenty of child-initiated play and choice making
- Some teacher-directed, skill-based learning experiences, such as fine motor art lessons, cooking experiences, and crafts
- Interacting with both children and adults in relaxed social groups

This framework is true for all early childhood programs; however, it becomes especially important in early intervention settings where the program is attempting to combat the effects of poverty or other risk factors. The early intervention programs that have proven to be the most successful are those that (Marcon, 2002; Parke & Agness, 2002)

- Are comprehensive (education and health components)
- Balance teacher- and child-initiated learning
- Are based on developmental theories
- Seek to support families and involve them meaningfully in children's school life
- Are implemented by trained and educated staff

Since its inception, Head Start program goals have taken a holistic view of children's needs, maintaining a broad perspective on all areas of children's development. "Head Start's commitment to wellness embraces a comprehensive vision of health for children, families, and staff" (Head Start Bureau, 1997, p. 5). Head Start addresses these goals through comprehensive, structured services, including

- Physical health and wellness
- Nutrition
- Mental health
- Medical and dental care
- Social, emotional, and cognitive stimulation
- Parent support, including education and networking
- Community-based service provision

Overall Health and Wellness

Without adequate nutrition, children's basic physiological needs are not being met. This results in lower cognitive functioning, poorer physical development, and social withdrawal (Aber & Palmer, 1999). Just think about how hard it is for you to concentrate when you are very hungry. Your mind wanders, your stomach hurts, you feel grouchy, and eventually you simply feel too tired to do much of anything. Multiply that feeling over an extended period of time and you can begin to imagine the chain reaction of negative effects that occurs for children who consistently do not receive the food needed by their bodies and minds. Head Start program standards require that one third to two thirds of children's daily nutritional needs be served through center meals and snacks (in part-day and full-day programs, respectively; Head Start Bureau, 2005).

Programming for children's nutrition includes engaging in warm social interactions during meals and snacks.

As well as meeting children's nutritional needs, attention to physical and mental health and wellness is a cornerstone of early intervention programming (Gershoff, 2003). Head Start Program standards provide a schedule of overall physical and mental health screenings and assessments of the children themselves and their home environments. These screenings are to be conducted at regular intervals beginning with the initial entrance into the program. Although a schedule is mandated, the program standards are flexible and do not stipulate a specific assessment tool. Children are to be screened within 90 days of program entrance for overall physical and mental health and wellness and within 45 days for disability assessment. Ongoing tracking in the form of observations, recordings, and home visits is conducted periodically to sustain an individualized service plan (Head Start Bureau, 1997).

Through this schedule of home and child assessment, Head Start programs seek to promote positive health behaviors as well as identify children's individual needs. Referrals are made as needed to a network of community health service providers, including psychologists or psychiatrists, physicians, dentists, and disability specialists.

Cognitive Stimulation

The learning environment in Head Start programs also maintains a holistic view of children's development. Curriculum planning is guided by a clear, broad mission. "The objective of [the education and development performance standard] is to provide all children with a safe, nurturing, engaging, enjoyable, and secure learning environment, in order to help them gain the awareness, skills, and confidence necessary to succeed in their present environment, and to deal with later responsibilities in school and in life" (Head Start Bureau, 1997, p. 58). Toward this end, the program performance standards offer several suggestions for practice. These include providing children with a variety of materials and progressively challenging individual and group activities to promote all areas of development. Relationships are valued, as are active learning experiences. The 2004 reauthorization of Head Start requires that any curriculum used be based on scientifically valid, evidence-based research; in other words that Head Start programs use proven methods and approaches to learning that are based on developmentally appropriate practice (USDHHS, 2009a). The classroom visit demonstrated these elements when the children's interests were valued, as in the food collage, and when the children's home lives were incorporated with learning experiences in the community walk.

Parent Involvement

MyEducationLab

Go to the Assignments and Activities section of Topic 3: Family/ Community in the MyEducationLab for your course and complete the activity entitled *Daily Conversations with Families.* Consider both the teacher's approach to welcoming parents and the parents' responses.

Within the scope of the comprehensive services, the family unit is always valued as a strong support network for the child. Respected in this way, parents are included in service provision and planning for children enrolled in intervention programming. Parents are encouraged to volunteer in classrooms, but they are also asked to take part in making program decisions. For example, Head Start mandates that parents hold the majority of governing board positions (Head Start Bureau, 2005). This ensures that parents have a voice and control over how programs serve their children.

Parents are also given preference when paid positions are available. Regular information and training sessions are held to encourage parents to take a role in improving their own situations for themselves and their children. Many parents report positive changes in their own lives, as well as their children's, as a result of being actively involved in the program's implementation. They also report a feeling of empowerment and community among program personnel and participants (Kagan, 2002). Visit MyEducationLab to view how families and teachers interact in the classroom setting.

Family Support Within the Community Context

By simultaneously empowering parents and children, Head Start programs seek to extend beyond the children's immediate needs and empower the family unit as a member of the larger social community (Peth-Pierce, 2000). The goal of eradicating poverty could not be met simply by sending children to preschool. Intervention efforts must maintain a connection to the culture of families and the community in which the programs are being implemented. Respecting the culture of both the families and the community ensures that services are provided within the context of children's lives. As such, they are, therefore, more meaningful and successful. This also allows for maximum community participation and integration, which serves the goal of supporting community revival. Eradicating poverty may start with classroom programming, but it also focuses on uplifting the entire community.

In support of this goal, Head Start program standards are specific in terms of the comprehensive scope of services but also are less defined in terms of actual implementation. This allows for maximum flexibility to tailor programming to the particular home and community culture. For example, in one program, the curriculum includes a bilingual component in Spanish and English; in a program in another community, Russian and English are incorporated. Head Start programs also encourage hiring staff from the immediate community to act as an employment resource within lower SES neighborhoods where employment is needed most.

These examples of a more comprehensive, family- and community-centered vision illustrate the philosophy behind Head Start and early intervention programs in general. It is a philosophy that employs a *change-from-within* process. This is based on the belief that real

Putting It Into Practice

Forming Parent Partnerships

Here are some ideas for forming parent partnerships:

- Ask for parent input. Parents know more about their own children than anyone else. Learning from them makes your job easier and also validates their role as their child's first teachers.

- Support parents' decisions for their children. Let parents know that their goals, beliefs, values, and choices are important to you. When there are conflicts between your practices and parents' goals (such as in academic expectations), discuss these. Start by listening. Share your beliefs and your rationale for your practice. Find ways to integrate both views. Communication is a two-way street!

- Let parents know that your door is always open and that they are welcome at any time.

- Communicate freely with parents about when their child has a good day, not just when there are problems. Send home "Great Moments" notes celebrating positive classroom experiences or funny anecdotes.

- Let them know your position: We're in this together!

social change can be effected only by empowering individuals to take control of their lives while working together to overcome adverse conditions (Rappaport, McWilliam, & Smith, 2004). Understanding this focus is crucial in recognizing how these programs have the potential to ameliorate widespread social problems as well as empower individual children and families.

Does It Work? Evidence of Effectiveness

One of the biggest challenges faced by early intervention programs like Head Start is the reality that children eligible for Head Start services are often lagging behind their peers in many areas of development. Scores on tests of cognitive development and language and literacy skills show consistent differences for children based on family income status. Children from families with limited incomes fare worse on these measures than their more affluent peers (Caputo, 2003; Champion, Hyter, McCabe, & Bland-Stewart, 2003; Children's Defense Fund, 2003; Rauh, Parker, Garfinkel, Perry, & Andrews, 2003; USDHHS, 2003a). Some researchers point to cultural biases within the test instruments; however, it is generally believed that at-promise children lag behind their peers developmentally (Champion et al., 2003). So the question remains: Can Head Start help?

Cognitive Development and Language Arts Skills

The Head Start FACES study is an ongoing evaluation of child outcomes in Head Start programs (USDHHS, 2006). The 2006 report includes longitudinal data collected from 1997 to 2003. Key findings reveal that, although children do enter Head Start programs significantly behind national averages in literacy and math skills, the gap is narrowed during program attendance. Children's cognitive development test scores and competence on vocabulary and early writing showed the most gains over time. The research also points out that children with the most significant delays were the ones who made the most gains on national norms. In addition, English Language Learners made significant progress in English vocabulary skills. Early Head Start has also recently reported evaluation data with similar positive results in receptive language. Yet, even with these positive gains in relation to control groups, the scores for Head Start program children still remain below national averages with reading skills remaining below expectation for kindergarten entrance (USDHHS, 2006).

Another recent study revealed that children enrolled in three different Head Start programs all scored significantly lower on a standardized test of vocabulary recognition than national averages. Further analysis revealed that Head Start teachers exhibited a lack of direct vocabulary instruction strategies. Study researchers suggest that more direct instruction on vocabulary could improve children's scores (Champion et al., 2003). The connection to quality, balanced instruction, and children's developmental outcomes is an important one to keep in mind both for evaluating programs and for shaping future policies on teacher qualification requirements.

Social and Behavioral Skills

Improving children's social competence is a key Head Start program goal. The mission to help children be ready to learn in school (*school readiness*) hinges on their social competence. Significant gains were found in Head Start participants in social development, and reduced hyperactive behavior, increased cooperative behaviors in the classroom (USDHHS, 2006). The importance of developing positive social skills as a precursor to being successful in later educational environments is a key foundation of all preschool programming, but it is especially important in a program that is seeking to ameliorate developmental delays prior to kindergarten. The impact of healthy socioemotional development in infants and toddlers is perhaps even more significant than in preschoolers. Strong attachments and healthy socioemotional development in infancy and toddlerhood lay the foundation for being ready and able to learn in preschool classrooms.

Early Head Start has reported improvements in parent–child relationships, children's responsiveness to parents and caregivers, and improvements in parenting skills and confidence (USDHHS, 2002b). According to many developmental theorists, healthy early attachments, fostered through responsive caregiving, can positively impact all later relationships (Vander Zanden, 2003). Given that socioemotional development is so influential in children's later school and life outcomes, this is a key goal of Head Start and Early Head Start programming.

Program Effects over Time

A primary concern of Head Start program evaluators is the fading of positive effects over time. There have been reports that improvements in children's development have faded by 2 years after leaving the program and entering public school. Some people

Cycle of Stress

Imagine a young single mother, living alone and struggling to maintain two low-paying part-time jobs while raising a toddler. She is often stressed about how she will provide food and shelter for herself and her child. Adding to her stress is the child's consistent fussiness; he often cries and refuses to be comforted by her. The more she is unable to console him, the more inadequate she feels as a mother. The more inadequate she feels as a mother, the more she herself withdraws from her child. The more she withdraws from her child, the more he is unable to be consoled by her. Soon this small family is entangled in an unfortunate, vicious cycle. Many parents may lack the knowledge, skills, and support networks necessary to handle the stresses that can be associated with poverty. Research has found that by specifically focusing on improving the dynamic of the mother-child relationship, early intervention efforts can have positive effects on the quality of that relationship (Blair et al., 2003). Improved relations between the mother and child then set the stage for a healthier socioemotional development that positively influences later social relationships. Given that strong parent support and involvement in the child's life are two of the best predictors of positive developmental outcomes, parent support and involvement are key features of most early intervention programming (Kagan, 2002).

point to these results as a failure on the part of Head Start programs to produce sustained benefits over time (Lee, Brooks-Gunn, Schnur, & Liaw, 1990). Other researchers, however, recognize that the comprehensive services provided under the auspices of Head Start are not necessarily continued through the public school years. As children enter classrooms with many more children and fewer teachers, the time and attention they need may not be available. In addition, access to health and welfare services may not be included in school programs in the same way. This drop-off in intervention services and supports is a factor that must be considered when interpreting the fade-out of positive effects (Rauh et al., 2003).

Recent research does demonstrate some promising longer term effects with the Head Start FACES study reporting that gains made during Head Start years in vocabulary, early writing, early math and social skills continue to grow in kindergarten (USDHHS, 2006). This report demonstrates the value of prekindergarten programming specifically designed to enhance these skill areas and the progress made in working toward closing the achievement gap between higher and lower SES children.

Current Trends and Implications

Originally, the Head Start curriculum focused more heavily on developing children's social competence. The last few years have seen the focus expanded to include a strong emphasis on language arts development. As national goals for school readiness become more defined (for example, specific skill expectations such as knowing 10 letters), Head Start child and program outcomes are continually revised to reflect these trends.

Trends in Teacher Credential Requirements

Improving program quality through curriculum reviews, increasing teacher credentials and salaries, and striving to reach all children in need of services are historic and current goals for the program (Jacobson, 2003). The 2004 reauthorization called for all Early Head Start teachers to have a child development associate (CDA) credential by 2010, at least half of all Head Start teachers nationwide to earn a bachelor's degree by 2013, and all Head Start teacher assistants to have a CDA by 2013. By 2011 all Head Start teachers will be required to have completed at least an associate's degree (2-year degree) in early childhood education with teaching experience (USDHHS, 2009a). (The CDA, a credential that combines minimal education and experience, was created as an entry-level credential for teachers and assistants.) Improving the education of Head Start teachers is a complex issue involving concerns about funding and timeliness but is a goal that is widely accepted as a viable means of improving quality programming for children. Remaining at the forefront of the field and supporting innovations in best practices have been part of Head Start programming since its inception. The program standards manual continues to be revised to remain current with new developments and research in the field of early childhood education.

Trends in Program Assessment

Periodic reauthorizations of the Head Start legislation also mean that the program is continually under review. The 2004 reauthorization requires at least one annual comprehensive self-assessment based on Program Performance Standards and monthly reports of enrollment (USDHHS, 2009a). This component is designed to evaluate program effectiveness. Evaluation of children's progress is addressed in the National Reporting System (NRS), which is a test of all 4- and 5-year-olds' performance on language, math, and socioemotional tasks upon entrance to the Head Start program and again prior to kindergarten entrance (USDHHS, 2003b). The results of these tests are connected to program goals and used to identify programs that are in need of additional technical assistance to support expected outcomes for children (USDHHS, 2007). In practice, this means that 4- and 5-year-old children are being assessed on a limited set of literary and numerical skills using a standardized test. The cognitively oriented testing component has been a source of major debate between advocates and policy makers (Zigler & Styfco, 2004). Head Start advocates maintain that it is the broader holistic view of children's development that makes it uniquely capable of meeting children's diverse needs. Their fear is that an emphasis on cognitive development would fail to adequately assess the broad effects the program is having on children and families (Jacobson, 2003; 2004). The debate continues as educators and policy makers seek fair, reliable, and accurate assessment tools.

Conclusion

Responsibility for ameliorating negative outcomes for children living with one or more risk factors is borne by all members of society. Current research promotes the theory that the most effective way to address social problems of poverty and inequality is by providing comprehensive support services to children and families. Head Start programs have remained at the forefront of the long-standing effort to combat poverty and give every child the best chance for success. Through research and responsive program implementation, Head Start also remains a leader in shaping future practices.

The implications for educators and policy makers are clear—it is essential to understand, validate, and support children's development within the context of the family and community through individualized, appropriate, comprehensive programs and services. By identifying and addressing children's and families' needs as early as possible, we stand the best chance for improving children's developmental outcomes. Also by improving children's developmental outcomes throughout school and later life, we stand the best chance of repairing torn communities and strengthening society as a whole.

REFLECTION QUESTIONS: LOOKING BACK AND LOOKING AHEAD

Now that you have a broader perspective on both the early intervention movement in general and the Head Start initiative in particular, consider their impact on both society and the field of early childhood education. Responding to social inequities and global demands may not be motivations you previously associated with teaching. Consider these perspectives as you reflect on the following questions, and make connections between concepts in development, education, economics, social welfare, and global competitiveness:

1. Have your views on children's needs changed?

2. List the five things you now think children need for healthy overall development. Have any changed from the beginning of the chapter?

3. Have your beliefs on public assistance, community responsibility, or family involvement changed?

4. Can you foresee any problems with the administration of early intervention programming (for example, diverse cultural values and talking with parents about sensitive issues like poverty and employment status)?

5. How would you manage goals of maintaining an inclusive class, individualizing for all children, reaching out to families (in school and in their homes), and keeping your own education and training updated?

SUMMARY

When research in the field of early brain development provided evidence about the importance of appropriate environmental stimuli during critical periods of development, concerns over children living in families with limited incomes grew. New evidence underscored the divide in developmental outcomes between lower SES children and their more affluent peers. Citing this evidence, concerned professionals began seeking solutions to problems of poverty and other risk factors. However, it was not until America faced extreme civil unrest as marginalized populations began to demand equality that policy makers began to take a more comprehensive, cultural view of educating all children.

In response to the growing developmental gap between socioeconomic classes, Head Start and Early Head Start were created in 1965 and 1994, respectively, to close the gap and help prepare all U.S. children for success in school. Head Start and Early Head Start programs integrate the following key elements of early intervention programming:

- Children learning within the interrelated contexts of the family, community, and school environments
- Strong partnerships with families and community members
- Comprehensive health, wellness, education, and sociocultural elements

Recent evaluations of the programs' effects on children's developmental outcomes yield marginally positive reviews. However, program administrators continually seek to research, evaluate, and modify the programs as needed to remain innovative and increase effectiveness. Increases in teacher qualifications, changes to the curriculum guidelines, and a commitment to reflective research all seek to initiate positive changes in program implementation.

Application Activities

MyEducationLab

Go to the Assignments and Activities section of Topic 3: Family/Community in the MyEducationLab for your course and complete the activity entitled *Family-Centered Practice in Head Start*. Review the key components of Head Start programming and history and think about the role of Head Start in early childhood education.

On the Web: MyEducationLab The activity entitled *Family-Centered Practice in Head Start* reviews the key components of Head Start programming and history and prompt you to think about the role of Head Start in the landscape of early childhood program options. Discuss the corresponding questions in small groups.

In Class In small groups, review the resources and information on the Head Start Early Childhood Knowledge and Learning Center website eclkc.ohs.acf.hhs.gov/hslc/ecdh/eecd. Select any of the topics that sound interesting to you and explore the linked content. There is a wealth of information available on the website that can be used by any teacher in any program.

In the Field Arrange a visit to a local Head Start program. Use the Head Start website, eclkc.ohs.acf.hhs.gov/hslc/hsd, to locate programs. Try to identify strategies the teachers are using to provide comprehensive supports to children and families. Talk to the teachers about their perspectives on working with families (including home visits), inclusion of children with disabilities, curriculum goals, and assessment.

For Your Portfolio Locate a current early intervention journal article on one of the following topics:

- Early intervention programs for preschool children at promise
- Bilingual education for young children
- Preschoolers with special needs

After reading the article, include the following sections in your two-page, double-spaced, word-processed review:

1. Complete reference in APA format
2. Brief summary of article ($\frac{1}{2}$ to 1 page), including the purpose and topic of the article, the main points, and the major findings
3. Your reaction to each article ($\frac{1}{2}$ to 1 page), including what you learned and whether you agreed with the author (This article can be added to your portfolio in a section on child development and learning or knowledge of the field.)

RELATED WEB LINKS

Center for Prevention and Early Intervention Policy
www.cpeip.fsu.edu

Circle of Inclusion
www.circleofinclusion.org/

Early Head Start National Resource Center at ZERO TO THREE
www.ehsnrc.org

Head Start information
www.acf.hhs.gov/programs/ohs/

The High/Scope Foundation: Planning, Implementing, and Reviewing Best Practices

Education is not the filling of a pail, but the lighting of a fire.

—W. B. YEATS

The name High/Scope is most often associated with an early childhood and elementary education curriculum based on Piagetian beliefs and constructivist learning principles. Developed as an intervention program, the curriculum seeks to instill in children a deliberate, active approach to learning. High/Scope teachers facilitate children's self-directed planning, which the children then carry out and later take time to reflect on. High/Scope is much more than just a curriculum model; the High/Scope Educational Research Foundation also publishes child and program assessment tools and conducts research on the effects of early childhood programs on children's later school and life success.

STARTING POINTS: QUESTIONS AND REFLECTIONS

Before you take a short trip to a High/Scope classroom, take a few moments to reflect on the following questions:

1. What purpose may be served by one organization's conducting educational research, creating a curriculum model, and preparing extensive assessment tools?

2. What challenges might this pose?

3. What might children gain from becoming deliberate, active agents in their education through planning, implementation, and reflection? Try to think about your own educational experiences—have you felt differently during activities that you plan and implement, for example, a group presentation or an individually selected report?

4. How does it make you feel to be able to choose your own learning activities or topics?

CLASSROOM VIEW

The rain is lightly falling as you pull up to the large facility that encompasses a High/Scope program in a small urban area. Through the swish of your windshield wipers, you note that the long driveway with the brick buildings on the hill makes it feel more like an old college campus than a preschool program. Most of the old buildings house other social service agency programs. The one that houses the preschool programs is new and boasts an inviting playground with large, wooden climbing equipment and flower gardens. You park your car and ring the bell outside the locked glass doors. Once inside, you are met with a smile, sign in at the reception desk, are given a visitor badge, and are escorted to the classroom that you will be observing. Although the safety of the children is clearly important, the program staff makes every effort to make invited visitors feel welcome. The classroom at the end of the hall has a small observation room with one-directional windows and speakers hooked up to the classroom, allowing unobtrusive observations. You settle in at the observation windows as the teacher is preparing for the children's arrival.

The classroom is quiet now, and you can see that the room is set up in distinct learning areas. Materials are grouped on low cubby shelves that are all labeled with pictures and words in English and Spanish. There are numerous open-ended materials, including blocks, dramatic play props, empty boxes and bottles, water and sand toys and tables, and art supplies. There is also an inviting book corner with tape players and headphones. In each learning area, posters are hung on the wall with descriptions of the kinds of developmental skills promoted by the area. Neat displays of children's work abound, and each one has a separate note card describing how the child completed the work or something the child said about it. There are several large display boards with photos of the children and their families around the room. The teacher is busy setting the tables with laminated place mats that include each child's name and outlines of eating utensils. Trays of cereal, juice, and milk are on the tables, ready for the children to eat breakfast.

The early morning quiet of the classroom soon gives way to a buzz of activity as children arrive from their buses and are walked to the room by the assistant teacher. A few children are brought to the classroom by their parents, but most children arrive by the buses provided by the center. The teacher has already set out place mats so each child can eat breakfast at one of the four tables. As the children enter, they deposit their coats into individual cubbies, wash their hands, and take their seats. The teachers and children (19 children present) eat breakfast together, along with another support staff who is visiting for the day. They all talk naturally and openly about life at home and their busy mornings getting ready for school. Several children speak in Spanish with the assistant teacher, who responds in Spanish. He then follows with English translation to the non-Spanish-speaking children to fill them in on the conversation. He encourages the children to use both languages, and he encourages non-Spanish speakers to repeat some of the Spanish words. You notice that the non-Spanish-speaking children appear to be interested in the new words, and the Spanish-speaking children are eager to praise their peers' efforts. The classroom feels warm and respectful.

After the children finish eating, they clean up and gather together on an open carpet space. The teacher brings over a large poster listing (with words and pictures) all the available centers and activities. The children begin to discuss which areas and activities they want to play with and work on for the morning. The teachers engage the children in dialogues about their choices and their plans.

KARISSA: *I want to work with the blocks.*

TEACHER: *Karissa, you want to work with the blocks again like yesterday? What do you want to do with the blocks? Are you going to build something today?*

KARISSA: *I want to build a bridge for the cars to go under.*

TEACHER: *A bridge? Great! What kind of blocks do you think you will need?*

KARISSA: *Um . . . long ones for across I think. (Pause.)*

TEACHER: *OK. How do you think the cars will fit underneath the long. . .*

KARISSA: *(Bursts in.) And tall ones for the sides!*

TEACHER: *OK. So you're going to the block area to build a bridge for the cars to go under and you're going to try using long blocks and tall blocks. Great! Let's see how it works!*

Karissa puts her nametag next to the blocks section on the chart and hurries off to carry out her plan. The rest of the children make similar choices during conversations with the teachers, each with specific plans. Before leaving the rug area, the children are reminded about the daily schedule, also written with words and pictures. After breakfast time, there is always a planning time, followed by individual and small-group activities for nearly 2 hours. After work time, the schedule indicates that all the children will come together again for a reflection time.

For now, the teachers circulate with the children as they carry out their plans, and the assistant teacher works with a small group of children who are planning to put on a talent show in the music area. They are listening to recordings of children's songs and singing and playing along with musical instruments.

One child excitedly talks about how he recently went to his cousin's school play and they gave them a paper (a program). The assistant teacher talks about programs and what information they provide for the audience. He asks the talent show group if they would like to design their own programs for their performance. They excitedly begin to make plans for using the writing center, and one child decides to make a collage from old magazines in the art area for the cover. Another child cautions her, "Don't forget to just look for pictures of music and instruments. This is a music performance." With a nod, she is off to gather magazines.

As the group continues their project, the assistant teacher talks to the teacher about a possible large-group activity involving singing and dancing. It would tie into the talent show group's interest and encourage other children as well. He mentions that Javier was able to apply classification concepts when he reminded Maria to only look for music pictures. The teachers discuss the progress he is making from his last observation report. Wanting to build on the children's interests, they agree to write up a music-related lesson plan for tomorrow. The teacher mentions the book on bridges she has brought in for large-group time today to connect to Karissa's ongoing interest in cars and bridges. She seems as excited as Karissa as she tells the assistant teacher about how the child is integrating more complex structures into her building and has begun using arch-shaped blocks as tunnels for the cars.

As work time winds down, children begin to gather at the table with the teachers. They talk about their experiences in their choice time, but it is more than just a review. Just as the teachers prompted children to make more detailed plans, they encourage deeper reflection during review time.

TEACHER: *Karissa, I noticed you started using some different-shaped blocks today. Why did you decide to do that?*

By guiding children's planning through dialogue and questioning, teachers can indirectly promote more complex thinking and more in-depth play in children.

KARISSA: I saw a picture in the Thomas book of a bridge for the trains. Underneath it was where cars go. But the tall parts weren't just straight like my tall blocks on the sides. They were curved in the book.

TEACHER: And you wanted to make the tall part of your bridge look curved like the book?

KARISSA: Yes.

TEACHER: How did you do that?

KARISSA: I remembered those curved blocks. Well, they have a curve on the underneath part, but the top part is flat. Just like in the picture. So I got some from the shelf and put them under the long blocks. It made it just like in the book!

TEACHER: I could see that! I took a picture of your bridge structure, so we can put that in your portfolio. You know, I also found another book about bridges I think you might like. We're going to read it together after rest time.

KARISSA: OK!

TEACHER: Can you think of anything else that you would like to put into your portfolio section on bridges?

The interactions between the teacher and Karissa are typical of those you hear with all the children. The classroom is abuzz with conversations; there is a lot of discussion happening in this classroom. You've observed active learning environments before, but with the deliberate planning and reflecting, these children are not only learning through hands-on activities but are actively in control of and aware of their own learning. As the children clean up the room and prepare to go outside, you look forward to sitting down with the teachers and hearing more about the High/Scope model.

Overview of High/Scope

Since 1970, the High/Scope Educational Research Foundation has been creating, implementing, and researching high-quality early childhood programs specifically targeting children living in poverty. The High/Scope demonstration preschool includes the following elements:

- A core curriculum that includes specific elements but encourages following children's interests
- A three-phase "plan-do-review" learning cycle
- Assessment tools and strategies

The High/Scope Educational Research Foundation publishes an extensive array of informational training videos and books and coordinates teacher trainings nationwide. The foundation also conducts research on the effects of High/Scope and other early childhood programs, collecting data for more than 40 years. Above all, the foundation seeks to inform practice and advocate for the right and need for all children to have access to high-quality early childhood programming. These are the methods they use to accomplish that task.

Educational Programming

Curriculum and Key Developmental Indicators

Key developmental indicators

Fifty-eight learning goals that serve as a foundation to the High/Scope curriculum.

The High/Scope preschool curriculum is based on 58 **key developmental indicators** (High/Scope Education Research Foundation, 2009b) and is organized in five curriculum areas covering nine content areas:

- Approaches to learning
- Language, literacy, and communication
- Social and emotional development
- Physical development, health, and well-being
- Arts and sciences
  - Math
  - Science and technology
  - Social studies
  - Arts

Within each learning area, specific skills and behaviors are identified that are appropriate outcomes for preschool-age children. These 58 key developmental indicators serve as the foundation for teachers' planning and design of the learning environment and material selection. Each of the five curriculum areas is made up of a number of specific key developmental indicators. Teachers use the extensive key developmental indicators to ensure that children are provided with opportunities to grow and develop fully in all learning domains and skill areas. Teachers also base their assessment of children on these milestones. High/Scope infant/toddler programs also include separate key experiences appropriate for that age group.

MyEducationLab

Go to the Assignments and Activities section of Topic 8: DAP/Teaching Strategies in the MyEducationLab for your course and complete the activity entitled *Developmentally Appropriate Programs for Various Ages.* Notice how the teacher facilitates simple social exchanges and encourages relationships in the first clip.

Putting It Into Practice

Infants and Toddlers

High/Scope also includes programming for infants and toddlers. The infant and toddler curriculum includes 41 key experiences covering the following content and developmental areas (High/Scope Educational Research Foundation, 2009a):

- Sense of self
- Social relations
- Creative representation
- Movement
- Music
- Communication and language
- Exploring objects
- Early quantity and number
- Space
- Time

Although the nature of teacher–child interactions is important at all levels of education, it is perhaps most important when working with infants and toddlers. Infants come to know about their world through active exploration. But this is made possible only when infants are encouraged and supported in their explorations by adults who love and care for them and who respond to their verbal and nonverbal cues. Adults must be in tune with infants' patterns of behavior, gestures, vocalizations, and eye movements. Looking toward sounds or objects indicates to the watchful caregiver that infants are interested in something. Looking away or raising their hands to their face can be an indication that they are not interested in something. Infants will also indicate different needs through different cries. Their willingness to explore their world is heightened by being surrounded by adults who learn how to read their signals and respond quickly and sensitively to their needs. This sensitive responsiveness is essential for infants' healthy attachments and willingness to explore.

In addition, infants and toddlers thrive in environments where adults engage them in conversations and interactions with words, gestures, and eye contact. Being an infant and toddler teacher in a High/Scope classroom involves much more than ensuring that children's needs are met. It is also about developing warm, reciprocal relationships with the children in your care, an essential foundation for learning (Girolametto, Weitzman, van Lieshout, & Duff, 2000). Relationships are important for all learning environments, but for infants and toddlers, education *is all about relationships.*

The companion piece to the key developmental indicators in the High/Scope curriculum is the plan-do-review routine. The overarching emphasis here is on encouraging children's active learning and meaningful involvement in their own education. The plan-do-review sequence is the mechanism by which learning goals are met (Schweinhart, 2003).

Time to Plan

As you read in the observation visit, the teachers and children gathered together prior to choice or center time and discussed their goals for themselves. The teacher prompted Karissa to make specific plans about which blocks she would use in her bridge building. In this way, Karissa learned to elaborate on her general plan to build a bridge. The teacher also helped expand Karissa's thinking about the bridge by including photos and making connections between the child's work and the books. During planning time, children are encouraged to

- Make plans
- Think about how they will use materials
- Consider ways to work together with other children
- Make predictions about what they expect to happen as they carry out their plans

It is through this thoughtful planning phase that children learn to be deliberate, active agents who are able to direct the course of their own learning. This is truly an empowering experience for children. Children see that they are in control of their time and actions and that their choices are respected. The planning phase also promotes higher order thinking and problem-solving skills as well as deliberate, purposeful action (Epstein, 2003). When children are in the driver's seat in terms of choosing activities, teachers find there are fewer discipline problems and are free to interact with the children as partners (Child Care Information Exchange, 2002). Many center programs offer children a free-choice time where they are allowed to choose among materials or learning centers, but High/Scope's method takes the notion of children's choice making to another level. Here the emphasis is on intention, thinking ahead, discussion of ideas, and more detailed planning. This thoughtful planning can lead to a more deliberate use of the materials and a deeper engagement with peers and adults.

Time to Do

When children are given choices about materials and activities to engage in, they are naturally empowered and more interested in their learning. When children thoughtfully plan details about their choices, they *think* more about their actions. There is a sense of ownership that comes with directing their actions. This ownership promotes autonomy (independence), initiative (willingness to try and do things), and industry (interest in being busy and active). Remember from Chapter 2 that Erikson's theory of socioemotional development states that achieving positive outcomes in these areas is essential for healthy development throughout life.

An important feature of the activity time is that children are given long periods of time to carry out their plans. By allowing children ample time in the "do" phase

Typical High/Scope Preschool Classroom Daily Schedule

8–8:30 A.M.	Arrival and Breakfast
8:30–9 A.M.	Self-Serve Breakfast for Latecomers
8:30–8:45 A.M.	Group Meeting: Planning Time
9 A.M.	Do Time (Center Activities)
10:45 A.M.	Wrap Up Learning Activities
10:50 A.M.	Group Meeting: Reflection Time
11:15 A.M.	Outside on the Playground
12 noon	Prepare/Lunch
1 P.M.	Rest/Quiet Activity Time
2:30 P.M.	Group Activities
3 P.M.	Outside on the Playground
4:30 P.M.	Prepare to Go Home

(nearly 2 hours in the observation classroom), teachers ensure that children have time to really get into their play and learning. Children are encouraged to engage deeply in their activities, revising and extending their plans as their play and work progress. They are encouraged to use materials from different centers—housekeeping, writing, blocks, and manipulatives—to add richness and detail to their play and work. In the

Teachers are active partners in children's dramatic play; participating and extending, helping them implement their plans.

opening classroom visit, the talent show group combined materials and activities in the music, writing, and art centers to elaborate on their play. Throughout the do time, teachers were actively participating with children in their play. Through interactions with peers and teachers, children are prompted to think actively about their learning experiences.

Time to Reflect and Review

When it is time to wrap up do time, teachers and children come together again to recap their experiences, reflect on how their predictions and outcomes aligned, and share the excitement of learning with peers and adults. Once again teachers encourage dialogues with children by

- Asking open-ended questions
- Making connections to prior learning
- Extending children's ideas with suggestions for future plans
- Pointing out similarities with projects other children have undertaken, encouraging collaborations

Teachers ask children cognitively challenging questions that reflect the children's activities and interests. This helps to promote language, social, and cognitive development (Trawick-Smith, 1994). In these conversations, children are encouraged to make connections between predicted outcomes and actual events. In this way casual, yet meaningful, interactions become a teaching tool that can be applied throughout the day to enhance children's skills and promote positive adult-child bonds (Child Care Information Exchange, 2002).

As children and teachers reflect on and analyze the do-time activities, children are encouraged to reflect and represent their experiences in a variety of ways. They may dictate a story, make a drawing, write or draw in a journal, or discuss their experiences. Through this review phase, children learn that

- Their actions have impact and consequences.
- They can direct their learning.
- Adults and peers are interested in their discoveries.
- Language is a powerful tool for reflecting on experiences, describing events, and organizing thought.

There is a growing body of research that shows the importance of responsive interactions, including authentic and conversational dialogues, for children's optimal development (for discussions, see File & Kontos, 1993; Girolametto et al., 2000). Through the active learning experiences, open-ended materials, responsive interactions, and personal goal setting, children's learning is supported on their own levels and at their own pace. With the plan-do-review sequence and the emphasis on social dialogues throughout the day, the High/Scope curriculum has integrated hallmarks of good practice into the structure of the model. To prepare teachers and ensure that the model is applied appropriately, High/Scope also provides initial and ongoing training, teacher certification, and regional and international conferences.

Teacher Roles

The primary role of the teachers in High/Scope classrooms is to facilitate children's active learning. This means providing hands-on learning experiences and materials as well as encouraging children's active thinking about their learning. Teachers use the plan-do-review sequence as a framework to promote children's deliberate, active involvement in learning. Teachers also use a lot of discussion to encourage children's thinking and build relationships. Recall from the observation vignette how the teacher prompted Karissa to make her block-building plans more specific and encouraged her to predict what would happen to the cars when she used the long blocks. The teacher also encouraged Karissa to reflect more deeply on how her bridge building went by asking open-ended questions, such as, "Why did you decide to do that?" Through their discussions with children and participation in their play, High/Scope teachers strive to increase children's thinking and active roles in their learning. The rich language environment that is created by these in-depth discussions is also a key ingredient in promoting language and literacy development. The processes of predicting and assessing children's own work assist in developing their logical thinking (Epstein, 2003).

High/Scope teachers are also active partners in children's play and learning experiences. For example, when children are engaged in a dramatic play scenario, adults may play a part in the stories. They may act as playmates or extend the child-directed play. Teachers do not take over children's play or try to direct it. Instead, they participate actively but in the background, taking advantage of moments to extend children's thinking by

- Suggesting new materials
- Expanding children's ideas with questions or comments
- Supporting children's social interactions with peers and adults

Visit MyEducationLab to watch a group of children engage in a dramatic play sequence with their teacher.

It is also important for teachers to watch and listen carefully to children's interactions, play, and work with materials. Through this keen observation, teachers are able to assess children's emerging interests and meaningfully integrate new materials, ideas, and activities that will maximize their internal motivation. The teacher in the opening observation did this by bringing in new books that related to a few children's interest in bridges and transportation. By integrating new materials that align with children's current interests, teachers facilitate children's deeper exploration of topics. This validation of children's interest promotes personal, authentic learning. These are the hallmarks of the High/Scope approach (Epstein, 2005).

Dovetailing with the teacher's role as an active participant and listener is the teacher's role as an observer. Observations are every teacher's best tool for

- Getting to know children
- Understanding children's needs and interests
- Planning meaningful instruction
- Individualizing instruction/materials
- Assessing children's progress

MyEducationLab

Go to the Assignments and Activities section of Topic 2: Child Development/ Theories in the MyEducationLab for your course and complete the activity entitled *The Restaurant*. Notice the role of the teacher and the level of interaction and problem solving among the children.

When teachers are not engaged in children's play or running group learning activities, they take time to watch children in action. They are careful to record children's language, details about their play, and their use of materials. Observations are essential for creating learning environments that reflect the individual children's unique lives and interests. When making choices of materials, designing classroom space, and even making the daily schedule, it is imperative that teachers use their knowledge of their children. Through observations and open two-way communications with families, teachers are able to learn much that they can use to plan engaging learning experiences for all children.

Assessment

For observations to be effective as an assessment tool, they must be conducted systematically over time at routine intervals. They must include key details and broad generalizations. They must also be related to developmental theories to determine children's healthy growth and progress toward age-appropriate milestones as well as to highlight unique paths individual children follow. In High/Scope programs, teacher observations are implemented with the help of the **High/Scope Child Observation Record** (COR). The COR includes informational packets, especially designed for families, to assist teachers and families in working together to facilitate and assess children's development.

High/Scope Child Observation Record

The assessment checklist, completed over time, which assesses children on 30 developmental outcomes in all domains.

Child Observation Record

The COR is a checklist that is completed over time and assesses children on 30 developmental outcomes in all domains (socioemotional, cognitive, language, and physical). The items align with the key developmental indicators (Schweinhart, 2003). Teachers use one checklist form for each child, and each checklist includes space for three separate observations over time. This allows for progress to be charted easily over time on one form. Each item includes five examples of behaviors, milestones, or skills teachers might observe from children at different levels—from simple to complex. Each item also includes space for open-ended notes. Here is an example of the range of sample behaviors in the COR for 2.5- to 6-year-olds in the social relations category (High/Scope Educational Research Foundation, 2005):

1. Child expresses an emotion.
2. Child comforts another child.
3. Child talks about an emotion.
4. Child represents an emotion through pretend play or art.
5. Child identifies an emotion and gives a reason for it.

As teachers observe children at play in natural and authentic situations, they make notes about the highest level of behavior or skill being exhibited by the child. Teachers are cautioned not to make the completion of the COR into a test situation unrelated to children's normal activities; rather, the COR is to be used as an authentic assessment during children's natural activities. In this way, teachers and children feel less pressure than when completing more formal, structured tests, and the results more accurately represent how children are actually developing and performing in their daily activities.

Program Quality Assessment

In addition to the COR, which is for use with individual children, High/Scope publishes a program assessment packet called the High/Scope Preschool Program Quality Assessment (PQA). The purpose of the PQA is to "evaluate the quality of early childhood programs and identify staff training needs" (High/Scope Education Research Foundation, 2003, p. 1). Completing the assessment includes conducting observations of individual classrooms as well as across the center. Interviews of teachers, administrators, and even children provide important information that could be missed in a single observation. All aspects of the program are reviewed, including (High/Scope Educational Research Foundation, 2003)

- Learning environments
- Schedules
- Interactions
- Curriculum
- Family involvement
- Staff development
- Program management

Each category includes several items, which are individually rated on a 5-point scale. Items marked with a 1 indicate poor performance and a need for improvement. Level 5 indicates high-quality programming. The PQA is designed to assess programs using the High/Scope or other curriculum model as well as align with Head Start Performance Standards. It can be a useful self-assessment tool for identifying strengths and weaknesses in a program and for identifying staff-training needs. The inclusion of several specific items addressing staff credentials, orientation, and ongoing training is a unique feature of this assessment tool compared to other rating scales. This emphasis reflects High/Scope's strong teacher-training programs and belief that increasing teacher credentials and training are keys to improving early childhood programming (Epstein, Schweinhart, & McAdoo, 1996).

Inclusion and Cultural Responsiveness

With roots in the social reform movement of the 1960s and its initial focus on early intervention, High/Scope programs are designed to meet the needs of diverse families. Underscoring High/Scope's commitment to quality is the belief that unique family culture is to be valued and preserved. Families and children are viewed as individuals, not defined by comparisons with others. As you read in the COR example, the expectations of children are broad and represent a range of abilities. Children scoring mostly at level 1 are not necessarily viewed as deficient but rather as being at different developmental points (Shouse, 1995). With an emphasis on viewing children as individuals within a broad developmental stage, teachers are able to value and support all children.

Home visits are an important component of intervention programs such as Head Start and High/Scope that foster strong family connections and involvement.

Another aspect of High/Scope's early intervention roots is the importance of meaningfully involving families in children's development (Schweinhart, 2003). High/Scope strongly advocates the use of home visits as a vehicle for developing open relationships with families. Families are validated as the child's first teachers. High/Scope teachers seek to support families as well as rely on families to support their work. Family literacy programs are also currently being implemented to encourage parents and children to learn together. With open communications, facilitated by outreach programs and formal and informal reports, each child's unique family culture is welcomed into the classroom.

Teachers also strive to maintain connections to the English-language learner's home language (Maehr, 2003). Remember the breakfast conversations in the opening classroom observation? The teachers were having conversations in Spanish with Spanish-speaking children and English with English-speaking children. They also involved all children in group conversation by translating between the two languages. The teachers do not try to push children to speak English; instead they engage in conversations in Spanish. By speaking in the children's native language, they are able to have more elaborate and meaningful conversations.

Just think about how limited the depth and meaning of conversations would be if the children could use only a handful of English words. These limited words and phrases could not adequately express the complex ideas they are capable of thinking. The difference between their thinking and speaking would leave these children at a great disadvantage in the classroom. Remember Vygotsky's work in promoting the connection between thought and language? He believed that children use language to organize thinking. To limit children's language by suppressing the use of their dominant language is to also limit their thinking. The preservation of the family's home language while the child and family learn English is an important part of supporting overall language development (NAEYC, 1995).

Putting It Into Practice

Strategies for Supporting Linguistic Diversity

Young children come to centers and schools with a variety of family culture and linguistic backgrounds. All children, regardless of their home language, bring with them a wealth of diverse experiences, knowledge, interests, and capabilities. Our responsibility, as early childhood educators, is to work to maximize each child's development and support each family's success. Children's home language is closely tied to their individual and family identity as well as their cognitive development. It is essential that all teachers remain sensitive and responsive to the unique family culture of all children. "For the optimal development and learning of all children, educators must *accept* the legitimacy of children's home language, *respect* (hold in high regard) and *value* (esteem, appreciate) the home culture, and *promote* and *encourage* the active involvement and support of all families, including extended and nontraditional family units" (NAEYC, 1995, p. 2, emphasis in original). NAEYC recommends the following strategies for appropriately working with linguistically and culturally diverse children and families:

- Recognize the connection between home culture and cognition and emotion.
- Understand that increasing proficiency in the child's first (home) language contributes to second- (English) language learning.
- Promote the many ways (or "languages") children use to share and represent their knowledge (including arts, movement, gesturing, etc.).
- Support and encourage family involvement in the classroom and English-language learning, while validating the importance of maintaining the home language.
- Become aware of available resources to help you and your families and children communicate together. This may include translators, dictionaries, translation software, and so on.

For more information, print and read the NAEYC position statement on responding to linguistic and cultural diversity from www.naeyc.org/positionstatements

Research

In addition to comprehensive academic programs, educational research and publication are important parts of High/Scope's efforts to empower children and families. A great deal of research has been published under the auspices of the High/Scope Educational Research Foundation. The reports shed light on outcomes for lower socioeconomic status children as well as on the efficacy of developmental-constructivist curriculum models in general and High/Scope programs in particular. Although some early research indicated a lack of significant effect of preschool curriculum models on children's outcomes (cited in Marcon, 1992), more recent reports indicate a stronger correlation between curriculum approach and child outcomes (summaries in Quindlen, 2001). High/Scope researchers have published results from studies of program quality and effectiveness as well as evaluations of program impact on child outcomes (Epstein et al., 1996; Schweinhart, 2003).

Results indicate positive short-term and long-term outcomes for children attending High/Scope and other high-quality early intervention programs in all developmental domains. Research projects include exploring teacher-training effectiveness and comparisons of curriculum models; however, High/Scope's best-known research project is the Perry Preschool Study (Bracey, 2003; Schweinhart, 2003).

Perry Preschool Study

High/Scope Perry Preschool Study

The longitudinal research project that tracks school and lifetime achievements for randomly assigned program or no-program participants.

"The **High/Scope Perry Preschool Study** identified young children living in poverty, randomly assigned them to a no-preschool group or a high-quality preschool program using the High/Scope Curriculum at ages 3 and 4, and collected data on them throughout their childhood, adolescence, and young adulthood" (Schweinhart, 2003, p. 8). The study, conducted during the children's preschool years from 1962 to 1965, included 123 African-American children who attended preschool 5 days per week in addition to receiving weekly home visits. Data on various academic, developmental, and lifestyle outcomes continued to be collected from program participants and parents annually during childhood and periodically through middle adulthood. This form of long-term data collection on one participant sample is called longitudinal research. The most recent report includes data from age 40 (Schweinhart et al., 2005). As research results have been published throughout the years, especially at the age 27 report, more and more attention has been drawn to quality early childhood programming in general and to early intervention programs in particular.

Several features of this research project make it especially important in the field, including elements of the research design and data-collection methods that are indicators of quality research:

- Random assignment of participants (so any differences between the program and no-program group are more likely to be due to the program, not sample bias)

- Longitudinal design (tracking the same participants over time, thus ensuring results are true to the intervention, not to differences between people)

- Low attrition rate (very few participants dropping out of the study; data collected from a high percentage of the original participants)

These are the behind-the-scenes quality indicators, so to speak. It is the actual impact on the program participants that has stolen the spotlight since the powerful "age 27" report. Researchers gathered data on school performance measures (special education services, graduation rates) through adolescence and lifestyle indicators (employment status, arrest rates, home ownership) through the most recent data-collection point at age 40. One of the most eye-catching components of the reports is the cost-benefit analysis: the actual dollar amount of return on the public investment in this early intervention program. Findings from the study are summarized in Table 7-1 (Schweinhart et al., 2005). General conclusions of the study indicate that there are positive lifetime effects of high-quality early intervention preschool programming for children of families living in poverty. Furthermore, these lasting effects impact school performance, economic welfare, and social functioning into adulthood.

TABLE 7-1   Summary of Key Findings of the High/Scope Perry Preschool Study Through Age 40

Outcome		Performance Comparison	Savings to Public
Education: In general, the program group required fewer special services for educable mental impairment; scored better at some data collection points on standard tests of intelligence and language; had more positive outlooks on school; and program parents had higher goals for their children (attending college, for example).	Special education services required	Program: 1.1 years No-program: 2.8 years	$7,303
	Attitude toward school (participants reporting preparing schoolwork at home)	Program: 68% No-program: 40%	
	Graduated from regular high school	Program: 65% No-program: 45% (higher program graduation rates due to much higher percentage of program females graduating vs. no-program females)	
Crime Rates: In general, participants in the program group were arrested fewer times; were arrested fewer times for violent, drug, or property crimes; and spent fewer months in prison or jail.	Average number of arrests	Program: 2.3 No-program: 4.6	$171,473
	Arrested 5 or more times	Program: 36% No-program: 55%	
Economic Welfare: In general, in middle adulthood significantly fewer program participants reported receiving social welfare services; held higher paying jobs; owned and paid more per month for residences; owned a car.	Employed at age 40 (continued trend from previous data collection)	Program: 76% No-program: 62%	$16,846
	Median annual salary	Program: $20,800 No-program: $15,300	
	Owned own home at age 40	Program: 37% No-program: 28%	
Health/Family: In general, program males reported better relationships with their families; raised their own children; and were married.	Male participants raising their own children	Program: 57% No-program: 30%	
	Males reporting getting along "very well" with families	Program: 75% No-program: 64%	
Total Cost-Benefit Ratio: In general, savings to the public for program participation was highest in reduced crime rates and associated costs (88%), increased payment of taxes from higher earnings, and reduced need for special education services. Reduced dependence on welfare services also contributed to public return. Worth noting is that male program participants account for 93% of the public return.		Cost of Program	$15,166
		Total return/savings of program at age 40	$195,621 to general public
		Return to public on program investment at age 40	$12.90 per dollar (compared to the $7.16 cost-benefit ratio at age 27)

Researchers caution, however, that the results should not be generalized too broadly (Schweinhart et al., 2005; Sylva & Evans, 1999). For example, many people compare the High/Scope Perry Preschool Program to Head Start programs and mistakenly assume the results also apply to Head Start programs. It is important to understand the specific elements of the High/Scope Perry program that are thought to be the key factors impacting the lifetime effects:

- The program was a 2-year education program for 3- and 4-year-olds living in families with limited incomes.
- The curriculum and schedule supported child-initiated learning and included small- and large-group activities.
- Program teachers held bachelor's degrees and teaching certification.
- Teachers received ongoing training and support in implementing the model.
- Each teacher served five or six children.
- Weekly home visits were conducted by classroom teachers.

In order to expect the same positive lifetime benefits seen in this study, other programs would have to be comparable—that is, equal on these specific elements. Remember from Chapter 6 that Head Start policy has only recently started working toward requiring bachelor's degrees of a percentage of its teachers. Also, Head Start programs usually have higher teacher-child ratios, which align with state requirements but do not compare with the 1:6 ratio of the classrooms in the Perry study. Interestingly, many Head Start programs across the country use the High/Scope curriculum and assessment tools, and High/Scope materials include connections to Head Start performance standards. Although the Perry research results cannot be generalized to all Head Start programs, there is some connection between High/Scope and Head Start history, goals, and implementation.

What researchers say can be concluded in a broader sense is that all children living in poverty should have access to high-quality early childhood programming with reasonably similar features. With other quality early intervention programs also producing research results with similar positive effects, the importance of investing in quality early intervention programming continues to be emphasized. The most basic implication is that we must continue to provide high-quality programming for the children who need it most. This call to action starts with early childhood professionals committed to high-quality programming, is supported by research results like the Perry study, and opens much-needed dialogue at local and national levels. The returns to program participants specifically and to society in general prove that the improvement of quality early childhood programming is everyone's business.

Considerations and Applications

The overarching framework of High/Scope's developmental-constructivist practice can guide practice in any setting. These applications can improve program quality and increase children's positive outcomes. The key is to maintain the emphasis on child-initiated play that is facilitated by supportive adults. The core structure of the plan-do-review

Teachers use pick-up times for informal meetings with families to ensure that daily contacts are made and relationships are continually strengthened.

sequence can be implemented whenever children are given time to engage in learning centers. Providing open-ended materials and ample time to explore them individually or in small groups is a hallmark of developmentally appropriate early childhood practices. Adding the child's own direction and responsive adult interaction strengthens the active learning environment.

Just as important as having children guide their own learning experiences and having teachers who actively support children's learning is having teachers systematically assessing children's interests and development. Accomplishing this important task is most effective when teachers and parents are able to build close relationships that include open communication. Teachers use classroom observation reports, notes, and work samples to share with parents to show how children are doing in school. But that's only half the story. Teachers also need to seek out more complete information from parents and validate the role of the parents as their children's first teacher. It is important that teachers take responsibility for encouraging parent involvement in a variety of ways that respect the home culture. Explore children's home life in open, nonjudgmental ways. Invite parents into school to share something special about their family culture. Opening the doors between home and school allows teachers to integrate authentic cultural experiences from a child's home life into the classroom. This is a key ingredient in making learning meaningful for children and validating for families.

Conclusion

The work of the High/Scope Educational Research Foundation serves as an example of what is possible when early childhood professionals maintain an unwavering commitment to children. With an emphasis on respecting children's interests and abilities to take an active role in their own learning, the High/Scope curriculum lays a foundation for the ability of children to grow into deliberate, responsible people.

High-quality early childhood programming continues to demonstrate significant benefit for lower SES families, but High/Scope's curricular approach provides a road map to achieve high standards of practice for programs serving diverse families. As professionals and advocates, all early childhood teachers must continue to remain current with new research. The High/Scope research projects and reports provide a place to start. The emphasis on meeting the needs of children living in poverty makes much of the High/Scope research particularly important for all teachers. The poverty rates among children continue to rise. Teachers in nearly every center or school setting will work with families living in poverty at some point in their careers. With such compelling evidence that quality early childhood programming can ameliorate the risks associated with living in poverty, it becomes the responsibility of all educators to understand how to give children the best possible chances for lifelong success.

REFLECTION QUESTIONS: LOOKING BACK AND LOOKING AHEAD

1. Think back to the observation at the start of the chapter. What lesson plan suggestions could you give the teachers to build on the music group's interests? Think about the key developmental indicators, the development of preschoolers, and their interests.

2. Why do you think researchers suggest that there are fewer discipline problems when children learn through the plan-do-review sequence?

3. In what ways do you think the plan-do-review sequence might contribute to later prosocial behavior (less crime, for example)?

SUMMARY

The High/Scope Educational Research Foundation is an organization that promotes best practices through research, training, and a published curriculum model. The High/Scope curriculum, which is based on a constructivist learning perspective, was originally designed as an early intervention program. The plan-do-review sequence encourages children to be deliberate in selecting activities and materials to work with, active in implementing their plans, and reflective in their subsequent review. The extensive key developmental indicators guide teachers in planning a range of activities to enhance all areas of development and skills. The formal observations, using the Child Observation Record, form the basis for assessment. Comprehensive assessments also include work samples, portfolios, and other authentic artifacts.

The longtime research efforts conducted through High/Scope have contributed to our current knowledge base and practices. The research-based suggestions enhance programs serving children from all economic levels and using a variety of curriculum approaches. Long-term effects of the Perry Preschool Study indicate significant positive outcomes for children in high-quality early childhood programs that last into middle adulthood. These results have been used to support high-quality programming for all children, particularly children from low socioeconomic families.

Application Activities

MyEducationLab

Go to the Building Teaching Skills and Dispositions section of Topic 8: DAP/Teaching Strategies in the MyEducationLab for your course and complete the activity entitled *Implementing Developmentally Appropriate Practice.*

On the Web: MyEducationLab Go to the Video Examples section of Topic 7: Curriculum/Content Areas in the MyEducationLab for your course and watch the video entitled *Group Time: Inquiry Activity*. In this video (viewed previously in Chapter 5), children engage in several different activities related to an insect project. Note the first-hand learning experiences and how the teacher facilitates children's reflection and review of their learning using journals and drawing. Regular self-reviews of learning are a key component of the High/Scope approach.

In Class Go to www.highscope.org to the research link and then to the Perry Preschool Study link. Locate the Perry Results Through Age 40 video, Lifetime Effects. Watch the video, making notes about the how the High/Scope program was designed to impact lives of children living in poverty. In small groups, discuss the research study results in light of the original program goals (www.highscope.org/Content.asp?ContentId=219).

In the Field Use the plan-do-review sequence in your own learning experience. Plan an appropriate lesson plan integrating at least four key developmental indicators. Include predictions of how the children will respond, potential problems and solutions, and desired outcomes. Implement the lesson plan at a local child-care facility or with a personal acquaintance or family member. Write up and present a review of your experience to the class. Include connections to your predictions, analysis of how your implementation went, and a representation of something you learned from the experience (use any media or format you choose).

For Your Portfolio Select a key developmental indicator learning area (creative representation, initiative and social relations, etc.), and design a learning center that supports each of the key developmental indicators associated with that learning category. Be sure to align with High/Scope's theoretical framework of developmental constructivism as well as goals for active learning experiences. Include a drawing of your learning center, list of materials, description of your goals, and purpose of the design. This activity can go in your portfolio in a section on learning and teaching.

RELATED WEB LINKS

High/Scope Educational Research Foundation
www.highscope.org

Information on the Child Observation Record
www.fpg.unc.edu/∼eco/assets/pdfs/High_Scope_Preschool-updated_3-07.pdf

Additional information on the High/Scope Preschool Curriculum
www.ed.gov/pubs/EPTW/eptw11/eptw11e.html

CHAPTER 8

The Project Approach: Active Inquiry in Early Childhood

Give the pupils something to do, not something to learn; and the doing is of such a nature as to demand thinking; learning naturally results.

—JOHN DEWEY

The idea of child-centered curricula is not new. The importance of creating authentic learning environments—those that are real to children and flow naturally from the context of their daily experiences—cannot be emphasized enough. Creating authentic learning environments is the most effective way to fully capture imagination and engage children's senses. Within the context of children's own experiences, learning can come alive. Many teachers struggle to keep children interested in classroom activities and feel challenged by disruptive behavior. All teachers strive to foster in children an internal (intrinsic) motivation that will keep them engaged in learning. The project approach is a framework that does just that: Children are engaged in personally meaningful, interesting activities that promote intellectual and social development. In project approach classrooms, children are valued as the driving force in their learning process and are empowered to engage thoughtfully with their world.

STARTING POINTS: QUESTIONS AND REFLECTIONS

Before we embark on the journey into project work with young children, carefully consider the following questions. Use them to reflect on your beliefs about children, how children learn, and how you want to teach them. As you read through this and the other chapters, keep in mind that your beliefs can and should change as you explore new methods and ideas about early childhood.

1. What do you think an active learning environment looks like? Sounds like?

2. What should be the goals of education?

3. How can we teach children to be inquisitive?

4. Reflect back on your own classroom experiences. Describe times when you felt empowered, excited, and interested in what you were doing.

5. What does it take for you to get enthusiastic about something you are doing in school?

6. How do you approach solving problems or taking on new challenges?

CLASSROOM VIEW

In order to more clearly envision what project work looks like, let's visit a first-grade classroom in which the children are learning through inquiry and investigation.

In a mid-sized public school in a shore community, the children in Miss Michelle's first grade have spent the last 2 weeks investigating the types of creatures that inhabit the seashore. Being an integral part of local culture and geography, the seashore is a topic that builds on widely shared experiences of both the children and their families. The shore is often a topic of conversation among the children as well as a popular spot for family vacations and class field trips. The **catalytic event** *for this particular study occurred 3 weeks earlier. Miss Michelle explains, "It all started when Chaelia came to school one Monday with a collection of shells and a horseshoe crab shell after a weekend trip with her family. The children were just enthralled with her treasures. They wouldn't stop talking about them! We call that kind of spark a catalytic event. It can be anything that sparks children's interest and that motivates them to want to know more."*

Catalytic event

An experience or material that sparks children's interest and motivates them to want to learn more.

Many of the children expressed interest in the shells and began asking questions about how Chaelia found them and about the nature of the creatures that had inhabited the shells. When questions and discussions dominated several days' group time and dramatic play, Miss Michelle decided to make a list of the children's questions and a list of what they already knew about seashore creatures. "We always start projects with a discussion about what the children already know about the topic, and then we discuss what they want to know more about. This is the beginning of the KWHL chart" (what we know, what we want to know, how we can find out, what we learned).

On the fourth day of discussion, Miss Michelle began making a **concept web** *with the class centered around the main topic of life at the beach. The web included subtopics such as animals with shells, plants, fish, and birds. Additional branches of sub-subtopics radiated out from these subtopics, forming a web of ideas and possible research areas. Children were interested in animal life both in and out of the water. The planning web also included the children's questions and initial ideas about how to find answers to those questions. (See Figure 8-1.) Miss Michelle explains that the web serves to guide the children's research and document the earlier stages of their understanding. "But the assistant teacher and I also use the web to document which state standards are being met. When the children are in the investigation phase, where they are actually doing their research, we go through our standards and mark down which ones are being addressed by which activities. It's a great way for us to see immediately which areas are being covered and which standards we may need to target during a teacher-directed activity. We keep making notes as the children complete new representations, too. It's really another assessment tool for us as well as being a planning tool for the children."*

Concept web

A visual mapping strategy that creates a web of related ideas.

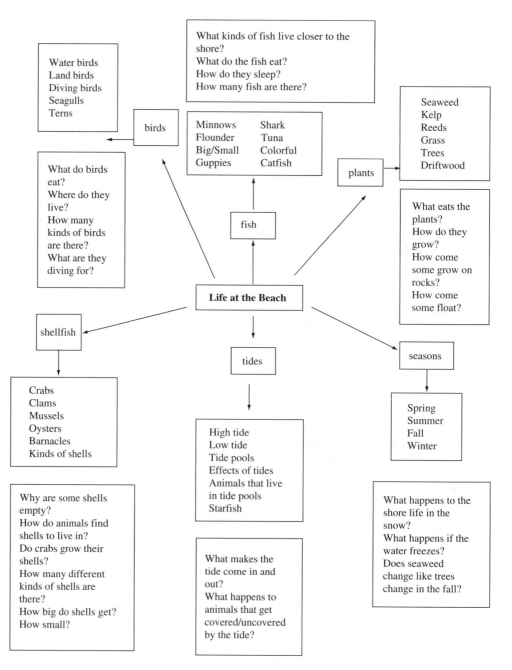

Figure 8-1 Life at the Beach Project—Phase I Planning Web

On the day of your visit to the classroom, some of the children are preparing for a visit to the beach, where they will conduct investigations in small groups. They all have clipboards, pencils, and paper. One group of children, who express interest in gathering shell specimens, will be collecting actual shells as well as making field sketches (drawing items they see on their field trip). Another group that wants to count the number of different kinds of birds they see will be listing and graphing their findings. Armed with a picture encyclopedia, they have marked the types of birds they predict they will see at the shore. A last group of children has been exploring the nature of tides and how the waters move in and out. This group will be taking measurements of the tide lines over the course of the field visit to note changes. Several parents are on hand for the trip, and Miss Michelle explains that many other parents have been involved in the development of the project by donating most of the materials the children are now using.

In addition to the children who are preparing for their field visit, another group of children will remain in the classroom. They have been working on representing their experiences from a recent aquarium trip, and they are currently engaged in transforming a section of their classroom into a replica of the aquarium. As you scan the walls behind an art area, you notice several paintings and drawings of different kinds of fish and shells, all labeled with the species names and parts. A picture dictionary and other photo books, lying open on the table, are being used along with the children's photos and sketches as references.

Three children are sitting in the art area having a discussion about their plans for their aquarium replica. The children have drawn and painted several different kinds of fish and crabs and have sculpted shells out of clay. They are now trying to figure out how to replicate the water. Mr. Dean (the other teacher) is sitting with them, transcribing their conversation in an observation notebook.

MICHAEL: *We need to have our fish and shells look like they are in the water.*

GREISAN: *Yeah, we need the water to be blue and see-through.*

NICOLA: *We could use blue paper.*

GREISAN: *(PAUSING) No . . . paper isn't see-through. We looked through the water at the fish and shells in the water. The water was right up against the glass and the fish were behind it.*

NICOLA: *So we need something clear but blue also.*

GREISAN: *Yeah, and shiny. To make it look wet. (The children pause and look around the room.)*

MICHAEL: *What about the blue plastic paper we painted on once? (referring to blue cellophane that was provided in the art area)*

NICOLA: *Yes! That was clear and blue and shiny. Just like the water behind the glass at the aquarium.*

GREISAN: *Yeah! Let's use that!*

Miss Michelle explains that keeping records of the children's discussions along with samples of their work and pictures of them investigating are all important pieces in their documentation. "We're lucky to have a video camera, digital camera, and tape recorder. We use all of those to record what the children do and say. But the children also use them to record things they think are important. I know it may seem odd to let the children use this kind of equipment, but we show them how to properly use and handle it. They know it is expensive, but they also know that the work they are doing is valuable. We respect them as capable of properly using the equipment, and in turn they respect class belongings."

By recording the class's activities and conversations, the teachers are able to capture their learning and progress. The children are also able to document for themselves the things that sparked their interest and thinking along the way. The children use the photos, work samples, videos, and transcriptions to revisit their experiences as their investigations progress. This process of revisiting and rerepresenting is an important part of how the children, parents, and teachers are able to see children apply their growing knowledge and skills. Miss Michelle emphasizes the term apply, pointing out that through this method, children are using their abilities as they are also learning and developing.

You look around the room at the documentation of the children's investigation journeys. You notice with some surprise that all the children are active and excitedly engaged in a variety of activities. Some are building the aquarium structure; others are writing signs for the aquarium, drawing fish, and sculpting shells from clay. Others are engaged in dramatic play, acting like crabs and fish. Some are categorizing and labeling the classroom shell collection. It really seems that all the children are actively exploring and representing in unique ways that satisfy their own styles. Everyone in the room seems engaged and abuzz with activity and discovery, and you take a few moments to just take in the whole scene.

Overview of the Project Approach

Historical Context

Many of the key elements of the project approach are not necessarily new or exclusive. The use of project-based curricula was influenced by the work of educators in the British Infant Schools in the early 1900s. A project method was also used by John Dewey in his lab school at the University of Chicago and promoted by William Kilpatrick during the Progressive Era. This emergent curriculum framework (emerging out of children's interests) of active inquiry and hands-on investigation has been practiced internationally for many decades. Considering the pendulum-like swings in educational practice, it is not surprising that project work has had periods in favor and periods out of favor within the field of education. Once considered at odds with more academic, skills-oriented instruction, project work was seen as conflicting with established formal education models. As the field now moves away from an "either-or" type of thinking toward a "both-and" philosophy, project work is once again finding favor in the field (Katz & Chard, 2000). Teachers at both preschool and primary grade levels are now making strong connections between project learning and state standards. With the integration of a balance of skill-based and interest-based activities and a focus on broad learning goals, the project approach is finding its place as a viable approach to engaging children in meaningful, purposeful learning activities.

What Is the Project Approach?

As the opening classroom story indicates, children who are learning through the project approach actively investigate topics that are meaningful to them. Topics can emerge from their own experiences or can be introduced by a teacher who has gleaned insight into the children's interests through observations. Whatever the topic of study, the basis of any good project is that the children are actively driving the investigation process while teachers support and facilitate the children's learning. "A key feature of project work is that it is an investigation—a piece of research that involves children seeking answers to questions they have formulated" (Katz & Chard, 2000, p. 2). Teachers and children work together to generate lists of questions and map out how concepts relate to one another within the scope of the project topic. Teachers use their ongoing observations of children to continually assess their abilities and interests, both to identify possible project topics and to evaluate the children's learning as they engage in project work.

At the heart of the project approach is the premise that children's learning is optimized when they are intellectually engaged in the learning environment (Katz & Chard, 2000). Children who are able to work on meaningful activities that allow them to explore topics of interest to them are, by definition, *interested*. Being interested is a powerful internal motivator that strengthens children's desire to explore, to ask questions and seek answers, and to be excited at discovery and sharing. Remember the children who were problem solving the aquarium design? They were focused on finding the best possible way to represent what they had experienced during their field visit. They were very clear about creating a representation that was as close to their inner vision as possible. The dialogue they went through as they sought to recreate their aquarium as accurately as possible illustrates their excitement and motivation to represent what they had learned and experienced. This emotional aspect of children's learning in project work (being excited, motivated, interested, etc.) is one of the four key learning goals addressed in the project approach. It is also an area that is often neglected in educational environments. In project work, the four learning goals must be explored individually (Katz & Chard, 2000):

- Knowledge
- Skills
- Dispositions
- Feelings

Learning Goals Supported Through Project Work

Knowledge   It is a widely accepted goal that children learn certain content, facts, concepts, and information that are part of the standard knowledge base (Gregory, 2002).

Putting It Into Practice

Sparking Interest

As you read in the life at the beach project, the children's interest was sparked when one child shared the collection of shells she found on a family trip to the beach. Sometimes worthy project topics flow easily out of children's lives: a walk through the park and a child sees a bunny family; a walk down the street and children see a fire truck or ambulance; a child has to visit the hospital; a family pet goes to the vet. Sometimes you can gently guide children's interest into a new topic. Perhaps you went to a new museum exhibit over the weekend. Bring in some artifacts to share with your children. Your ticket stub, brochure, postcard prints, or posters may just catch their attention as you vividly tell them about what you saw and did there. Or maybe you have a friend or parent in the class who works at a supermarket and can be a guest in the class and arrange a store tour. Parents can be great resources with their work and hobbies. You can also try bringing in a unique item like a horseshoe crab shell or special stones. By sharing your own interests you may spark your children's next project.

This knowledge is the foundation that helps students grow into functional members of society. Standard concepts children learn through preschool and the early primary grades include differentiating colors and shapes; understanding concepts in arithmetic, local geography; understanding the relationship between sounds, words, and sentences; and so on. Often related to state or national curriculum standards, the particular knowledge set to be explored at certain ages should be decided based on developmental appropriateness and children's readiness.

Skills   Skill development and mastery are also familiar elements of educational settings. When children perform certain tasks they are utilizing their skills. Being able to cut with scissors is a fine motor and coordination skill. Drawing an object from the environment or a scene from the imagination demonstrates motor, cognitive, and aesthetic skills. Being able to use written words to communicate and number sense to add items shows a growing competence in literacy and numeracy skills. Children also learn self-care skills, such as learning to use a spoon to eat fruit salad.

Dispositions   Perhaps a less familiar learning goal, building positive dispositions in children relates to temperaments or habits toward learning and experiencing new things. Although we may be familiar with the desire to develop in children a love of learning, an interest in reading, or a willingness to take on challenges, many educational approaches do not clearly address these goals. The child-driven, meaningful, authentic nature of project work ensures that children's interests are engaged. Their excitement about exploring and representing knowledge is fostered by their internal motivation. Project work provides the opportunity for children to build dispositions in the following ways:

- Continually make predictions (through initial webbing and dialoguing about a topic)
- Actively explore and test those predictions (through fieldwork)
- Synthesize information (through representing and sharing newfound knowledge)

Sometimes it is a challenge for teachers to motivate children, to hold their attention, and to control their behavior. Resorting to using such external rewards as stickers, points, or candy may seem like the only way to keep them focused. One of the biggest benefits teachers find in using projects, however, is that children are naturally more focused because the work comes directly from their interests and their own ideas and questions. Teachers often report fewer behavior problems as a result of the children being more in control of their learning.

Feelings   As a learning goal, promoting positive feelings about classroom experiences is difficult to overtly address. Simply teaching children about feelings of self-esteem, competency, acceptance, and comfort does not actually promote those feelings in them. Children need real, authentic opportunities to engage in classroom experiences that serve to promote those feelings. A key criterion for selecting topics (as discussed later) is that the children have some familiarity with the topic; that is, that the topic is a meaningful part of their lives.

The children discussed in the classroom visit at the beginning of the chapter live near the seashore, and the topic of life at the beach is one that is familiar to nearly all of them. Conducting an investigation on this topic allows the children to start from a place of confidence and competence—they have some personal experience with this topic and

Putting It Into Practice

Projects and Classroom Management

"Once our camping project got under way, I could barely keep up with the children! They were really into it—really thinking about what they were going to do to set up their campsite in the dramatic play area. Children were telling stories, like campfire stories. Some children were making a collage mural on the wall. They made one part out of darker papers and put on stars and a moon. On the other part they used lighter papers and put on a sun and birds. One child painted a dog and attached it to the mural at the bottom when the other children were done. They made rocks out of papier-mâché, and I helped them tape blue paper on the floor where they wanted to make a stream. There were so many little projects going on at once, you know, that it would seem hard to manage, but really it was like they were managing themselves. We gave them materials, made suggestions when they needed help to construct their vision, and helped them find resources.

One of the parents drove his camper to school for the children to go in. We were able to take some space on the playground and 'camp' there one afternoon for lunch; then we napped in tents. After that trip the children made a graph of who preferred tents or campers. When they learned that tents didn't have bathrooms, most of them voted for campers! One small group decided to build a camper from a clothes washer and dryer box. With so many subprojects going on, all the children found something that they were really into. We [the teachers] were able to watch it all unfold and document their learning and excitement. The parents even had a good time when we invited them for a campout lunch to wrap up the project!"

knowledge to contribute to the project. Through the initial planning, webbing, and listing of what the children know and what they want to know, children's existing knowledge is highlighted and valued. Through the engagement in self-selected activities, children apply skills competently to new situations. This strengthens their feelings of accomplishment and satisfaction.

Through their in-depth investigations, the children engage in a wide variety of activities. They work in groups, all together as a whole class, or individually on tasks that support their growing knowledge base and skill development, promote positive learning dispositions, and increase emotional satisfaction. Children in the life at the beach project are learning meaningful knowledge about the ecosystem at the seashore by learning names and parts of different animals and by exploring the nature of tides. In the same project, we saw children using skills such as counting and classifying, drawing, and language to interview experts and dialogue with each other. Children's dispositions to be inquisitive, interested in exploring, and able to actively problem solve as they develop new ways to represent their research findings are strengthened as their project unfolds.

The aquarium group exemplifies this problem solving and persistence as the children generate ideas of how to achieve their goal of representing the water. One of the most special

Project work can include individual, small-, and large-group work, promoting children's knowledge acquisition as well as social skills.

elements of project work is the positive emotional climate generated by the children's satisfaction, feelings of competence, and group acceptance. Children's individual styles of processing and representing are valued through the many different project activities and forms of representation. Each child's place in the group is strengthened as each individual contributes something to the whole. Through this variety of activity and expression, project work celebrates, values, and supports the many diverse ways in which children think and process information and experiences. You know from Chapter 5 how important it is to support diverse learning styles and multiple ways of thinking. It is this feature of project work that makes it particularly attractive as an integrated approach to learning.

Explanation of the Parts and Process: How It All Fits Together

When you think about children working on projects, perhaps you think about sitting together at a table with a variety of materials where children are making some kind of teacher-directed craft activity. Perhaps you think about a science fair–type process in which children independently design and create a display to illustrate a particular phenomenon. Under the framework of the project approach, however, the children's experiences progress through a more structured system.

As soon as a topic has been selected, teachers and children engage in activities structured in three distinct phases. Although each project will inevitably entail different kinds of activities and representations owing to the specific group of children doing the investigation, the categories remain the same:

- Phase I (planning)
- Phase II (investigation)
- Phase III (culmination)

It is important for teachers to keep detailed records of the children's activities during each phase of the project. As Miss Michelle explained in the opening story, these records will

- Chronicle the path of the project
- Illustrate the process the children went through on their project journey
- Provide authentic documentation of the children's learning, including standards covered

Let's explore each phase in more detail, including how projects get started and examples of children's activities and strategies for teachers to use as they support and document children's progress.

Getting Started

Often referred to as a *catalytic event*, many projects begin with an experience that sparks a great deal of interest with all or a part of the class (Chard, 1998a, 1998b). There may be a shared group experience, such as seeing a fire truck during a walk (Helm & Katz, 2001) or children getting haircuts over the weekend (Gallick, 2000). By observing children's play and dialogues, teachers are able to determine the level of children's interest and potential for the project topic. Documenting children's questions and things they wonder about the topic is an important start to any project by providing direction and ensuring that the investigation is based on the children's interests. It is worth keeping some anecdotal records about how the initial interest was generated—whether it was through a whole-class or individual experience or even a teacher-prompted topic. View a class project on caring for a hatchling bird that falls from a nest at MyEducationLab to see how teachers capitalize on catalytic events, engage children's interest, and facilitate project learning.

Phase I: Planning and Questioning

Phase I marks the official beginning of the project, where the project really starts to take shape and definition. Teachers may observe children expressing interest in a topic through discussion, questions, manipulating materials, or even by reliving an event through dramatic play. As teachers take note of the children's interest and excitement building around a worthy topic, planning can begin (Edwards & Springate, 1993). A hallmark of the project approach is that children drive the investigation process with support and, sometimes, leadership from adults. One way that the children truly direct the project is by generating the questions that will shape the course of the investigation. Teachers and children work together to write down the children's questions along with statements about what they already know or think they know. Often this process reveals misconceptions on the children's part, but it is important that those misconceptions are still included in the lists. Documenting all the children's initial conceptions allows teachers to address erroneous beliefs as children's misconceptions are challenged through their own investigations.

While the children's questions and conceptions are being chronicled, the class can begin to map out their investigation. *Concept webbing* is a visual way to represent ideas and

MyEducationLab

Go to the Video Examples section of Topic 6: Curriculum Planning in the MyEducationLab for your course and watch the video entitled *A Theme is Hatched*. Observe how an event in the children's environment becomes a catalyst for a unit of study.

the relationships between those ideas. Beginning with the main topic in the center of a large piece of paper, children and teachers brainstorm as many related subtopics as possible. These are then written on the paper in a radiating web that lays out progressively more specific related concepts. (Figure 8-1 from the opening classroom view is an example of a concept web.) The initial web serves as a visual guide to where the children's investigations can take them, but it also acts as a documentation of the preinvestigation beliefs. As the investigation progresses, the web can be revisited, modified, and added to as children's knowledge and experience grows. This can be quite an involved process, so it helps to start with a big piece of paper.

KWHL From the Life at the Beach Project, Phase I

What Do We *K*now?	What Do We *W*ant to Know?	*H*ow Can We Find Out?	What Did We *L*earn?
• Shells live at the beach • Fish live in shells • Some shells are empty • Fish need water to live • Some birds fly, some birds swim	• Why are some shells empty? • Why do some fish swim and some live in shells? • What do fish eat? • Do birds eat fish? • What are the shells on the rocks; what happens when the water covers them? • How many kinds of shells are there? • How big do shells get? • How do fish breathe underwater?	• Go to the beach • Ask a marine biologist (one of the children's parents; most children did not know these words) • Books • Internet • Go to the zoo (aquarium)	

Primary sources

Firsthand sources of information, such as field visits and expert interviews, which allow children to interact personally with the information source.

Secondary sources

Secondhand sources that provide information in a one-way flow, such as books and other printed materials.

As children are generating questions, making predictions, and planning out how they will investigate their topic, teachers are busy gathering resources to fuel their inquiry. An essential element of project work is the use of **primary sources** of information. In primary sources children gather firsthand experiences. Primary sources include field visits where children personally engage with places and materials as well as experts. Experts are the people who provide firsthand information through interviews and visits.

Books and online sources, or **secondary sources**, are used in concert with primary sources to round out children's understanding. It is important that the content of books be as realistic as possible to provide accurate, authentic information. A photo-rich picture dictionary is a key resource to have in the classroom. This is also the optimal time to encourage parent involvement. A letter home can engender parent support by sharing the children's interest and excitement and outlining ways in which parents can help with the unfolding project. Often parents can serve as primary sources and make a guest visit to the classroom. Sometimes parents can even provide ongoing help with children's representations and classroom constructions. With a roster of children's questions and a handle on the resources that are available, the investigation can begin.

Primary sources—those with which children can interact face-to-face—are essential in project investigations and help children learn on a more meaningful, personal level.

Phase II: Investigating and Researching

Phase II activities generally revolve around the children's research of their topic and questions. This is the heart of the investigation of the topic. This is the time when children go on field visits and interview guest experts. Children seek out answers to their questions and use a variety of media to represent their knowledge and re-create their experiences. Children investigate the topic on field visits by seeing, touching, drawing, manipulating, counting, measuring, taking things apart, and fully engaging with the environment at the field site. Field visits can also offer chances for children to interview and dialogue with experts. During a project on a fire truck, the preschool children's field visit to a firehouse allowed them to explore all the ladders, hoses, buttons, and levers of the truck and question a firefighter about his job and his life. The children were able to try on the coat, hat, and boots and role-play being a firefighter (Helm & Katz, 2001). This role-playing provided the children, especially the younger children, with a means to explore the related topic more deeply.

Another important aspect of Phase II work is the children's representations of their experiences. As the children in the life at the beach project explore the seashore during their field visit, they are able to document from their firsthand experiences a more in-depth understanding of how shore creatures live. Although they may have spent time at the shore before, through their research and investigation they are constructing a far more detailed knowledge of their community. They are also applying a host of skills that are being strengthened by their meaningful application to real-life situations. The classroom view provides a snapshot of Phase II activities. In the course of the project, children are actively learning by

- Graphing
- Measuring
- Drawing

Building and Representing Knowledge

Project work often lends itself to the building of some kind of group construction. This offers a valuable opportunity for children to engage in three-dimensional representation. For example, the children in a camping project decided to build a camper from large boxes. The older children built the frame and added lots of the details. The younger children enjoyed driving it and sleeping in the back. Through construction and dramatic play, children of different developmental levels were able to represent their knowledge in diverse ways.

- Labeling specimens from encyclopedia sources
- Writing signs
- Role-playing
- Problem solving
- Seeking answers to their questions
- Building replicas of what they have seen

Teachers' Roles in Phase II   Through the children's revisiting and revising of their earlier representations, children, teachers, and parents all are able to see how their understanding has changed over the course of the project. Being able to demonstrate changes over the course of a project is another important reason why teachers have to be diligent and systematic about chronicling the children's representations, activities, and dialogues (Edwards & Springate, 1993). This is also the time when teachers can guide children's explorations to help them uncover misconceptions that may have been revealed during Phase I. For example, through the visit from a parent-expert in the beach project, the children learned about the differences in mollusks and fish. This related directly to their own questions about fish and shells. By continually reviewing the progress of the children's project, teachers are also able to notice content or standards that need more emphasis.

Teachers are active in orchestrating the children's activities and encouraging their dispositions to question, investigate, and problem solve. They are often coordinating multiple small-group projects within the larger project, keeping track of needed materials and resources. Teachers are also continually staying in contact with parents to update them on the children's progress as well as to continue to seek their involvement in the project (Beneke, 2000). Teachers assist children in recalling their field experiences when they are back in the classroom, and they prompt children's questions and exploration should they need it. By encouraging frequent drawing (in field sketches and later representations), teachers are able to capture illustrations of children's changing knowledge and abilities (Beneke). By analyzing and comparing children's drawings and representations over time, teachers make children's learning visible.

Children are engaging with each other and the community to share ideas, challenge beliefs, and create new understandings. There is a real potential for strong bonds to develop

Teachers use children's work samples and documentation panels to share their learning with parents and involve them in class projects.

in the classroom community through this kind of experiential learning. As the children's questions are being answered and their investigations begin winding down, teachers develop a sense that the project is ready to be concluded. This is the opportune time to shift into Phase III activities, which give children the chance to wrap up their investigation and share what they have learned.

Phase III: Concluding and Culminating

Just as the project began with children and teachers dialoguing about the shaping of the project, the decision to wrap it up can be made together. As teachers notice that children's investigating and playing are diminishing, it is a good point to ask the children if they would like to review and wrap up their work (Katz & Chard, 2000). This has been a big undertaking for the whole class, and a satisfying culminating process is important. This allows the class to reflect on the journey and take pride in sharing what has been learned. By posing the question to the children about how they might like to share their project, their satisfaction with the closing phase will be enhanced. After all, this has been *their* project all along, so it follows that the culminating phase should stem from their ideas.

In the same way that initial brainstorming revealed questions and beliefs about the topic, a group discussion session can reveal creative ways for the children to share the project. Ideas for a culminating event might include (Helm & Katz, 2001)

- Museum opening with children's work displayed
- Documentary book
- Documentary movie
- Family and community open house
- Slide show

The possibilities are numerous, and together teachers and children can explore the execution of the most popular suggestions. The goal of Phase III is to realize the journey, share what they have experienced, and provide closure for this particular project (Edwards & Springate, 1993). Keeping a record of the culminating event is another way for teachers to gather evaluative data on the children's progress. Video cameras and digital cameras are indispensable equipment that can capture children's progress and help them remember trips and expert visitors. Using tape recorders regularly also allows teachers to capture authentic samples of children's dialogues. Transcripts of children's conversations can reveal great insights into their thinking processes.

The following points on engaging in the project approach with young children are important considerations to keep in mind in regard to how this approach fits into current frameworks about best practices in teaching young children.

Applications With Young Children

Selecting Topics

Although the balance of project activities remains key to successful learning outcomes for children, the selection of the project topic is perhaps even more important. Teachers maintain responsibility for making a decision about the project topic; however, most of the time they base the initial idea for the topic on the real or potential interest of the children. There are several important criteria teachers need to keep in mind as they weigh the value of a particular topic in addition to the children's interest (Helm & Katz, 2001; Katz, 1998; Katz & Chard, 2000):

- Are there opportunities for primary sources of investigation, including field sites and experts?

- Is the topic worthy of teachers' and children's time and effort—is there enough to generate an in-depth investigation?

- Does the topic engender an interest in making an in-depth investigation?

- Is the topic relevant to the children's day-to-day life—is it something they can get their hands on?

- Do many of the children have shared experiences that provide a starting place?

- Will the topic contribute to curriculum standards and learning goals?

- Does the topic lend itself to representations through a variety of media?

- Is the topic neither too broad nor too narrow (for example, are children engaged in a project on a fire truck, which is concrete, not the topic of fire safety, which may be too abstract for young children)?

With these main criteria in mind, teachers use their dialogues with and observations of children to determine suitable topic options. In addition, projects will be enhanced by the teacher's own interest, experience, and knowledge about the topic. This may mean that teachers need to conduct some research on their own while the children's interest in the topic is building in the early phases (Katz & Chard, 2000). Being knowledgeable about the topic and available resources (consider parents and community members and sites) is an important teacher responsibility and one that will help in the planning and successful implementation of projects. Visit MyEducationLab to view a teacher-led group discussion on apples that started a project on apples and supermarket food shopping as well as a teacher involved in a small group creating a block structure.

Cultural Responsiveness and Inclusiveness

Projects are based on children's worlds and emerge from their lives, interests, and conversations. From the start of Phase I discussions, children share their personal family experiences and knowledge, empowering them as important sources of information from the beginning. Children may share family norms, events, and traditions as part of the groundwork of KWHL and brainstorming sessions. Although children may have very different life experiences, the emergent nature of projects embraces this diversity. This authenticity provides a perfect opportunity for individualized, inclusive learning through

- Integrating home, community, and school into the classroom
- Valuing the context of each child's unique family, culture, and abilities
- Tapping families and community members to bring their expertise to the project
- Valuing all children's contributions equally
- Validating what children already know

As children get into the heart of investigations during Phase II, the many ways to represent their thinking support varying abilities. Some children may enjoy literacy or numerical activities; others may prefer dramatic play or sensory activities. Each child can engage in activities that demonstrate his or her own capabilities. This bolsters children's confidence to continue investigating and wondering about the world, no matter what level their learning or scope of their ability. Working in groups allows children to share tasks, problem solve together, and build on each other's strengths. One child's strengths can support another child's weaker area. It is the supportive, collaborative nature of project work that enables all children to participate in their own unique ways. It is essential that all teachers remain vigilant about facilitating participation at a variety of levels so that all children feel competent and valued.

MyEducationLab

Go to the Assignments and Activities section of Topic 6: Curriculum Planning in the MyEducationLab for your course and complete the activity entitled *Effective Teaching Strategies in Early Childhood Classrooms*. Observe how the teacher prompts interest and questions from the children.

Putting It Into Practice

Listen

In order to identify topics that are meaningful, interesting, and reflect children's lives, teachers must become adept listeners. Listen to children's conversations. Listen to their play. What themes, topics, ideas, or events are they talking about? Their spontaneous play can provide clues as to what they are most interested in at the moment. Those are the topics you can seize for potentially great projects.

Teachers create documentation panels with photos of children working, quotes from children's conversations, and notes, all carefully laid out on large posters or wall space.

Assessment

Assessment is a constant activity of teachers in a project classroom. Right from the very beginning, artifacts are being created that are useful tools in documenting children's learning. The first conversations, webs, and KWHL charts indicate where children are starting from; revisited at the end of the project, they provide a great comparison to show how far the children's learning has progressed. Teachers act as data collectors from the very first catalytic event through the close of the culminating activity.

The variety of children's investigation activities and knowledge representations provides a rich array of authentic assessment documentation. Teachers can use portfolios to compile and chronicle project artifacts such as

- Drawings
- Graphs or charts
- Photographs
- Transcriptions of dialogues
- Notes from expert interviews (children's); notes from observations (teacher's)
- Field sketches
- Stories from children and families

Documentation panels

Displays of children's work, conversations, photos, and teacher notes that describe the process children engaged in throughout a project.

A more public way to chronicle active learning is the use of **documentation panels**. Documentation panels are carefully designed displays chronicling the progress of the children's projects and the process they went through in their explorations. They can be created on cardboard trifold presentation panels or poster board, or they can be mounted directly on an open wall. The panels include photos of children working, webs, work samples, drawings, paintings, other graphic representations, teacher's notes, and transcriptions of children's dialogue.

Documentation panels or walls create attractive and informative displays, both showcasing and chronicling children's process and work.

How Project Work Fits Into Current Beliefs About Good Practice

Based on what we currently know about developmentally appropriate practice, constructivism, social learning, and diverse learning styles, there are several ways in which the project approach dovetails with many of the current beliefs about how young children learn best. Generally accepted frameworks of good practice embrace the following practices:

- Balance skill and interest-based classroom activities
- Foster an atmosphere of curiosity and discovery
- Provide ample opportunities for active, hands-on learning experiences
- Maintain responsive and supportive social interactions among children and between children and teachers
- Maintain an open link between school and home
- Support children's play as a vehicle for learning

We know that children are active explorers of their environments from their earliest days. We know that as toddlers, they are full of questions and can become enthralled with exploring even the smallest details. We know that children need positive guidance and careful scaffolding from adults to reach their full learning potential (Vygotsky, 1978). And we know that young children need more concrete experiences that are meaningful to their own lives and provide continuity between time, content, and environment (Katz & Chard, 2000). All these elements can be found within project work.

Proponents of the project approach promote the idea that children need to learn some basic skills through teacher-directed activities but also become engaged in many child-initiated and child-directed activities (Katz & Chard, 2000). By allowing the path of the project to emerge from children's own interests, children's motivation remains high and learning remains meaningful. Also, by keeping the focus of projects centered on topics that are a part of their lives, the context remains authentic. This also allows for easier parent involvement, because topics are also a part of families' lives and communities. The nature of in-depth investigations of familiar topics also ensures that there is continuity between children's lives in and out of school (Trepanier-Street, 1993).

Think back to the children in the life at the beach project. The topic was a familiar feature of their family and community life, one that parents and children alike had experienced. Consider how their curiosity and natural inclination to find out more was fostered through their project work as they made predictions and discoveries throughout their field visits. Some children were wondering about bird life, making predictions from their encyclopedia research, and testing those guesses with their real data. Because the direction of projects springs from children's own questions, their inquisitiveness is naturally encouraged.

Beyond Play: How Is the Project Approach Different?

One of the contrasts between the project approach and other play-based approaches lies in the emphasis on the value of play as a primary vehicle for children's learning. Often a play-based philosophy is grounded in the belief that early learning environments should be solely child centered as opposed to strictly teacher directed. A worthy mission, keeping children at the center of educational planning is certainly an accepted hallmark of good practice and also a part of the project approach. However, whereas project work is child initiated, the emphasis is placed more heavily on engaging the child's intellect and developing the four prime learning goals: knowledge, skills, dispositions, and feelings. Project approach proponents also believe that children's play is natural, is necessary, and has a key place in early educational settings. However, they also point out that play is not the only way to engage children in the deeper intellectual activities of questioning, problem solving, researching, and representing. Focused, active inquiry is combined with play to ensure deeper engagement and learning in developmentally appropriate ways.

Children are certainly capable of inquiry-based learning, researching, and active investigation, but too often their capabilities are underestimated and teachers make decisions for them and limit their intellectual engagement. It is through inquiry-based project activities that positive dispositions and feelings are promoted and strengthened. And it is through the balance of skill-based instruction, interest-based activities, play, and socialization that the four learning goals are integrated into the learning environment in meaningful ways.

Conclusion

Project approach teachers strive to create learning environments that truly value and support children's capacities for complex thought. At the heart of the approach is the goal of engaging children in interesting, personal, meaningful investigations of their world. Through a three-phase structure and web-planning strategies, teachers support and foster children's active explorations. Because the project topics emerge from children's interests and are driven by the children's questions, this approach can be tailored to any age level. From toddlers to elementary school children and beyond, project work provides an opportunity for truly active learning.

REFLECTION QUESTIONS: LOOKING BACK AND LOOKING AHEAD

Now that you've read an example and overview of the project approach, take some time to reflect on what you've read, thinking back to the children exploring the life at the beach project.

1. How have your ideas about active learning changed after reading this chapter?
2. How do the children drive the learning process in project work?
3. Describe ways that diverse learning styles and intelligences are supported through projects?
4. How is learning from primary sources different from learning from secondary sources in terms of the children's constructing meaning and understanding for themselves?
5. How do you think you would learn through a project approach?

SUMMARY

According to the project approach framework, children's learning experiences are optimized when they are actively engaged in meaningful, authentic explorations of their day-to-day world. Children's interests and inquiry drive these explorations and in-depth investigations of topics. The investigations promote positive outcomes on four main learning goals:

- Knowledge
- Skills
- Dispositions
- Feelings

Engaging children in project work integrates curricular learning goals and standards and maximizes children's natural curiosity and internal motivation.

Projects permit children to work together and sometimes individually to satisfy their inquiry and interact with their environment. Through this interaction with each other and their environment, children's ability to interface with their world is developed. This strengthens feelings of community inside and outside the classroom. Implementation of the project approach follows three distinct phases that help organize the children's journey:

- Planning (Phase I)
- Investigation (Phase II)
- Culmination (Phase III)

Through a careful balance of skill- and interest-based classroom activities throughout the project process, teachers can successfully address all areas of children's learning while supporting children's diverse learning and representation styles.

Application Activities

MyEducationLab

Go to the Video Examples section of Topic 7: Curriculum/Content Areas in the MyEducationLab for your course and watch the video entitled *Integrated Curriculum.* How did the teachers integrate the theme across curriculum areas, and how is this beneficial to children?

On the Web: MyEducationLab Visit MyEducationLab to view teacher interviews explaining ways to integrate curricular areas to make learning more meaningful and connected. Make some notes about the class project on the body, making connections to the phases and activities of the project approach. Use the following questions as a guide for generating small group discussion:

1. In what ways did the teachers integrate the topic across curriculum areas?
2. What content or subject areas were integrated?
3. Why do the experts feel this type of learning is beneficial to children?
4. Brainstorm at least three other topics that can be integrated across the curriculum, making notes about key activities in several content/subject areas. Share these with your group.

In Class One of the benefits of engaging children in project work is the ability to support diverse processing styles and the many different ways children can represent their learning. Using the opening project story (life at the beach) or the bridge project that follows, analyze the investigation, children's activities, and representations. Identify as many different kinds of thinking/processing styles at work as you can. Use Gardner's Multiple Intelligences framework or another learning styles model to categorize the children's activities. For example, did you notice activities that would support verbal processing? Mathematical or logical processing? Naturalistic? Spatial? Feel free to use the following chart to analyze the diverse array of activities in the target project.

Processing Style	Supporting Activities or Representations

Sally and Barbara's Class Builds Bridges

One morning Luci came into the class with one of her favorite books. It was a book of paintings by Impressionist painter Claude Monet. She had marked her favorite page, a print of an arching bridge over a pond with water lilies (*The Water Lily Pond*). Luci shared her picture during circle time. Teachers Sally and Barbara were excited at the idea that the children might become interested in exploring the life and work of Monet.

But the children's interests took a different turn. The children became very interested in the bridge, asked questions about it and the water underneath, and shared stories of when they had walked on bridges. Following their lead, the teachers encouraged this questioning and sharing throughout the circle time. The next day, when children's interests were still high, Sally and Barbara began making lists of children's questions and began a concept web. Soon the children decided they wanted to find more bridge pictures.

They started sketching their own bridges and replicas of bridges from books, including the Golden Gate Bridge in San Francisco. The children learned new words like truss, suspension, cable, and foundation. In addition to sketching, some children began making tally mark charts, counting the number of foundation legs, the number of cables, and so on. Some children wrote stories and journals about their own experiences with bridges, sharing stories from family vacations and trips around town. Children began constructing models from blocks and craft sticks. This evolved into beginning to build a small, straight bridge from scrap pieces of wood. The children made plans and decisions about how it would be elevated and how to make it strong enough for people to walk on.

The teachers began planning for a field trip to a small footbridge on the grounds of the school. On the field trip, the children took videos and photos and sketched what they saw. Some children measured length and height, marking the arch and other dimensions on large butcher paper. Sally and Barbara also discussed the developing project with the parents. One of the parents, Marty, who works in construction, volunteered to assist with the project. He was also able to facilitate donations of supplies from a local lumber yard.

Marty became an integral part of the project and facilitated the children's planning and building of a life-sized footbridge to go in the children's play yard and garden. The children interviewed Marty, asking questions about how bridges were built and general building questions. With Marty's help, the children explored the building process, including tool safety, blueprints, and plans, through to actual construction. Several children, who took charge of overseeing various aspects of the project, became project managers. They facilitated class decisions about design, size, shape, and placement. When the children had designed their bridge, several weeks of construction began. The children were involved in all aspects of the construction. They took turns and used authentic tools.

One small group of children went back to the original inspiration print and began to find interest in the flowers. This group embarked on a subproject of designing flower gardens to go around the bridge in the play yard. They reviewed garden books, spoke to gardeners, and enlisted parent help in finding plants and bulbs. They decided to plant one area with vegetables and one with flowers. They made sketches, selected color schemes, and ultimately worked on planting the actual garden in raised beds built by another family member.

The children's bridge construction, with surrounding gardens, culminated their Bridge Project.

Throughout the project, Sally and Barbara were busy providing resources as the children's interests evolved. They located materials, planned the trip and parent involvement, and supported group and individual activities. They were also carefully documenting the process. Sally took photos, Barbara collected work samples, and both teachers made notes about children's dialogues and questions. Ultimately, the teachers created a large documentation panel to chronicle the project. When they reflected on their documentation, they highlighted each of the developmental domains and state learning standards areas that were fostered with each activity. They smiled as they spoke about how children's personal family stories (through vacation stories and photos) were integrated. They also nodded as they talked about how each child, regardless of abilities and skill levels, had an important role and made valuable contributions in his or her own way.

When the children's bridge was complete, the class came together to decide how to share what they had learned and created. The children chose to hold a garden party, where families, children, teachers, and visitors could come and traverse the bridge and see the artifacts of the project. On party day, the children excitedly shared their experiences, reliving the project and revisiting their work.

In the Field In the spirit of engaging minds in meaningful, constructivist learning, one of the best ways to really understand the structure, process, and potential of the project approach is to actually *do* a project. As a class or in groups, consider topics that are interesting and worthy of in-depth study. Keep in mind the same criteria teachers use to decide on topics to investigate with children.

For each topic, begin documenting what members of the group already know and then generate questions that address what you want to know more about. View this segment as a webbing/KWHL brainstorming session. Come up with as many related ideas, concepts, and questions as possible. Ask one person to keep a running list to document responses. Begin to organize ideas into a web to see possible directions and relationships between responses. Once the web begins to take shape, smaller groups may want to break off to explore particular ideas or concept branches.

In small groups, explore possible primary sources where you could conduct your investigations—think about possible field visit sites and possible experts to talk to. Continue Phase I activities until you and your group feel ready to embark on your investigation. Move into Phase II, remembering to keep notes and records of activities and investigations as they take place. Keep photos, notes, sketches, writings, and transcriptions of interviews and dialogues for your documentation panel and/or culminating event. Let your initial questions from your KWHL and web guide your investigations. Move into Phase III as time dictates or as your investigations begin to wind down. Plan and implement your culminating event as a whole class or as small groups. Your culminating event should answer this question: How can we share what we've learned and how we learned about our topic?

For Your Portfolio When you have completed your project, reflect on the following questions in a brief paper:

- Were you surprised by how much you knew about your topic or how many questions you had while you planned in Phase I?
- How did Phase I activities help guide your investigations?
- How did you feel as you engaged in your investigation?
- Was a certain energy or excitement generated by your group?
- What can you say about the experience of getting out in the community to do fieldwork? How was this different than using secondary sources?
- Did you find out new information through your investigation? Describe it.
- What kinds of representations did you enjoy? Did you find yourself using a variety of skills and knowledge?

As a final group activity, make notes on your documentation panel, web, or KWHL chart about which of your state standards were covered. You will need to find your state learning standards for K–3 or preschool. If your state does not have standards for your age group, consider using another state (Pennslyvania, Colorado, Arizona, and North Carolina are some states with extensive early learning standards).

Include photos and descriptions from your project in your reflective paper. This artifact can be added to your portfolio in a teaching and learning section.

RELATED WEB LINKS

Project Approach home page
www.projectapproach.org

Clearinghouse on Early Education and Parenting
ceep.crc.uiuc.edu/poptopics/project.html

Issues in Selecting Project Topics
ceep.crc.uiuc.edu/eecearchive/digests/1998/katzpr98.html

9

The Schools of Reggio Emilia: A Child's World

Each child is unique and the protagonist of his or her own growth. Children desire to acquire knowledge, have much capacity for curiosity and amazement, and yearn to create relationships with others and communicate.

—LORIS MALAGUZZI

In the small, wealthy, northern Italian town of Reggio Emilia, a community of early care and education centers embodies the epitome of exceptional practice in teaching young children. Numerous books, exhibits, and observation reports have been published about their approach in the past two decades. The international educational community has become captivated by this aesthetically beautiful, professionally collaborative place. From the first illustrations of life in the Reggio schools, early childhood professionals in America have developed a vision of Reggio practice as a romantic ideal. With core values affirming a deep respect for children's capabilities and families' influence and an attention to beauty and detail, the Reggio philosophy, teaching methods, and environment are highly attractive yet also require tremendous effort. This chapter presents an introduction to the history, philosophy, and practice of the infant through preprimary schools of Reggio Emilia, Italy. Challenges and possibilities for successfully integrating the Reggio spirit and inspiration into U.S. programs are also presented.

STARTING POINTS: QUESTIONS AND REFLECTIONS

The schools of Reggio Emilia, Italy, offer a unique approach to nurturing and educating young children. Open yourself up to considering the values of other cultures as you think about the following questions:

1. What would you describe as the most important elements of classroom design (lighting, furniture, layout)?

2. Close your eyes and imagine your ideal preschool classroom. Think about the room construction, the choice and placement of furniture, the kinds of materials on the shelves, the wall decorations, and anything else that comes to mind. What were the key features you envisioned?

3. How important do you feel creative activities are for young children? Why?

4. How important do you think it is for teachers in a center to work together as a team? Do you think you see this happening in your observations or teacher interviews?

Overview of the Reggio Emilia Philosophy

Overarching everything Reggio teachers do is the guiding belief that children are capable and competent. They are capable of responding to each other and to richly detailed, authentic artwork. They are able to create complex, beautiful, meaningful work either individually or in collaboration with teachers and peers (Gandini, 2002). Although the Reggio philosophy integrates developmental theories, their perspective is on children's potential development rather than norms of ages and stages (Warash et al., 2008). In other words, the Reggio Approach is based on seeing each individual child as capable of much more than expected when provided the right opportunities for engaging with his or her world in creative ways. Reggio teachers take children's aesthetic (sense of beauty) development as seriously as their development in every other domain. It is this respect for and valuing of the arts in children's lives that make possible the uncommonly expressive, aesthetically striking representations created by Reggio children.

Reggio Emilia schools focus learning experiences on allowing children to experience the world with all their senses. Teachers give children the opportunity and tools to explore the world at their will—to be the captains of their own learning. In turn, Reggio children's understanding reaches deeper and becomes much more personal to them. The themes of their study can last for months, continuing as long as the children need to squeeze all the juice out of the topic and feel satisfied that they have a real understanding of it (Seefeldt, 1995). The depth of their comprehension is most evident in the rich detail, variety, and maturity of the expressive works used by the children to give form to their individual awareness.

Small-group interaction is also an important element of the Reggio approach. Classrooms are busy places where groups first engage in discussion and debate and then embark on the task

Reggio-inspired teachers take great care in presenting children's work, illustrating how children are respected for their amazing capabilities.

of exploring the topic of their discussion (Gandini, 1997). Throughout their investigations, teachers carefully document the children's process so that all—teachers, children, and parents—are able to see children's learning and revisit and reflect on their process (Warash et al., 2008). This is a great example of the social construction of knowledge you read about in the constructivism chapter. In this environment, children's unfolding thought processes lead to the advancement and testing of their understanding. This is possible because the teachers and children promote an environment of value and respect for each other's ideas, differences, and expressions.

Reggio teachers, who teach in an area rich in traditions of art and social relationships, take great care in preparing children's environments to be places of beauty, complexity, comfort, and visual interest (Edwards, 2003). Teachers focus on aesthetic elements of light and shadow, texture, shape, dimension, color, and composition in the design of displays, presentation of materials, project experiences, and selection of classroom furnishings. The environment is viewed as the third teacher, and, as such, it is given careful, deliberate consideration (Danko-McGhee & Slutsky, 2003). Most importantly, teachers carefully focus children's attention and provoke interest through choice of material and classroom display.

Materials may be found, purchased, donated, or natural, but they are all displayed in organized, organic, unusual groupings that draw the children into activity with them (Tarr, 2003). Teachers select, prepare, and present materials to challenge children "to respond deeply to the natural world, their cultural heritage, [and] to their inner worlds" (Tarr, p. 37). Through the use of materials, displays, and conversations, teachers act as **provocateurs**, seeking to provoke children's thought.

A full understanding, appreciation, and knowledge of the Reggio Emilia approach (REA) require an awareness of the forces that built and shaped the schools as well as of the motivations and efforts that perpetuate them so successfully. Before you launch into the historical overview, take a moment to visit a Reggio-inspired school.

Provocateurs

Teachers view their role as provokers of thought. They seek to spark children's interest and motivation to explore materials, ideas, relationships, and events by posing engaging questions and presenting interesting materials.

CLASSROOM VIEW: A VISIT TO AN AMERICAN REGGIO-INSPIRED CLASSROOM

In a small, close-knit town, the director of an established child-care center became intrigued by the richly detailed, beautiful images publicized by the schools of Reggio Emilia. What transpired over the course of several decades embodied the emergent, dynamic, reflective, collaborative nature of the Reggio Emilia spirit. The center's transformation was made possible by a passionate commitment to the community, to the children, and to the beauty that could be created together.

Imagine you are visiting this center early one sunny, cold, winter day. The center is located in what looks from the outside like a house, now converted to a preschool. There is a welcoming entrance foyer with a couch, tables of informational pamphlets, and reference books on Reggio Emilia schools. The lighting is soft, and the room feels lush with several floor plants. There is a small table with tea and coffee near the couch. An office adjoins the space, allowing for visitors to be greeted upon arrival. A hallway leads from the entrance to three classrooms, accompanied by a large community room and an art studio. Throughout the center, the walls are painted white and the wood floors gleam in the streams of sunlight shining through the many windows. The sound of children engaged with each other is immediately noticeable—many conversations and bubbling laughter echo through the hall.

From the entrance and all throughout the center the walls are adorned with framed, lighted prints. With such care given to the placement, framing, and lighting of the work, the space resembles a museum. These carefully displayed works are, in fact, representations the children have created using a variety of media in the course of their long-term projects. Near many of the pictures are small plaques of transcriptions of children's dialogue to serve as accompaniment and provide additional information.

Framed photos of children at work creating sculptures, drawings, and paintings; engaging in dialogues; and observing their world with rapt attention punctuate the project documentation. The expressions on their faces begin to reveal the deeply personal, authentic, engaging atmosphere that has been carefully and deliberately created by the teachers. This is clearly a child's world. It is made beautiful, nurturing, and exciting by a group of teachers who have committed themselves to valuing and celebrating the amazing potential of children.

The first classroom down the hallway is empty; the children, bundled against the cold, are outside in the snow-covered garden. A small group of children is gathered around a pine tree. They are pointing to a bough heavily weighed down with snow. They turn and talk to one another and the teacher nearby. Other children are busy scooping snow and shaping it into sculptures. You see animals and towers, not just the usual snowball snowman. One little girl takes deliberate steps and looks back to see her footprints in a patch of untouched snow. She creates a dotted pattern by varying between big and small steps. She laughs and sings in time to her stepping.

Inside, the classroom is lit by a full wall of windows on one side and three large windows on the other. There is a large, open space on one side of the room, with several small alcoves and three clusters of small tables and chairs. Adjoining the room is a small art room, called the mini-atelier in Italian. This studio room is lined with floor-to-ceiling shelves. One entire wall of shelves is stocked with clear jars holding collections of items, including naturally found items such as shells, stones, pinecones, leaves, twigs, sawdust, nuts, and seeds as well as manufactured materials, including flat wooden sticks, cotton balls, pom-poms, scraps of fabrics, sequins, glitter, pipe cleaners, yarns, cookie-cutters, wire, and beads. Recycled materials fill another series of jars: bottle caps, various packing materials such as Styrofoam peanuts, starch noodles, and pieces of bubble wrap. Other shelves hold baskets of artists' instruments, including clay tools, paintbrushes of all sizes, sponges, pens, pencils, crayons, pastels, different forms of paint (water color, tempera, powdered, acrylic, finger), paper of all sizes and colors, clear plastic bins of clay, small trays, and small jars and cups. On one shelf, children's paintings are still drying; other paintings are hung by clothespins from a string stretched across the room. The classroom illustration depicts this room.

The children's paintings are a study in composition. They are all done in shades of white and light grey, blue, and lavender. These are the colors the children chose to represent the snow outside and their experiences with it. There are two sinks, one low for children and one higher for adults, and a counter and cabinet for teachers' materials. In the center of the room is a long, wide, low table with small chairs around it. Despite being filled with objects, the small room appears organized, spacious, and inviting. Materials are grouped in collections and arranged in an orderly fashion.

In the main classroom, evidence of typical preschool centers appears in the form of blocks, dramatic play clothes, kitchenwares, a pillowed alcove surrounded by bookshelves, a table with puzzle racks, and low shelves housing manipulatives, dolls, cars, paper, and pens. An overhead projector and a screen are set up in a corner near a basket filled with a variety of items of different shapes and opaqueness. A tank with one fish is located in the far corner of the room. A class book has been placed next to the tank. You flip through the book and read the children's story about the death of one of the class pets. The book includes scanned pictures of the children discovering the fish in the morning, the fish's funeral and burial, and children's drawings of their memories of the fish. Quotes of children's comments and dialogue, printed alongside the pictures, include memories of the fish and feelings about the loss. The teacher later explains that this two-day project was discussed with families first and that they had all decided to let the children experience this loss as an opportunity for authentic learning.

*As the children return from their snowy outing, there is a sound of dialogue from the large art studio (**atelier**) down the hall. Children use the studio to work on long-term projects. The large art studio is similarly well stocked, but it has larger collections of supplies and materials. There are several long, wide tables with groups of small chairs and a higher table for the art teacher (**atelierista**). A long*

Atelier

The art studio space—within the classroom or in a central location—which provides the children with space to create over time.

Atelierista

A teacher who is also trained as an artist. The atelierista provides instruction on the use of art media, supplies, and tools and supports the evolution of class projects. He or she also serves as a key resource and partner with classroom teachers.

Reggio-inspired classroom.

Sample Class Schedule

8:30 A.M.	Arrival and greeting, play
9 A.M.	Circle meeting and project discussions
9:20–10:40 A.M.	Children's choice, project work, art, play
10:40 A.M.	Snack together
11 A.M.	Outdoors
11:30 A.M.	Prepare for lunch (bathroom, washing, setting table)
11:45 A.M.–12:45 P.M.	Group meal
12:45–1:30 P.M.	Rest time
1:30 P.M.	Snack
2–3:20 P.M.	Play, choice, art, project work
3:20 P.M.	Clean up, come together, story
3:45 P.M.	Outside, play
5 P.M.	Pick up, good-byes

wall of windows with wide ledges allows for plenty of natural lighting. The ledges are lined with pinecones, acorns, and smooth river stones. These collections of materials were found by the children on a recent nature walk.

In the middle of one of the tables, there is a book of bridges, opened to an overhead view of the cables on the Golden Gate Bridge in San Francisco. Two children are seated around the book with large, thick paper and a variety of pencils and markers. They are intently focused on drawing their own bridges, attending to the shapes and lines of the cables and the overhead perspective. One teacher, who is sitting with them, shows the children how to use a smudging technique with their fingers to create soft shadows.

At another table, three children have gathered a variety of pieces of flat wooden sticks, string, toothpicks, and brown river stones. They are deep in debate about how to create three-dimensional models of their own bridge. They are talking about how to make it stand tall enough to span the stones. Another teacher is cutting ample pieces of clay for two children to use to sculpt more bridges. Three other children are gathered on the floor near a window, where they are working on a weaving they began yesterday. Integrated into the alternating strips are twigs, leaves, pinecones, and other found items. The children chose soft hues of greens and blues for their strips to represent the way the colors of the water and the grass looked when they blended at the riverbank on a recent field trip to a nearby footbridge. They talk as they work, animatedly describing qualities of each shell, seaweed, and twig as though it had a personality.

"This little pinecone is a baby, let's tie it on by its mother."

"This piece of wood looks like it is dancing. Turning, turning, turning." The child moves the small piece of wood in a spiraling motion.

"This leaf is blowing bubbles under the water. Blub, blub, blub." The child runs her hand along the bumpy surface of the large leaf.

The building of a personal relationship with the things they encounter in their world is considered a valuable part of the learning process and is encouraged by Reggian teachers. "We believe in the power of the relationships children create with their world," the teacher explains. "It's not strange that they talk about pinecones and twigs as if they had personalities. To the children, they do. They are living elements in their daily lives, characters in their stories. This personal relationship makes their learning, their engagement with their world, so much more meaningful to them." The children and teachers will continue their explorations of building bridges as they work toward designing and building their own footbridge in the play yard. This kind of long-term project is fueled by the children's interest and motivation to process and represent new experiences in their world. In many ways, the projects undertaken by Reggio children align with the principles presented in the project approach, as with this bridge project.

The Schools of Reggio Emilia, Italy: History, Influences, and Relationships

This brief snapshot of school community life in a U.S. Reggio-inspired center illustrates the practical application of the core values of Reggio Emilia schools:

- Children's rights and capabilities
- Collaboration among all members of the school community
- Relationships among children, teachers, families, experiences, and materials

Children's rights and capabilities are respected through the sharing of power and control over classroom experiences. This respect for children includes teachers allowing children to fully participate in all facets of classroom life and drive the topic and length of group projects. Children are viewed as powerful and capable of generating complex, meaningful ideas. Through careful, systematic observations and recording of children's conversations, teachers pick up on key topics of interest to the children. Using this information, they may present materials or plan a trip around the unfolding interests. In this way they are able to guide children's explorations and enhance their natural curiosity about their world.

Children are also validated as unique individuals within a social group. They are provided with space and time to work alone and in small groups and also to come together as a community. Most of their classroom time is spent working in naturally forming groups. Teachers encourage collaboration through the design of the classroom (group tables, for example). They also embody a collaborative spirit by working together as a centerwide team and with the families and the community. In the bridge project, for example, a parent was enlisted to help with the construction of the children's life-size bridge. A contractor by trade, he was knowledgeable about tools and architecture. As a father, he was keenly aware of safety issues and supportive of having the children take an active role in planning and construction. He continued his collaborative relationship by working with the children on other projects.

The relationships children create with peers, adults, their environment, and materials are viewed as the very heart of education. The relationships among teachers, children, parents, and administrators are valued and promoted through active interaction and open dialogue. Collaborations between school staff and parents are firmly ingrained in the school culture, and parents are viewed as valuable resources and supports. Parents are routinely welcomed to the center for open-house events and are continually participating in project activities.

Italian Influences: A Cultural Context of Caring

Successfully translating Reggio Emilia values into the unique U.S. educational context requires careful, critical reflection and a rethinking of traditional norms of practice. This is no small task for new teachers, although it is one that is worth your effort on behalf of all children. Many U.S. educators have tried to import the REA into their classrooms, with varying success. Teachers in Reggio are the first to caution that the importance of cultural context cannot be overlooked. Their unique cultural surrounding is foundational to their approach.

Italy is a country with a long tradition of appreciating beauty, art, food, family, and communication (Edwards, 2003). Architecturally, the country is filled with simple, ancient dwellings and churches still in use, as well as cosmopolitan cities demonstrating new and ornate designs. Geographically diverse, the mountainous north falls away to rolling, fertile hills and ends in the hot, rocky southern "boot" and the island of Sicily, both encircled by the brilliance of the Mediterranean Sea. Beauty surrounds Italians in the picturesque countrysides, the plethora of museums, and the murals and mosaics in local churches. It also lives in the warm closeness of family, the heart of the Italian way of life.

Of utmost importance in Italian culture is the celebration of the family as the core of any community. Children are celebrated as the promise of a beautiful future. Given this context it is no surprise that the schools are carefully and thoughtfully designed to be places where children and adults alike cultivate a sense of wonder as they learn to look at, listen to, and feel the world around them from infinite perspectives (Caldwell, 1997).

Historical Perspectives: A Community Continues Its Tradition

During World War II, Italians witnessed firsthand the tragedy and decimation of the war. The citizens of Reggio Emilia played a significant role in the anti-Nazi-Fascist movement. They were active in working to restore order from the chaos that followed the end of the war (Caldwell, 1997). Spurred on by a vision and dedication to reconstruct their society as a place of freedom, equality, and community, a group of parents set out to build new schools and a new world for their children (Gandini, 1997). Using proceeds from the sale of abandoned war equipment, parents secured the resources needed to begin forming their schools. In 1945 the first parent-run preschool of the common people opened in Reggio Emilia (Gandini, 2002).

Loris Malaguzzi, then a teacher and student of education and psychology, soon became committed to the effort. He was impressed with the passion of the parents and attuned to the vision of education as a force for social change (Day, 2001). With Malaguzzi's organization, additional schools soon opened. After nearly two decades of advocacy, in 1963 the city of Reggio Emilia instituted support for opening the first municipal preschool and within 5 years had played a major role in establishing a national early education system (New, 2003). Continuing a tradition of reflection and study, the Reggio teachers remained active scholars in education and related fields. Influenced by theorists such as Piaget, Vygotsky, Bruner, and Dewey, they became involved in exploring and promoting innovations in education, which garnered public support in the 1950s and 1960s (Gandini, 1997).

In 1968, national legislation was passed in Italy providing for public funding for preschools for all children from 3 to 6 years of age (Hewitt, 2001). This public funding structure is very different from that of most preschools in the United States. Adequate funding for facilities, programs, and teacher salaries is an ongoing challenge for many U.S. early childhood centers today. Many teachers feel hopeless about being able to apply Reggio principles in other contexts, particularly without ample resources, but many programs are currently finding inspiration from Reggio and successfully embracing the spirit of their approach. In many ways, the Reggio community relies on the creative use of available resources, even when they are scant. Recall their humble beginnings financed through the sale of cast-off war equipment and fueled by the efforts of volunteers and their reliance on "found materials" to stock classroom shelves.

Amid the backdrop of the grassroots efforts to create a place of beauty and learning for their children, the schools of Reggio Emilia continue to self-reflect and evolve in pursuit of that goal. They remain fueled by the dedication and involvement of parents. Now with more than 36 preschools and infant-toddler centers, roughly 50% of the city's preschool children and 35% of infants and toddlers are enrolled in the municipal schools (Hewitt, 2001; New, 2003). Nearly 99% of the young children in Reggio Emilia attend some kind of schooling (municipal, private, or parochial) (Gandini, 2002). These impressive numbers demonstrate a firmly entrenched family and community commitment to optimizing children's development. This is one city that truly embodies the African proverb, "It takes a village to raise a child."

In response to a growing interest in their schools, in 1981 Malaguzzi and the Reggio Emilia school community created an exhibit illustrating the spirit of their school. Echoing their belief that children have multiple ways of communicating, they titled the exhibit "The Hundred Languages of Children." The exhibit traveled internationally, and along with the documentary book, brought international attention to the philosophy, culture, and practice of Reggio schools (Edwards, Gandini, & Forman, 1996). Malaguzzi's final effort to disseminate information about the Reggio schools came with the 1994 formation of the Reggio Children organization. Malaguzzi died the same year (Gandini, 1997). Reggio Children continues to promote the REA through books and videos and sponsors annual study tours to the Reggio schools. Through all these efforts, their guiding principles of collaboration and emphasis on the value of relationships are promoted and encouraged among professionals in the field.

Guiding Philosophical Framework: Capturing an Evolving Perspective

Reggio teachers consider their current philosophy to be a reflection and reinvention of innovations in education. They continue to be inspired by a variety of theorists and borrow pieces from traditional and contemporary educational approaches. You are doing the same thing here by exploring a variety of theories, frameworks, methods, and approaches and deciding what aspects of each work with your own personal philosophy of education. The guiding framework in Reggio schools is heavily influenced by social constructivist theory, which is embodied in their belief that learning is based on relationships (Edwards, 2003). The key principles that were the motivation for starting the schools remain foundational to current practice. The REA is "a tightly connected, coherent philosophy, in which each point influences, and is influenced by all the others" (Gandini, 2002, p. 16). Thus, the interrelatedness of the REA does not lend itself well to having its parts separated from the vision of the whole. However, a more in-depth look at the key elements of the underlying views on children, teachers, and the community, within the context of the program as a whole, serves to illustrate guiding views.

View of Children To fully appreciate the REA, visitors are first introduced to their image of the child. Reggio Emilia educators validate all children as competent, resourceful, and curious (Gandini, 2002). Inspiring everything Reggio teachers do is an immense respect for children's potential to

- Interact with their world (people, events, and materials)
- Develop personal, meaningful relationships in their world
- Construct new, complex meanings and knowledge

The environmental design, the selection of materials, and the interactions and guidance in activities are all interrelated to an utmost respect and appreciation for the capabilities of children (Bredekamp, 1993).

A visit to a Reggio infant-toddler center will reveal toddlers sculpting with wire, clay, and small beads. These materials would be forbidden in U.S. centers on the basis of safety. Likewise, preschool children, in investigation of a large lion statue in a town square, freely climb atop the 6- or 7-foot statue. They want to see what the top looks like, feel what it is like to ride on the lion, and experience the lion's perspective (Reggio Children, 1980). Reggio teachers support them in their interest. Concerns over safety would prevent U.S. teachers from allowing children to experience such perspectives (Tarr, 2003).

Overarching all teaching practice is an emphasis on fostering children's learning to look at their world and see it in as many ways as possible. In essence, children are encouraged to look at, and really *see*, their world. It is this carefully trained eye, tied closely to an

Light tables are used to explore light and shadow and create tabletop shadow compositions.

inner vision and imagination, that allows children to engage in deeply involved explorations and relationships. Reggio teachers remain present, involved, and ready to provide support and guidance as needed, but they make every effort to interfere as little as possible in the work of the child. Any such interference would deny the child's role as a powerful and capable individual (Reggio Children, 1994).

Teacher's Roles   Teachers are viewed as partners within children's learning, not as the external forces directing it. They provoke children's thoughts, ask open-ended questions, display materials that satisfy children's requests or extend their thinking (called provocations), and continuously observe children's progress (Caldwell, 1997). Their participation may be more or less active, depending on the stage of children's processing at the moment. In addition to facilitating projects, the other two primary roles of the teacher—observing and listening to the children—define their level of activity and nature of involvement in children's activities (Danko-McGhee & Slutsky, 2003). View teachers guiding children's discussion and learning at MyEducationLab and identify strategies that you can use to enhance children's active learning.

When they are not facilitating children's project work, teachers are carefully documenting the unfolding process of the children. Even when they are engaged in children's work, they often use tape recorders to capture children's dialogues to be transcribed later. The important learning revealed in listening to children's dialogue is always present in the teacher's mind (Caldwell, 1997). In this way, teachers also act as researchers. They are continually gathering data, analyzing it, and reflecting on it in collaboration with other teachers and the children themselves (Gandini, 2002; Hughes, 2007).

The guiding principle of "education as relationships" also holds true for teachers. Teachers work in close relationship to children, fellow teachers, parents, and the community. They engage in a reflective self-discovery learning process alongside the children. Special time is set aside in the regular schedule for teachers, *atelieristi* (art directors), and

MyEducationLab

Go to the Assignments and Activities section of Topic 6: Curriculum Planning in the MyEducationLab for your course and complete the activity entitled *Using Guided Learning in a Unit of Study*. Focus your observation on the role of the teacher and what strategies she uses to guide the children's learning and thinking.

Light Tables

One of the materials employed in the Reggio Emilia schools as a provocation is the light table. In the classroom visit you read about the overhead projector and screen setup. Projectors, screens, and light tables are used to provide children with an interesting space to create compositions focusing on shadow, shape, light, dark, and levels from opaqueness to transparency. By placing items on the lighted surface (either lighted from above or below, like the light table), children are able to focus on the bulk or shape, not all the three-dimensional details. This is just one way that materials provoke children's visual perception and promote aesthetic development.

Pedagogisti

The pedagogical coordinators work as part of the collaborative team to guide and support learning activities throughout the center. Their role is to help teachers extend children's learning experiences and projects as far as they can go in meaningful, worthy directions.

pedagogisti (pedagogical coordinators) to come together to discuss their practice and the children's work. These honest, open exchanges often include confrontation and conflict over certain issues. However, the culture of respect and collaboration encourages these open dialogues as being necessary to the work of reflection and evolution. Suggestions are met with openness, just as they are offered in respect.

This level of passionate, respectful exchange, a natural part of Italian culture, is not routinely experienced in U.S. culture (Caldwell, 1997). Imagine yourself facing a conflict with a colleague at work. It probably does not conjure up pleasant feelings and may be something you would prefer to avoid. Reggio teachers embrace the potential for growth that is inherent in conflicts, and they negotiate through them respectfully and openly. This perspective allows teachers to learn from each other just as conflicts in the classroom can be great opportunities for children to grow. Remember how Piaget felt that cognitive conflict was essential for development? This perspective certainly rings true for Reggio teachers.

Weaving provocation.

Weaving Provocation

The teachers in the Reggio-inspired classroom visit noticed their children were becoming interested in entwining strings. They would twist them and showed the beginnings of weavings. Wanting to support and extend this, the teachers decided to create a weaving provocation. They found a beautiful storybook about a South American grandmother and granddaughter who create elaborate traditional woven blankets and read the book to the children. The teachers placed the book next to a wall-hanging weaving station. At the base of the frame on the wall, they placed a basket with a variety of string, ribbon, fabric strips, twigs, leaves, beads, feathers, and other crafting items. They placed this display in the hallway where all the children would have access to it. They showed the children where the display was and encouraged them to visit and add to the communal weaving. Over the course of several weeks, they noticed that the weaving was growing as children from all the rooms added pieces here and there. When the space was full, they talked about what they had created, took some photos, and then unwove it so that they could start a new work.

Likewise, open dialogues are fostered with parents through informal exchanges during the day or meetings scheduled to discuss pedagogy, children's work, and community issues. The heart of these dialogues, indeed the heart of all endeavors in Reggio schools, is to be in continual reflection in the ongoing effort of self-improvement. Teachers' pedagogy of listening promotes reciprocal relationships with children just as it does with fellow teachers and parents. With the dedication to providing the best possible experience for children at the heart of their work, teachers are motivated to remain open, collaborative, and mutually supportive of each other (Gandini, 2002).

Most teachers in Reggio Emilia begin their work with minimal preservice education, and the schools are viewed as laboratories where teachers are learning as well as the children. This is viewed as desirable because all Reggio teachers work together and, in effect, all new teachers are mentored. In Reggio schools, the right kind of spirit, heart, and attitude is as important as formal credentials. Within the context of the collaborative school community and through professional development and experience, Reggio teachers develop an advanced degree of understanding of children's development and learning (Bredekamp, 1993). It was only in 1998 that Italy passed a law requiring college-level teacher education for early childhood teachers (New, 2003).

View of Children's Learning Process   Teachers believe that children's learning is developed primarily through discourse, representations, and relationships. Reggio teachers operate within the philosophy that the focus of education must be on the social context of the child's world. This means that the child's relationships with peers, teachers, family, and the community shape his or her learning (Caldwell, 1997; Krechevsky & Stork, 2000). Opportunities for small-group investigations and discourses are continually presented by teachers and propelled by the children. Even the architecture of the building prompts dialogues: Small windows join adjacent rooms and a central communal play space, called the **piazza** in Italian. It is during small-group exchanges that Reggio teachers anticipate challenges and

Piazza

The town square at the center of the village. In this case, the communal gathering place at the heart of the preschool center.

cognitive conflicts. These settings prompt the group members to explore concepts more deeply to create a new understanding (Gandini, 2002).

Throughout each day, fluid conversations happen everywhere. Children converse with each other, discuss things with teachers, and also create conversations with and through their representations. Keep in mind that relationships overarch everything. Relationships spring from communication—from dialogues. Dialogues are supported through the opportunities for multiple representations and modes of communication: painting, drawing, dance, shadow theatre, sculpture, discussion, music, and dramatic play. Each of these expressive activities allows the children to process their own experiences as well as share their thoughts with others. Through their art, the children dialogue with their ideas as well as communicate with those who view their work.

The spiraling process of verbal dialogue, graphic representation, more verbal dialogue, and so on, is the communication cycle through which children act on information. It is through this cycle that they are deconstructing and reconstructing as they process and represent. Children are thus empowered in their world by being given a myriad of languages through which to construct meaning and to communicate with themselves and others. Remember the view of "the hundred languages of children."

Reggio teachers believe that it is through graphic representation that children create order out of the chaos of new experiences (Reggio Children, 1994). You, too, might find that making notes, sketches, maps, or diagrams helps you make sense of new information. On one level, you might make those kinds of graphic representations to keep track of information or remember things. On a deeper level, you might use graphic representations to rethink something or reflect on your understanding using a language other than words.

In Reggio schools, long-term projects emerging from the children's interests are the primary vehicles for classroom learning activities. Ample space and time are given for children's unfolding projects. Because children are the directors of their group projects, they are empowered as negotiators of their own learning with teachers reflectively and thoughtfully supporting and guiding their explorations (Edwards, 2003). Just as in the project approach discussed in Chapter 8, Reggio teachers believe that good projects (Reggio Children, 1994)

- Have a high level of personal interest
- Are thoughtfully carried out by the children with intention
- Revolve around the potential for developing relationships with people and materials

Documentation: A Tool for Assessment and Planning   As projects unfold, teachers capture children's processes and developing and changing ideas through careful documentation. The documentation sources (photos, videos, drawings, transcriptions of dialogues) are then used to promote teachers' and children's reflections on their process. This, in turn, leads to new directions for investigation, discoveries of thinking errors, and future planning. The use of documentation as a reflecting and planning tool differs from the common U.S. practice of using documentation primarily for evaluation purposes (Turner & Krechevsky, 2003). One step beyond simply using documentation for teachers' planning purposes, artifacts from classroom experiences are used by the children themselves as tools for reflection and future planning (Warash et al., 2008). So just as teachers review samples of children's work to "see" their learning, children are able to do the same. The importance of careful documentation is evident in the Reggio teachers' belief that only through collecting and reflecting on relevant documents or traces of children's work does learning become visible and knowledge construction possible (Rinaldi, 2001).

Documentation Panels

Remember from Chapter 8 that documentation panels are carefully designed displays that chronicle the progress of the children's projects and the process they went through in their explorations. The panels include photos of the children working, work samples, drawings, paintings, or other graphic representations, teacher's notes, and transcriptions of dialogue. Capturing children's dialogue is a primary way teachers glimpse children's unfolding thought processing, learn about children's interests, and glean insight into future possibilities (Tarr, 2003).

Because of the emphasis on the whole child and the complex processes unfolding within them, paper-and-pencil tests are inappropriate for assessments. Teachers seek to capture richly detailed, personally meaningful pictures of the children at various stages of learning and growing. These assessment goals require much more in-depth observations and conversations than any simple test could provide. If you have ever been frustrated because you felt that you knew more than a single test could accurately reflect, you probably can understand the Reggio teachers' choice of authentic assessment techniques. They would agree with you that you are more than a number.

View of the School Environment, Parents, and Community   Reggio teachers believe strongly in the instructive power of the learning environment. They view the environment as the child's third teacher (after parents and teachers) (Gandini, 1997). Beauty and complexity as key components permeate the Reggio classrooms. The learning spaces are carefully designed with two overarching goals in mind (Edwards, 2003):

- Encourage children to sense their world through new perspectives (see things differently, hear new sounds or combinations of sounds, think about something familiar in a new way, etc.)
- Provoke their thinking, questioning, hypothesizing, representing, and sharing

Much of the children's project work revolves around the life of their surrounding community. Viewed as interrelated to life at school or at home, the school grounds and surrounding city often serve as the spark of interest for a project. Children have become entranced by the birds in the play yard, the mother cat and kittens outside their window, the streets and buildings on their way around town, the crowds in the streets, and everyday events like trips to the market (Edwards et al., 1996; Reggio Children, 1980). An Alaskan Eskimo village preschool using a Reggio-inspired approach embarked on a journey exploring how life in their village had changed over generations, and the children's investigative journey brought them to the tradition of fishing. The children explored frozen lakes, fishing tools, stories from families, and the rich history of this core part of life in their village (Hughes, 2007). The connection between their learning environment and life outside the classroom is viewed as an interrelated, interdependent one. Reggio teachers use these connections to maintain an emphasis on education as a series of relationships.

IN YOUR OWN WORDS

Now that you have explored the key principles that underscore the spirit and practices in the schools of Reggio Emilia, do any of these principles and practices seem applicable in your own work or future work? Are there any facets of Reggio practices that you think would pose challenges for early childhood educators in the United States? Take a moment to reflect on the observations you have made of early childhood classrooms and compare them to your developing vision of Reggio schools. What similarities or differences can you see? What changes could you imagine making to either setting that would improve the beauty, learning, and overall quality of the children's experiences? Keep these ideas in mind as you read about the applications of the Reggio Emilia approach in U.S. schools.

Challenges to Reggio-Inspired Practice in the United States: Lost in the Translation?

One of the overarching premises of the REA is valuing and respecting the unique context of children's lives. Much of the framework of the REA, as well as its success in garnering support and respect for the framework, comes from working in concert with the beliefs, values, and goals of the surrounding community. To simplify the REA into a checklist of beliefs and technical elements would be contrary to the spirit of the schools, which focus on the unique cultural context of the school community. Attempting to simply transplant the Reggio framework into a U.S. context is counterproductive, futile, and strongly cautioned against by Reggio advocates (Linn, 2001). This contextualization of learning experiences within the community is often a challenge to appropriately applying a Reggio approach in other cultures. Understanding the REA as a flexible framework, a system of beliefs, and an example of a collaborative process is necessary to learn useful lessons from the approach.

REA: Is a Philosophy, Not a Curriculum

The first mistake many visitors to Reggio schools make is assuming that what happens in Reggio schools is a curriculum. The term *curriculum* has been defined as "an organized framework that delineates the content that children are to learn, the process through which children achieve identified curricular goals, what teachers do to help children achieve these goals, and the context in which teaching and learning occur" (Bredekamp & Rosengrant, 1992). The REA is fluid, emergent, dynamic, and responsive to the unique context of the children's lives and open to changes based on teachers' continued observation and reflection of children. There is not the kind of recipe for practice that would be the hallmark of a prescribed, preplanned curriculum.

Instead of viewing their program as a curriculum, Reggio educators suggest that the core beliefs and guiding principles be used as a means of generating reflection and dialogue among other educators in their own pursuit of a uniquely responsive approach (Goffin, 2000). When the parts that are interdependent and intertwined within the context of the school culture are viewed as a whole, valuable lessons and possibilities for inspiring U.S. practice emerge.

REA Requires Family Involvement

One of the most impressive characteristics of the schools of Reggio Emilia is the exceptionally strong support and interaction from parents and the community. Reggio teachers believe that parents have rights, just as children do. Parents are respected for being their children's first teachers and for having the right to participate actively and freely in their children's educational lives. This open collaboration is viewed as vital to children's emotional security and requisite for optimal learning (Gandini, 2002).

With its very foundation built on the tireless efforts of parents in the design of both physical space and philosophical beliefs, it is not surprising that parents remain highly involved and respected in the school collaborative. This level of involvement and respect may be a foreign concept to many American educators. Building bridges toward a true collaboration among school, home, and community is a challenge, but the possibilities are also there when schools and families build relationships of trust, mutual respect, and a shared goal of providing the very best care and education of their children. This collaborative relationship is even more important when working with children with special rights, as they are called in Reggio schools. For those children who may need adaptations, special attention, or modifications of some kind, close communication with families is imperative and can make all the difference in creating a fully inclusive classroom community (Gilman, 2007). The Reggio approach lends itself well to meaningful inclusion due to the emphasis on all children as competent, powerful individuals.

In several ways, the principles of Head Start programs are similar to Reggio principles. Both Head Start and Reggio programs share the following key principles:

- An eclectic mix of theoretical perspectives, including Montessori, Piaget, Vygotsky, Dewey, Froebel, and research from the High/Scope foundation, is synthesized to create a unique approach to educating young children.

- Continued self-reflection and critical analysis are viewed as necessary to keep teachers and programs current with research in the field.

- Staff are encouraged to learn from other related fields to ensure a comprehensive, holistic picture of children's learning in the context of their lives (psychology, social work, health).

- Space is reserved so children with handicaps can be fully included.

- An emphasis on family involvement is embedded as a core component of the program.

In the case of Head Start, parental involvement is mandated by national program guidelines (USDH HS, 2005). Some Head Start programs are also making changes to their program structure and practice in ways that align with Reggio principles (Hughes, 2007). Although teachers and parents report some challenges related to understanding about Reggio principles, many also report satisfaction with the changes in the program and their children's choices and interest in school. However, it is essential that teachers maintain a high level of communication with parents about changes in practice to ensure successful implementation of the REA (McClow & Gillespie, 1998).

REA Is About Context

Ultimately, the lessons learned from Reggio Emilia concern context. The schools of Reggio Emilia enjoy a long history that is rich with the eloquent interplay of parents and teachers working together to create beautiful, enriching spaces for their children. They are founded on collaboration and a singular focus on creating the absolute best environment for children. Housed in a culture that historically values the family as a whole (children in particular) and is rich in beauty and generous in resources, Reggio schools thrive in part because of their context and history. Supported by national funding legislation, parent involvement, and staff commitment to ongoing self-reflection, the cultural context is one of the key relationships that shapes and perpetuates Reggio schools.

A major part of the REA is the validation of the context of children's lives and an unwavering effort to integrate that context into the learning environment (Strozzi, 2001). This emphasis on emergent, authentic learning does not necessarily align with a reliance on predetermined outcomes and universal standards. U.S. education systems rely heavily on the use of standards and preset curricula as tools to plan and evaluate learning experiences for children. This process of planning based on end results poses a real challenge to embracing an emergent learning model (New, 2003). Implicit in an emergent model is a respect for children's interests, motivations, and inner processes. Power is shared, and teachers focus on carefully listening to children's words and rhythms to guide learning. This level of responsiveness requires a great deal of ongoing reflecting and planning and takes up a fair amount of time.

For example, Reggio teachers embed 6 hours a week into their schedules for collaborative teacher planning and discussion (Gandini, 2002). That's almost an entire day's worth of hours. The time involved often feels like an insurmountable challenge for already stressed U.S. educators. It remains a key component, however, because emergent models take a great deal of planning and guiding despite seeming on the surface to require less planning on the teacher's part. The Reggio emphasis on taking time for thoughtful discussions and planning is another way of embodying its core belief that education is deeply entwined within social relationships.

In a broader view, U.S. early childhood professionals are continually battling for national validation and recognition, usually in the form of funding and professional credibility. Many caring, capable teachers leave the field, feeling frustrated, disempowered, and unable to effect positive change (Linn, 2001). This disillusionment arises when the divide between motivation to provide nurturing educational experiences and external pressure to conform to sometimes questionable standards feels unbridgeable. This negative cycle contrasts sharply with the Reggio approach. In Italy, early childhood education funding, extended family leave laws, and equal pay for men and women have been part of national legislation since the late 1960s (Gandini, 1997). Also, teachers there are part of a culture that respects them as thoughtful, deliberate, caring professionals (New, 2003).

Within this idyllic context, it is easy to dismiss the REA as simply not feasible within the U.S. context. Even Reggio teachers are clear in their caution that the REA is not a recipe or a prescribed curriculum to be copied and transplanted elsewhere (Linn, 2001). Nevertheless, the spirit, core values, and guiding processes of the REA hold valuable lessons for all early childhood educators. At the very heart of the REA are the processes of

- Social interaction
- Meaningful engagement
- Thoughtful reflection
- Respectful collaboration

Think about these four key principles as elements of any learning process for a moment. Perhaps these are processes through which you yourself learn best: working in groups, sharing personally interesting and meaningful discussions, investigating authentic topics through hands-on activities, seeing connections to your previous experiences and learning, and being free to ask questions, wonder, try, and succeed. These are worthy endeavors for any student or teacher and are the inspirations educators from around the world are finding in the schools of Reggio Emilia. Watch a teacher in action as she scaffolds and extends children's learning in the block area at MyEducationLab.

Inspired Applications: How Some U.S. Educators Are Making the Leap

Over the past few decades, U.S. educators have become increasingly interested in the practice and philosophy of the schools of Reggio Emilia. The intensely emotional response to the practices and agreement with the core values has sparked a passion and commitment that are driving a growing movement to integrate the REA in U.S. preschools and elementary schools. Preschools are demonstrating success in embracing the Reggio spirit through the translation and reinvention of key components:

- Careful meshing between school and community
- Validation of the reflective, analytical, and collaborative nature of teaching practices
- Willingness to take risks and learn from failures

Embracing core values and deriving inspiration from the beauty, relationships, and energy of the schools of Reggio Emilia are fitting ways to honor the commitment to provide children with the highest quality education possible.

Suggestions From the Field: Embracing the Spirit

The self-reflective exercise many U.S. teachers have engaged in since exploring the REA offers a starting point for the journey. First, educators must carefully consider their own vision of the child and what implications this has for their practice. Recognizing how deeply entrenched traditional deficit models of children and transmission models of teaching can be is an important part of freeing negative images and reenvisioning children, learning, and teaching in a more positive, collaborative light.

IN YOUR OWN WORDS

One way to start this awareness process is to consider well-known metaphors used to describe children and learning, such as children are like sponges, the early childhood center should be like a garden, or children are like angels. While reflecting on these metaphors, certain inherent implications may emerge. Regarding children as sponges may imply that they soak up their surroundings passively. How does this fit with a view that they actively deconstruct and construct their environment, experiences, and ideas in their formation of new knowledge?

If early childhood centers should be like gardens, the message may be that children need protected spaces in which they should be left to grow, although the role of the teacher is not so clear. Viewing children as angels may imply an innocence and a romantic notion that hinders their capacity to benefit from negotiating conflict, working through problems,

MyEducationLab

Go to the Assignments and Activities section in Topic 2: Child Development/ Theories in the MyEducationLab for your course and complete the activity entitled *Promoting Children's Play*. What strategies does the teacher use to promote collaborative play?

constructing knowledge, and being present in the realities of life. When children are viewed as powerful, capable, intelligent partners, possibilities arise for engaging in complex, authentic, worthy, meaningful experiences as part of a social group. Continuing to reflect critically on your beliefs is the first step in shaping or reshaping your practice.

Reflective Practice, Resourceful Practice

In reflecting on practice, teachers must consider what messages the environment conveys. The level of attention to detail (color, design, material selection and placement, aesthetics) sends a palpable message as to a teacher's level of commitment to children. Realistically, learning spaces may not be ideal homelike structures with lots of windows and light. The realities of early childhood practice are that centers operate wherever they can. The suggestion to carefully construct the environment does not imply building new centers or equipping classrooms with fancy, expensive furniture and materials. Resourcefulness is the first skill in any good teacher's toolbox.

An attention to detail, thoughtful design, and attractive arrangement of materials can happen within small budgets and architectural constraints. It is about the intention put forth. It is about the deliberate environmental design meant to convey a message of invitation, engagement, and genuine interest. This is possible with recycled or secondhand materials enriched by simple found objects like collections of natural resources (sticks, stones, shells, leaves, nuts). In fact, interesting displays and combinations of natural materials spark children's interests more than just being handed a fancy toy. By participating in children's experiments and explorations of the world around them, teachers affirm the message that children are valued, respected, and empowered. Encouraging and facilitating children's representations through a variety of "languages" gives children the tools they need to process

Displaying children's three-dimensional work, like block sculpture and branch/gauze sculptures, in interesting places sparks visual interest.

information and experiences more fully and deeply and to communicate ideas more skillfully. The goals of increased ability to process and communicate are timely and meaningful for all children, regardless of where they are living.

A final suggestion is to make connections and relationships with fellow teachers and parents. These are your partners in the quest to create the most beautiful, highest quality learning experiences for children. Relying on parents as resources for information and connections to the community expands children's learning. It also validates that the context of children's lives includes school, home, and community. As parents participate in children's learning, they should also participate in the documentation-reflection process. By engaging in a collective documentation-reflection process, each member of the team continues to see children and his or her own teaching from new perspectives (Grieshaber & Hatch, 2003). This process of seeing things in a new way is the heart of the REA. It is the result of careful, deliberate, collaborative reflection on the endless possibilities for improving practice for all children.

Conclusion

The schools of Reggio Emilia operate within a unique context that also shares many similarities with U.S. ideals and practice. There are challenges but also rich possibilities in exploring the REA as a way to reflect on and improve the status of U.S. early childhood education. To fully understand and successfully apply Reggio practices in U.S. schools requires that teachers explore lessons from Reggio within the context of the culture of their own area. By examining their beliefs about parents' role in schools and promoting reciprocal partnerships with families, U.S. teachers can begin the process of forging new, more open relationships between parents and schools. Although Reggio practice cannot be simply transplanted to foreign communities, the spirit of partnership, the emphasis on relationships, and the commitment to children's rights are all goals that can make any program more successful.

Acknowledging the REA as an example of a nurturing, emergent, collaborative, reflective, reciprocal learning environment allows educators to explore Reggio traditions as a catalyst for change in their own programs. The true inspiration of the schools of Reggio Emilia rests in the ability of outside educators to embrace the spirit of the approach. The spirit is one that echoes all educators' goal of providing all children with a beautiful, respectful place. It celebrates the importance of social relationships and engenders meaningful, collaborative learning experiences for children and teachers alike.

REFLECTION QUESTIONS: LOOKING BACK AND LOOKING AHEAD

We hope this chapter has made you think about your own vision of young children, your beliefs about family partnerships, and the opportunities inherent in exploring innovative programs from around the globe. Consider the following questions in light of what you have read in this and other chapters:

1. List the core values of the Reggio Emilia approach. List your own core values relating to your own work with young children (current or future). Which elements are similar and which are different?

2. How did you determine your own values and beliefs about education?

3. What challenges do you think U.S. educators face in applying the REA in their own schools? How can these be overcome?

4. After thinking about the environment and experiences in the schools of Reggio Emilia, what ideas do you have for infusing beauty and aesthetics into young children's lives in your own classroom?

SUMMARY

The municipal schools of Reggio Emilia have earned a great deal of international attention in recent decades from educators interested in exploring innovative approaches to teaching young children. Nestled among the picturesque countryside of northern Italy and imbued with the traditions of beauty and family, the Reggio Emilia schools began as the vision of a group of dedicated parents and continue as a collaborative effort on behalf of all children.

After the decimation resulting from World War II, a small group of families bonded together in defiance of then-current Nazi-Fascist regimes and created a school of hope, promise, possibility, and beauty. Their mission was to create a better future for their children through education. Loris Malaguzzi became involved in the growing effort, and by the 1960s additional schools were opening and legislation was being written affording public funding for preprimary schools. Currently, more than three dozen infant-toddler schools and preschools are operating within the city of Reggio Emilia.

The Reggio Emilia approach holds several core values at its heart:

- Children are strong, powerful, and capable.
- Children learn through active, social, constructive processes.
- Art and beauty should be the foundations of the educational environment.
- Families are essential partners in the education process.
- Relationships are the foundation of learning.

Children in Reggio Emilia schools learn primarily through investigating emergent projects, through dialogues, and through representation and reflection experiences. Their projects stem from their daily lives, their surrounding environment and community, and their everyday experiences. The primary roles of the teachers are to observe and listen to children, to provoke their thinking, and to document their processes by collecting representative works and dialogues of the children. Teachers routinely engage in observations and reflections of the children at work and in reflective discussions on their own teaching methods.

MyEducationLab

Go to the Assignments and Activities section of Topic 4: Observation/ Assessment in the MyEducationLab for your course and complete the activity entitled *Opportunities for Authentic Assessment.* Consider the teacher's assessment methods.

Application Activities

On the Web: MyEducationLab Go to the Video Examples section of Topic 7: Curriculum/ Content Areas in the MyEducationLab for your course and watch the video entitled *Creativity and the Arts in a Study of Birds.* Keeping the Reggio-inspired emphasis on the arts as a valuable means of representing knowledge and expression, respond to and discuss the following questions in small groups:

1. What can the children's art tell us about their learning and thinking?
2. What can teachers learn about children's development from observing them as they create their artwork?
3. How do you think children's learning was impacted by including real-life birds in the classroom as they created their art?

In Class Think about metaphors you have heard or other phrases that come to your mind that describe young children. While working in small groups, write down at least three ways that children and learning are described. Discuss what these phrases or words might be subtly conveying and how they might be impacting practice. Select your own image or metaphor and create a visual representation to share your image of the child.

In the Field With a heavy emphasis on aesthetics, or art experiences, Reggio schools seek to hone children's ability to really look at the world around them from many different perspectives. One activity you can do with children is to use 2-inch × 2-inch viewers to focus children's looking. Use an empty slide holder or make a viewer from a 2-inch × 2-inch card with a 1-inch square cut out of the middle.

Try it yourself first. Hold your viewer about 12 inches from your eye. Close one eye and look through the open space in the center of your viewer, focusing your attention on just the contents of your viewer. Look carefully and make some mental notes about what you see. Note shapes, lines, colors, forms, and so on. Once you have really looked, take 10 minutes to sketch what you see in your viewer. Do not try to reconstruct what the portion in your viewer is supposed to be (a table, a window) but rather just re-create the lines, shapes, colors, shades, and so on, from your viewer as though those parts existed separately from the whole. This exercise allows you to see something familiar in a new way, as a new piece of your world. It also takes your focus away from drawing a table or a window and prompts you simply to explore the composition of this isolated series of lines, shapes, and shades. Seeing a small part of something whole in your world makes you stop and really look at an item that you glance at or see only as a whole every day. In other words, you see it from a new perspective through your viewer. Keep refocusing your viewer around your world and see just how much you can see!

For Your Portfolio The underlying beliefs and values teachers hold about children are the driving forces for interactions, planning, and teaching approaches. These values serve to guide teachers but also ultimately impact children's experiences and learning. It is essential

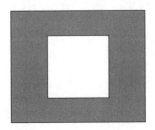

Slide viewer.

that teachers are clear in articulating their values and beliefs about children. In keeping with the Reggio approach to viewing all children as having rights, think about the very core rights that you believe ALL children should be endowed with. Many educators and communities think about this in terms of our own Constitutional rights. Review a collaboratively created version of a Children's Bill of Rights at www.newciv.org/ncn/cbor.html and www.boulderjourneyschool.com/Pages/Home/Charter_of_Rights.htm for inspiration as a starting point to create your own statement. Your statement is a good addition to your professional portfolio in an introductory or professionalism section.

RELATED WEB LINKS

North America Reggio Alliance
www.reggioalliance.org

Boulder Journey School
www.boulderjourneyschool.com

Reggio Children USA
zerosei.comune.re.it/inter/index.htm

CHAPTER 10

Montessori Education: Environment, Materials, and Methods

The greatest sign of success for a teacher . . . is to be able to say, "The children are now working as if I did not exist."

—Maria Montessori

Montessori education, a household phrase in the United States today, has had a significant impact on the fields of education and child development. Maria Montessori began her groundbreaking work with impoverished and developmentally delayed children and later devised methods to use with all children. Her well-documented theories about the development of the child's will and intellect have been impacting teacher practice for more than a century. Many of Montessori's once-radical views have become accepted components of all good practice. Thousands of Montessori schools, some serving infants through high school–age children, are found all over the world, with more than 5,000 in the United States alone.

Because Maria Montessori plays such a key role in the way we think about and teach young children, it is important for educators to become more familiar with her as well as with her method of teaching. To truly understand her method requires that you have a foundational understanding of her beliefs about how children develop, how she came to hold those beliefs, and how her theories guided her practice in teaching young children. This chapter presents the historical background of Montessori and her theories and then explores the key elements in her method, including the materials, environment, and teacher's role. Ongoing debates concerning divergent beliefs about the role of play in Montessori programs and other early childhood programs are also presented.

STARTING POINTS: QUESTIONS AND REFLECTIONS

By this point in your studies, even if you have just begun learning about early childhood education, you probably have done at least one observation but possibly many. Think about the purpose of observations as well as your role as an observer. Think about how teachers conduct and use observations to plan and assess learning and development.

1. How involved with children should a teacher be while observations are being conducted? Would there be a difference between actively teaching or refraining from contact during observations?

2. Why do you think a teacher would follow the same prescribed routine when demonstrating new materials to children?

3. How do you feel about teachers being given detailed, scripted routines for presenting materials? In what ways could you see this helping or hindering the teacher and/or children?

CLASSROOM VIEW: MONTESSORI IN ACTION

In order to better visualize the basic framework of Maria Montessori's method of education, take a moment to step into a carefully prepared Montessori preschool classroom. It is a bright, sunny fall

Montessori classroom.

day as we enter the houselike structure of the Montessori school. Today you are going to visit the 3- to 6-year-olds' mixed-age preschool room. The space is large and open, with a bathroom area sectioned off by half walls at one side of the room. There is also a minikitchen space adjoining the bathroom that includes a sink and counter space for adults and a smaller one for children. Next to the kitchen there is a small table on which orange quarters and a plate of crackers, small spreaders, and a tub of jam have been set out for an hour for those children who choose to help themselves to snack at their will.

The teachers explain that by letting children snack when they please, they do not have to interrupt children's work for a designated whole-group snack time. "As Montessori teachers, above all else, we are careful not to interrupt children's work," one teacher explains. "It is a way of respecting their process. We believe that the children's internal process is engaged when they work with the materials. I don't disrupt that because of a schedule we've set for them. We strive to allow close to 3 hours of children's choice time in the mornings. This allows children the time to get deep into their work. Here, the children drive their learning."

As you glance around the room, you notice the clean, pleasing appearance of the pink-and-white striped curtains and matching child-sized wicker sofa set. It is located in what seems to be a house area in the far corner of the room. The walls are white and are sparsely adorned with framed Monet and Van Gogh prints. The classroom space is well lit by both large windows and overhead fluorescent lights. The room has an overall feeling of order, brightness, and neatness. It strikes you as a little unusual for a room filled with preschool children in the midst of morning activity. It seems even quieter than the other classrooms you have visited.

As you continue to survey the scene, you notice that there are three-step climbers at one side and low shelves and small tables that divide the open space. There is a large, solid-green carpet under a wall of windows. The carpet is lined with low shelves containing neatly stored block sets. Next, you begin to notice the children. Most of them are working individually with the self-correcting materials on trays placed on small carpet squares. They are intently focused on their respective tasks—some are pouring water from one small glass pitcher to another; others are stacking pink blocks of successively smaller dimensions into a tower. Others work at lacing, snapping, tying, and zipping, and still others intently focus on moving their hands over letters cut out of sandpaper with a gentler touch than you can recall ever seeing in a 4-year-old. In fact, you are surprised at the quiet intensity of all the children as they focus all their attention on the materials in their hands.

The teachers, too, seem to be unusually quiet, closely watching specific children who are intently and repetitively working. One teacher is slowly and deliberately modeling the correct use of a new material. She silently shows the child how to pick up a cylinder and place it in the empty space on the base. When she has completed putting the series of cylinders in their holes, she asks the child if he would like to try this work. He nods and quietly replicates her actions.

The children move about their space with care, quietly helping themselves to trays of materials stored on the low shelves. They deliberately and repetitively manipulate the materials. When the children

Children use knobless cylinders to develop fine motor skills and work on seriation.

Sample Daily Schedule

Montessori believed children should be allowed to work at self-selected activities with little interference from teachers. This translates into a long block of time for child-selected work.

8:00 A.M.	Arrival, Bathroom, Wash up, Breakfast (if desired)
8:30 A.M.	Children Select Work (snack available)
11:00 A.M.	Circle Gathering
11:15 A.M.	Outdoors—Free Play, Gardening, Exercise
12:15 P.M.	Clean up, Set Table, Prepare for Lunch
Lunch	
12:45 P.M.	Quiet Rest
2:15 P.M.	Bathroom, Clean up, Outdoors
2:30 P.M.	Children Select Work (snack available), Some Free Play
5:00 P.M.	Clean up, Prepare for Departure

decide that they are finished with a particular work, they return the pieces to the tray and return the tray to the exact location from which they took it. The materials look new, and you are surprised to later find out that they have been in this classroom for more than 15 years. The children clearly demonstrate that they have the utmost respect for their environment and understand that the materials will be used by children for years and years to come.

One of the teachers notices your surprise and explains, "Instilling in each child a reverence and respect for themselves, each other, and their environment is one of our most important tasks as teachers. A big part of each day is spent working on self-care skills and also work that takes care of this space. Children clean the tables and materials and dust the plants. They learn how to dress and serve themselves. Montessori considered these skills essential work for preschoolers."

After their rather intense period of mostly independent work, the children are called to the carpet space, where they converge with the teachers and participate in a circle time. Today the children are being introduced to a new object—a pineapple—and they are encouraged to feel and smell the fruit while the teacher talks about where it came from. Later on the children will have an opportunity to taste the fruit in an afternoon snack. After a relatively brief circle period, the children and teachers get ready for an outing to their outdoor playground. After such an intense independent work time, the children and teachers alike are eager to enjoy the fresh air, sunshine, social interaction, and physical exercise of the climbing equipment.

Who Was Maria Montessori? Auspicious Beginning and Lasting Legacy

Maria Montessori was born in Italy in 1870 to a wealthy family, and even as a child she became known for her superb intellect. In a time when women were not traditionally afforded the same kinds of educational or professional opportunities as men, Montessori demonstrated a competency and capability worthy of special recognition. While attending an all-boys technical school, she settled on the pursuit of medicine, although she had to complete clinical studies alone due to social decorum of the time relating to men and women studying together (Lascarides & Hinitz, 2000; Shute, 2002). Montessori quickly demonstrated unusual strength as a student and clinician even in her first year (Gettman, 1987). Thus began the recognition of her unusual capabilities.

Montessori became the first female doctor to graduate from the University of Rome. She subsequently spent a decade practicing surgical medicine and advocating equal rights for women (Gettman, 1987). As her studies and work branched out into psychology and she began teaching at the nearby psychiatric clinic, Montessori became intrigued with the so-called defective and insane children housed in the institution. In all likelihood, these children today would be classified as *developmentally delayed*. Montessori was deeply influenced by the work of Romantic philosophers Rousseau, Pestalozzi, and Froebel (Elkind, 2003) and the growing constructivist theory base (Edwards, 2002). But she was perhaps most profoundly inspired by the work of Jean-Marc-Gaspard Itard and his student Edouard Seguin. Both physicians, Itard and Seguin promoted the radical belief that mental deficiencies were more problems of the way in which "defective children" were being taught and less a medical problem (Cossentino, 2006; Lascarides & Hinitz, 2000).

With a scientific rigor typical of Montessori, she observed and documented how the institutionalized children fought over the tiniest crumbs and dust fluffs. She set out to prove her hypothesis that these children were starved for stimulation and not biologically defective. Montessori began a 2-year experiment in which she observed the children engaging with a variety of hands-on materials that she created (Gettman, 1987). After 2 years of work with the materials, these defective children were able to pass age-level school competency exams as well as any typically developing child (Shute, 2002). This finding fueled her belief that stimulating environments and focused, purposeful activity could promote cognitive growth in any child.

Energized by this success, Montessori turned her attention to the current educational system. She believed that educational environments were stifling and suppressing the child's will, inner drives, and naturally unfolding development. She began to crusade for educational programs for young children that were not merely smaller-sized versions of the elementary education programs (Shute, 2002).

Putting It Into Practice

Make Your Own Sandpaper Letters and Numbers

Montessori created thin wooden tablets that had numbers or letters written in sandpaper to provide texture and sensory experience. You can easily stencil and cut out letters and numbers from medium-grit sandpaper and glue them to heavy cardstock or wood pieces. Invite children to trace the sandpaper shapes with their eyes open or closed. This experience gives them a physical, tactile sensation of the lines and shapes of letters and numbers.

Absorbent mind

Montessori's description of how children soak up their surroundings and experiences.

Casa dei Bambini

Montessori's first Children's House opened in 1907 as her first educational program for impoverished children in an area of Rome, Italy.

Montessori validated young children's instinct to touch any material they could get their hands on and soak up any stimulation in their environment (the **absorbent mind**). At the heart of her new model of early childhood education was the belief that children learn through purposeful work on sensory experiences and by absorbing their surroundings. This prompted her to be concerned with the careful design of the child's space and careful selection of manipulative materials. She also recognized the highly active, physical nature of young children and sought to celebrate this nature instead of try to suppress it. Montessori's first opportunity to work with community children came in 1906, when she was asked to take charge of nearly 50 wayward children of the tenement families living in a low-income area of Rome. Montessori regarded this as another opportunity to practice and expand her theories about children's learning and development. The opening of her **Casa dei Bambini** (Children's House) in 1907 marked the beginning of a theory and method of teaching that has had an enduring and significant impact on teaching practices for more than 100 years.

Montessori employed a scientific approach through the presentation of materials and objective observation of children's activity. Through her carefully documented observations, Montessori began to notice amazing discoveries. She found that these tearful, frightened children, ranging in ages from 2 to 6, could become intently engaged with her purposeful materials, not the irrelevant toys which she quickly removed, and preferred to work on meaningful tasks free from adult intrusion. She saw an inner calm come over them as they worked, repeatedly and with greater competence, with their chosen materials (Gettman, 1987). Building on her observations, Montessori refined the environment and materials to maximize each child's own spontaneous activity within a carefully prepared environment and structured materials. This system of *freedom with limits* became a hallmark of her method.

Montessori further chronicled the different activities and levels of competence in the children of various ages. Through these notes, she began to notice what she called *sensitive periods* in the children, which you read about in Chapters 6. Montessori believed that maximizing development required sensitivity on the adults' part—an awareness that came from respecting the child's own inner forces and from observing the child freely engaged with materials of his or her own choosing (Montessori, 1966). Out of this belief came Montessori's view of the teacher as an observer and preparer of the environment, rather than an imparter of knowledge.

Montessori teachers demonstrate the correct use of materials and then observe children's work.

Putting It Into Practice

Make Your Own Color Chips

Montessori created color chips of varying hues so children could discriminate from lightest to darkest. You can create your own by using paint swatches readily available at paint stores or home improvement stores. Get two of each color palette you choose. Cut one so that each hue is separated. The task then is to match them, using the whole card as a template. Or, for a more advanced work, cut one card in pieces and have the children seriate the shades (put them in order from lightest to darkest).

Montessori continued developing and promoting her method and was both applauded and criticized throughout her career. During her visits to the United States in 1913, Montessori's ideas were fairly well received by the public. In particular, her 1915 World's Fair exhibit, in which children silently and intently worked on independently selected activities with remarkable attention, caused a great public buzz (Sobe, 2004). Kindergarten advocates and teachers such as Patty Smith Hill and William Heard Kilpatrick, however, rejected the rigid, structured work children methodically repeated with the materials (Cossentino, 2006; Lascarides & Hinitz, 2000). Concerns were raised over the lack of creative expression, the absence of play, and the strict use of *didactic* materials (which you read about in Chapter 2). Although some upper-class families accepted the method and even founded several Montessori schools and a professional association, for the most part, the Montessori method remained an unpopular choice among early childhood educators in the Progressive Era.

Her method did not become really popular until years after her death (in 1952), when, during the 1960s, three key shifts opened the door for new interest in her methods. At that time, more theorists were beginning to make connections between early experiences and later success, the early intervention movement for at-risk children was beginning to take hold, and educators were searching for a more scientific method of child development and education. With Montessori's strong science background, the emphasis on naturalistic observation, and the origins in special education, Montessori's method was once again in the U.S. spotlight in both the 1960s and again in the 1980s. Independent Montessori schools quickly opened under the auspices and direction of such agencies as the newly formed American Montessori Association and the Association Montessori Internationale (AMI). Both associations advocate close alignment with Montessori's writing. Although Montessori schools do not necessarily have to align with her method (there is no trademark on the name), those who are affiliated with one of these agencies will more closely adhere to Montessori's own design.

As more and more Montessori schools opened, public knowledge of Montessori's method increased. In recent decades, the number of Montessori-inspired schools has grown to more than 5,000 in the United States, and Montessori methods have been implemented in more than 300 public elementary school settings (Lillard & Else-Quest, 2006). After Montessori's death in 1952, her only son, Mario, took over control of the AMI and continued to promote the Montessori method until his death in 1982 (Gettman, 1987; Henry-Montessori, n.d.). Visit MyEducationLab to watch a video of a Montessori classroom, including a description of her unique materials.

MyEducationLab

Go to the Assignments and Activities section of Topic 1: History in the MyEducationLab for your course and complete the activity entitled *Montessori Classroom*. Notice how the teacher describes the purpose, use, and care of materials.

Basic Principles of the Montessori Method

Throughout her career, Montessori took advantage of any opportunity she could to observe children in their natural environment. She made insightful connections from these extensive observations and began to be increasingly concerned at how adults seemed to be misinterpreting and thwarting children's needs and drives. A highly spiritual person, Montessori was concerned for the psychic well-being of children. She wrote extensively about her observations of children's distress when adults did not recognize the spiritual basis for children's outward expressions (Montessori, 1966). She was so committed to reinventing early childhood practice that she painstakingly documented her method with prolific writings, teacher training, and sometimes inordinate numbers of steps scripted for every activity in which children engage. She prescribed teacher's actions and words for every step of an activity—from the introduction, demonstration, and invitation to the child to try the work. Montessori insisted on strict adherence to her method because she was certain that her method was the single best way to maximize children's innate abilities to foster their own development (Goffin, 1994). Her method can perhaps best be understood by exploring the key principles that guided her work with children, which include Montessori's

- Beliefs about children's development
- Vision of the teacher's role and function in the classroom
- Original materials for which she has received much acclaim

We explore each principle in turn as it relates to our overall understanding of Montessori's method and her contributions to the field of early childhood education.

View of Children and Their Development

Montessori believed that children come into this world with a natural sense of spirituality, inquisitiveness, capability, and purpose, all of which act as driving forces in their development and learning. Montessori also believed that at birth children are in a state of internal chaos, out of which they strive to make sense and order. She believed this effort is manifested by their increasing purposefulness and productive behavior. A great deal of her writing chronicled her belief that the "secret of childhood" was that children, when unfettered by inappropriate adult demands, would naturally and spontaneously engage in activities that guided their development toward becoming ordered, productive adults. According to Montessori, development is an internally regulated process that requires carefully planned interaction with the environment and materials (Montessori, 1966).

Contrary to the currently and widely held belief that children learn through play, Montessori viewed play, imagination, toys, and games as frivolous to learning. She regarded these activities as counterproductive to the young child's own drive to purposefully engage with realistic, practical activities (Cossentino, 2006). Through her observations, she noted that children appeared to be entertained for a brief period by play and toys, yet remained somehow unsatisfied. She believed that the adult ideal of learning through play and letting childhood be a time of fun and imagination was nothing more than that: an adult ideal that was in conflict with the child's need for productive developmental "work" (Gettman, 1987). Montessori considered frivolous play—as well as stifling advanced academic lessons—as something the teacher ought to redirect children away from (Montessori, 1967). Born out of a tremendous respect for children's capabilities, Montessori's method seeks to value the child's ability to become intently and joyfully focused in productive exploration. She felt that it was these explorations that served a mysterious inner developmental need that arose within the child (Montessori, 1965a).

Sensitive Periods

Montessori believed that children naturally pass through phases that prepare them for learning in certain areas. During these phases, called *sensitive periods*, the child is ready to master particular skills or concepts that cannot be fully mastered at other times. Beginning in infancy, these sensitive periods allow the child to soak up stimulation and cues in their world that, when subjected to the child's internal processes, result in developmental growth. In this way, Montessori viewed the young child's mind as *absorbent*, eager to take in, model, and imitate any stimulation that is put before it (Montessori, 1966).

We can see this idea illustrated in an infant's mimicking of a facial expression made by an excited caregiver, in a toddler's gleefully repeating a word or phrase just heard from an adult, or in a preschooler's imitation of an older sibling's physical actions. Through these examples, we see how a child is influenced by his or her environment. This also emphasizes what tremendous responsibility teachers have in presenting only the most appropriate model for children to imitate.

As we know from commonly observed milestones in development, an enormous amount of developmental growth is seen in the first 3 years of life. It is in this formative period that children learn to speak in their culturally accepted language and command their physical actions with relative control. Advances in these two major developmental domains enable the organization of all later cognitive, social, and emotional development. Thus, the early years represent a critically important period in terms of the child's later development. Montessori felt problems resulted from an adult's view of the infant as being completely dependent, resulting in an overbearing, overprotective—albeit loving—desire to do everything for an infant. She felt that doing too much thwarted the infant's own innate drive to make sense of his world. In turn, this would render the infant out of touch with his own tools of self-education. Out of respect for the child's inborn capabilities, Montessori sought to reempower infants and children to be able to guide their own development through self-sufficiency (Montessori, 1966).

Have you ever witnessed a battle of wills between an adult and a motivated toddler? Perhaps you've seen a child who refused to settle down into a stroller, insisting on walking instead. Or maybe you've seen an infant desperately reaching for food during feeding time, wanting to feed herself or perhaps smear food on her hair. If so, you can begin to understand that even young children have internal processes that are extremely important to them, even though they lack an adult framework for describing them. Montessori wrote passionately about what an offense to the child it was to exert unnecessary authority over the child in such a battle. She firmly believed in limits, but she insisted they be reasonable and not undermine the will and self-determination of the child. She viewed these as two essential components of development and learning (Lascarides & Hinitz, 2000).

Montessori also believed that the preschool years (3 to 6 years old) were years that were essential in developing a sense of order about the world that would lay a foundation for later rational thought. Although the belief that the child's early experiences have great impact on their later functioning is now widely accepted, in her time Montessori's emphasis on the early years was met with skepticism. Ever the pioneer, Montessori maintained her conviction and developed materials and prescribed activities that would allow optimal natural development as it unfolded from within the child.

In order for the child's innate developmental plan to be realized, Montessori realized that the child needed to be able to function with independence. She defined this as the freedom for a child to take care of his or her own needs as well as the freedom from being dependent on assistance from others. She believed that, if children mastered some basic

Putting It Into Practice

Make Your Own Dressing Frames

Using purchased wood frames (discard the glass) and old shirts and jackets, you can create your own set of dressing frames. You can find old clothes at thrift shops if you do not have clothes with a variety of fasteners. Or you can sew zippers, buttons, and snaps onto purchased fabric. Cut the fabric/shirts to fit over the frame, hemming the tops and bottoms if desired. Use a staple gun or upholstery tacks to attach the clothing/fabric to the right and left sides of the frame, centering the fastener/closure in the middle of the opening. Children can unfasten and refasten the buttons, zippers, and other fasteners and develop self-care skills (learning to dress themselves) as well as fine motor skills.

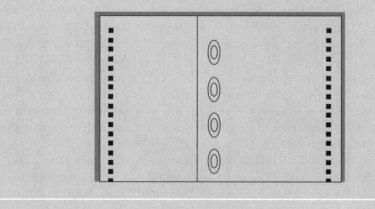

Children use work with the dressing frame to learn self-care skills and develop fine motor skills like buttoning, zipping, lacing, or buckling.

self-sufficiency skills, they would be at liberty to self-select materials, activities, and experiences. This self-direction using didactic materials, or **auto-education**, would naturally maximize the developmental outcomes of the particular sensitive period which they were experiencing at the moment (Goffin, 1994). This belief served as the framework for the first phase of her curriculum plan, which she referred to as *practical life*. Practical life focuses on the skills of daily living: dressing, washing, and ordering one's environment.

Auto-education

Self-directed action using didactic (self-correcting) materials.

Montessori also observed that young children are innately driven to handle and physically explore their world and everything in it. She became increasingly dissatisfied with parents and teachers who always seemed to be at odds with their children who were not listening, sitting quietly, or keeping their hands off adult valuables. Ultimately convinced that these battles of will were detrimental to the child's naturally occurring sense of purpose, Montessori became outspoken in her disagreement with current practices of care and education for young children (Rambusch, 1992). For example, think about that toddler who resists being strapped into a stroller. Although a parent may insist the child remain there because the parent has a busy schedule and it is faster to push him, the child has a burning desire to test out his developing walking skills. The toddler does not necessarily understand the parent's schedule; instead, he is aware only that at this point in his life, he needs practice to master walking. Montessori would have advocated allowing the child to walk for a while, even though the parent's schedule would be delayed. Montessori reported that in these battles of will, when the child is once again on his own developmental path, there is an immediate shift in the child from inconsolable to joyful and bright-eyed (Montessori, 1966). It is with this perspective in mind that we now explore Montessori's vision of the role teachers should play in the child's educational development.

Teachers' (Directress') Roles and Functions

Teachers in a Montessori program are carefully trained in a prescribed, approved Montessori teacher-training program. Here they learn the basic principles of child development and Montessori's view of children, as well as the proper scripts to use when working with and talking to the children. Montessori's vision was that all schools and teachers would look and act in a similar way—carefully following her model.

Montessori constructed materials to act as the child's teacher, meaning that children could use the materials without teacher direction or assistance. She discovered that when children were properly introduced to the use of the materials deliberately and carefully, they could select and work with the materials at their own will (Montessori, 1965a). This allowed the teacher to step back and let the child guide his or her own learning, serving as director of the classroom activities (thus her title of "directress") and observer. The teacher should remain a background part of the environment, guiding and supporting the child's unfolding development without pushing or imposing the teacher's own desire on the child. Montessori explained that "our intention in this marvelous process is *indirect*; we are here to offer to this life, which came into the world by itself, the *means* necessary for its development, and having done that we must await this development with respect" (Montessori, 1965a, p. 134).

Along with the emphasis placed on the correct use of the didactic materials, the teacher, or *directress*, is an influence of primary importance in the child's life (Lascarides & Hinitz, 2000). The teacher's influence could have either positive or negative effects on the child's developmental and psychic outcomes. Montessori believed that the teacher should start with a tremendous respect for children's rights and abilities and be responsible for three primary functions:

- Carefully preparing the environment
- Appropriately introducing and modeling the didactic materials
- Closely observing the children and documenting learning

Preparing the Environment

Although it may seem obvious to early childhood educators today, making the classroom and materials accessible to children was not a well-understood idea before Montessori. She insisted that children not be made to exist in an adult-oriented environment. To foster independence, she created classrooms for children that included lightweight, scaled-down furniture that could be easily moved about and from which children could easily take and replace materials (Mooney, 2000). Building on her beliefs that children craved order in their world, creating an aesthetically pleasing space that was neat, ordered, and free from undue clutter became a trademark of her vision.

Contrary to what we may commonly find in preschool classrooms today, Montessori did not believe in using intricate wall decorations and brightly colored paint. Her clean, white spaces presented an organized design in which carefully chosen materials and artwork were displayed in moderation. Montessori strove to provide an environment that was not overstimulating and distracting, but instead provided a clean backdrop for the internal work in which the child would engage. Shelves were to be stocked but not overstocked, and materials were to be clean and in good condition. This order and visual harmony was extremely important to Montessori. She wrote passionately about her belief that children's development was strongly influenced by their environment and experiences as well as by their internal drives (Goffin, 1994). It was important to cultivate a psychological space in which children were respected and free. In this way there would be a great deal of individualization to children's learning.

Instead of supporting a laissez-faire, or hands-off attitude, Montessori believed that it required great training and work to understand the child's innate drives and needs. She felt it demanded even more effort on the teacher's part to create a classroom space that offered appropriate experiences that could support drives and meet needs. This, she felt, was accomplished through

- Setting clear limits
- Modeling proper use of materials
- Backing away to allow the child to explore the materials and environment

The Teacher as Model and Director

It may sound like a contradiction to talk about teachers as directors in a classroom where children are to be free from adult interference. Montessori was careful to point out, however, that the child is freed from dependence on others when he or she is able to act independently in his or her world. And independence is learned through skills acquired by imitating teacher directions. To support this independence in children, Montessori developed materials and instructions for their use that focused initially on developing self-sufficiency skills in children. Although many of her practical life materials address fairly common activities, such as dressing and cleaning, Montessori insisted that teachers follow her detailed method for introducing the work.

Knowing that young children are neither interested in sitting quietly in large groups for long periods of time nor capable of developing at the same rate, Montessori believed that individual instruction was the primary means to introduce the materials. Considering her preferred practice of mixed-age grouping, not all children would be ready to use the same materials at the same time; therefore, the introduction and use of materials was to be a very individualized endeavor. Specific materials were presented only to children who were ready and interested to receive them. Through their observations and insight into each child, teachers become familiar with each child's readiness for work with specific materials. If a material was introduced and the teacher observed that the child was uninterested or unable to work with it properly, the teacher was simply to remove the work, allowing the child to freely choose another work, and reserve the new material for another time (Montessori, 1965b). Visit MyEducationLab to view a child working with sand scoops and a sieve as he intently, independently explores the sensory nature of the sand and the use of the tools. This kind of independent intensity is commonly seen in Montessori students.

Also keeping in mind that Montessori viewed the child's work with the materials as the primary vehicle for learning (not the teacher's lessons themselves), she insisted that the introductory lessons were to be brief, simple, objective, and use as few words as possible (Montessori, 1965b). A teacher slowly demonstrates the correct use of a material, such as the button dressing frame, by

- Carefully removing the frame from the shelf
- Saying simply, "This is the button dressing frame."
- Placing it on the table with the child seated to her left
- Quietly announcing, "I will now show you how to button and unbutton."
- Instructing the child. "Watch me do this work first and then you can try it if you like."
- Silently completing the button dressing frame work

MyEducationLab

Go to the Video Examples section of Topic 2: Child Development/ Theories in the MyEducationLab for your course and watch the video entitled *Child in the Sand*. Observe how the child demonstrates his interest in the sand and the tools he is using.

Teacher Training

To ensure accurate presentation, Montessori insisted that all teachers who sought to teach through her method be trained under her own supervision. As the popularity of her method grew and as a way to maintain consistency after her death, approved institutions assumed responsibility for carrying on the work of teacher training. In addition to an emphasis on understanding the child, teacher training involved strict guidance in regard to exactly how teachers are to present the didactic materials. Remember that Montessori believed that children's minds were absorbent and highly influenced, positively or negatively, by their environments and adult interactions. Considering this framework, it naturally follows that the method of introducing the materials that will guide the child's development must be carefully and deliberately demonstrated. Visit www.montessori-ami.org to learn more about the history and practices of Montessori teacher training.

Then the teacher slowly and deliberately demonstrates unbuttoning and rebuttoning the series of buttons, labeling both the unbuttoned and buttoned positions. When she has finished, she invites the child to try this work on his or her own, either at that time or later. Although the action of buttoning and unbuttoning may seem like a simple enough task, the teacher has 25 steps to follow according to Montessori's script for introducing this work. In fact, every lesson, including sweeping sawdust (34 steps), handling a book (42 steps), saying thank you (16 steps), and pouring between two jugs (26 steps), has a very detailed method of presentation to the child (Gettman, 1987). Limiting the amount of teacher talk is a part of Montessori's effort to free the children from undue teacher control (Cossentino, 2006).

After the presentation is complete, the teacher leaves the child to his or her independent work, either with the new material or with something else of the child's choosing. For the better part of the morning (3-hour work periods being ideal), children are independently engaged in working with materials of their choosing and are usually intently focused their work. The child's independence, in turn, leaves the teacher free to address the last, equally important, of her primary tasks: the focused observation of the child engaged in work.

The Teacher as Observer

Throughout her career, Montessori fought against dissenting public opinion about her program model. One of the main arguments she made in favor of the validity of her approach was the fact that this was a scientific model (Rambusch, 1992). Her work was based on many years of work with children from a medical, psychiatric, and educational perspective. Montessori's emphasis on the teacher as a trained, objective observer was one of the main components of the professional, scientific model. She insisted that childhood was a special period and that children demonstrated unique processes, not merely scaled-down versions of adult needs and abilities (Goffin, 1994; Montessori, 1966). This intimate knowledge of children and the ability to observe them carefully were also aspects of prime importance in teacher training.

Putting It Into Practice

Make Your Own Smelling Jars

Use old film canisters or small bottles to create pairs of matching smells. Label one set with colored tape or some other distinctive mark so the child knows one is a tester and one is a matcher. Using a variety of extracts, spices, coffee grounds, or other safe items, put a scented cotton ball in each of two containers (making pairs). Glue a piece of mesh or screen over the can, fitting under the lid. Children then choose one match can and smell each of the tester cans to identify the correct match. You can use the same process to make sound cylinders. Use a variety of materials to make different sounds when shaken.

Only through the careful study of scientific methods of inquiry and observation and only through the complete divorcing of one's personality and ego could a teacher truly observe and see children's development unfold. This separation of one's self was critically important in the Montessori teacher. The Montessori teacher was instead trained to focus solely on the child as the director of his or her own development and learning (Swan, 1987). Although this may sound radical, in essence it is the same motivation in practice in today's child-centered programming.

First, the stage was set through the careful preparation of the environment and deliberate instruction on the self-correcting materials. Then, the teacher was free to occupy her time not in detrimental interference of the child's work, but rather in watching the child's unfolding developmental path with reverence and care. Furthermore, having taken the time to witness this unfolding, the teacher was trained to carefully document her observations of the children's actions (Montessori, 1966). The teacher's analyses of the observations then served as a guide in the planning and assessing of instruction and material selection for each child.

This intense observation and documentation allowed the teacher to come to know each child's abilities and needs intimately. As with all quality early childhood practice, you can see the emphasis on using observations and documentation of children as a means of assessment and planning. We hope you are starting to see why your professors give you so many observation assignments in your classes!

Montessori Materials and Activities

This research-oriented practice elevated the status of the teacher's work from the more custodial nature of ensuring safety and care to the highly professional work of ensuring optimal, healthy development of the body, mind, and spirit. This attitude of professionalism, combined with the strict training teachers received, was necessary to maintain Montessori's vision just as she crafted it, even as her method was spreading internationally.

Perhaps also compelled by the fact that her materials were carefully designed after years of observing children engaged with their explorations, Montessori was also adamant that only her original materials be purchased and used with her method (Goffin, 1994). Authentic, well-crafted Montessori materials can be a significant expense. Equipping a classroom with a complete repertoire of materials can cost up to $25,000 (AMS, n.d). True Montessorians would not promote cutting corners; however, substitute materials can be crafted to achieve similar learning goals when expense is an issue.

Over the years there has been much discussion about Montessori's self-correcting materials. Based on her observations and beliefs about children's development, the materials are purposeful, realistic, and concrete. They are designed and sequenced to provide children with experiences to satisfy their current developmental tasks. They are also designed to lay a foundation to prepare children for later academic and life tasks. When children enter the Montessori program, they are to begin with the simpler activities and progress to more challenging materials and activities as their own individual pace dictates, as observed by the teachers.

There are five overarching curricular areas that are addressed at increasing levels in the method and materials:

• Practical life activities

• Sensorial activities

• Cultural activities

• Language activities

• Mathematics

Although most of the levels of activity include experiences in each of these areas, within the child's initial experience in the Montessori environment there are no mathematics activities per se. Instead, the child's experiences with some of the materials in other areas prepare the child for later mathematical activities (Gettman, 1987).

Practical Life Activities

Within the scope of early practical life activities, some of the tasks children engage in include tasks of pouring from one pitcher to another; completing simple dressing frames (buttoning, buckling); courtesy tasks such as saying thank you; self-care tasks such as hanging and folding clothes and brushing hair; and movement tasks such as sitting and rising from a chair, lifting and carrying a tray, and dusting. As children become more familiar with the Montessori environment, they progress to more advanced practical life activities such as polishing and cleaning different surfaces, being silent, greeting people, handling a book, using more difficult dressing frames like tying and lacing, ironing, and simple cooking. Once children progress into the upper age of the mixed-age group, practical life activities include caring for and comforting younger children, caring for the environment, serving snacks and meals, and ultimately presenting early practical life activities to new children.

Throughout the sequence of practical life activities we can see an emphasis on positive social behaviors, self-care, care of the environment, and consideration of others. The children's demonstration of respect for themselves, their environment, and the people around them often seems remarkable to visitors to Montessori classrooms. Remember from the classroom observation that the teacher described these qualities as essential and as being at the core of their classroom experience. When Montessori created her method for the impoverished children in the Casa dei Bambini, these skills were absolutely necessary for their success in life and basic health.

The Pink Tower develops sight discrimination and motor skills.

Sensorial Activities

Sensorial activities are designed to awaken and train children's senses. Montessori firmly believed that children learn best through their senses. Activities in the early sensorial domain include exploring size and dimension with a series of cylinder blocks that fit into precise holes based on their size; working with the pink tower (solid blocks in successively smaller units); using geometric solids, sound boxes, and bells tuned in a scale; and working with cubes and numeric rods. More advanced sensorial experiences include exploring a square of Pythagoras; discriminating a variety of fabrics by touch; exploring a mystery bag and other blindfolded discrimination work; using smelling jars and tasting cups; performing advanced sound work with the bells; and ultimately presenting early sensorial activities to younger children.

Even in the earliest sensorial activities we can see the groundwork for later mathematical, logical, and spatial thought. Children learn to identify shape, order, size, and volume. As children progress to increasingly more difficult tasks and levels, as their development begins to move from concrete to more abstract, the emphasis shifts away from sensorial and practical life activities to the cultural, language, and mathematics domains.

Cultural Activities

Montessori advocated that humans learn not solely through biology, as other animals do, but through our shared culture and individual adaptations of our cultural experiences. These tendencies include affective characteristics like curiosity and a desire to explore, the need to communicate and share experiences, an interest in calculating, and working toward lofty goals in the pursuit of independence. These qualities are indeed many of the forces that make us uniquely human. Within the cultural area, children explore concepts such as land and water, maps, classification pictures, past and present, air, gravity, sound, optics, plant life cycles, geography, and nature and human history studies. In this area, we can see how Montessori sought to address dispositional and affective needs of the child, along with instilling a respect for the environment and humankind (Williams & Keith, 2000).

Language Activities

In addition to these cultural qualities, our ability to master and use language allows us to connect in social groups, communicate and share on surface and profound levels, and organize our thoughts into coherent, complex forms. As we know from observations, the task of mastering language (in all its forms) is a major developmental endeavor of the young child. As such, it occupies a prime place in the young child's educational life. Montessori developed language activities that, in the early levels, begin with exploring pictures, books, and sounds. Later language experiences progress to exploring the written word through tracing sandpaper letters and metal shape insets and eventually to manipulating and outlining movable alphabet letters to make words and sentences.

Language activities ultimately culminate in the child's ability to write down thoughts, and to read and understand the writing of others. Children in Montessori classrooms can be observed using their communication skills to engage in group dialogues and, in early primary grades, in fantasy play. Even though there are no dramatic play areas in the early classrooms (Montessori did not value fantasy play for young children), children still develop imaginary stories and tell them to each other (Soundy, 2003). Through the activities in this domain, children's linguistic and related cognitive skills are encouraged as the children are continuing to become more and more independent within their world.

Mathematics

The final area of Montessori activities falls within the mathematical concepts of counting and arithmetic. Montessori noticed, as many parents and teachers might, that children actually embrace activities of sorting, categorizing, quantifying ("His piece is bigger than mine!"), and performing basic arithmetical functions ("Now I'm going to take one away from him so I have more.") and have a natural inclination toward exploring many mathematical concepts. These natural tendencies are enhanced through carefully timed introduction of sequential number rods, sandpaper numbers, bean sorting and counting, number cards, memory games using numbers, more complex decimal counting beads, fraction exercises, more complex arithmetical functions with beads (subtraction, multiplication, and division), and the use of charts and boards to explore multiplication and division.

As mentioned previously, several of the earlier explorations with sensorial activities, such as geometric solids and sequential blocks, build a conceptual foundation for later, more abstract mathematical skills. Planning that builds earlier experiences as a foundation for later, more complex tasks is seen throughout the Montessori curriculum. The process of later skills building on previously accomplished skills is one of the hallmarks of any developmental program, since this process is at work in all human development. (For example, we learn to balance upright prior to standing, then learn to walk, and walk prior to running, etc.) This is another example of how Montessori's method strives to be in balance with the child's natural developmental processes.

Reflections, Controversies, and Accolades

Throughout our introduction to Montessori's unique method of working with young children, you may have noted some surprising elements that may have seemed contradictory or controversial. Think about what you know about lesson planning or perhaps your own teaching. Do you analyze every aspect to the degree that Montessori did in her detailed step-by-step system? Montessori's detailed procedure for presenting lessons is one aspect of her method with which contemporary teachers and teacher education students may disagree. Montessori's restriction on teacher-child dialogues is also at odds with many researchers who advocate for plentiful, warm teacher-child interactions. Many early childhood education programs today promote more of a loud, busy, joyfully boisterous classroom environment in which children are encouraged to play and explore learning centers in small and large socially interactive groups. Play as the primary vehicle for children's learning and development is routinely promoted as a benchmark of high-quality practice.

There are many people in the field of early childhood education who show concern over the seemingly rigid, narrow way in which the children are directed to use the materials. These concerns are not easily resolved, and as reflective practitioners it is important for educators to continually analyze alternative methods and theories. Through your reflections you will find elements you choose not to utilize, but you will also find elements to embrace that enhance your own perspective on teaching. This is your task throughout this text and your education studies.

Montessori's Enduring Legacy

Amid criticism, the Montessori method has contributed aspects worthy of recognition to nearly all early childhood classrooms. Her series of blocks in sequential order (short to long, low to high, thin to wide), geometric solids, sense-discrimination tasks (smell, touch, taste, hearing), dressing frames, and sorting tasks—to name just a few—are widely considered staples in most preschools. Her theories concerning children as active, sensory learners have also greatly contributed to current practice and understanding in the field. Her goals to have teachers carefully understand each child's development and individualize planning are keys to quality care and education within any approach.

Student Outcomes

Teachers and prospective teachers studying Montessori's method often wonder about comparative research exploring effectiveness of her programs. Although the research base is relatively small, one study reported higher academic achievement on math and science tests for Montessori graduates who attended Montessori public school programs from ages 3 to 11 (Gartner, Lipsky, & Dohrmann, 2003). Another study of 5-year-olds attending a public Montessori program demonstrated significantly higher achievement in language and math skills and, most notably, in children's reasoning, fairness, and social problem solving (Lillard & Else-Quest, 2006). Montessori programs' emphasis on culture studies and conflict resolution, such as the use of a Peace Table for children to independently resolve social conflicts together, have been applauded as innovative contributions to positive social change and education for democracy (Williams & Keith, 2000).

Montessori wrote extensively about children deeply engrossed in their work, intently focused on an unfolding inner process. In essence, she reported that children seemed to get into a "flow." Recently, researchers have taken an interest in this intent work, this flow, and have sought to evaluate this and other dispositional or emotional experiences in the classroom. In a study of more than 300 middle school students' reports demonstrated higher affective (emotional) satisfaction in the Montessori programs (Rathunde, 2003). Montessori students reported feeling more comfortable, supported, and successful than their traditional school counterparts. Among these important findings were increased student reports of intrinsic motivation in Montessori programs. In other words, students in Montessori programs reported feeling more internally driven and personally satisfied with their schoolwork and school experiences. As the research base continues to build, more specific effects of Montessori education will be explored and identified.

Application Ideas

Some general applications of Montessori's method in any early childhood setting include the following ideas:

- Use trays, small baskets, placemats, or carpet squares to organize the environment to clearly define space for individual materials and individual children's work.
- Integrate materials that focus on addressing concrete self-help skill building (dressing, cleaning).
- Provide long blocks of time for children to engage with materials.
- Maintain an orderly, cleanly designed environment.
- Promote respect for environment, self, and others through caretaking messages and lessons.
- Take time to observe individual children, taking careful notes on their actions and language to determine developmental progress and plan for next steps.
- Provide materials and experiences in an array of curricular areas.

Conclusion

There is much to be learned from Montessori's philosophy and methods, which have endured for more than 100 years. Above all else, we can embrace the reverence and respect for children that is such an integral part of Montessori's theory and practice (Williams & Keith, 2000). Montessori's emphasis on a carefully prepared environment, deliberate interactions, and use of observations to assess and plan for children remain respected elements of quality, developmentally based practice.

Although some elements of her method may not fit in with your own personal philosophy, it is important to carefully consider her beliefs, philosophy, and practice as you continue to develop your own eclectic approach to teaching young children. Yours will be an approach that will combine key elements of many exemplary models and is tailored to suit the individual children with whom you work. It is this sharing of ideas and individualizing of our approaches that make the professional practice of education a dynamic, progressive field.

REFLECTION QUESTIONS:
LOOKING BACK AND LOOKING AHEAD

Teachers' experience, attitudes, philosophy, and beliefs are all strong influences on their practice; who you are or will be as a teacher is very much connected to these things. This is one reason why it is so important for you to continue to actively reflect on your own beliefs, experiences, and philosophy about teaching. Continue the reflection process by considering your beliefs about how children learn and trying to identify how those beliefs guide your own method of instruction.

1. What elements of Montessori's method and theories do you agree with? Why?
2. What elements do you disagree with? Why?
3. Identify other teacher roles that you feel are important and plan to utilize in your own teaching.

SUMMARY

Maria Montessori's work with and for children has left an indelible mark on the practice of early childhood education since the opening of her first early childhood center in 1907. Because of her respect for children's innate abilities, her beliefs that all children can learn, and her groundbreaking work with disabled children, the field of education has made tremendous progress in the endeavor to raise healthy, capable adults. In reviewing Montessori's beliefs and the development of her method of teaching young children, you must remember several key elements and principles in order to fully understand her method.

- Children develop through spontaneous, sensory activity that is free from undue adult interference.
- Children's minds absorb the stimuli in their environment.
- Children develop through sensitive periods when learning in specific domains is optimal.
- Children intuitively seek order and structure.
- Children desire to be engaged in purposeful work.

When you consider these points, you can see the implications her philosophy and model have for educators. Through her careful documentation and prolific writing, she has reshaped the role of the teacher and the design of the child's environment to better reflect children's needs. Classrooms are now routinely places where children can independently choose and access materials. Materials and activities are sensory based, and teachers continue to carefully train themselves to be objective observers of children's independent, active engagement. Teachers use their observations of children to plan for them and guide their work with the materials.

There are five overarching curricular areas that are addressed at increasing levels through her carefully designed hands-on materials:

- Practical life activities
- Sensorial activities

- Cultural activities
- Language activities
- Mathematics

MyEducationLab

Go to the Video Examples section of Topic 5: Program Models in the MyEducationLab for your course and watch the video entitled *Montessori Classroom* again. Focus specifically on the materials and spatial organization.

Application Activities

On the Web: MyEducationLab Go to the Video Examples section of Topic 5: Program Models in the MyEducationLab for your course and revisit the video entitled *Montessori Classroom*. Focus your observation on the materials and spatial organization. Discuss the corresponding questions in small groups.

In Class Working in pairs, identify three questions you would ask Montessori if you could have lunch with her right now. Write them down. Share them in class with your instructor. Using Internet sources, such as various Montessori associations and articles, as well as any local Montessori schools you may have available, try to find the answers to your questions.

In the Field Arrange to visit a Montessori program in your area. During your visit, try to interview an administrator or a teacher as well as observe a classroom. If you do not have a Montessori center near you, arrange a phone interview. Is the center associated with a Montessori organization? What ages does the program serve? Are the teachers Montessori trained? If so, where did they complete their training? Identify aspects of the classroom and school that illustrate Montessori principles and methodology. Identify and describe authentic Montessori materials.

For Your Portfolio Montessori insisted on the use of her commercially available materials, but many can be made on your own. Research her materials (try www.montessori-ami. org) and make substitutes for two of them. Try to make your own version as close as possible to her version.

For example, make your own shape inserts. (Purpose: Children learn shapes and can trace insert.) Using heavy cardstock squares, cut out exact shapes using a razor knife so that the shape and frame are intact. Glue a small knob, such as a pencil eraser or bead, to the insert so children can pick it up out of the frame. Children then can remove the shapes from the frames and practice finding the correct frame for each shape.

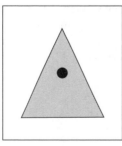

RELATED WEB LINKS

North American Montessori Teachers' Association
www.montessori-namta.org/

Association Montessori Internationale
www.montessori-ami.org/

American Montessori Society
www.amshq.org/

CHAPTER 11

Waldorf Education: Harmony and the Whole Child

Our highest endeavor must be to develop free human beings who are able, out of their own initiative, to impart purpose and direction to their lives.

—RUDOLF STEINER

Waldorf education is a unique approach that views children as complex, whole human beings developing in mind, body, and spirit—or head, hands, and heart. The Waldorf philosophy is based on this holistic approach to education and operates under the often-used principle of education toward freedom. Waldorf schools strive to foster an environment in which children are free to explore themselves and their world and ultimately develop into capable, competent, caring adults. This approach to education strives to develop children's ability to think creatively and analytically. In this highly creative model of education, early childhood classrooms are routinely abuzz with dialogue, storytelling, building, painting, creative fantasy play, and representation of individual knowledge and experience. Waldorf education is an approach that seeks to offer a model of education with the goals of social renewal and strengthening society.

Throughout the educational experiences of all students, Waldorf education is designed to develop well-rounded individuals. This chapter presents the key elements that make up the Waldorf education approach, including its history, philosophy, and pedagogy, with a particular emphasis on the early years.

STARTING POINTS: QUESTIONS AND REFLECTIONS

You may be unfamiliar with many aspects of the Waldorf approach but be familiar with some of the underlying goals and principles. As you explore the Waldorf classroom and philosophy, think about the following questions:

1. In what ways does the learning environment embody the philosophy of a school, teacher, or approach? What environmental elements might give you clues to the program's or teacher's beliefs?

2. What kinds of activities, subjects, or skills do you think are the most important parts of a well-rounded, developmentally based education for young children?

3. As you read, think about the theories you read about in Chapter 2. What connections can you make to those theories?

CLASSROOM VIEW: THE WALDORF NURSERY-KINDERGARTEN

Imagine a room softly lit by the early fall morning sunshine peeking through large, arching windows. The morning sun shines through the tall trees outside the windows, making dappled marks on the earth-toned area carpet. The windows are gently draped in a soft pink silk fabric. The walls are painted in a light peach color using a fluid color-washed technique to create a feeling of blended waves of peach tones. Wooden support beams rise from the wooden floor to the high ceiling at obtuse angles, not the usual 90-degree angles. The gentle arch of the beams, the roundness of the room, and soft colors foster

Waldorf classroom.

an embracing feeling. The space smells warm, like bread is rising, nearly ready for baking. All these sensations make the space feel very homelike: warm, gentle, cozy, and inviting.

The natural wood shelves, which line the space, are filled with rocks, crystals, pinecones, baskets of beads and blocks, soft handmade dolls, and the occasional knitted gnome peering out from among the organic material. There are baskets cradling balls of soft-colored knitting yarn. A child's kitchen area is sectioned off by low wooden dividers. The dividers are draped with colored silk fabric clipped with oversized clothespins. A row of small white slippers is lined up at the door near the children's personal cubbies. The cubbies are labeled with a hand-painted drawing with each child's name and a special design. There are a few low tables at one side of the room. In the open center of the room there is a round, low, tree stump topped with an unlit beeswax candle surrounded by rocks, sticks, leaves, and small felt gnomes. The children's chairs form a ring around the candle. You take in this scene with a deep breath that both relaxes your body and spirit and fills you with the soft scents of bread, beeswax, and pine needles.

The children arrive, replace their shoes with slippers, and begin to quietly enter the room. The classroom teachers warmly greet every child individually in melodic voices. The children move about the room and begin to engage with materials of their choosing. Several children converge in the kitchen area, taking soft, faceless dolls from a shelf and beginning an imaginative play with them. Other children quietly gather around the teacher as she rocks in her rocking chair, sewing more felt dolls. She sings softly, and the children, who are gathering around her feet, take up vegetable-dyed yarn and begin finger knitting.

After all the children have arrived, the teacher sings a song to gently guide them over to their chairs around the candle. She lights the candle to help the sun bring light into the classroom. The children gather, settle into their seats, and wait eagerly while the teacher offers each child a piece of beeswax from a fabric-lined basket. The children take the sculpting material with reverence and delight, cup it in both hands, and watch the teacher as she finishes her round. She takes a deep breath, welcomes the children together, and then introduces the story of the day.

While the teacher quietly tells the story of gnomes, fairies, and life in the forest, the children cup the beeswax, occasionally moving their hands as directed in the story. Their hand movements are deliberately directed to warm the wax and make it ready for sculpting. After the story concludes, the teacher brings the children's attention to the now-softened wax in their hands, and they are invited to begin to work with it. The teacher gently guides the children's sculpting: "Children, move the beeswax in your hands this way and that. Let it bend and stretch as the form waiting inside takes shape." As the children complete their sculpting, the teacher extinguishes the candle and talks to the children about their creations. Each sculpture is different. Some children make animals, one child makes a tree, and another makes a bowl-shaped object.

Thus begins a typical day in a Waldorf early childhood room. It is a day that is filled with nature, harmony, song, social interaction, play, and fantasy. This environment is full of reverence for life and nature. It celebrates the innocence and wonder of childhood and embodies the belief that children's play is of the utmost importance.

IN YOUR OWN WORDS

Take a moment now to reflect on some of the early childhood environments you have seen. Make some comparisons to the scene you created in your imagination as you journeyed into a Waldorf classroom. Think about these spaces and the emotional environment that you sensed.

- Do you feel any differences between this early childhood classroom and others you have experienced before?

- What are your beliefs about play and young children's learning?

- How does this environment compare with your own educational experiences?

The History and Philosophy of Waldorf Education

The Waldorf education movement was born during a time of collective social crisis. During the chaos in the early decades of the twentieth century, much of Europe struggled to cope with the devastation in the aftermath of World War I. It was during this era that Austrian philosopher Rudolf Steiner devoted his life to exploring human potential, spirituality, and growth and development. Steiner believed that human beings were truly complete only when the three main parts of their being—the body, mind, and spirit—were developed. In the wake of the devastation of World War I, Steiner embarked on a quest to educate the European community on the necessity to reunite the whole human being as a collective effort toward social renewal (Oberman, 1997). Steiner's golden opportunity came in the form of a request to develop a school program for the children of the factory workers at the Waldorf Astoria cigarette factory in Stuttgart, Germany.

Waldorf in Theory

A highly spiritual man, Steiner developed his own form of *spiritual science*, called *anthroposophy* (human wisdom). **Anthroposophy** is a movement described as the knowledge and awareness of humanity, with a belief that there is a spiritual world that can be accessed by the highest intellectual faculties (Steiner, 2005). It is a philosophy based on examining more deeply the three parts of the human being (body, mind, and spirit) and the connections that bond humanity together. Although anthroposophy forms the basis of Steiner's educational plan, it is not explicitly taught in Waldorf schools (Nicholson, 2000). Because he believed in a holistic (whole-person) perspective, Steiner asserted that life and education called for schools to address all three elements of the human being. The holistic educator strives towards "the cultivation of a receptive, compassionate awareness, an attitude of wonder, awe and reverence for life" (Miller, 2006, p. 8). Based on his life's work, the educational curriculum he developed reflects his beliefs that

- Children grow through three distinct developmental phases.
- The highest pursuit of education should be to develop the whole child to become a free and creative thinker capable of self-actualization.
- All children should have the right and access to this form of schooling.

And so it was that the first Waldorf school was opened in Germany in 1919; the first Waldorf school in North America opened in New York City in 1928 (Nicholson, 2000). Steiner insisted that Waldorf schools operate under four key conditions, which were quite radical for the day:

- The school was open to all children (race, class, ethnicity, ability level).
- The school was coeducational (accepting boys and girls).
- The K–12 curriculum was viewed as a unified, complete program.
- The teachers bore the primary responsibility for control of the administration of the school, with minimal outside interference.

Anthroposophy

The philosophy developed by Rudolf Steiner, described as the knowledge and awareness of humanity, with a belief that there is a spiritual world that can be accessed by the highest intellectual faculties.

Steiner firmly believed that the social renewal that society so badly needed could be achieved only through the careful education of the whole child (Fenner & Rivers, 1995; Steiner, 1997). His purpose in developing this radical alternative education model "was to create a new impulse in education that would enable children from diverse backgrounds to develop the capacities necessary to cope with the demands and challenges of a post-industrial world" (Easton, 1997, p. 88). Steiner believed that each school should maintain some commonalities but should also reflect the particular culture and needs of the community in which it was located. In this way, Steiner sought to ensure the relevance, authenticity, and service of each school as it responded to the unique community. Since the opening of the first Waldorf school in 1919, the movement has spread internationally and has become one of the largest independent school movements in the world. As of 2009, there were approximately 900 schools and 1,600 kindergartens operating in 83 countries worldwide. The Association of Waldorf Schools of North America (AWSNA) lists 107 Waldorf teacher-training centers worldwide and reports 250 Waldorf schools and 102 early childhood programs affiliated with the Association in North America alone (United States, Canada, and Mexico; AWSNA, n.d.).

Waldorf in Practice

In the nursery-kindergarten room, the Waldorf school classroom is designed to be a place of harmony, beauty, and gentle guidance. It is a place where the innocence of childhood is protected and revered. Specially trained teachers, who believe that the first phase children grow through is that of imitation, serve as the purest form of model. All the materials in the child's world are natural and inspire creative play. The foods served are organic, nutritious, and often grown by the class members themselves. Children are provided with long periods of outdoor play to encourage healthy physical development and a spiritual connection to nature. The open-ended, hands-on design of the materials and the aesthetic focus of the curriculum encourage development in all children, including children with special needs (Edwards, 2002). Take a closer look at the key principles that form the foundation of the program:

- View of child development
- Programs and teacher's role
- Waldorf curriculum

View of Child Development

Steiner's theory of child development lays the foundational framework for the development of the curriculum, the design of the classroom space, and the general focus of the approach. As did several other key developmental theorists (e.g., Piaget, Erikson, Kohlberg), Steiner believed that children grow and develop through distinct stages:

- Early childhood (birth to 7 years old)
- Middle childhood (7–14 years old)
- Adolescence (14–21 years old)

Early Childhood

The early childhood phase extends from infancy to roughly 7 years of age, when baby teeth are beginning to be replaced by adult teeth. Before this milestone of physical development, Steiner believed that children were still connected to the spiritual world from which they were born (Iannone & Obenauf, 1999). During this formative period, Steiner believed that children were deeply influenced by their environment. Evidence of this is the child's unquestioning imitation of adult models and susceptibility to external stimuli. Consider the toddler who crawls across the floor following the family dog or the preschooler who repeats everything he or she hears. Protecting the child from unhealthy, unnatural, or inappropriate experiences, models, and stimuli—while embodying a reverent teacher archetype—is of the highest importance for the adults in the child's world. As in any developmentally appropriate approach, the heart of Steiner's early childhood practice is focused on teacher-child relationships. Waldorf teachers achieve strong bonds with children through deliberate story-telling, dramatic play, and creative expressions (Mitchell, 2007).

Steiner firmly believed that during the early years children's energies needed to focus on developing their physical bodies and imagination. He strongly cautioned against pushing children's development of intellectual skills. This resistance to a so-called push-down effect, or early academic instruction, is supported by educators and researchers (the NAEYC, Lillian Katz), as well as education policy makers across the world (Clouder, 2003). For example, children's early literary experiences in Waldorf kindergartens include oral storytelling, not formal training in decoding words or forming letters. Experiences of **emergent literacy** abound, however, through listening to teacher storytelling, fine motor development through painting and sculpting, and children's own storytelling. These experiences are viewed as a foundation of thinking and feeling that enable later development in the academic skills required to read and write. The opening classroom visit illustrates the Waldorf emergent literacy process. There, you saw the children listening to a short story, learning about story structure and plot while creating images in their minds to illustrate what they hear. Their imaginary illustrations then come to life in their fine motor work with the beeswax.

Steiner recognized learning and development as a lifelong process, and he was consequently resistant to pushing children into experiences that were beyond the scope of their naturally unfolding development. This is similar to Froebel's view of a child's garden. Steiner believed intellectual skill building would take the child's natural energies away from their endeavors in creative play, imitation, and refinements in physical development (Steiner, 1997). Steiner believed that the development of a healthy, coordinated body was a necessary foundation for all later learning. He further explained that the child's innate intelligence of his or her developmental needs and energy to work on those needs must not be "siphoned off too early from this essential task [physical development] into intellectual learning. Therefore, in the Waldorf Kindergarten no academic instruction takes place" (Schmitt-Stegmann, 1997, p. 4). Instead, children's imaginative play in a carefully crafted environment serves as the foundation for later academic knowledge and skill building.

Emergent literacy

Knowledge and skills that lay the foundation for reading and writing. Emergent literacy skills and behaviors, which can be seen in infancy and throughout the preschool years, are built on early experiences with written and oral language.

Middle Childhood

According to Steiner, as children begin the transition into middle childhood, which is marked by the transition from baby to adult teeth, their developmental process lies firmly within the domain of imagination. He believed that it was through imagination that children learn the cognitive tasks of concentration, mental imagery, and more complex thinking. It is during this phase that language is refined to adult levels, academic and intellectual work begins, and children are ready to experience their world on a deeper, more conscious level. Here teachers introduce alphabetic and numeric symbols, which are explored throughout all disciplines including literature, drama, stories, art, movement, and languages (Fenner & Rivers, 1995).

In this fully integrated curriculum, conceptual connections are made across disciplines and throughout the child's school years, thereby allowing for a deeper, richer understanding. Children are routinely engaged in creative, hands-on activities that allow them to hold and manipulate concrete examples of more abstract concepts (Nicholson, 2000). This can be seen in the emphasis on art, music, handcrafting (knitting, sewing), woodworking, and dance, which all align with academic subject matter. For example, as children learn basic mathematical concepts, they are simultaneously applying them in their knitting projects as they are planning and counting and increasing and diminishing stitches and rows. Geometric forms are being explored in math classes through painting, drawing, and sculpture and in a special form of dance called **eurythmy**, in which the arms reach out in different angles. Eurythmy is a form of dance in which body movements correspond to musical tones and spoken words. This careful integration of the body and mind is a hallmark of the integrated Waldorf curriculum.

Whereas the early years are focused on imitation of the physical surroundings, the middle childhood years emphasize explorations through language, feelings, and imagination. Throughout the Waldorf school experience, teachers embrace multiple representation methods for exploring content. Teachers routinely use storytelling, song, music, visual art, drama, movement, written word, and diagrams to present content (Nicholson, 2000). In turn, students are able to use multiple forms of representation to explore and share their understanding.

Adolescence

Often noted for its turbulent nature, adolescence marks the rocky transition from child to young adult. Steiner saw this as a time when youths are forming strength in their individual identity at the same time that they are developing feelings of social connectedness. It is during this time that youths could develop a deep and abiding love of humankind—a fraternity that would allow for the development of respect, morality, character, and social consciousness (Steiner, 1997). Although all the traditional academic areas are required parts of the curriculum (sciences, mathematics, English, arts, technology, and also foreign language, health, etc.) a holistic approach to learning continues throughout the high school years. Along with academic expectations, social consciousness remains a focus for Waldorf high school teachers today. This can be seen in the community service component of the high school curriculum and in the international exchange programs that are promoted in most Waldorf schools.

Waldorf Early Childhood Programs

Like Montessori, Steiner observed that young children unquestioningly imitate and absorb their surroundings. Thus, he believed that adults, through careful and deliberate action, should prepare and present an environment worthy of children. Unlike Montessori, however, he asserted that the child's early years should be a time of creative play and imaginative fantasy

Eurythmy

The art of movement that attempts to make visible the tone and feeling of music and speech. Eurythmy is helpful in developing concentration, self-discipline, and a sense of beauty. This training of moving artistically with a group stimulates sensitivity to others' as well as one's own individual mastery. Eurythmy lessons follow the themes of the curriculum, exploring rhyme, meter, story, and geometric forms (www. AWSNA.org).

These simple hand-knitted dolls, with their formless bodies and blank faces, are typical toys Waldorf teachers make for their children. The lack of form is meant to be suggestive rather than explicit so children can use their imagination to create features.

play. We could see this emphasis during the opening visit to the Waldorf nursery-kindergarten as the children transitioned to their beeswax-modeling activity after hearing a gnome story.

Other familiar characters the children come to know through the teachers' stories and displays include angels, fairies, fairy tales, and other stories about animals and woodland spirits. Traditionally, fairy tales are told from their original version (Grimm and Anderson, for example). These versions include graphic parts about death and suffering that may concern some early childhood teachers. In their storytelling process, however, Waldorf teachers skim such details in a matter-of-fact way that does not dramatize them or emotionally arouse the children (Astley & Jackson, 2000). Waldorf teachers prefer this authentic, gentle retelling as opposed to editing stories, which changes their deeper meaning and intentions.

Waldorf early childhood teachers are also adamant about not hiding academics in their curriculum or trying to mask academic lessons through play. Steiner believed that education should fit the child, not the other way around. Because he cautioned against pushing children before they are developmentally ready (Ogletree, 1975), there are usually no books, letters, or printed numbers in the nursery-kindergarten classroom. However, the nurturing of naturally unfolding development in young children is part of the complete academic curriculum for nursery-kindergarten to 12th grade. It is carefully constructed to develop strong cognitive, social, emotional, and physical development throughout the child's early life into young adulthood. Recall that one of Steiner's four key conditions set at the time he created the model was that the school be a unified K–12 program. The foundations that are laid in the early years are built on in later years and seek to instill a lifelong love of learning more than just attainment of certain skills. This big picture, or awareness of what lies ahead for the developing child, is always in the forefront of Waldorf educators' minds.

The experiences in early childhood are meant to develop a strong intellect through

- Imitating exemplary models in carefully constructed environments
- Communing with nature through ample daily outdoor play and gardening
- Fostering the child's imagination through storytelling and play
- Creative experiences such as painting, movement, and drawing, which build skills for later literacy

Children's self-initiated play with natural, open-ended materials is viewed as the most appropriate means of development at this phase. Nursery-kindergarten materials include

Waldorf Nursery-Kindergarten

Sample Half-day Daily Schedule

8:00 A.M.	Teachers Prepare for Children's Arrival
8:20 A.M.	Children Arrive, Begin Engaging with Materials Such as Finger Knitting; Children Gather with Teachers for Oral Storytelling; May Include Beeswax Modeling, Movement and Music, Special Celebrations
8:50 A.M.	Free Play, Dramatic Play, Cooking or Baking Activities
10 A.M.	Snack Together
10:20 A.M.	Outdoors, Free Play, Gardening
11:30 A.M.	Lunch Together
12:30 P.M.	Prepare for Departure

yarns, blocks, dolls, paints, sculpting materials, household artifacts, instruments, natural elements, and dress–up scarves.

Children's play is allowed to flow freely from the children as much as possible. They are given long, uninterrupted blocks of time and ample open-ended materials to engage in child-initiated social or individual play experiences. The children engage in a great deal of dramatic play, which may entail building tentlike homes from lengths of silk fabric and clothespins and caring for cloth dolls. Blocks (often made from smoothed slices of tree branches) and collections of natural materials are on hand for other constructions. Sculpting with beeswax, knitting, gardening, and sewing are routine activities. Teachers remain in the background, modeling such tasks as cooking, baking, knitting, tidying, and gardening; the children are free to move about the classroom at their will. There is a pervasive feeling of harmony, gentleness, dreaminess, and calm that surrounds children in the Waldorf nursery-kindergarten. This is promoted through soft lighting, muted colors, melodic singing, and the slow, deliberate actions of the teachers.

Early Childhood Teachers' Roles

Steiner observed that children were deeply affected by their surroundings and experiences. He became increasingly concerned with tracing later adult dysfunctions to negative experiences of children reared in a careless environment (Waldorf Kindergarten Association, 1994). Thus, especially in the Waldorf nursery-kindergarten, the role of the teacher is viewed as particularly important. As you explore this role more deeply by revisiting our focus on the early childhood years, keep the broader contexts of the whole child and unified K–12 perspectives in mind.

Teacher Preparations: Self and Environment

As mentioned previously, early childhood teachers recognize children's early years as a period in which children deeply absorb their surroundings and imitate the adults in their

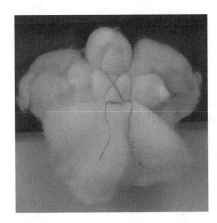

A wool angel created by a Waldorf parent for a classroom display.

world. The teacher is entrusted with the task of serving as an ideal model (in action and words) and the protector of children's innocence. Above all else, teachers strive to provide children with a sheltered environment. Much preparation goes into being a Waldorf teacher. There are special training institutes, and a specialized teaching certification is required. Part of this training focuses on the philosophical underpinnings of Steiner's work. Another part of it focuses on nourishing the teacher's creative skills so that he or she may, in turn, model these qualities for the children (Oberski, Pugh, MacLean, & Cope, 2007).

During the Waldorf teacher training, in addition to learning about anthroposophy, the teacher would explore the roles of

- Storyteller
- Embodiment of the parent figures
- Protector of the child's innate drives and creativity
- Nurturer of children's play

The teacher spends a great deal of time lovingly preparing the classroom environment to feel like a household. Teachers make cloth dolls and collect materials from nature to enhance the children's play. Teachers learn poems, stories, and songs to fill the children's day with fantasy and wonder. They create works of watercolor art to enrich the aesthetic beauty surrounding the classroom. Teachers learn how to knit, weave, sew, and create pictures using pieces of fluffy colored wools (a handcraft called *felting*: Waldorf Kindergarten Association, 1993).

Teacher as a Model

Steiner envisioned an early childhood teacher as one who embodies the ideal parental persona: loving, deliberate, careful, watchful, supportive, and present but not imposing. Early childhood teachers express delight and inner satisfaction as they engage in daily activities that mimic home life: gardening, baking, woodworking, caring for the classroom space, and interacting meaningfully with the children (Fenner & Rivers, 1995). When the teacher wants the children to do something (clean up, gather together, prepare for an outing), he or she begins by modeling the action and gently using a song to verbally draw the children to the activity.

Teachers strive to maintain a harmonious, peaceful space by using song and story to direct the children. They would never use a harsh or raised tone of voice or a forceful movement. Indeed, all movements are deliberate and pensive, always keeping in mind that young children take every aspect of their surroundings into themselves and seek to preserve a dreamy quality. When watching Waldorf teachers, you have the sense of the movements of a graceful, deliberate dancer. All these aspects of the teachers' roles of creating the environment and being a model are carried out with care and reflection (Astley & Jackson, 2000). Waldorf teachers strive to be thoughtful in all their actions, always aware of the children in their care. Watch how a teacher uses singing and gentle touch to engage infants and build loving bonds at MyEducationLab.

Teacher as an Observer

During the hours the children are in the classroom, the teachers engage in purposeful activity as well as careful observation of the children. Knowing each individual child is an essential aspect in the Waldorf teacher's role, and this is often accomplished through observation, strong parent relationships, and communication. It is through an intimate knowledge of each child's unique personality that the Waldorf teacher is able to support each child's growth and celebrate the individuality of each. To allow for the child's true spirit and nature to be exercised, as well as for ample teacher observation, the schedule in the early childhood classroom is fairly open.

Each day begins with a long period of free play, later accompanied by such outdoor experiences as gardening, nature walks, and playing on the school grounds. The class also comes together to share poems, songs, and a nutritious snack consisting of bread or soup made by the teachers or fruits or vegetables grown in the class garden (Waldorf Kindergarten Association, 1993). When space or season makes home growing of food impossible, the children are still given organic, whole foods from local farms. The closeness children feel to nature is preserved throughout all activities as well as in the selection of materials and foods.

The activities of daily life, focus on routines, and explorations of nature largely make up the basic elements of the curriculum in the early childhood classroom. As such, the teachers do not rely on standardized tests or intelligence measures to assess children's development. Beginning in early childhood, observations and portfolios of children's work are used. Teachers throughout all the grades write reflective statements about each child's progress, which are compiled with work samples to demonstrate developmental progress. As you read in Chapter 1, it is important with any assessment plan that the methods used reflect the educational experience. By using authentic assessment methods like observations and work samples, Waldorf teachers strive to validate each child's unique characteristics and progress.

Curriculum

By working with their hands while gardening, modeling, painting, or sewing, children develop the capacity for later writing, dance, and visual lessons. Through their creative play and sharing of stories, children develop the capacity for later intellectual, social, and imaginative tasks. In this way, the early childhood teacher lays the groundwork for the child's

MyEducationLab

Go to the Assignments and Activities section of Topic 9: Guiding Children in the MyEducationLab for your course and complete the activity entitled *Nurturing Relationships.* Observe how the teacher uses gentle touch and soft song to encourage loving bonds with and among infants.

later experiences in elementary classrooms. Teachers at all levels are intimately knowledge-able about the entire curriculum, and they are in close contact with each other. In keeping with Steiner's original condition that school administration be part of the teachers' role, teachers meet regularly to plan and discuss instructional and curricular goals. This is one small way in which teachers view their work as a part of a larger, unified program that is embodied in the view of the curriculum as an *ascending spiral* (Nicholson, 2000).

The curriculum in the Waldorf school is carefully and thoughtfully designed to be viewed as a unified whole from kindergarten to the 12th grade. Content, skills, attitudes, and knowledge areas are visited and revisited at different levels in what is referred to as an ascending spiral. This means that as children explore topics and their world at earlier ages; similar topics are repeated and explored as the children's maturity levels change and their cognitive processes develop. This ensures that children are continually engaged in authen-tic experiences that are both familiar and new, and they are engaged at a level that pro-gresses with them. In this way, the curriculum is developmentally appropriate and addresses the most important criteria required for learning to occur: that learning activities be mean-ingful and appropriate for children's age and developmental level. This also allows for later academic experiences to build on early experiences, giving children a frame of reference with which to better understand increasingly complex ideas.

Cultivating Imagination as a Precursor to Intellect

The early childhood classrooms are generally structured as a nursery school model, in which children come to school for the morning, sometimes only two or three mornings a week. In addition to presenting pure and idealistic models and protecting the innocence of childhood, teachers endeavor to celebrate and revere children's fantasy and creative play. To this end, teachers do not expose children to printed literature, which includes only illus-trations generated by adults. As noted earlier, children are continually exposed to language through oral storytelling, which is believed to allow their own mind's eye to create images of their own design. This resistance to early academics also means that children are not pushed to read and write in the early childhood classroom.

Formal training in reading and writing is reserved for introduction later in the second or third grade (Oppenheimer, 1999). However, children are routinely developing and re-fining their fine motor skills and exploring shape through sculpting and painting and in their play. Young children draw with blocks of beeswax crayons, as opposed to stick-shaped crayons, which more closely resemble writing implements. They are routinely exposed to different forms of stories, characters, and authors through the storytelling. These experi-ences are viewed as the appropriate early foundations that support later reading and writ-ing when the children's intellect is developmentally ready (Fenner & Rivers, 1995).

This point is often surprising to outsiders, and it can be a source of concern in today's academically focused early childhood world. Despite ample support by prominent early childhood experts on the potentially negative impact of pushing academics too early (re-ferred to in Oppenheimer, 1999, and Clouder, 2003), some people are critical of this prac-tice. Take a moment to close your eyes and conjure up an image of a talking mouse that has all kinds of adventures. Did you immediately think of Walt Disney's Mickey Mouse? In-deed, you would not be alone—many people would. But this image was just Disney's vi-sion of a mouse, so why should so many of us conjure up the same image? Why are we not able to develop our own vision?

Block crayons are made from beeswax and designed to encourage shading, not line drawing.

Waldorf educators believe that early exposure to print and media images can have detrimental effects on our ability to create our own ideas, vision, and imagination. When we are not allowed or encouraged to develop strong imagination skills, we may never hone this active, creative potential. This may leave us instead passively relying on someone else's vision through the variety of media forms that abound. Remember that Waldorf education seeks to develop independent, creative thinkers. Thus, the loss of our unique power of creative imagination is something that the curriculum is designed to prevent. Certainly, advocating for a resistance to early academics, technology in classrooms, and media influences like television and movies may not be the most popular position today. On the other hand, it is important to keep in mind that Waldorf early childhood classrooms value children's play, social interactions, and inquisitive explorations of their world. And, these are widely considered to be important characteristics of good practice that may be jeopardized when media and technology bombard the senses.

Recent research on academic proficiency of students attending four public schools using Waldorf methods found that although language and mathematics test scores of the Waldorf-method school second-graders were "far below their peers[,] by eighth grade, however, they were on par with the top 10 peer-alike public schools. Overall, the Waldorf eighth-graders often performed a tiny bit lower on the language arts (reading and writing), and moderately better on mathematics" (Oberman, 2008, p.12). Furthermore, other studies of private Waldorf graduates revealed that the Waldorf school students earn SAT scores above the national average, but Waldorf schools also instill in students critical thinking skills, global awareness and concern for others, stronger relationships, and dedication to lifelong learning (Mitchell & Gerwin, 2007; Oppenheimer, 1999). Coupled with strong academic achievement in the later grades, these attitudes and dispositions are widely valued in schools and society.

The Integrated Curriculum

The Waldorf K–12 curriculum also takes an integrated approach, recognizing that content must be meaningful, applicable, and used in context. In this way, children explore content and topics through multiple modes, including foreign languages, literature, arts, movement, discussion, experiment, debate, and so on. A truly hands-on model, Waldorf education

Pages from an elementary Waldorf student's main lesson book.

seeks to develop in all children the ability to engage with the world on a concrete level and later to expand that experience to an abstract, thoughtful, spiritual level. The curriculum allows for an exceptional degree of individual expression. This also contributes to the personal meaning and relevance of all studies. One of the ways in which Waldorf education integrates the individual into all learning is through the reliance on the student's writing and illustrating of his or her own "textbooks" (blank artist's sketchbooks), commonly called **main lesson books**.

Much of the content in the elementary grades is explored through lectures, discussions, and active experiments. Rarely will children be seen passively relying solely on a textbook as the main source of information (Nicholson, 2000). Rather, teachers and children actively explore their world, finding primary sources of information. Recall from Chapter 8 that project work also embraces the use of primary sources and active exploration over secondary (printed) sources. Children chronicle their newfound knowledge in their blank sketchbooks, in which they write, draw, or paint as they represent their knowledge. Children prepare a new book for each new course of study they undertake (AWSNA, 1996). In this way, Waldorf education utilizes principles of project work both in the nature of classroom activities and in the myriad ways experiences are represented. Through the use of multiple modes of learning and representation, Waldorf education also aligns with principles of multiple intelligence theory.

Main lesson books

Blank books that each student fills with information and self-generated illustrations that align with each new course of study.

Daily Structure

In the elementary schools, the schedule is constructed around a 2-hour block of study each morning. It is out of this focused study that the student's main lesson books are created. This allows for a more focused, intense experience in which children and teachers concentrate on topics covering all disciplines in turn. The rest of the day is generally divided into the familiar 50-minute periods in which courses in academic subjects such as languages, sciences, and mathematics, as well as creative subjects such as handwork, woodwork, dance, movement, and music, are studied (Fenner & Rivers, 1995). For the most part, all children participate in all classes together, strengthening their bonds as an extended family.

Looping

The practice of having the same teacher move through ages or grades with the same class for 2 years or more.

Throughout the first- through eighth-grade years, Waldorf teachers ideally remain with the same class. This practice is called *looping*. **Looping** refers to having the same teacher move through ages or grades with the same class for 2 or more years. This continuity of care is used in various programs from infant care through elementary school grades, although it is practiced more frequently in European and Japanese schools (Hegde & Cassidy, 2004). In Waldorf schools, teachers loop from first grade through eighth grade. Many teachers and parents report increased satisfaction because they are able to develop more profound relationships with each child (Cicala Filmworks, n.d.). Obviously, not every Waldorf teacher remains with the same class. The same issues of relocation, staff changes, and so on can be found in individual schools, but looping remains the goal of all Waldorf elementary schools. Although this practice is not unique to Waldorf schools, it is certainly a notable feature of the approach resulting from the scope of the span of grades.

Many people new to Waldorf education are surprised by this practice, expressing concern over the ability of one teacher to provide comprehensive learning experiences for such a range of ages. Newcomers have also raised the potential for personality conflicts to fester for long periods of time as a concern of long-term looping. Imagine if you were in this situation, facing many more years with a student who routinely gave you trouble—the one who just pushed your buttons everyday. Or, imagine yourself having to be an expert in the advancing content of 8 years of study. A daunting task!

Proponents of Waldorf education cite the practice of looping as a valuable asset in teacher satisfaction, in building social connections, and in managing the inevitable conflicts that arise from such close contact. When teachers or children experience social conflicts, it is not an option to passively wait until the end of the year to avoid resolving the issues. The last day of the school year does not mean "that child" will become someone else's problem in September. Teachers are keenly aware that personality conflicts among students or with them will have to be resolved directly. Through the productive resolution of problems as they arise, both teachers and children learn positive, necessary skills in conflict resolution and how to get along with diverse personalities. In terms of teacher satisfaction, many teachers report that the continual change in grade levels pushes them to continue to enhance their own knowledge and to remain creative in designing successively more skilled lesson experiences; in addition, it reduces the monotony of repeating the same content year after year. Many looping teachers report that this practice helps keep their teaching fresh and interesting (Fenner & Rivers, 1995).

Diversity and Inclusion in Waldorf Education

The Waldorf education model is well suited to serve children from families with limited incomes and children with special needs because of the

- Hands-on manipulative activities prominent throughout the grades
- Focus on individual expression through the creative arts
- Integral part that music and eurythmy (used as a form of curative dance) play in the curriculum
- Unified nature of the K–12 curriculum

Today Waldorf schools are serving children from all socioeconomic backgrounds and are found in rural, suburban, and urban settings. The Waldorf model has been employed in public education as charter schools in seven districts, including an urban district in Wisconsin that was plagued by poverty, violence, and low student achievement. Soon after the school's opening, the school district, parents, community, and teachers witnessed remarkable changes in students' attitudes, motivation, abilities, and academic achievement scores (Byers et al., 1996). Called "healing education" by administrators and faculty alike, the hallways now ring with song and music, are veritable museums of students' watercolor paintings, and are no longer places of violence and tension (Cicala Filmworks, n.d.). Stories of such transformation are shared by educators in other schools as well (Mollet, 1991).

Additional intervention applications of Waldorf education in the United States can be found in California, where a juvenile correctional facility has adopted a Waldorf approach (Cicala Filmworks, n.d.; Oppenheimer, 1999). The results have been favorable. Teachers, students, and parents alike have praised the arts-based curriculum as having opened pathways of communication between once-rival gang members, troubled teens, and violent repeat offenders. Perhaps most meaningful to students, teachers, parents, and administrators is the sense of pride that the students begin taking in their creations. This feeling then spills over into the sense of pride and responsibility in themselves that is often lacking in children, whether at risk or at promise.

Several Waldorf charter schools in California have reported that the curricular methods specific to Waldorf education, such as integrating the arts into all subject areas, the hands-on methods of all subjects, and the social dynamics of the classrooms, have made learning English easier for their linguistically diverse students (Cicala Filmworks, n.d.). The variety of expressive activities, including music, dance, art, story, and handcrafts, allows children at all levels of language learning to find ways to communicate.

In addition to the modifications made to suit specific applications, such as public schools, the Waldorf education model has been used to address the wide range of needs of diverse students. Steiner called his approach *curative education*, emphasizing the powerful role education can have in healing and promoting development. Remember from Chapter 10 that this is similar to Montessori's early experiences with institutionalized children. Although some schools are not well equipped to handle children with special needs, for the most part Waldorf schools welcome all children, and there are currently programs that exclusively serve children with developmental and physical disabilities in New Hampshire, that serve children in an impoverished community in South Africa, and that serve abandoned, extremely poor children in the most destitute area of Nepal.

The Children of Nepal program was established through grants made available by the Rudolf Steiner Foundation in 1996 as a means to counteract the extreme poverty and destitute conditions faced by Nepalese children, many of whom had been abandoned. Of primary importance for the founders of the Tashi (Tibetan for "all that is good") Waldorf School located outside Katmandu is building a strong foundation in all areas of development for young children to improve their chances of gaining a full education (Rudolf Steiner Foundation, n.d.). Where parent partnerships are possible, the Tashi School strives to include all members of the children's family in the care and education of the family as a whole. Despite being a relatively new facility, they have already added a free medical clinic for children and families, a cooperative farming program, and parent-education sessions. By working in partnerships with parents, the school hopes to support responsible parenting and decrease the high rates of child abandonment.

Like the U.S. Head Start programs you read about in Chapter 6, the Tashi Waldorf School is comprehensive in its intervention approach. Through a comprehensive scope of health, family welfare, and education, the school hopes to improve the self-confidence and self-efficacy of each child and family and, ultimately, effect real change in this most needy community. These, of course, are the driving goals of all Waldorf schools, built on the commitment to improve society through education for the head, heart, and hands.

Contemporary Issues: Debates about Waldorf Education

The vast majority of families and teachers involved in Waldorf schools report success and satisfaction with children's outcomes. Waldorf graduates are frequently referred to as *well-rounded people*, able to think, manage challenges, and lead successful adult lives (Almon, 1992; Mitchell & Gerwin, 2007). Some reports indicate that, in addition to being more reflective, deliberate thinkers and strong students, Waldorf students' Scholastic Aptitude Test scores are above national averages (Oppenheimer, 1999). In addition, roughly 94% of Waldorf high school graduates go on to 4-year colleges, an impressive rate compared to the national average of 64% of 2007 high school graduates attending 4-year colleges (BLS, 2008; Dancy, 2004; Enten, 2005; Mitchell & Gerwin, 2007). Nonetheless, criticism of the application of the Waldorf philosophy in public schools is growing.

Criticism mostly centers around the argument for the division of religion and public schools. Although Waldorf educators do not promote any one religion, there is a strong spiritual component, grounded in the anthroposophy roots, that has contributed to the criticism (Ruenzel, 2001). Many of the traditional Waldorf songs and poems learned in the nursery-kindergarten and repeated throughout the years include reference to various gods and saints. Many of the rituals and festivals, so important to life in the Waldorf school, center around such events as Advent, solstices, and spiritual awakenings. Even such things as the use of candles during some festivals, the recitation of poems, and the celebrations of earth changes generally stray from mainstream religious holidays and are, therefore, sometimes surprising to people new to Waldorf education.

However, it is this separation from mainstream (religious) holidays that, Waldorf education proponents point out, makes them not a religious program. Proponents point to the difference between religion and spirituality. Religion is defined by specific texts and beliefs, and it is often exclusionary to other religions. Spirituality is a more personal set of beliefs and reverence for all life and it does not necessarily align with one formal religion (Miller, 2006). When viewed in this way, spirituality—as an individual construct—allows for an openness and acceptance that some religious faiths may not have room for. Advocates of Waldorf education point to the emphasis on education that frees each individual to think for himself or herself as a counter to this criticism (Ward, 2005).

Public school systems have circumvented this issue by successfully modifying the curriculum and practice to better fit their communities' needs and expectations. Some schools may refrain from using certain verses and celebrations. Most Waldorf schools, whether public or private, do not engage in formal religious teaching and do not tolerate discrimination or exclusivity. Recently, the Waldorf education community crafted and adopted a statement against all forms of discrimination in any Waldorf school, referred to as the Stuttgart Declaration. The statement includes a commitment that "Waldorf schools do not select, stratify or discriminate amongst their pupils, but consider all human beings to be free and equal in dignity and rights, independent of ethnicity, national or social origin, gender, language, religion, and political or other convictions" (ECSWE, 2007).

Inspirations for Application From Waldorf Practices

When introduced to the foundational beliefs and practices of Waldorf education, many early childhood teachers find inspiration for their own practice in diverse early childhood education settings. Some simple ideas for Waldorf-inspired applications include

- Integrate more natural materials into the classroom for children to explore and create with
  - Sections of tree branches
  - Collections of leaves, shells, stones, crystals
  - Seasonal collections such as pine cones and boughs; flowers and dried grasses; moss-covered rocks; abandoned birds' nests; gourds
  - Balls of wool yarns
  - Beeswax for sculpting
- Replacing finished, formed, plastic, or battery-operated toys with open-ended materials
  - Simple dolls sewn from organic cottons and wools
  - Large squares of soft material or silk scarves
  - Homemade blocks from wood or fabrics
  - Variety of items and materials for sculpting and building
  - Items reminiscent of home such as cooking utensils, simple tools, sized-down bedding or dress up items
- Encourage constructive, social play
  - Providing materials and prompts to foster imagination (What can we make out of this? What shape do you see hiding in that clay? I wonder . . .)
  - Giving children ample time, space, and freedom to build imaginary worlds together
  - Allowing fantasy play (fairies, gnomes, talking animals, etc.)
  - Sewing simple dolls with twist or braid yarn for hair
  - Making characters from natural materials (corn husks, twigs, pine cones, wool)
  - Baking and cooking nutritious snacks (bread, soup, fruits)
  - Providing outdoor time as much as possible, preferably with access to natural areas
- Slowing down your actions, being deliberate in gesture and voice
  - Integrating soft, slow songs throughout the day and for transitions
  - Moving in fluid, graceful gestures and deliberate movements (no yelling across the room or running down halls)
  - Modeling kind language and gentle touches of friendship
  - Integrating oral storytelling with simple props and hand gestures

Conclusion

Waldorf education is a significant educational movement, and it has important implications for all educators. Many elements of this approach can influence practices in child development and learning, including

- The way adults structure the environment and teaching to protect childhood
- The emphasis on preserving the developing imagination by resisting offensive media influences
- The view of education as a means of strengthening society

By exploring the Waldorf education model, several key themes emerge as important contributors to Steiner's goals for the education of the whole child:

- Children are valued as threefold individuals (body, mind, spirit).
- Early experiences focus on play and imitation.
- Classroom activities are hands-on and meaningful.
- Learning is developmental and content is integrated.
- Children demonstrate their understanding through multiple, creative representations.
- Children's classroom experiences become increasingly more global throughout the years.

Bearing these foundational elements in mind, you can begin to see the comprehensive, complex interplay between philosophy and practice. It is a philosophy that began with one man's vision of empowering individuals through holistic education. It has progressed into a worldwide, independent movement that is committed to the practice of educating well-rounded individuals ready to reshape and reform society.

REFLECTION QUESTIONS: LOOKING BACK AND LOOKING AHEAD

Take a moment now to reflect back on some of the surprising or unique features of the model. Ask yourself if there are any elements in the view of childhood, teacher's role, or curriculum with which you particularly agreed. Reflect on how these elements could be incorporated into your own philosophy and practice of teaching. You may want to make some notes on key phrases or aspects that you would like to include in your own teaching philosophy statement. By this point in your readings, your own personal teaching philosophy should be growing and becoming clearer to you. Continue reflecting on the many approaches and models of teaching as well as your own beliefs about children as you construct your teaching philosophy.

1. What elements did you read about in the Waldorf schools that are similar to other theories, approaches, or frameworks you have explored so far? Think about DAP, MI, constructivism, and the project approach in particular.

2. Look back at the classroom view from the start of the chapter. In what ways can you identify aspects of the Waldorf philosophy illustrated in this classroom visit?

3. Are there elements that you strongly agree or disagree with about the philosophy and application of Waldorf education? Describe these.

SUMMARY

The first Waldorf school opened in 1919 in Germany. Based on the work of philosopher Rudolf Steiner, Waldorf education is a unique kindergarten-to-12th-grade model that seeks to develop independent, creative thinkers through a carefully designed school environment and curriculum that nurtures the head, heart, and hands of each individual child. Waldorf education emphasizes the use of hands-on learning and integrates the arts throughout all subject areas.

In the early childhood years

- Teachers seek to preserve children's naturally unfolding processes in physical development and their awakening to the physical world around them.
- Early childhood is a time of play, imagination, creation, and nature.
- Teachers provide open-ended materials and model appropriate behaviors.
- Songs, stories, dramatic play, and games are the basis of the curriculum.
- Teachers maintain a harmonious, peaceful atmosphere in the classroom and within the child.
- Teachers hone their skills as observers and indirectly encourage children's play.

Waldorf education began as a program for lower-socioeconomic-class families, but over time it became more and more an exclusive alternative program. Recent applications in impoverished communities have seen a rekindling of Steiner's initial vision: education as a force for social renewal. Although the transformative power of Waldorf education has been reported in these intervention schools, parents and educators alike are seeing positive impacts in all schools.

Application Activities

On the Web: MyEducationLab Go to the Video Examples section of Topic 5: Program Models in the MyEducationLab for your course and revisit the video entitled *Waldorf Classroom*. Focus your observation on the environment and materials, making notes as the narrator describes how the unique features embody Steiner's philosophy of education. Discuss the corresponding questions in small groups.

In Class Find a Web source for more information on Waldorf education. Find a journal article online or explore a website that has information about Waldorf schools, criticisms of Waldorf education, parent information, teacher trainings, and so on. Bring a copy of the source you found and a one-page summary of your findings. In small groups, share the site you explored, what you learned, and your thoughts about Waldorf education.

In the Field Storytelling is a key part of the early childhood classroom. All teachers can use some practice to hone their storytelling skills. For this activity, choose a well-written children's book and prepare a storytelling session based on the book. Practice using your tone of voice, facial expressions, and body gestures to bring the story to life. You may want

MyEducationLab

Go to the Video Examples section of Topic 5: Program Models in the MyEducationLab for your course and watch the video *Waldorf Classroom*. Observe the environment and materials, noting how the unique features embody Steiner's philosophy of education.

to observe a storyteller for ideas. Locate a child-care center, family care program, or library where you can present your storytelling session to a group of children.

For Your Portfolio Interview an early childhood teacher from a local program in your area. This does not have to be a Waldorf teacher. Ask about the teacher's beliefs about the following concepts and compare the responses to what you've read about Waldorf education:

- Academic programming for pre-kindergarteners
- Development of literacy
- Young children and imagination
- Aesthetic environments for young children
- Teachers as role models
- Media and technology in the classroom

Write a two-page summary of your comparisons. This paper can be added to your portfolio in the teaching and learning or professionalism section.

RELATED WEB LINKS

Association of Waldorf Schools of North America (AWSNA)
www.whywaldorfworks.org

Waldorf Answers
www.waldorfanswers.org

Waldorf Early Childhood Association of North America (WECAN)
www.waldorfearlychildhood.org

Waldorf Home Schooling
www.waldorfhomeschooling.org

Nova Natural Materials
www.novanatural.com/creativity/waldorf-materials

CHAPTER 12

Bringing It All Together: Imagining and Becoming

If a child is to keep his inborn sense of wonder, he needs the companionship of at least one adult who can share it, rediscovering with him the joy, excitement and mystery of the world we live in.

—RACHEL CARSON

You have taken a long journey through some of the events, lives, and practices that continue to shape the field of early childhood education. Set against the backdrop of a long history rich in discourse, innovation, debate, and challenges, your task now is to reflect on who you are becoming as an early childhood professional. I use the term *becoming* even considering the many experiences and skills you may already bring to your professional persona. I choose this word to convey the dynamic, active, transformational state in which all educators live. Through our continued reflection, risk taking, trying, testing, inquiring, and introspection, we are all on the ever-stretching path to "becoming." This is the work of the caregiver, the educator, the advocate, the professional—the passionate life-long learner.

The people and practices in this book have shared with you what they have learned during their own course of becoming. Their stories and histories are like a lantern illuminating our shared history. Now it is passed to you to carry it forward into the as yet uncharted future. Standing on the solid foundation of our past, now it is up to you to imagine who you are becoming.

Looking forward, there are some familiar topics that remain timely as well as some new issues that we face in our changing world. As technological and social advances have created an increasingly global society, we find ourselves with more access and open communications than ever before. Communications have indeed brought the world together in many respects. And yet we still see vast divides in economic classes, access to quality education, and cultural practices, values, and beliefs. Teachers continue to see dramatic changes in culturally and linguistically diverse student populations. Families and communities struggle to find successful schools and quality programs. In addition, we continue to see increasing inclusion of children with broader ranges of abilities and needs in all classrooms. Teachers must be sensitive to the unique resources and needs of the families they work with, while always respecting the increasing diversity of education environments. As you move forward in your journey, these issues will be your companions and will guide the nature of your work.

Guiding Principles for the Future: Respect, Enthusiasm, Commitment

One of the most important guiding principles all teachers must bring with them is an awareness of and respect for working with diverse people. Many new teachers may not have experienced opportunities to interact with diverse people. It is natural to develop deeply held beliefs, habits, and biases based on your own past experiences. As you move forward into the classroom as a teacher, how you teach will be greatly affected by how you were taught and raised. It is imperative that you continue to reflect on the connections between your past and your teaching style. You may make deliberate choices about how you want to teach, about how you want your students to learn, that are different from your own school experiences. You will be able to make these conscious choices only if you are aware of your past and you create a vision of your future.

Each child who comes into your classroom will bring a unique perspective and set of experiences. Finding ways to connect new learning with familiar experiences is a key to being a successful educator. In order to do this you will need to get to know your children and truly value each child's background. Regular communication with families is the first step to integrating children's home culture into the classroom. Families have a wealth of resources to offer and are often flattered and proud to share them with your class. Just be sure to welcome their input in meaningful activities, not merely as an extra set of hands.

At different times in your career, you will also undoubtedly work with colleagues who bring very different backgrounds and beliefs to their teaching. You may not always agree with them, but there is always something to learn from the people who cross your path. As you read about in the chapter on the National Association for the Education of Young Children (NAEYC) Code of Ethics, part of being a professional educator is respecting and supporting colleagues. Seek out advice, share strategies, and develop open communications. Creating mutually respectful, supportive relationships in your center or school is a primary way to nurture your satisfaction and enthusiasm for teaching. Throughout many of the chapters in this book, you read about the importance of teachers working collaboratively. Making meaningful connections with families and colleagues is challenging at times, but it is at the heart of best practices.

Enthusiasm for Teaching

Remember the activity you did in Chapter 1 when you remembered your favorite teacher? Most likely you remember qualities of enthusiasm, energy, and genuine caring.

Great early childhood teachers find joy in exploring the world, just as their children do.

The affective disposition you bring to your classroom sets the tone for all your interactions with your children. Children, especially very young children, need caring, energetic teachers. They need to feel that they are with adults who, first and foremost, want to be there with them. The way you tell and read stories, build villages from blocks, and play restaurant or house while skillfully negotiating conflicts, challenges, and collaborations conveys your enthusiasm for your work. Considering there will always be rough days, try to retain a childlike energy, curiosity, and wonder as you work with and for children. Cultivate a vivid imagination, just as your children are exploring theirs.

Being enthusiastic about your work not only benefits your children but also helps improve your own work satisfaction. When you feel that our work is meaningful and that your dedication is recognized, you naturally feel more personally and professionally fulfilled. Your energy and enthusiasm can also translate into a willingness to imagine, wonder, and try. Being open to new experiences in teaching, just as reading this book opened you to new methods and approaches, keeps your work fresh and interesting. Some ideas or strategies may not work the way you thought they would, just as some lessons will not go as planned. But even in the "flops," you learn and grow. You will develop new twists on old ideas and discover new directions for your teaching. This process truly gets at the heart of the lifelong journey of being a professional educator.

Commitment to Professionalism

As you read in Chapters 2 and 3, the field of early childhood education has not always been a highly regarded profession. In recent decades, however, great strides have been made nationally to increase standards, teacher credentials, teacher salaries, and professional

MyEducationLab

Go to the Assignments and Activities section of Topic 12: Professionalism/ Ethics in the MyEducationLab for your course and complete the activity entitled *Characteristics of the Early Childhood Professional.* Consider the various ways you can grow as a professional.

NAEYC Membership

Go to the NAEYC website at www.naeyc.org and look up the section on membership. Study the costs and benefits of being an NAEYC member. Think about the benefits listed on the site as well as others, such as the feeling of being part of a large national group with shared commitments.

development. It is essential that new teachers entering the field continue this important work. Teachers promote the increase in professionalism by carrying out their work with ethics and care and by continuing the learning process.

By now you have heard people encourage you to be a lifelong learner. This is also a call to be a professional. By attending conferences, joining professional organizations, networking with other professionals, and completing workshops and seminars, you can keep yourself current on new research and innovations in the field. As you gain classroom experience and research knowledge, you will be able to contribute to future research and innovations. This cycle of learning, growing, exploring, and sharing is the epitome of professional collegiality. As you can see, this is just the beginning of a long, exciting journey.

Congratulations on making this commitment to becoming a professional educator. Now let the real journey begin!

The important thing is not to stop questioning. Curiosity has its own reason for existing.

—ALBERT EINSTEIN

Culminating the Text and Creating Your Portfolio

MyEducationLab

Go to the Resources section in the MyEducationLab for your course to access the Portfolio Builder and gain insights for creating your own professional portfolio.

In the following series of activities, you will explore your ideas, beliefs, goals, and vision as you imagine and define yourself as an educator. These will help you not only synthesize what you have read about in this text, but also continue to refine your vision of education and of being a teacher. You may decide that several of these activities fit into your professional portfolio and provide evidence of your teaching philosophy, style, and skills. Thoughtfully select and organize the work you choose for your portfolio based on categories or standards, such as those you read about in Chapter 1. The NAEYC standards provide a recognizable, professional organization for your portfolio and may be your College or University's preferred framework, particularly if your program is part of the NCATE or NAEYC accreditation process (NAEYC, 2008). Visit the Resources link at MyEducationLab to access the comprehensive Portfolio Builder tool for additional ideas and tips for pulling your professional portfolio together.

NAEYC Standards for Early Childhood Professional Preparation Programs

Standard 1: Promoting Child Development and Learning
Artifacts: analysis of metaphor describing children; statement of beliefs about teaching and learning; brochure highlighting development in each domain

Standard 2: Building Family and Community Relationships
Artifacts: family workshop outline; family brochure or newsletter; community needs survey; community resource list/brochure collection for agencies serving families and children

Standard 3: Observing, Documenting, and Assessing
Artifacts: observation reports; program comparison report; assessment tools; rubrics and checklists created to evaluate classroom environments and children's progress; child study

Standard 4: Using Developmentally Effective Approaches to Connect with Children and Families
Artifacts: lesson plans; review journals or self-evaluations; learning center designs; planning webs and charts; photo documentation panels

Standard 5: Using Content Knowledge to Build Meaningful Curriculum
Artifacts: content-area lesson plans; planning webs and charts;

Standard 6: Becoming a Professional
Artifacts: multiple intelligence self-test and response; NAEYC membership; NAEYC position statement review; journal article reviews; theorist studies; conference attendance records; teacher interview report including questions on law and policies affecting families and children

Application Activities

Activity 1, Meshing approaches Using the charts in the appendixes or another graphic organizer of your choice, identify key elements of each of the theories, frameworks, methods, and approaches you have read about. This will help you keep everything straight and will also help you pick out aspects of practices you agree with most and want to integrate into your own beliefs and practice. Highlight elements that speak to you, energize you, and empower you. Share your chart with a small group or your class and compare which elements you highlighted.

Activity 2, Ideal environment visual In small groups, decide what you believe educational environments for young children should look like. Think about how past theorists have described ideal settings. Come up with some descriptions that you agree with from their work or your own ideas. Create a visual representation of your own ideal educational environment for young children using large paper and a variety of art supplies (markers, collage, sculpture, painting). Or, if you prefer, create a skit/play to illustrate your vision.

Activity 3, Philosophy of education Throughout this book you have stopped along the way and thought about your own beliefs and ideas about early childhood education. You may want to flip back to some of the starting or ending reflection questions in each chapter to refresh your memory. Using your responses to these questions, create your own philosophy of education statement. This statement is an important part of all teachers' professional identity, and it should be put in your professional teaching portfolio. As you gain more experience and learn more about the field of education, your philosophy statement will evolve. Think of this as a living, breathing, working document. This is just a start. Or, if you already have one from previous classes, take this time to revise it and change things as you see fit. Your statement will say many things, but at the heart of it is sharing your vision of how theory is translated into practice. Some important aspects you may want to convey are

- Your beliefs about best practices in early childhood education?
  - What do you believe are the rights of all children?
  - How does teaching look when children are valued and respected?
  - What qualities make a "great teacher" in your view?
- Your vision of the ideal learning environment?
  - How do environments look when children are valued and respected?
- Your beliefs about children
  - How do children grow, learn, think, and feel?
  - Are children active in driving their own learning or building their own knowledge?
- The role teachers play in young children's lives
  - In what ways do you hope to impact children's lives?
  - What do you believe are teachers' responsibilities to children?
- The role teachers play in families' lives
- What it means to work collaboratively in planning, teaching, and assessing
  - Do you view teachers as a team? How will you embody this team-approach?
- Why you want to be a teacher
- The strengths you possess or are honing that will make you a great teacher

To get started, you can brainstorm a list of key words and phrases that embody your beliefs and ideals about teaching and education and write them on small adhesive notes. Organize these words in categories that make sense, such as teachers, children, learning, teaching, environment, your own skills, your motivations, and so on. After your sections are grouped, you can start writing paragraphs and organizing your material into a logical statement.

Activity 4, Vision of the child In small groups, think about all the images of children and teachers you have read about throughout the book. Recall how key theorists described their beliefs about children and teachers. What ideals do you believe in? These may be your own ideas or the ideas of those about whom you have read in this book or other books. Create a visual representation of your vision of children as well as your vision of

Creating your professional portfolio is a reflective, ongoing process.

early childhood teachers. Use any materials you have available—paper and marker, collage, sculpture, papier mâché, or perhaps even a dance, poem, or skit. Be sure to make your beliefs and ideals clear.

Activity 5, Ideal school In small groups, create your own ideal school. Pull together the elements from the programs you have read about that appeal to you and align with your own beliefs about best practice and what early childhood should be all about. Create your own personal method and approach to teaching young children. You can use the charts to give you ideas of key elements you want to include. Be sure to identify which program/method/theory (which chapter) your specific elements/ideas come from.

Include the following structural elements:

- A name and logo
- A mission or program philosophy
- Overarching goals: How will your mission be achieved?
- Expectations of teachers: teacher roles, credentials
- Expectations of children: behavior, performance, place in the school community
- Expectations of families: What role will families play in the school?
- Daily schedule
- Basic curriculum plan: What kinds of experiences will be provided for children? What will children learn? How will you promote learning and development?
- Administration: How will your schools' administration be handled? Teacher-run, parent-run, or administrative professionals?

Now start having some fun! Make a brochure to educate the public about your program. Make an ad campaign to market your new school. Make floor plan designs of your school building(s). Let your imagination run wild.

Activity 6, Partnering With Families Working in small groups, identify a topic that is important in the lives of children and their families. Consider the topics you've read about or select one that is interesting to you. Here are some examples:

Understanding behavior

Healthy nutrition

Kindergarten readiness

Toilet training

Promoting literacy at home

Home safety

Accessing community resources

After you have selected your topic, create a workshop that could be presented at a parent evening. Include the following components:

   I. Workshop Topic
- What is your workshop topic?
- Make a workshop title that will grab attention.

  II. Workshop Goals
- What three things do you hope your workshop attendees will get from the workshop?

 III. Methods of Instruction
- What techniques are you going to employ to keep the attendees' attention?

 IV. Workshop Content
- How will you guide your participants through the session? What information will you cover?
- Content outline

  V. Ending the Workshop
- How are you going to wrap up the workshop?
- How are you going to evaluate the workshop to assess effectiveness? (Consider a participant survey or checklist or a question session.)

To accompany your parent workshop, create an information brochure that briefly presents the highlights from your topic. This should be a pamphlet that educates parents about the topic and provides them with sources for more information. You can hand out your brochure at the parent meeting. Create brochures in English and Spanish or another language spoken in your community. If you are not bilingual yourself, this part of the activity will include researching resources to help you communicate in another language. Check out Internet sources, student language groups at your school, language faculty members, and other community resources. It will be important to know how to find resources to facilitate communications with linguistically diverse families when you become a teacher.

Activity 7, Child Study You probably have already completed at least one observation of a classroom or child. These one-time visits provide only a glimpse into children's lives and learning and are made truly effective when completed systematically and repeatedly over time and when they are included with other sources of information about the child.

Parent interviews or checklists, informal notes about highlights from the child's day, and checklists help round out the picture of who the child is and how development is progressing. For your child study activity, select a child (with parent permission) to observe over a few months. Complete the following for your focus child:

- Biweekly observations where you document as many details as possible about what the child does and says for a 30-minute time period
- Weekly anecdotal records (brief notes capturing a highlight from a day—something the child did or said)
- Formal developmental checklist (covering all developmental domains)
- Parent interview/home visit; write up a one-page summary of the experience and what you learned from the family (Be sure to remain positive, supportive, and respectful when working with families; even if their home environment is different than what you are used to, be sure to hold back from making judgments!)
- Work samples—drawings, photos of block structures or clay sculptures, writing sample, dictated story, and so on.

Write a summative evaluation statement at the end of your observation period where you tie all your artifacts together and provide a snapshot of your focus child's development and describe your focus child's progress and change over time. Try to keep your reports as objective as possible; meaning that you report what you observe and not your opinions about what you saw. Teachers' analyses can add valuable insight to children's assessments, but at this point in your professional development, focus on making more objective reports.

Think about your images of children in all kinds of contexts, including home, school, on the playground, or in the community.

Activity 8, "Look what's developing . . ." wall charts Many teachers struggle to share with families the valuable and important learning and development that happens in a classroom that is organized in centers or activity areas and schedules long blocks of time for center choice time. One way to emphasize the value of learning/activity centers is to post charts on the walls in or near the centers that lists the key goals reached by playing or working in that area. Appendix E provides an example of a poster that can hang in a creative arts center. Using this as an example, create your own series of posters for the following centers: Creative Arts, Language Arts, Manipulatives, Blocks, Sensory, Science, Dramatic Play, and Outdoors. Use your observations, online sources, interviews, and video clips to guide you.

Activity 9, Article Review/Research Summary Using your school's library system or online professional journal (NAEYC offers select copies of its professional journal, Young Children, online at www.naeyc.org/yc/ or find the entire Early Childhood Research and Practice journal online at http://ecrp.uiuc.edu), locate a recent article on an issue relating to policies or laws affecting early childhood practice and write an article review paper. Be sure to include a copy of the article and the following components in your 2-page report:

1. Reference (author, date, article title, journal/source title, volume/issue, page numbers)

2. Brief summary of article (what were the key points or findings of the article)

3. Your response to article (what did you learn from the article, did you think the article is useful for early childhood teachers, what new points can you apply in your work with young children)

Activity 10, Sharing Who You Are in Families' Lives Now we can roll all these activity experiences together. You have read about authentic assessments and portfolios in several chapters. Now it is your time to create your own portfolio. You can use any format to compile your information, but keep in mind that you will want to add and change artifacts throughout your studies and career. Aim for a flexible format such as a three-ring binder, accordion file, or even a website.

Start by thinking about who you are as a student, teacher, and person. Your philosophy statement is a good start. Think about what other items you would like to add that create as true, detailed, descriptive, and vivid a picture of yourself as possible. Be reflective, selective, and creative with this. Think about the following items to get you started, and try to come up with others that share who you are and where you are going. Be sure to include a paragraph statement about why each artifact is significant as a cover page for each entry.

Sample Portfolio Outline:

Table of Contents

Autobiography

Goal statement

Résumé

Transcripts

Beliefs statements

Photographs

Artifacts with reflective statements (from activities in this chapter, chapters throughout the text, other classes, or your own work experience)

Now go for it! Start gathering, creating, organizing, embellishing, and refining your portfolio. This is your masterpiece; let your personality shine through.

The ultimate aim of education is to enable individuals to become the architects of their own education and through that process to continually reinvent themselves.

The important outcomes of schooling include not only the acquisition of new conceptual tools, refined sensibilities, a developed imagination, and new routines and techniques, but also new attitudes and dispositions. The disposition to continue to learn throughout life is perhaps one of the most important contributions that schools can make to an individual's development.

—Elliot W. Eisner

Related Web Links

Early Childhood and Parenting Collaborative
http://ecap.crc.uiuc.edu/projects.html

Parent Information Center
www.parentinformationcenter.org/

Resource for Portfolios, Lesson Plan Ideas, Homemade Toys, and More
www.teachnet.com

Language-Translation Services
www.babelfish.com

Early Childhood Research Quarterly
http://ecrp.uiuc.edu

Early Childhood Education Historical Time Line and Notes

Date Period	View of Children	Education Practices	Societal Influences	Key People
1600–1700	–Viewed as small adults	–Harsh punishment	–Emphasis on Bible and morality	–Locke
1700–1800				
1800–1900				
1900–2000				
Current Issues				

Key Contributors

Who Was the Theorist?	What Did He or She Do in His or Her Own Time?	Where Was He or She Influential or From?	When Was He or She Active in the Field?	How Has He or She Impacted the Field Now or Then?
Rousseau	–Author of several education books— proposed children be educated in rural, harmonious envi- ronments free from adult dominance	–Influential in Europe and America	–Mid to late 1700s	–Emphasized out-of- home schooling— viewed children as innately good
Pestalozzi				
Froebel				
Hall				
Dewey				

Who Was the Theorist?	What Did He or She Do in His or Her Own Time?	Where Was He or She Influential or From?	When Was He or She Active in the Field?	How Has He or She Impacted the Field Now or Then?
Mitchell				
Piaget				
Vygotsky				
Montessori				
Steiner				
Gardner				

Guiding Principles: Meshing Approaches

Use the following chart or your own graphic organizer to identify aspects from the chapters that you might use in teaching. For each item you select, create one concrete strategy that you can apply that addresses the item. Identify the origin of the idea (theorist/approach).

Teacher's Role	View of Children	Environmental Design	Philosophy, Mission, Program Goals	Cultural/Individual Responsiveness and Inclusion
–Spark children's thinking, curiosity, desire to know more (constructivism)	–Powerful and capable (Reggio)	–Beautiful, gentle, hands-on (waldorf)	–Parents are essential, valuable partners (Head Start)	–Validating each child's abilities and potential, not in comparison with others (High/Scope)

Multiple Intelligence Planning Web

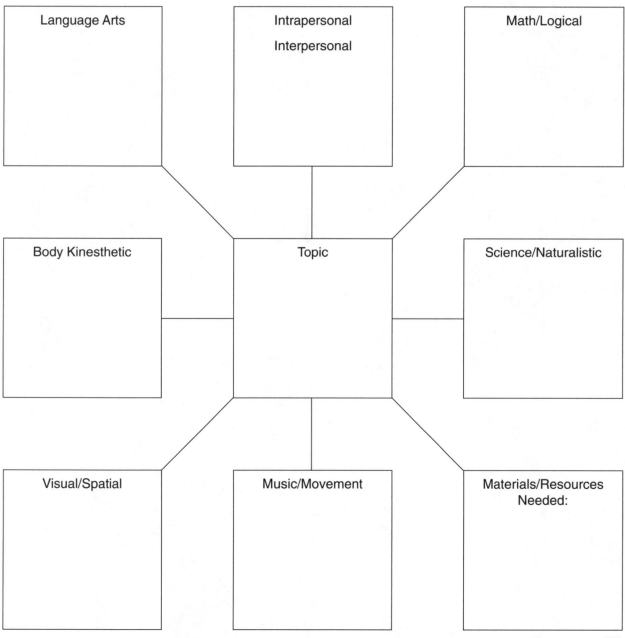

Language Arts

Intrapersonal
Interpersonal

Math/Logical

Body Kinesthetic

Topic

Science/Naturalistic

Visual/Spatial

Music/Movement

Materials/Resources
Needed:

Sample Professional Portfolio Rubric

Early Childhood Education Programs—Student Assessment

Based on NAEYC, state, and CDA standards and requirements

Certificate level completes partial portfolio with additional Degree-level portfolio requirements in bold

Component	Courses Artifact Assigned To	Purpose of Artifact	Exceeds Expectations–15	Meets Expectations–10	Does Not Meet Expectations–5
Section I- Intro. Materials - Résumé - Autobiography - **Transcripts** - **2 references**	Intro to ECE Practicum I, II	Self-reflection Professional identity development Credential review	All present Well-written, typed Formatted for easy reading	Two present Few minor writing errors Typed or clearly printed	One or fewer Many writing errors Not Presented in an organized way
Section III- Standards 1. Child Development - Two resources for coping with challenging behaviors - One assessment tool to document children's behavior; one copy blank one completed - Weekly learning plan (inclusive) - Four pamphlets or articles informing families how 3-5 year olds develop and learn	Child Growth and Development or Developmental Psych Observation, Guidance, and Assessment EC Curriculum Diversity in ECE	Demonstrate knowledge of general and unique attributes of growth Reflect competence in guiding child's development Apply principles of development to learning experiences	Four artifacts Typed and clearly formatted Accurate and up-to-date information (current years) Pamphlets demonstrate foundational knowledge of child development and how theories relate to practice Learning plans are inclusive, tied to appropriate developmental expectations and include appropriate assessment and reflection	Three artifacts Typed or clearly printed Accurate information from within the past 5 years Pamphlets demonstrate foundational knowledge of child development Learning plans are inclusive and tied to appropriate developmental expectations	Two or less artifacts Hard to read (penmanship or copies) Inaccurate and/or out-of-date information Pamphlets demonstrate lack of foundational knowledge of child development Learning plans are not inclusive and tied to appropriate developmental expectations

- Poster series documenting development and learning in classroom centers - Developmental theorist review chart - Family literacy brochure	Child Growth and Development or Developmental Psych	Apply knowledge to classroom settings	Seven artifacts Typed and clearly formatted Accurate and up-to-date information Artifacts demonstrate knowledge of developmental theories	Five artifacts Typed or clearly printed Accurate information from within the past 5 years Artifacts demonstrate knowledge of developmental theories	Three or fewer artifacts Hard to read (penmanship or copies) Inaccurate and/or out-of-date information Artifacts demonstrate lack of knowledge of key developmental theories
2. Family and Community - Contact information on family nutrition education agency - Contact information for family counseling referrals - Resource contacts for non-English speaking families - Parent handbook	Diversity in ECE Practicum I, II Administration of EC Programs	Knowledge of community resources Apply knowledge of community resources	Four artifacts Typed and clearly formatted Accurate and up-to-date information (current years) Resources and handbook demonstrate family-centered, supportive, inclusive attitude and practice	Three artifacts Typed or clearly hand-printed Accurate information from within the past 3 years Resources and handbook demonstrate family-centered, supportive, inclusive attitude	One or no artifact Hard to read (penmanship or copies) Inaccurate and/or out-of-date information Resources demonstrate student bias
- NAEYC position statement on ELL children - Plan for a family workshop	Diversity in ECE Administration of EC Programs	Apply knowledge of family needs and skills in interacting with families	Six artifacts Typed and clearly formatted Accurate and up-to-date information (current years)	Four artifacts Typed or clearly hand-printed Accurate information from within the past 3 years	Two or fewer artifacts Hard to read (penmanship or copies) Inaccurate and/or out-of-date information
3. Observe & Assess - 3 record keeping form samples (accident report, emergency contact form, and one other) - Copies of two developmental checklists (one blank and one completed)	Observation, Guidance, and Assessment	Awareness of assessment tools	Two artifacts Appropriate resources Typed and clearly formatted Developmental checklist demonstrates clear knowledge of assessment purpose and practice	Two artifacts Typed or clearly hand-printed Appropriate resources Developmental checklist completed appropriately	One or no artifact Hard to read (penmanship or copies) Inappropriate resources Developmental checklists not completed/missing

- Two sample standardized assessments designed for young children - NAEYC position statement on Kindergarten screening - Photos of documentation panel chronicling children's group project (including analysis)	Intro to ECE EC Curriculum	Demonstrate knowledge of and application of authentic assessment Awareness of professional policies	Five artifacts Accurate and up-to-date information (current years) Appropriate resources Typed and clearly formatted Documentation panel is organized, neat, includes a variety of forms of data, comprehensively chronicles children's learning process	Four artifacts Typed or clearly hand-printed Accurate information from within the past 3 years Appropriate resources Documentation panel is organized, neat, includes some forms of data, chronicles children's learning process but leaves some gaps that require explanation	Two or fewer artifacts Hard to read (penmanship or copies) Inaccurate and/or out-of-date information Inappropriate resources Documentation panel is unorganized, cluttered, does not include variety of data, does not clearly chronicle children's learning process or is missing
4. Using Developmentally Effective Approaches - 4 songs, poems, or fingerplays to promote phonological awareness - Bibliography of 10 books helping children cope with challenging situations	Infant and Toddler Programs Children's Literature	Demonstrate knowledge of DAP	Typed and clearly formatted Accurate and up-to-date information (books within past 5 years) Appropriate resources Book list includes diverse topics	Typed or clearly hand-printed Accurate information within the past 8 years (8 books included) Appropriate resources Book list includes few diverse topics	Hard to read (penmanship or copies) Inaccurate and/or out-of-date information (5 or fewer books included) Inappropriate resources Book list does not include diverse topics
- Project documentation including web, KWHL, doc panel, and notes - Behavior plan for addressing challenging behavior	Intro to ECE EC Curriculum	Apply DAP through project with children	Appropriate resources Typed and clearly formatted Project is clearly and thoroughly documented and clearly demonstrates children's learning process, includes dialogues, photos, teacher reflections, child artifacts	Typed or clearly hand-printed Appropriate resources Project is partially documented and demonstrates some of the children's learning process, does not include variety of data sources	Hard to read (penmanship or copies) Inappropriate resources Project documentation fails to demonstrate children's process, does not include data

			Behavior plan integrates 3 positive guidance strategies	Behavior plan integrates 1 positive guidance strategy	Behavior plan incomplete, does not include positive guidance strategies
5. Using Content Knowledge - 9 learning plans covering NAEYC content areas (defined in Standards)	Language Arts Birth-8 EC Science, Math, and Social Science	Demonstrate content knowledge	Learning plans demonstrate theoretical knowledge and practical applicability (9 included)	Learning plans demonstrate theoretical knowledge and practical applicability (7 included)	Learning plans fail to demonstrate knowledge of appropriate theory and practice (6 or fewer)
6. Professionalism - Current CPR certification - Summary of child abuse and neglect reporting requirements - Two resources from national ECE association websites (NAEYC and one other) - Child Care licensing agent contacts - Copy of Child Care licensing manual and NAEYC accreditation standards for teacher qualifications - Written statement relating at least two important requirements to your practice - Contact info for 2 agencies serving children with special needs	Basic Emergency Care (or private CPR class) Administration of EC Programs	Demonstrate standard of professional knowledge and credential	Eight artifacts Accurate and up-to-date information (current years) Appropriate resources Typed and clearly written/ formatted statement Statement reflects complex analyses and applications of advocacy and professionalism issues	Six artifacts Typed or clearly hand-printed Accurate information from within the past 3 years Appropriate resources Statement includes 4 or more grammatical errors Statement reflects basic knowledge of central policy and advocacy and professionalism issues	Four or fewer artifacts Hard to read (penmanship or copies) Inaccurate and/or out-of-date information Inappropriate resources Statement poorly written, not typed Statements demonstrate lack of understanding of central policy issues and advocacy and professionalism issues

- NAEYC/ state (or other professional association) student membership - Copy of state Early Learning Standards	Administration of EC Programs	Engage in profession	Ten artifacts Accurate and up-to-date information (current years) Appropriate resources	Seven artifacts Typed or clearly hand-printed Accurate information from within the past 3 years Appropriate resources	Five or fewer artifacts Hard to read (penmanship or copies) Inaccurate and/or out-of-date information Inappropriate resources
Level of reflection in entire portfolio			Very well developed, complete, clearly written, and includes insights of personal growth and understanding	Well developed and contains good insights into growth and understanding, most items well-written	Not well developed. Lacks insights and connections to practice, many items contain writing errors
Portfolio organization and presentation			Clearly marked with dividers and tabs, sections easy to locate, well organized Very aesthetically pleasing (all typed, proper formatting, clear copies)	Marked with dividers, sections easy to locate, most sections organized Aesthetically pleasing (neat writing, most copies clear)	Not clearly marked or sections hard to find, not organized with tabs or dividers Poor penmanship, copies marked up, smudged, or unclear, items not typed
Score at certificate level			_____ /	_____ /	_____ /
Score at Degree Completion Level			_____ /	_____ /	_____ /

NAEYC (National Association for the Education of Young Children). (2008). NAEYC Standards for early childhood professional preparation. 2008 Revision Draft. Retrieved on June 25, 2009 from www.naeyc.org/positionstatements/prepstds_draft.

The Child Development Associate/ Assessment System and Competency Standards for Preschool Caregivers. (1999). Washington, D.C.: The Council for Professional Recognition.

Look What We Are Developing in the Creative Arts Center!

Knowledge	Skills
• Colors and Shapes • How different tools make different textures and lines • How shape, color, texture, and line combine to affect composition • Color mixing • Physics of how different materials move, are shaped, and their different qualities	• Fine motor—grasping, pinching, squeezing • Drawing, forming shapes • Gross motor—mixing, kneading, molding • Turn taking, sharing • Caring for materials and space • Pouring • Measuring • Stacking, rolling, pounding, stretching
Dispositions	**Feelings**
• Persistence • Risk-taking • Willingness to try new things • Wondering • Willingness to express ideas • Sharing • Validating multiple perspectives	• Sense of accomplishment • Validation of unique ideas • Joy of making something new • Caring about own ideas and those of others • Enjoyment—the fun and freedom of creating, getting messy, and experimenting!

References

Chapter 1

Allen, K., & Marotz, L. (2003). *Developmental profiles: Prebirth through twelve* (4th ed.). Clifton Park, NY: Delmar Learning.

Baker, A., & Manfredi/Petitt, L. (2004). *Relationships: The heart of quality care.* Washington, DC: NAEYC.

Barnett, S., Jung, K., Yarosz, D., Thomas, J., Hornbeck, A., Stechuk, R., & Burns, S. (in press). Educational Effects of the Tools of the Mind Curriculum: A Randomized Trial. *Early Childhood Research Quarterly.*

Bodrova, E. & Leong, D. J. (2007). *Tools of the mind: The Vygotskian approach to early childhood education* (2nd ed.). Upper Saddle River, NJ: Prentice Hall.

Bredekamp, S., & Copple, C. (Eds.). (1997). *Developmentally appropriate practice in early childhood programs* (rev. ed.). Washington, DC: NAEYC.

Bullock, A., & Hawk, P. (2001). *Developing a teaching portfolio: A guide for preservice and practicing teachers.* Upper Saddle River, NJ: Merrill/Prentice Hall.

Burchfield, D. W. (1996). Teaching all children: Four developmentally appropriate curricular and instructional strategies in primary-grade classrooms. *Young Children, 52*(1), 4–10.

Campbell, D., Cignetti, P., Melenyzer, B., Nettles, D., & Wyman, R. (2004). *How to develop a professional portfolio: A manual for teachers.* Boston: Allyn and Bacon.

Cassidy, D., & Buell, M. (1996). Accentuating the positive? An analysis of teacher verbalizations with young children. *Child and Youth Forum, 25*(6), 403–414.

Darragh, J. (2007). Universal Design for early childhood education: Ensuring access and equity for all. *Early Childhood Education Journal, 33*(2), 167–171.

Dyson, L. (2005). Kindergarten children's understanding of and attitudes toward people with disabilities. *Topics in Early Childhood Special Education, 25*(2), 95–105.

Eisner, E. (2004). Multiple Intelligences: Its tensions and its possibilities. *Teachers College Record, 106*(1), 31–39.

Elkind, D. (2003). Thanks for the memories: The lasting value of true play. *Young Children, 58*(3), 46–50.

Fraser, S. (2007). Play in other languages. *Theory Into Practice, 46*(1), 14–22.

Gargiulo, R. (2006). Homeless and disabled: Rights, responsibilities, and recommendations for serving young children with special needs. *Early Childhood Education Journal, 33*(5), 357–362.

Geist, E., & Baum, A. (2005). Yeah, but that keeps teachers from embracing an active curriculum: Overcoming the resistance. *Young Children, 60*(1), 28–36.

Gelfer, J., Xu, Y., & Perkins, P. (2004). Developing portfolios to evaluate teacher performance in early childhood education. *Early Childhood Education Journal, 32*(2), 127–132.

Girolametto, L., Weitzman, E., & Greenberg, J. (2003). Training day care staff to facilitate children's language. *American Journal of Speech Pathology, 12*(3), 299–311.

Hirsh, R. (2004). *Early childhood curriculum: Incorporating multiple intelligences, developmentally appropriate practice, and play.* Boston: Allyn and Bacon.

Hyun, E. (2003). What does the No Child Left Behind Act mean to early childhood teacher educators?: A call for a collective professional rejoinder. *Early Childhood Education Journal, 31*(2), 119–125.

Jalongo, M.R., Fennimore, B., Pattnaik, J., Laverock, D., Brewster, J., & Mutuku, M. (2004). Blended perspectives: A global vision for high-quality early childhood education. *Early Childhood Education Journal, 32*(3), 143–155.

Jenkinson, S. (2001). *The genius of play.* Gloucestershire, UK: Hawthorn Press.

Jones, J. (2004). Framing the assessment debate. *Young Children, 59*(1), 14–18.

Landerholm, E., Gehrie, C., & Hao, Y. (2004). Educating early childhood teachers for the global world. *Early Childhood Development and Care, 174*(7–8), 593–606.

NAEYC (National Association for the Education of Young Children). (2008). NAEYC Standards for early childhood professional preparation. 2008 Revision Draft. Retrieved on June 25, 2009, from www.naeyc.org/positionstatements/ prepstds_draft.

Nikolaraizi, M., Kumar, P., Favazza, P., Sideridis, G., Koulousiou, D., & Riall, A. (2005). A cross-cultural examination of typically developing children's attitudes toward individuals with special needs. *International Journal of Disability, Development and Education, 52*(2), 101–119.

Noddings, N. (1995). Teaching themes of caring. *Education Digest, 61*(3), 24–29.

Noddings, N. (2005). What does it mean to educate the whole child? *Educational Leadership, 63*(1), 8–13.

Pool, C. (1997). Brain-based learning and students. *Education Digest, 63*(3) 10–16.

Ryan, S., & Grieshaber, S. (2004). It's more than child development: Critical theories, research, and teaching young children. *Young Children, 59*(6), 44–52.

Stanford, P. (2003). Multiple intelligence for every classroom. *Intervention in School and Clinic, 39*(2), 80–85.

U. S. Department of Education (2004a). *A guide to No Child Left Behind.* Washington, DC: U.S. Department of Education, Office of the Secretary, Office of Public Affairs.

U. S. Department of Education (2004b). *Overview: Four pillars of NCLB.* Washington, DC: U.S. Department of Education, Office of the Secretary, Office of Public Affairs. Retrieved on May 25, 2009, from www.ed.gov/nclb/overview/intro/4pillars.html.

Chapter 2

Adelman, C. (2000). Over two years, what did Froebel say to Pestalozzi? *History of Education, 29*(2), 103–114.

Aldrich, R. (2002). The first 100 years. *Education Journal, 65*, 8.

Antler, J. (1987). *Lucy Sprague Mitchell: The making of a modern woman.* New Haven, CT: Yale University Press.

Archambault, R. (Ed.) (1964). *John Dewey on education: Selected writings.* Chicago: University of Chicago Press.

Beatty, B. (1995). *Preschool education in America: The culture of young children from the colonial era to the present.* New Haven, CT: Yale University Press.

Berk, L., & Winsler, A. (1995). *Scaffolding children's learning: Vygotsky and early childhood education.* Washington, DC: National Association for the Education of Young Children.

Blow, S. E. (1900/1999). Kindergarten education. In K. M. Paciorek & J. H. Munro (Eds.), *Sources: Notable selections in early childhood education* (2nd ed.). Guilford, CT: Dushkin/McGraw-Hill.

Bowers, F., & Gehring, T. (2004). Johann Heinrich Pestalozzi: 18th century Swiss educator and correctional reformer. *Journal of Correctional Education, 55*(4), 306–319.

Bredekamp, S. (1997). NAEYC issues revised position statement on developmentally appropriate practice in early childhood programs. *Young Children, 52*(2), 34–40.

Bronfenbrenner, U. (1986). Ecology of the family as a context for human development: Research perspectives. *Developmental Psychology, 22*(6), 723–742.

Bruner, J. (1991). The narrative construction of reality. *Critical Inquiry, 18*(1), 1–21.

Corso, R., Santos, R., & Roof, V. (2002). Honoring diversity in early childhood education materials. *Teaching Exceptional Children, 34*(3), 30–36.

Dewey, J. (1899/1999). Three years of the university elementary school. In K. M. Paciorek & J. H. Munro (Eds.), *Sources: Notable selections in early childhood education* (2nd ed.). Guilford, CT: Dushkin/McGraw-Hill.

Dewey, J. (1938). *Experience and education.* New York: Touchstone.

Dombrowski, K. (2002). Kindergarten teacher training in England and the United States 1850–1918. *History of Education, 31*(5), 475–489.

Gesell, A. (1940/1999). Early mental growth. In K. M. Paciorek & J. H. Munro (Eds.), *Sources: Notable selections in early childhood education* (2nd ed.). Guilford, CT: Dushkin/ McGraw-Hill.

Goswami, U. (2001). Cognitive development: No stages please—we're British. *British Journal of Psychology, 92*(1), 257–278.

Gregory, M. R. (2002). Constructivism, standards, and the classroom community of inquiry. *Educational Theory, 52*(4), 43–51.

Grinberg, J. (2002). "I had never been exposed to teaching like that": Progressive teacher education at Bank Street during the 1930s. *Teachers College Record, 104*(7), 1422–1460.

Hacsi, T. (1995). From indenture to family foster care: A brief history of child placing. *Child Welfare, 74*(1), 162–181.

Hall, G. S. (1907/1999). The contents of children's minds on entering school. In K. M. Paciorek & J. H. Munro (Eds.), *Sources: Notable selections in early childhood education* (2nd ed.). Guilford, CT: Dushkin/McGraw-Hill.

Hall, J. (2000). Psychology and schooling: The impact of Susan Issacs and Jean Piaget on 1960s science education reform. *History of Education, 29*(2), 153–170.

Henson, K. (2003). Foundations for learner-centered education: A knowledge base. *Education, 124*, 5–16.

Hill, P. S. (1941/1999). Kindergarten. In K. M. Paciorek & J. H. Munro (Eds.), *Sources: Notable selections in early childhood education* (2nd ed.). Guilford, CT: Dushkin/McGraw-Hill.

Horn, D. M., Caruso, D. A., & Golas, J. (2003). Head Start teaching center: Differential training effects for Head Start personnel. *Child & Youth Care Forum, 32*(1), 23–40.

Hoxie, F. (1984). *A final promise: The campaign to assimilate Indians.* Lincoln: University of Nebraska Press.

Hulbert, A. (1999). The century of the child. *Wilson Quarterly, 23*(1), 14–30.

Hyun, E., & Marshall, J. (2003). Teachable-moment-oriented curriculum practice in early childhood education. *Journal of Curriculum Studies, 35*(1), 111–127.

Isaacs, S. (1966/1999). Childhood and after: Some essays and clinical studies. In K. M. Paciorek & J. H. Munro (Eds.), *Sources: Notable selections in early childhood education* (2nd ed.). Guilford, CT: Dushkin/McGraw-Hill.

James, W. (2008). Jerome Bruner, born 1915. *Times Educational Supplement. Issue 4816*, special section 3, 24.

Kontio, K. (2003). The idea of autarchy in Rousseau's natural education: Recovering the natural harmony? *Scandinavian Journal of Educational Research, 47*(1), 3–19.

Lascarides, V., & Hinitz, B. (2000). *History of early childhood education.* New York: Falmer Press.

Lindqvist, G. (1995). *The aesthetics of play: A didactic study of play and culture in preschools.* (Report no. ISSN-0347-1314). Uppsala, Sweden: Uppsala University. (ERIC Document Reproduction Service no. ED396824).

Margolis, E., & Rowe, J. (2004). Images of assimilation: Photographs of Indian schools in Arizona. *History of Education, 33*(2), 199–230.

Matthews, W. (2003). Constructivism in the classroom: Epistemology, history, and empirical evidence. *Teacher Education Quarterly, 30*(3), 51–64.

McMillan, M. (1919/1999). The nursery school. In K. M. Paciorek & J. H. Munro (Eds.), *Sources: Notable selections in early childhood education* (2nd ed.). Guilford, CT: Dushkin/ McGraw-Hill.

Montessori, M. (1966). *The secret of childhood.* New York: Ballantine Books.

Moran, R. F. (2005). Undone by law: The uncertain legacy of Lau v. Nichols. *Berkeley La Raza Law Journal, 16*(1), 1–10.

NAEYC (National Association for the Education of Young Children). (1995). *Responding to linguistic and cultural diversity: Recommendations for effective early childhood practice.* Washington, DC: Author.

Null, J. W. (2004). Is constructivism traditional? Historical and practical perspectives on a popular advocacy. *Educational Forum, 68*, 180–188.

O'Connor, S. M. (1995). Mothering in public: The division of organized child care in the kindergarten and day nursery, St. Louis, 1886–1920. *Early Childhood Research Quarterly, 10*(1), 63–80.

Owen, R. (1857/1999). The life of Robert Owen. In K. M. Paciorek & J. H. Munro (Eds.), *Sources: Notable selections in early childhood education* (2nd ed.). Guilford, CT: Dushkin/ McGraw-Hill.

Peabody, E. P. (1877/1999). Guide to the kindergarten and intermediate class. In K. M. Paciorek & J. H. Munro (Eds.), *Sources: Notable selections in early childhood education* (2nd ed.). Guilford, CT: Dushkin/ McGraw-Hill.

Piaget, J. (1929). *The child's conception of the world.* London: Rutledge & Kegan Paul.

Piaget, J. (1954). *The construction of reality in the child.* New York: Basic Books.

Piaget, J. (1961/1999). The stages of the intellectual development of the child. In K. M. Paciorek & J. H. Munro (Eds.), *Sources: Notable selections in early childhood education* (2nd ed.). Guilford, CT: Dushkin/McGraw-Hill.

Piaget, J. (1969). *The psychology of the child.* New York: Basic Books.

Piaget, J. (1975). *The development of thought.* New York: Viking Press.

Powell, M. (2000). Can Montessorians and constructivists really be friends? *Montessori Life, 21*(1), 44–51.

Procher, L. (1998). Missing pieces: A review of history chapters in introductory early childhood education textbooks. *Journal of Early Childhood Teacher Education, 19*(1), 31–42.

Read, J. (2003). Froebelian women: Networking to promote professional status and educational change in the nineteenth century. *History of Education, 32*(1), 17–33.

Reynolds, A. J., Miedel, W. T., Mann, E. A. (2000). Innovation in early intervention for children in families with low incomes: Lessons from the Chicago Child-Parent Centers. *Young Children, 55*(2), 84–88.

Sameroff, A., & McDonough, S. C. (1994). Educational implications of developmental transitions: Revisiting the 5- to 7-year shift. *Phi Delta Kappan, 76*(3), 188–193.

Sandsmark, S. (2002). A Lutheran perspective on education. *Journal of Education and Christian Belief, 6*(2), 97–106.

Saracho, O. N., & Spodek, B. (1995). Children's play and early childhood education: Insights from history and theory. *Journal of Education, 117*(3), 129–148.

Schickedanz, J. (1995). Early education and care: Beginnings. *Journal of Education, 177*(3), 1–7.

Spodek, B. (1985). Early childhood education's past as prologue: Roots of contemporary concerns. *Young Children, 40*(5), 3–7.

Sullivan, K. (1996). Progressive education: Where are you now that we need you? *Oxford Review of Education, 22*(3), 349–356.

Swiniarski, D. (2005). Elizabeth P. Peabody's bi-centennial birthday: A celebration of a past legacy and a future vision for kindergarten. *Early Childhood Education Journal, 34*(4), 219–220.

Takanishi, R. (1981). Early childhood education and research: The changing relationship. *Theory Into Practice, 10*(2), 86–92.

Trotter, A., Keller, B., Zehr, M., Manzo, K., & Bradley, A. (1999). Lessons of a century: Faces of a century. *Education Week, 19*(16), 27–38.

Turnbull, R., & Cilley, M. (1999). *Explanations and implications of the 1997 amendments to IDEA.* Upper Saddle River, NJ: Merrill/Prentice Hall.

Vander Zanden, J. (2003). *Human development.* Boston: McGraw-Hill.

Vygotsky, L. S. (1962/1999). Thought and language. In K. M. Paciorek & J. H. Munro (Eds.), *Sources: Notable selections in early childhood education* (2nd ed.). Guilford, CT: Dushkin/ McGraw-Hill.

Vygotsky, L. S. (1978). *Mind in society: The development of higher psychological processes.* Cambridge, MA: Harvard University Press.

Chapter 3

ACEI (Association for Childhood Education International). (n.d.). *The ACEI experience.* Retrieved on April 23, 2009, from www.acei.org/history.htm.

ACEI (Association for Childhood Education International). (2006). Global guidelines for early childhood education and care in the 21st century. Retrieved on April 23, 2009, from www.acei.org/wguides.htm.

Baptiste, N., & Ryes, L. (2002). *Ethics in early care and education.* Upper Saddle River, NJ: Merrill/Prentice Hall.

Bredekamp, S. (1987). *Developmentally appropriate practice in early childhood programs.* Washington, DC: NAEYC.

Bredekamp, S. (1997). NAEYC issues revised position statement on developmentally appropriate practice in early childhood programs. *Young Children, 52*(2), 34–40.

Bredekamp, S., & Copple, C. (Eds.). (1997). *Developmentally appropriate practice in early childhood programs* (rev. ed.). Washington, DC: NAEYC.

Caulfield, R. (1997). Professionalism in early care and education. *Early Childhood Education Journal, 24*(4), 261–263.

DEC (Division for Early Childhood, Council for Exceptional Children). (n.d.). About DEC. Retrieved on April 23, 2009, from www.dec-sped.org/index.aspx/About_ DEC.

Diamond, M., & Hopson, J. (1999). *Magic trees of the mind: How to nurture your child's intelligence, creativity, and healthy emotions from birth through adolescence.* New York: Plume.

Dickinson, D. (2002). Shifting images of developmentally appropriate practice as seen through different lenses. *Educational Researcher, 31*(1), 26–32.

Dunn, L., & Kontos, S. (1997). What have we learned about developmentally appropriate practice? *Young Children, 52*(5), 4–13.

Feeney, S., & Freeman, N. K. (1999). *Ethics and the early childhood educator: Using the NAEYC code.* Washington, DC: NAEYC.

Freeman, N. K. (2000). Professional ethics: A cornerstone of teachers' preservice curriculum. *Action in Teacher Education, 22*(3), 12–18.

Jambunathan, S., Burts, D., & Pierce, S. (1999). Developmentally appropriate practices as predictors of self-competence among preschoolers. *Journal of Research in Childhood Education, 13*(2), 167–174.

Katz, L., & Ward, E. (1978). *Ethical behavior in early childhood education.* Washington, DC: National Association for the Education of Young Children.

Moore, K. (1999). Constructing appropriate curriculum. *Scholastic Early Childhood Today, 14*(3), 8.

Moore, K. (2000). Assessing children's learning and development. *Scholastic Early Childhood Today, 14*(4), 14–15.

Moyles, J. (2001). Passion, paradox, and professionalism in early years education. *Early years, 21*(2), 81–95.

NAEYC (National Association for the Education of Young Children) Ethics Panel. (1995). How many ways can you think of to use NAEYC's Code of Ethics? *Young Children, 51*(1), 42–43.

NAEYC (National Association for the Education of Young Children). (2004). About NAEYC. Retrieved on August 30, 2009, from www.naeyc.org/content/about-naeyc.

NAEYC (National Association for the Education of Young Children). (2005). Code of ethical conduct and statement of commitment. Retrieved on August 30, 2009, from www.naeyc.org/positionstatements/ethical_conduct.

NAEYC (National Association for the Education of Young Children). (2009). Developmentally appropriate practice in programs serving children from birth to age eight. A position statement of the National Association for the Education of Young Children. Retrieved on August 30, 2009, from www.naeyc.org/positionstatements/dap.

Quick, B. (1998). Beginning reading and developmentally appropriate practice: Past, present, and future. *Peabody Journal of Education, 73*(3/4), 253–272.

Serpell, R., Sonnenschein, S., Baker, L., & Ganapathy, H. (2002). Intimate culture of families in the early socialization of literacy. *Journal of Family Psychology, 16*(4), 391–406.

Spodek, B., & Saracho, O. (2003). "On the shoulders of giants": Exploring the traditions of early childhood education. *Early Childhood Education Journal, 31*(1), 3–10.

U.S. Department of Education. (2007a). Common core of data; public school student membership by race/ethnicity and State or jurisdiction. Washington, DC: United States Department of Education, National Center for Educational Statistics. Retrieved on April 21, 2009, from nces.ed.gov/ccd/tables/2009305_02.asp.

U.S. Department of Education. (2007b). Status and trends in the education of ethnic and racial minorities. Washington, DC: United States Department of Education, National Center for Educational Statistics. Retrieved on April 21, 2009, from nces.ed.gov/pubs2007/minoritytrends/ind_2_7.asp.

Chapter 4

Anderson, R. (1998). Why talk about different ways to grade? The shift from traditional assessment to alternative assessment. *New Directions for Teaching and Learning, 74,* 5–16.

Arcaro-McPhee, R., Doppler, E.E. & Harkins, D. A. (2002). Conflict resolution in a preschool constructivist classroom: A case study in negotiation. *Journal of Research in Childhood Education, 17*(1) 19–25.

Berk, L., & Winsler, A. (1995). *Scaffolding children's learning: Vygotsky and early childhood education.* Washington, DC: National Association for the Education of Young Children.

Castle, K. (1997). Constructing knowledge of constructivism. *Journal of Early Childhood Education, 18*(1), 55–67.

Davis, B., & Sumara, D. (2002). Constructivist discourses and the field of education: Problems and possibilities. *Educational Theory, 52,* 409–428.

DeVries, R., & Zan, B. (1995). Creating a constructivist classroom atmosphere. *Young Children, 51*(1), 4–13.

DeVries, R., & Zan, B. (2003). When children make rules. *Educational Leadership, 61*(1), 64–67.

Dewey, J. (1938). *Experience and Education.* New York: Touchstone.

Dixon-Krauss, L. (1996). *Vygotsky in the classroom: Mediated literacy instruction and assessment.* White Plains, NY: Longman.

Ediger, M. (2000). Purposes in learner assessment. *Journal of Instructional Psychology, 27*(4), 244–250.

Gregory, M. R. (2002). Constructivism, standards, and the classroom community of inquiry. *Educational Theory, 52*(4), 43–51.

Green, S., & Gredler, M. (2002). A review and analysis of constructivism for school based practice. *School Psychology Review, 31*(1), 53–70.

Henson, K. (2003). Foundations for learner-centered education: A knowledge base. *Education, 124,* 5–16.

Knight, C. C. & Sutton, R. E. (2004). Neo-Piagetian theory and research: Enhancing pedagogical practice for educators of adults. *London Review of Education, 2*(1), 47–60.

Low, J. M., & Shironaka, W. (1995). Letting go—Allowing first graders to become autonomous learners. *Young Children, 51*(1), 21–25.

Marcon, R. (1992). Differential effects of three preschool models on inner-city 4-year-olds. *Early Childhood Research Quarterly, 7,* 517–530.

Marcon, R. (2002). Moving up the grades: Relationship between preschool model and later school success. *Early Childhood Research and Practice, 4*(1). Retrieved on December 9, 2002, from ecrp.uiuc.edu/v4nl/marcon.html.

Matthews, W. (2003). Constructivism in the classroom: Epistemology, history, and empirical evidence. *Teacher Education Quarterly, 30*(3), 51–64.

McAfee, D., Leong, D. J., & Bodrova, E. (2004). *Basics of assessment: A primer for early childhood educators.*

Piaget, J. (1929). *The child's conception of the world.* London: Routledge & Kegan Paul.

Piaget, J. (1969). *The psychology of the child.* New York: Basic Books.

Piaget, J. (1975). *The development of thought.* New York: Viking Press.

Powell, M. (2000). Can Montessorians and constructivists really be friends? *Montessori Life, 21*(1), 44–51.

Ray, J. (2002). Constructivism and classroom teachers: What can early childhood teacher educators do to support the constructivist journey? *Journal of Early Childhood Teacher Education, 23,* 319–325.

Richardson, V. (2003). Constructivist pedagogy. *Teachers College Record, 105,* 1623–1640.

Schuh, K. (2003). Knowledge construction in the learner-centered classroom. *Journal of Educational Psychology, 95,* 426–442.

Schweinhart, L. J., Barnes, H., & Weikart, D. P. (1993). Significant benefits: The High/Scope Perry Preschool study through age 27. (Monographs of the High/Scope Educational Research Foundation, 10). Ypsilanti, MI: High/Scope Press.

Simpson, T. (2002). Dare I oppose constructivism? *The Educational Forum, 66,* 347–354.

Suizzo, M. (2000). The socio-emotional and cultural contexts of cognitive development: Neo-Piagetian perspectives. *Child Development, 71*(4), 846–849.

Vygotsky, L. S. (1978). *Mind in society: The development of higher psychological processes.* Cambridge, Mass: Harvard University Press.

Chapter 5

Armstrong, T. (1994). *Multiple intelligences in the classroom.* Alexandria, VA: Association for Supervision and Curriculum Development.

Bredekamp, S. (1993). Reflections on Reggio Emilia. *Young Children, 49*(1), 13–17.

Calvin-Campbell, K. (1998). *Supporting the development of the whole child through Orff Schulwerk, Montessori, and multiple intelligences.* ERIC document ED417030.

Campbell, L. (1997). Variations on a theme: How teachers interpret MI theory. *Educational Leadership, 55,* 14–19.

Campbell, L., Campbell, B., & Dickinson, D. (2004). *Teaching and learning through multiple intelligences.* Boston: Allyn and Bacon.

Carlisle, A. (2001). Using multiple intelligences theory to assess early childhood curricula. *Young Children, 56*(6), 77–83.

Davis, J., & Gardner, H. (1993). The arts and early childhood education: A cognitive developmental portrait of the young child as artist. In B. Spodek (Ed.), *Handbook of research in early childhood education* (2nd ed.). New York: Macmillan.

Edwards, C. P., Gandini, L., & Forman, G. (Eds.). (1996). *The hundred languages of children: The Reggio Emilia approach to early childhood education.* Norwood, NJ: Ablex.

Emig, V. (1997). A multiple intelligences inventory. *Educational Leadership, 55,* 47–50.

Erickson, E. (1950). Growth and crises of the "healthy personality." In M. Senn, *Symposium on the healthy personality.* Oxford, England: Josiah Macy, Jr. Foundation.

Flohr, J. (1999). Recent brain research on young children. *Teaching Music, 6*(6), 41–45.

Fox, D. (2000). Music and the baby's brain. *Music Educators Journal, 87*(2), 23–29.

Gardner, H. (1993a). *Frames of mind.* New York: Basic Books.

Gardner, H. (1993b). *Multiple intelligences: The theory in practice.* New York: Basic Books.

Gardner, H. (1995). Reflections on multiple intelligences: Myths and messages. *Phi Delta Kappan, 77,* 200–203.

Gardner, H. (1997). Multiple intelligences as a partner in school reform. *Educational Leadership, 55,* 20–21.

Greenhawk, J. (1997). Multiple intelligences meets standards. *Educational Leadership, 55,* 62–64.

Guild, P., & Chock-Eng, A. (1998). Multiple intelligence, learning styles, brain-based education: Where do the messages overlap? *Schools in the Middle, 7*(4), 38–40.

Hoerr, T. (2003). It's no fad: Fifteen years of implementing multiple intelligences. *Educational Horizons, 81*(2), 92–94.

Katz, L., & Chard, S. (2000). *Engaging children's minds: The project approach.* Stamford, CT: Ablex.

Krechevsky, M. (1991). Project spectrum: An innovative assessment alternative. *Educational Leadership, 98,* 43–49.

Miller, S. (2003). Encouraging exploration in young children. *Scholastic Early Childhood Today, 17*(6), 28, 30.

NEA (National Education Association). (1998). Hot on multiple intelligences. *NEA Today, 16*(7), 19–20.

Nuzzi, R. (1997). A multiple intelligence approach. *Momentum, 28,* 16–19.

Pool, C. (1997). Maximizing learning: A conversation with Renate Nummela Caine. *Educational Leadership, 54,* 11–15.

Reiff, J. (1996). Multiple intelligences: Different ways of learning. Association for Childhood Education International. Retrieved on May 28, 2003, from www.udel.edu/bateman/ acei/multint9.htm.

Rush, J. (1998). The arts and educational reform: Where is the model for teaching "the arts"? *Arts Education Policy Review, 98,* 2–10.

Salter Ainsworth, M. (1989). Attachments beyond infancy. *American Psychologist, 44*(4), 709–716.

Stanford, P. (2003). Multiple intelligence for every classroom. *Intervention in School and Clinic, 39*(2), 80–85.

Torrance, E. P. (2003). The millenium: a time for looking forward and looking back. *Journal of Secondary Gifted Education, 15*(1), 6–13.

Vander Zanden, J. (2003). *Human development*. New York: McGraw-Hill.

Vygotsky, L. S. (1978). *Mind in society: The development of higher psychological processes*. Cambridge, Mass: Harvard University Press.

Chapter 6

Aber, L., & Palmer, J. (1999). Poverty and brain development in early childhood. National Center for Children in Poverty, Mailman School of Public Health, Columbia University. Retrieved on March 13, 2004, from www.nccp.org/pub_ pbd99.html.

Beasley, T. M. (2002). Influence of culture-related experiences and sociodemographic risk factors on cognitive readiness among preschoolers. *Journal of Education for Students Placed at Risk, 7*(1), 3–23.

Blair, C., Peters, R., & Lawrence, F. (2003). Family dynamics and child outcomes in early intervention: The role of developmental theory in the specification of effects. *Early Childhood Research Quarterly, 18*, 446–467.

Bloom, B. (1964). *Stability and change in human characteristics*. New York: Wiley.

Bondy, E., & McKenzie, J. (1999). Resilience building and social reconstructionist teaching: A first-year teacher's story. *Elementary School Journal, 100*(2), 129–151.

Caputo, R. (2003). Head Start, other preschool programs, and life success in a youth cohort. *Journal of Sociology and Social Welfare, 30*(2), 105–126.

Champion, T., Hyter, Y., McCabe, A., & Bland-Stewart, L. (2003). "A matter of vocabulary": Performances of low-income African-American Head Start children on the Peabody Picture Vocabulary Test-III. *Communication Disorders, 23*(3), 121–127.

Children's Defense Fund. (2003). *Head Start reauthorization: Questions and answers*. Washington, DC: Children's Defense Fund.

Diamond, M., & Hopson, J. (1998). *Magic trees of the mind: How to nurture your child's intelligence, creativity, and healthy emotions from birth through adolescence*. New York: Plume Books.

Elliot, J., Prior, M., Merrigan, C., & Ballinger, K. (2002). Evaluation of a community intervention programme for preschool behaviour problems. *Journal of Pediatric Child Health, 38*, 41–50.

Gershoff, E. (2003). Living at the Edge Research Brief No. 4: Low income and the development of America's kindergarteners. National Center for Children in Poverty, Mailman School of Public Health, Columbia University. Retrieved on August 30, 2009, from www.nccp.org/publications/pub_533.html.

Hanson, M. (2003). Twenty-five years after early intervention: A follow-up of children with Down syndrome and their families. *Infants and Young Children, 16*(4), 354–365.

Head Start Bureau. (1997). Head Start program performance standards and other regulations (Health and Developmental Services). Washington, DC: Head Start Bureau, Administration on Children, Youth, and Families, U.S. Department of Health and Human Services. Retrieved on May 21, 2004, from www.acf.hhs.gov/programs/hsb/pdf/1304_ALL.pdf.

Head Start Bureau. (2005). Head Start program performance standards and other regulations (Health and Developmental Services). Washington, DC: Head Start Bureau, Administration on Children, Youth, and Families, U.S. Department of Health and Human Services. Retrieved on August 30, 2009, from www.access.gpo.gov/nara/cfr/waisidx_07/45cfrv4_07.html#1301.

Hume, K., Bellini, S., & Pratt, C. (2005). The usage and perceived outcomes of early intervention and early childhood programs for young children with Autism Spectrum Disorder. *Topics in Early Childhood Special Education, 24*(4), 195–207.

IDEA (2004). Individuals with Disabilities Education Improvement Act of 2004, Pub. L. No. 108-446, §2, 118 Stat. 2647 (2004).

Jacobson, L. (2003). Head Start reauthorization goals detailed. *Education Week, 23*(9), 23–25.

Jacobson, L. (2004). Criticism over new Head Start testing program mounts. *Education Week, 23*(4), 10–12.

Kagan, J. (2002). Empowerment and education: Civil rights, expert-advocates, and parent politics in Head Start, 1964–1980. *Teachers College Record, 104*(3), 516–562.

Knitzer, J. & Lefkowitz, J. (2006). Helping the most vulnerable infants, toddlers, and their families. National Center for Children in Poverty, Mailman School of Public Health, Columbia University. Retrieved on August 30, 2009, from www.nccp.org/publications/pub_669.html#1.

Lascarides, V., & Hinitz, B. (2000). *History of early childhood education*. New York: Falmer Press.

Lee, V., Brooks-Gunn, J., Schnur, E., & Liaw, F. (1990). Are Head Start effects sustained? A longitudinal follow-up comparison of disadvantaged children attending

Head Start, no preschool, and other preschool programs. *Child Development, 61*(2), 495–507.

NCCP (National Center for Children in Poverty). (2008). Basic facts about low-income children: Birth to age 6. National Center for Children in Poverty. Mailman School of Public Health, Columbia University. Retrieved on May 4, 2009, from www.nccp.org/publications/pub_847.html.

Nord, C., & Rhoads, A. (1992). *The survey of income and program participation as a source of data on children: A statistical profile of at-risk children in the United States.* Washington, DC: U.S. Department of Education. ED415992.

Parke, B., & Agness, P. (2002). Hand in hand: A journey toward readiness for profoundly at-risk preschoolers. *Early Childhood Education Journal, 30*(1), 33–37.

Peth-Pierce, R. (2000). *A good beginning: Sending America's children to school with the social and emotional competence they need to succeed.* Bethesda, MD: Child Mental Health Foundations and Agencies Network (FAN), National Institute of Mental Health.

Powell, M. (2000). Can Montessorians and constructivists really be friends? *Montessori Life, 21*(1), 44–51.

Rappaport, M., McWilliam, R., & Smith, B. (2004). Practices across disciplines in early intervention: The research base. *Infants and Young Children, 17*(1), 32–44.

Rauh, V., Parker, F., Garfinkel, R., Perry, J., & Andrews, H. (2003). Biological, social, and community influences on third-grade reading levels in minority children: A multi-level approach. *Journal of Community Psychology, 31*(3), 255–278.

Schweinhart, L. J., Barnes, H. V., & Weikart, D. P. (1993). *Significant benefits: The High/Scope Perry preschool study through age 27.* (Monographs of the High/Scope Educational Research Foundation, 10). Ypsilanti, MI: High/Scope Press. PS 021 998.

Smith, B. J. (1988). Does early intervention help? *ERIC Digest* No. 455. ED295399.

USDHHS (U. S. Department of Health and Human Services). (2002a). Head Start history. Washington, DC: U.S. Government Printing Office. Retrieved on August 30, 2009, from www.acf.hhs.gov/programs/opre/hs/ch_trans/reports/transition_study/trans_study_pt1.html.

USDHHS (U.S. Department of Health and Human Services). (2002b). Making a difference in the lives of infants and toddlers and their families: The impacts of Early Head Start. Washington, DC: U.S. Government Printing Office. Retrieved on October 23, 2002, from www.acf.hhs.gov/programs/opre/ehs/ehs_resrch/reports/impacts_exesum/impacts_exesum.html.

USDHHS (U.S. Department of Health and Human Services). (2003a). Head Start FACES 2000: A whole-child perspective on program performance. Washington, DC: U.S. Government Printing Office. www.acf.hhs.gov/programs/opre/hs/faces/.

USDHHS (U.S. Department of Health and Human Services). (2003b). *The national reporting system.* Washington, DC: U.S. Government Printing Office.

USDHHS (U.S. Department of Health and Human Services). (2006). Head Start fact sheet. Retrieved on August 30, 2009, from www.acf.hhs.gov/opa/fact_sheets/headstart_ factsheet.html.

USDHHS (U.S. Department of Health and Human Services). (2006). Faces findings: New research on Head Start outcomes and program quality. Retrieved on May 5, 2009, from www.acf.hhs.gov/programs/opre/hs/faces/reports/faces_findings_06/faces_findings.pdf.

USDHHS (U.S. Department of Health and Human Services). (2007). Report on Head Start assessment system. Retrieved on May 20, 2009, from www.acf.hhs.gov/news/press/2007/head_start_assessment_system.htm.

USDHHS (U.S. Department of Health and Human Services). (2008). Head Start statistical fact sheet. Retrieved on May 3, 2009, from www.acf.hhs.gov/programs/ohs/about/ fy2008.htsml.

USDHHS (U.S. Department of Health and Human Services). (2009a). Head Start reauthorization: P.L. 110–134. Retrieved on May 19, 2009, from www.acf.hhs.gov/programs/ohs/policy/im2008/acfimhs_08_01_a1.html.

USDHHS (U.S. Department of Health and Human Services). (2009b). The 2009 poverty guidelines. *Federal Register, 74*(14), 4199–4201. Retrieved on May 4, 2009, from http://aspe.hhs.gov/poverty/09poverty.shtml.

Vander Zanden, J. (2003). *Human development.* Boston: McGraw- Hill.

Zigler, E. & Styfco, S. (2004). Head Start's National Reporting System: A Work in Progress. *Pediatrics, 114*(3), 858–859.

Chapter 7

Bracey, G. W. (2003). Investing in preschool. *American School Board Journal, 190*(1), 32–35.

Child Care Information Exchange. (2002). Celebrating a life for children: An interview with David Weikart. *Child Care Information Exchange, 144,* 30–31.

Epstein, A. S. (2003). How planning and reflection develop young children's thinking skills. *Young Children, 58*(5), 28–36.

Epstein, A. S. (2005). *All about High/Scope.* Ypsilanti, MI: High/Scope Educational Research Foundation. Retrieved from www.highscope.org/about/allabout .htm.

Epstein, A. S., Schweinhart, L. J., & McAdoo, L. (1996). *Models of early childhood education.* Ypsilanti, MI: High/Scope Press.

File, N., & Kontos, S. (1994). The relationship of program quality to children's play in integrated early intervention settings. *Topics in Early Childhood Special Education, 13,* 1.

Girolametto, L., Weitzman, E., van Lieshout, R., & Duff, D. (2000). Directiveness in teacher's language input to toddlers and preschoolers in day care. *Journal of Speech, Language, and Hearing Research, 43*(4), 1101–1104.

High/Scope Educational Research Foundation. (2003). *Preschool program quality assessment* (2nd ed.). Ypsilanti, MI: High/Scope Press.

High/Scope Educational Research Foundation. (2005). *Child observation record information for decision makers.* Ypsilanti, MI: High/Scope Press. Retrieved on May 23, 2009, from www.highscope.org/file/Assessment/ cor_decision_maker.pdf.

High/Scope Educational Research Foundation. (2009a). *Infant and toddler key experiences.* Ypsilanti, MI: High/Scope Press. Retrieved on May 23, 2009, from www.highscope.org/Content.asp?ContentId = 94.

High/Scope Educational Research Foundation. (2009b). *Key Developmental Indicators.* Ypsilanti, MI: High/Scope Press. Retrieved on May 23, 2009, from www.highscope.org/ Content.asp?ContentId = 275.

Maehr, J. (2003). High/Scope preschool key experiences: Language and literacy [Videotape]. Ypsilanti, MI: High/Scope Educational Research Foundation.

Marcon, R. A. (1992). Differential effects of three preschool models on inner-city 4-year-olds. *Early Childhood Research Quarterly, 7,* 517–530.

NAEYC (National Association for the Education of Young Children). (1995). *Responding to linguistic and cultural diversity: Recommendations for effective early childhood practice.* Washington, DC: NAEYC.

Quindlen, A. (2001). Building blocks for every kid. *Newsweek, 137*(7), 68–69.

Schweinhart, L. J. (2003). *Validity of the High/Scope preschool education model.* Ypsilanti, MI: High/Scope Educational Research Foundation.

Schweinhart, L. J., Montie, J., Xiang, Z., Barnett, W. S., Belfield, C. R., & Nores, M. (in press). *Lifetime effects: The High/Scope Perry Preschool Study through age 40.* (Monographs of the High/Scope Educational Research Foundation, 14). Ypsilanti, MI: High/ Scope Press.

Shouse, A. C. (1995). *High/Scope preschool curriculum: Educational programs that work.* Ypsilanti, MI: High/ Scope Educational Research Foundation.

Sylva, K., & Evans, E. (1999). Preventing failure at school. *Children and Society, 13,* 278–286.

Trawick-Smith, J. (1994). Authentic dialogue with children: A sociolinguistic perspective on language learning. *Dimensions of Early Childhood, 22*(4), 9–16.

Chapter 8

Beneke, S. (2000). Implementing the project approach in part-time early childhood education programs. *Early Childhood Research Quarterly, 2*(1). Retrieved on July 11, 2003, from http://ecrp.uiuc.edu/v2n1/beneke.html.

Chard, S. (1998a). *The project approach: Book 1.* New York: Scholastic Inc.

Chard, S. (1998b). *The project approach: Book 2.* New York: Scholastic Inc.

Edwards, C., & Springate, K. (1993). Inviting children into project work. *Dimensions of Early Childhood, 22*(1), 9–12 and 40.

Gallick, B. (2000). The hairy head project. *Early Childhood Research Quarterly, 2*(2). Retrieved on July 11, 2003, from ecrp.uiuc.edu/v2n2/gallick.html.

Gregory, M. R. (2002). Constructivism, standards, and the classroom community of inquiry. *Educational Theory, 52*(4), 43–51.

Helm, J., & Katz, L. (2001). *Young investigators: The project approach in the early years.* New York: Teachers College Press.

Katz, L. (1998). Issues in selecting topics for projects. *ERIC digest* no. ED424031 1998-10-00. Retrieved on August 30, 2009, from www.eric.ed.gov/ ERICDocs/data/ericdocs2sql/content_sto age_01/ 0000019b/80/16/f2/ed.pdf.

Katz, L., & Chard, S. (2000). *Engaging children's minds: The project approach.* Stamford, CT: Ablex Publishing.

Trepanier-Street, M. (1993). What's so new about the project approach? *Childhood Education, 20,* 25–28.

Vygotsky, L. S. (1978). *Mind in society: The development of higher psychological processes*. Cambridge, MA: Harvard University Press.

Chapter 9

Bredekamp, S. (1993). Reflections on Reggio Emilia. *Young Children, 49*(1), 13–17.

Bredekamp, S., & Rosengrant, T. (Eds.). (1992). *Reaching potentials: Appropriate curriculum and assessment for young children* (Vol. 1). Washington, DC: NAEYC.

Caldwell, L. B. (1997). *Bringing Reggio Emilia home*. New York: Teachers College Press.

Danko-McGhee, K., & Slutsky, R. (2003). Preparing teachers to use art in the classroom: Inspirations from Reggio Emilia. *Art Education, 56*(4), 12–18.

Day, C. B. (2001). Loris Malaguzzi, founder: The Reggio Emilia approach, believing in the power of the child. *Scholastic Early Childhood Today, 15*(8), 46.

Edwards, C. P. (2003). "Fine designs" from Italy: Montessori education and the Reggio Emilia approach. *Montessori Life, 15*(1), 34–39.

Edwards, C. P., Gandini, L., & Forman, G. (Eds.). (1996). *The hundred languages of children: The Reggio Emilia approach to early childhood education*. Norwood, NJ: Ablex.

Gandini, L. (1997). The Reggio Emilia story: History and organization. In J. Hendrick (Ed.), *First steps toward teaching the Reggio way*. Upper Saddle River, NJ: Merrill/ Prentice Hall.

Gandini, L. (2002). The story and foundations of the Reggio Emilia Approach. In V. Fu, A. Stremmel, & L. Hill (Eds.), *Teaching and learning: Collaborative exploration of the Reggio Emilia approach*. Upper Saddle River, NJ: Merrill/ Prentice Hall.

Goffin, S. G. (2000). The role of curriculum models in early childhood education. Washington, DC: Office of Educational Research and Improvement. (ERIC Document Reproduction Service no. ED 443597). Retrieved on August 30, 2009, from www.eric.ed.gov/ERICDocs/data/ericdocs2sql/content_storage_ 01/0000019b/80/16/57/e9.pdf.

Grieshaber, S., & Hatch, A. (2003). Pedagogical documentation as an effect of globalization. *Journal of Curriculum Theorizing, 19*(1), 89–102.

Hewett, V. M. (2001). Examining the Reggio Emilia approach to early childhood education. *Early Childhood Education Journal, 29*(2), 95–100.

Krechevsky, M., & Stork, J. (2000). Challenging educational assumptions: Lessons from an Italian-American collaboration. *Cambridge Journal of Education, 30*(1), 57–75.

Linn, M. I. (2001). An American educator reflects on the meaning of the Reggio experience. *Phi Delta Kappan, 83*, 332–335.

McClow, C. S., & Gillespie, C. W. (1998). Parental reactions to the introduction of the Reggio Emilia approach in Head Start classrooms. *Early Childhood Education Journal, 26*(2), 131–136.

New, R. S. (2003). Reggio Emilia: New ways to think about schooling. *Educational Leadership, 60*(7), 34–38.

Reggio Children (Producer). (1980). *To make a portrait of a lion* [Film]. Reggio Emilia, Italy: Reggio Children.

Reggio Children (Producer). (1994). *A message from Loris Malaguzzi* [Film]. Reggio Emilia, Italy: Reggio Children.

Rinaldi, C. (2001). In Project Zero & Reggio Children (Eds.), *Making learning visible: Children as individual and group learners*. Reggio Emilia, Italy: Reggio Children.

Seefeldt, C. (1995). Art—serious work. *Young Children, 50*(3), 39–45.

Strozzi, P. (2001). Daily life at school: Seeing the extraordinary in the ordinary. In Project Zero & Reggio Children (Eds.), *Making learning visible: Children as individual and group learners*. Reggio Emilia, Italy: Reggio Children.

Tarr, P. (2003). Reflections on the image of the child: Reproducer or creator of culture. *Art Education, 56*(4), 6–11.

Turner, T., & Krechevsky, M. (2003). Who are the teachers? Who are the learners? *Educational Leadership, 60*(7), 40–44.

USDHHS (U.S. Department of Health and Human Services). (2005). Head Start program performance standards *(45-CFR 1304)*. Washington, DC: U.S. Department of Health and Human Services. Retrieved on April 13, 2006, from www.acf.hhs.gov/programs/hsb/performance/index.htm.

Chapter 10

AMS (American Montessori Society). (n.d.). Essential elements of public Montessori schools. Retrieved on April 21, 2006, from www.amshq.org/schools_public.htm.

Cossentino, J. (2006). Big work: Goodness, vocation, and engagement in the Montessori Method. *Curriculum Inquiry, 36*(1), 63–92.

Crain, W. (2004). Montessori. *Encounter, 17*(2), 2–4.

Edwards, C. P. (2002). Three approaches from Europe: Waldorf, Montessori, and Reggio Emilia. *Early Childhood Research and Practice, 4*(1). Retrieved on

August 30, 2009, from http://ecrp.uiuc.edu/v4n1/edwards.html.

Elkind, D. (2003). Montessori and constructivism. *Montessori Life, 15*(1), 26–29.

Gartner, A., Lipsky, D. K., & Dohrmann, K. R. (2003). *Outcomes for students in a Montessori program: A longitudinal study of the experience in the Milwaukee public schools.* Rochester, NY: Association Montessori Internationale.

Gettman, D. (1987). *Basic Montessori: Learning activities for under-fives.* New York: Saint Martin's Press.

Goffin, S. (1994). *Curriculum models and early childhood education.* Upper Saddle River, NJ: Merrill/Prentice Hall.

Henry-Montessori, M. (n.d.). Portrait of Mario Montessori. Association Montessori Internationale. Retrieved on April 21, 2006, from www.montessori-ami.org.

Lascarides, V., & Hinitz, B. (2000). *History of early childhood education.* New York: Falmer Press.

Lillard, A., & Else-Quest, N. (2006). Evaluating Montessori education. *Science, 313,* 1893–1894.

Montessori, M. (1965a). *Dr. Montessori's own handbook: A short guide to her ideas and materials.* New York: Schocken Books.

Montessori, M. (1965b). The Montessori method: Scientific pedagogy as applied to child education in the Children's Houses. In M. Paciorek & J. Munro (Eds.) (1999), *Sources: Notable selections in early childhood education.* Guilford, CT: McGraw-Hill.

Montessori, M. (1966). *The secret of childhood.* New York: Ballantine Books.

Montessori, M. (1967). *The discovery of the child.* New York: Ballantine.

Mooney, C. G. (2000). *Theories of childhood: An introduction to Dewey, Montessori, Erikson, Piaget and Vygotsky.* St. Paul, MN: Redleaf Press.

Rambusch, N. (1992). Montessori's "method": Stewardship of the spirit. *ReVision, 15*(2), 79–81.

Rathunde, K. (2003). A comparison of Montessori and traditional middle schools: Motivation, quality of experience, and social context. *NAMTA Journal, 28*(3), 12–52.

Shute, N. (2002). Madam Montessori. *Smithsonian Magazine,* September, 70–74.

Sobe, N. W. (2004). Challenging the gaze: The subject of attention and a 1915 Montessori demonstration classroom. *Educational Theory, 54*(3), 281–297.

Soundy, C. (2003). Portraits of exemplary Montessori practice for all literacy teachers. *Early Childhood Education Journal, 31*(2), 127–131.

Swan, D. (1987). Forward. In D. Gettman, *Basic Montessori: Learning activities for under-fives.* New York: Saint Martin's Press.

Williams, N., & Keith, R. (2000). Democracy and Montessori education. *Peace Review, 12*(3), 217–222.

Chapter 11

Almon, J. (1992). Educating for creative thinking: The Waldorf approach. *ReVision, 15*(2), 71–79.

Astley, K., & Jackson, P. (2000). Doubts on spirituality: Interpreting Waldorf ritual. *International Journal of Children's Spirituality, 5*(2), 221–227.

AWSNA (Association of Waldorf Schools of North America). (n.d.). (About AWSNA). Retrieved on February 1, 2009, from www.awsna.org.

Association of Waldorf Schools of North America. (Producer). (1996). *Waldorf education: A vision of wholeness* [Film]. Available from Association of Waldorf Schools of North America, 3911 Bannister Road, Fair Oaks, CA 95628, 916-961-0927.

BLS (Bureau of Labor Statistics), 2008. College enrollment and work activity of 2007 High School graduates. Retrieved on February 6, 2009, from www.bls.gov/news.release/ hsgec.nr0.htm.

Byers, P., Dillard, C., Easton, F., Henry, M., McDermott, R., Oberman, I., & Uhrmacher, B. (1996). *Waldorf education in an inner city public school: The Urban Waldorf School of Milwaukee.* Spring Valley, NY: Parker Courtney Press.

Cicala Filmworks, Inc. (Producer). (n.d.). *Taking a risk in education: Waldorf-inspired public schools* [Film]. Available from Cicala Filmworks, Inc., 115 W. 29th Street, Suite 1101, New York, NY 10001.

Clouder, C. (2003). The push for early academic instruction: A view from Europe. *Encounter, 17*(1), 10–16.

Dancy, R. B. (2004). The wisdom of Waldorf. *Mothering, 123,* 62–73.

Easton, F. (1997). Educating the whole child, "head, heart, and hands": Learning from the Waldorf experience. *Theory Into Practice, 36*(2), 87–95.

ECSWE (European Council for Steiner Waldorf Education). (2007). Waldorf Schools Against Discrimination: Stuttgart Declaration. Retrieved on February 1, 2009, from.

Edwards, C. P. (2002). Three approaches from Europe: Waldorf, Montessori, and Reggio Emilia. *Early Childhood Research and Practice, 4*(1). Retrieved on December 9, 2002, from http://ecrp.uiuc.edu/v4n1/edwards.html.

Enten, A. (2005). Life after Waldorf High School. *Renewal Magazine*. Retrieved on December 14, 2005, from www.awsna.org/renlifeafter.html.

Fenner, P. J., & Rivers, K. (1995). *Waldorf education—A family guide*. Amesbury, MA: Michaelmas Press.

Hegde, A., & Cassidy, D. (2004). Teacher and parent perspectives on looping. *Early Childhood Education Journal, 32*(2), 133–138.

Iannone, R., & Obenauf, P. (1999). Toward spirituality in curriculum and teaching. *Education* (Chila Vista, CA), *119*(4), 737–743.

Miller, R. (2006). Reflecting on spirituality in education. *Encounter, 19*(2), 6–9.

Mitchell, D. & Gerwin, D. (2007). Survey of Waldorf Graduates, Phase II. Research Institute for Waldorf Education. Retrieved on February 1, 2009, from www.waldorfresearchinstitute.org//pdf/WEPhaseII 0307.pdf.

Mitchell, R. (2007). Seeking the archetype of the teacher. *Encounter, 20*(2), 27–35.

Mollet, D. (1991). How the Waldorf approach changed a difficult class. *Educational Leadership, 49*, 55–56.

Nicholson, D. (2000). Layers of experience: Forms of representation in a Waldorf school classroom. *Journal of Curriculum Studies, 32*(4), 575–587.

Oberman, I. (1997). *Waldorf history: Case study of institutional memory*. Paper presented at the annual meeting of the American Education Research Association, Chicago, Il. (ERIC Document Reproduction Service No. ED409108).

Oberman, I. (2008). Waldorf Education and its spread into the public sector. *Encounter, 21*(2), 11–14.

Oberski, I., Pugh, A., MacLean, A., & Cope, P. (2007). Validating a Steiner-Waldorf teacher education programme. *Teaching in Higher Education, 12*(1), 135–139.

Ogletree, E. (1975). Geometric form drawing: A perceptual-motor approach to preventive remediation (the Steiner approach). *Journal of Special Education, 3*, 237–243.

Oppenheimer, T. (1999). Schooling the imagination. *Atlantic Monthly, 282*(3), 71–83.

Rudolf Steiner Foundation. (General information). (n.d.). Retrieved on October 23, 2002, from www.refoundation.org/index2.asp.

Ruenzel, D. (2001). The spirit of Waldorf education. *Education Week, 20*(41), 38–46.

Schmitt-Stegmann, A. (1997). *Child development and curriculum in Waldorf education* (ERIC Document no. ED 415 990).

Steiner, R. (1997). *Education as a force for social change*. Hudson, NY: Anthroposophic Press.

Steiner, R. (2005). *Encyclopedia britannica*. Retrieved on December 14, 2005, from Encyclopedia Britannica Premium Service www.britannica.com/eb/article-9069553.

Waldorf Kindergarten Association. (1993). *An overview of the Waldorf kindergarten*. Silver Spring, MD: Waldorf Kindergarten Association.

Waldorf Kindergarten Association. (1994). *Understanding young children: Excerpts from lecture by Rudolf Steiner*. Silver Spring, MD: Waldorf Kindergarten Association.

Ward, W. (2005). Is Waldorf education Christian? *Renewal Magazine*. Retrieved on December 14, 2005, from www.awsna.org/renchristian.html.

Chapter 12

NAEYC (National Association for the Education of Young Children). (2008). NAEYC Standards for early childhood professional preparation. 2008 Revision Draft. Retrieved on June 25, 2009, from www.naeyc.org/positionstatements/ prepstds_draft.

Index